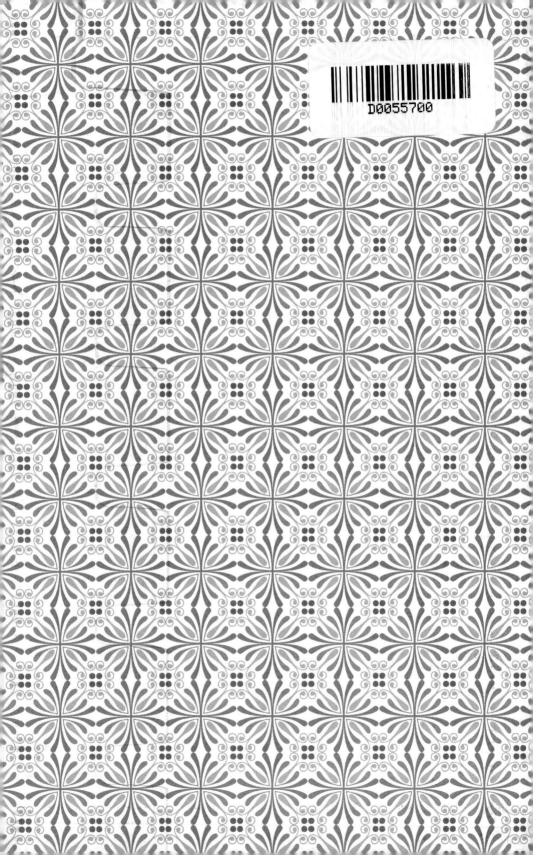

The Book of

Random Oddities

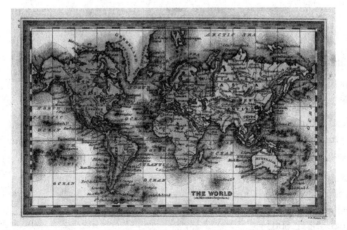

Publications International, Ltd.

Contents

❋ ❋ ❋ ❋

Highlights Include: Everything from A to Z ✦ Spoonerisms ✦ Aptronym: Thy Name Is Destiny ✦ Hinky Pinky and Holorimes ✦ Wordly Wisdom: African Proverbs ✦ Mrs. Malaprop and Her Friends ✦ If I'm Reading This Article Correctly, I Would Be Very Surprised ✦ Famous First Lines ✦ An Eye for an I ✦ Acrostics ✦ Kangaroo Words ✦ Vowel Play ✦Chronograms: Timeless Wordplay ✦ The People's Prefix ✦ Famous Last Words: Presidents ✦ M*ss*ng the Po*nt ✦ 'Scuse Me While I Kiss This Guy ✦ Word Pluses and Minuses ✦ A Hodgepodge of Reduplications ✦ It's What's Inside that Counts

Highlights Include: Seeking Heaven's Aid ✦ From Little Eggcorns Grow… Great Jokes ✦ Words of Wisdom: Mistakes ✦ Almost, but Not Quite ✦ Don't Have Anything Nice to Say? Use a Euphemism ✦ It's Not That Bad ✦ The Illusion of Allusion ✦ Missing Word Puzzles ✦ No Need to Be Nice ✦ Snap! Crackle! Pop! ✦ Words of Wisdom: Advertising ✦ got snowclones? ✦ That's What They All Say ✦ Ambiguous Amphibology ✦ Why Bother? ✦ In Error, Sometimes Deliberately ✦ It Would Be Superfluous to Say… ✦ The Music of Assonance ✦ Words of Wisdom: Music

Highlights Include: Cupertino Effect: The Corrections ✦ A Devilish Dictionary ✦ Positively Confounding ✦ Words of Wisdom from Mark Twain ✦ Don't Take Things So Literally ✦ Jargon: How the Meaningless Can Mess with Your Mind ✦ Snack Attack ✦ The 411 on Texting ✦ Words of Wisdom: Family ✦ Janus Words ✦ Translating Across the Galaxy ✦ Infixes: Getting Into Words ✦ Famous First Lines ✦ Eponyms: A Rose by Anyone Else's Name… ✦ Words of Wisdom: Friendship ✦ Sickening English Usage ✦ Indefinite Words Are Definitely Useful ✦ What's in a Name?

Highlights Include: Odd Jobs ✦ Words of Wisdom: Work ✦ The Longest Words ✦ Going Green ✦ In Vino Verbitas ✦ Words of Wisdom: Raise Your Glass ✦ No Offense Intended ✦ Words of Wisdom from Oscar Wilde ✦

The Color Purple ✦ A Lot of -*Auto* ✦ Pardon Me? Words with No English Equivalent ✦ Kench and the World Kenches with You ✦ Words of Wisdom: Laughter ✦ The Germans Have a Word for It (and Now We Do Too) ✦ Don't Let These Words Confuse You ✦ W-I-N-N-I-N-G W-O-R-D-S ✦ Fear and Loathing ✦ Love and Marriage ✦ Words of Wisdom: Marriage

Random World of Words

✳ ✳ ✳ ✳

ARE YOU A whiz when it comes to word games? Do you find yourself wondering where words come from? Maybe you're consistently searching for unusual language to wow your friends, or perhaps you're just confused about the difference between *affect* and *effect*. Whether you're a textbook wordsmith or a casual bookworm, *The Book of Random Oddities* is here to lead you through the strange, odd, wonderful world of words.

With 16 chapters crammed full of delightful logodaedaly, including turns of phrase, figures of speech, recently coined terms, spelling tips and mnemonics, unusual vocabulary, cool language tricks, word games, and more, this is a book designed for those who are curious about language and wild about wordplay.

Read about:

✳ The U.S. congressman who single-handedly introduced the word *bunkum* to the English vernacular

✳ Mrs. Malaprop from the play *The Rivals*, whose name has come to identify an entire genre of humorous lexical mistakes

✳ The Cupertino Effect, or, Why Spell-Checker Is Not Always Your Friend

✳ Crash blossoms (poorly worded headlines) such as "Prostitutes Appeal to Pope" and "Kids Make Nutritious Snacks"

✳ Unusual insults like *blatherskite* (a babbling, foolish person), *dowfart* (a stupid, dull person), and *quakebuttock* (a coward)

The Book of Random Oddities is a celebration of the English language and a witty, entertaining treasure trove of information containing just about everything you ever wanted to know about words.

Chapter 1

Wordplay

Everything from A to Z

A **pangram** *is a sentence that uses every letter of the alphabet at least once. (It's also known as a holoalphabetic sentence.) Besides having wordplay value, pangrams also have usefulness in the real world—for example, a pangram will often be used to show what all the different characters in a font look like. The best-known pangram is probably "The quick brown fox jumps over the lazy dog," which fits all 26 letters of the alphabet into a 35-letter sentence.*

✳ ✳ ✳ ✳

Two traits are valued highly in pangrams: brevity and coherence. The pangram above is a good example of one that reads fairly naturally. Generally, the shorter a pangram gets, the less sense it makes.

Here's a list of some notable pangrams, eventually getting all the way down to exactly 26 letters.

✳ Watch *Jeopardy!*, Alex Trebek's fun TV quiz game. (37 letters)

✳ Jinxed wizards pluck ivy from the big quilt. (36 letters)

✳ The quick brown fox jumps over the lazy dog. (35 letters)

✳ Kvetching, flummoxed by job, W. zaps Iraq. (32 letters)

✳ Pack my box with five dozen liquor jugs. (32 letters)

✳ The five boxing wizards jump quickly. (31 letters)

* Five quaking zephyrs jolt my wax bed. (31 letters)

* Two driven jocks help fax my big quiz. (30 letters)

* Sphinx of black quartz, judge my vow. (29 letters)

* Quick zephyrs blow, vexing daft Jim. (29 letters)

* Waltz, bad nymph, for quick jigs vex! (28 letters)

* New job: Fix Mr. Gluck's hazy TV, PDQ! (26 letters)

Translation, Please!

Trying to find a 26-letter pangram that uses no proper nouns is difficult indeed, especially if you want it to make sense. This one contains only dictionary words but requires a bit of explanation: "Jumbling vext frowzy hacks PDQ" (or, translated, "Being bounced around annoyed the unkempt taxi drivers very quickly").

Sometimes pangrams naturally occur in published writing. When such a pangram is found, the sequence of characters within it that uses all 26 letters is called a "pangram window." Such a window may start and end in the middle of words. One very short pangram window was found in a blurb from *Entertainment Weekly*, which described the time director Werner Herzog rescued actor Joaquin Phoenix from a car crash (brackets indicate the beginning and ending of the window): "Then on Jan. 26, Her[zog happened by Joaquin Phoenix's car wreck and pulled the actor from the v]ehicle." No doubt, Mr. Herzog deserves thanks for his altruism—and his contribution to wordplay.

---

* **The pangram "The quick brown fox jumps over the lazy dog" has been used to test keyboards to make sure all of the keys work, and it is often used by graphic designers and to see how every character in a font is drawn.**

Spoonerisms

If you've hot nerd... that is, if you've not heard of **spoonerisms** *before, today's your ducky lay—er, lucky day.*

✳ ✳ ✳ ✳

SPOONERISMS ARE SLIPS of the tongue named after the Reverend William Arthur Spooner, longtime dean of New College, Oxford University in the late 1800s and early 1900s. He was renowned for verbal fumbles in which he swapped sounds between pairs of words—so renowned that his students made up their own examples for fun, and now it's difficult to know which (if any) he actually said and which were merely attributed to him. One spoonerism thought to have been uttered by Spooner himself was his announcement of a hymn as "Kinkering Congs Their Titles Take" instead of "Conquering Kings Their Titles Take"; another, "It is kisstomary to cuss the bride."

Examples in which the swapped sounds create new words are more likely the result of deliberate effort from others, such as "Three cheers for our queer old dean!" (ostensibly a toast to Victoria, the dear old queen); "You have hissed all my mystery lectures," to a student who had missed many history lectures; "The Lord is a shoving leopard" (rather than a loving shepherd); and so forth. The most common form of spoonerism involves swapping initial consonant sounds, but internal sounds may be swapped as well, as in the "Kinkering Congs" and "kisstomary to cuss" examples, or the time Spooner is said to have called, when his hat was blown off by the wind, "Will nobody pat my hiccup?" Entire words may be swapped too, as in "Time wounds all heels."

Say What?

Spoonerisms figure in the punny punch lines of many a joke ("People in glass houses shouldn't stow thrones," or the tale of the seabird-hater who left "no tern unstoned"). Someone had to be the first person to say, "I'd rather have a bottle in front of me than a frontal lobotomy," but apparently they were too busy drinking to make sure their witticism was properly credited—it's been attributed to Dorothy Parker, W. C. Fields, and Fred Allen, among others. But as we've seen, the truth rarely gets in the way of a good attribution. Or to put it another way, when it comes to popular quotations, few tracts contain true facts.

This Is the Pun Fart: A Mew for Spoonerisms

* Chewing the doors (doing the chores)

* Clappy as a ham (Happy as a clam)

* Fighting a liar (Lighting a fire)

* Know your blose (Blow your nose)

* Jing of the Kungle (King of the Jungle)

* Lack of pies (Pack of lies)

* Nick your pose (Pick your nose)

* Pull a habit out of a rat (Pull a rabbit out of a hat)

* Ready as a stock (Steady as a rock)

* Pleating and humming (Heating and plumbing)

* Skipping the tails (Tipping the scales)

* Sparking pace (Parking space)

* Time to shake a tower (Time to take a shower)

* Tips of the slung (Slips of the tongue)

* Wave the sails (Save the whales)

---

* Children's author Shel Silverstein wrote a book of poems composed entirely of spoonerisms. The book is called *Runny Babbit: A Billy Sook,* and sample poem titles include "Runny's Rig Bomance," "Runny's Jig Bump," and "Runny Loes to Gunch."

Aptronym: Thy Name Is Destiny

Dr. Payne ... paging Dr. Payne. Ouch!

✳ ✳ ✳ ✳

IN THE PAST, people's last names reflected their occupations. The surname *Cooper* means "barrel maker," *Chandler* means "candle maker," and *Smith* means, well, "smith" (as in a blacksmith). Nowadays, though, when someone's last name and their occupation have a particularly symbiotic relationship, it's generally a coincidence—and a cause for amuse-ment, as you probably know if you've ever had a dentist named Dr. Payne or known a lawyer named Sue. Such names are called **aptronyms**, from the Latin word for "exactly suitable" or "appropriate" and the Greek *onuma* ("name").

Strange But True

Of the many true-life examples, here are a few of the more humorous: There was army surgeon Dr. James Bird Cutter. (That name was probably even more amusing when he carved the Thanksgiving turkey.) Or what about Patricia Feral, an ani-mal rights activist? Besides the aforementioned Dr. Payne, there's more than one dentist named Dr. Toothaker and also many a Dr. Hertz out there. Russell Brain was a neurologist, poet William Wordsworth made wordcraft his life's work, William Headline was CNN's Washington bureau chief for 12 years, and spokes-person Larry Speakes was the voice of Ronald Reagan's White House. Unfortunately, Honor Blackman was not a civil rights activist, but the actress who played Cathy Gale in the original *The Avengers* and Bond girl Pussy Galore in *Goldfinger*.

Those are just a few that we could confirm: One problem with lists of aptronyms is that it's impossible to know, once they've been passed around enough times, which are real discoveries and which are just clever inventions. There may very well have been a barber named Dan Druff, but it's difficult to be sure. However, it's likely that Graves Funeral Home gets its moniker from the family surname, and Dr. Nutter, according to his business card, is a family psychologist.

Names of Fame

Celebrity aptronyms are more easily confirmed. There's Olympic sprinter Usain Bolt, the fastest man in the world. In other sports, you'll find tennis legend Margaret Court, father-and-son first basemen Cecil and Prince Fielder, Buffalo Bills cornerback Reggie Corner, Miami Dolphins kicker Jim Kiick, and onetime Chicago Bears quarterback Willie Thrower. Golfer Tiger Woods uses plenty of woods on the course (too bad Jeremy Irons pursued acting instead of golf). Someone with a good acting aptronym was *Little House on the Prairie* child actor Brian Part. And actress Megan Fox . . . well, just look at her! There's a reason her name has appeared on lists such as Moviefone's "25 Hottest Actors Under 25." It's no small irony that convicted scam artist Bernie Madoff "made off" with a lot of people's hard-earned cash.

Finally, let us not forget Thomas Crapper, who really did exist, though he did not actually invent the toilet. He did, however, manufacture toilets and make improvements to them, which is enough to merit his place on the (porcelain) throne of aptronym history.

✳ **Did you know that many last names derive from occupations? Here's a sampling: Baxter (baker), Collier (coal miner), Crocker (maker of pottery), Faulkner (keeper of falcons), Fletcher (maker of bows and arrows), Porter (doorkeeper), Slater (roofer), Thatcher (roofer), Webster (weaver), and Wright (workman).**

✳ **Aptronyms are sometimes referred to as *aptonyms, name-phreaks,* or *PFLNs,* which stands for "perfect-fit last names."**

✳ **A fancy word for surname is *cognomen.***

Hinky Pinky and Holorimes

*Rhymes are essential to poetry and song lyrics, but what happens when you keep the rhymes and ditch everything else? You end up with **hinky pinkies** and **holorimes**.*

✳ ✳ ✳ ✳

IN THE GAME *Hinky Pinky*, players think of a rhyming phrase and come up with a clue for it, and the other players try to guess the phrase. For instance, the answer to the clue "elitist backwoods group," is "hick clique," while "in debt to an airplane manufacturer" is "owing Boeing." "Flag that's been smeared by the media" would be a "slandered standard"; and "mistake made while playing 'You Are the Sunshine of My Life'" leads to the answer "Wonder blunder." Whoever guesses the phrase thinks of the next one, and you can award points for correct guesses.

If you're a fan of long, ambitious rhymes, you may wish to try your hand at *holorimes,* which are actually more like *homonyms* (words that sound the same but are different in meaning or spelling) than rhymes. A holorime consists of two lines of poetry that sound exactly alike, syllable by syllable. Holorimes are very difficult to write, as they require a careful marriage of form and meaning. "For I scream / For ice cream" and "Isle of view / I love you" both work, but neither is very impressive. Longer holorimes tend toward incoherency even when they sort of make sense on the surface, as in this example:

> *All afternoon I told tales. / Ah, laughter: new night, old tails.*

Another take on holorime indicates that the lines may rhyme on every syllable without necessarily being homophonic throughout. This definition is a secondary one, but it allows easier construction of comprehensible examples, such as:

> *Today will bring you sorrow, yet. / You may still sing tomorrow, pet.*

Worldly Wisdom: African Proverbs

✳ ✳ ✳ ✳

✳ If you can walk you can dance. If you can talk you can sing. (*Zimbabwe*)

✳ However long the night, the dawn will break.

✳ If you climb up a tree, you must climb down the same tree.

✳ When two elephants fight, it is the grass that gets trampled.

✳ Peace is costly but it is worth the expense.

✳ Sticks in a bundle are unbreakable. (*Kenya*)

✳ Because a man has injured your goat, do not go out and kill his bull. (*Kenya*)

✳ Wood already touched by fire is not hard to set alight. (*Ashanti*)

✳ Rain beats a leopard's skin, but it doesn't wash off the spots. (*Ashanti*)

✳ Evil enters like a needle and spreads like an oak tree. (*Ethiopia*)

✳ When spider webs unite, they can tie up a lion. (*Ethiopia*)

✳ A man on the ground does not fall.

✳ Little by little fills up the bowl. (*Kenya*)

✳ Never mind if your nose is ugly as long as you can breathe through it. (*Zaire*)

✳ Do not blame God for creating the Tiger, be thankful he didn't give him wings. (*Ethiopia*)

✳ Don't sweep another's house whilst your own is dirty. (*Kenya*)

Mrs. Malaprop and Her Friends

Richard Brinsley Sheridan's first play, The Rivals, *was first performed in 1775, establishing him as a successful playwright and, more important for the purposes of this book, introducing to the world the character of Mrs. Malaprop.*

✳   ✳   ✳   ✳

MRS. MALAPROP WAS prone to misspeaking, often substituting words she meant to use with words that sounded similar but were very different in meaning. These misstatements, delightful in their inanity and humor, are now known as *malapropisms.* Mrs. Malaprop's name was deliberately chosen to evoke her talent for choosing the wrong word. It's derived from *malapropos,* meaning "inappropriate" (from the French *mal à propos*). But she's hardly the only (or even the first) character to stumble over their word choices—Dogberry from Shakespeare's *Much Ado About Nothing* predated Mrs. Malaprop by more than 150 years when he said that "comparisons are odorous" (meaning *odious*).

Straight from the Horse's Mouth

Here are a few examples of malapropisms from Mrs. Malaprop herself: "He can tell you the perpendiculars," in which Mrs. Malaprop has confused *perpendiculars* with *particulars*. Or here's a line that includes two examples: "As she grew up, I would have her instructed in geometry, that she might know something of the contagious countries." (*Geometry* has been used instead of *geography,* and *contagious* instead of *contiguous*.) Another gem is "He is the very pineapple of politeness!" (Presumably she meant to say *pinnacle*.)

Another Type of Superhero

The comic strip *Frank and Ernest,* which was created in 1972 and relies heavily on wordplay for its humor, introduced the "superhero" "Malaprop Man," who, as a doctor, wrote a few "drug subscriptions" (*prescriptions*) and performed "taser surgery on a patient with slurred vision" (*laser; blurred*); didn't want to get "edited for his tax returns" (*audited*); and planned to run "the 26-mile telethon" (*marathon*).

Who's the Meathead Now?

Archie Bunker from TV's *All in the Family* was prone to malapropisms of his own, including "groinocology" (*gynecology*), "battery-operated transvestive radios" (*transistor*), and "patience is a virgin" (*virtue*). That the malapropisms often emphasized his tendency toward blustery racism ("In closing, I'd like to say 'Molotov'" [*Mazel tov*]) often added to the humor. The technique never gets old, as modeled in later television sitcoms such as *Modern Family*, as when Gloria says, "It's a doggy dog world" (*a dog-eat-dog world*).

I Resemble that Remark

Some real-life people are famous for their frequent use of malapropisms. Baseball's Yogi Berra dropped the ball when he said, "He hits from both sides of the plate. He's amphibious" (meaning *ambidextrous*). Berra misspoke frequently enough to earn his own eponym (*Yogi-isms*), as did George W. Bush. (For more on eponyms see page 136; for *Bushisms*, page 482.) But possibly the person who aligns most closely with Mrs. Malaprop herself is former vice president Dan Quayle, who claimed: "I stand by all the misstatements that I've made."

✳ **Cross a malapropism with folk etymology, and you get an *eggcorn*. An eggcorn occurs when someone mishears or misremembers a phrase, but the new phrase makes enough sense to seem correct. One very common eggcorn is *tow the line*, which invokes images of obeying orders by pulling a rope— which seems at least as logical as the real phrase, *toe the line*. Malapropisms, on the other hand, make no sense at all. (For more on eggcorns, see page 60.)**

Word Squares Are Hip

Is it hip to be square? The ancient Greeks thought so.

✳ ✳ ✳ ✳

A WORD SQUARE IS a venerable old puzzle dating back to ancient times. In its simplest form, a square arrangement of letters forms an identical set of words across and down, as in the following example:

```
S T U N G
T E N O R
U N T I E
N O I S E
G R E E T
```

Every letter is used in two different words except the letters along the diagonal extending from the upper left to lower right; but in one variant, an extra word is spelled along that diagonal:

```
C R A B
R A C E
A C R E
B E E T
```

In another variant, different words appear going across and down (with or without a word on the diagonal):

```
H E A R T       B A R N
E N T E R       A R E A
A D O R E       L I A R
V E N U E       L A D Y
E D E N S
```

These might start looking like proto-crosswords to you, as they should. Word squares began as feats of construction and evolved into puzzles, with definitions given as clues. Constructors didn't limit themselves to square shapes. In 1913, puzzle developer Arthur Wynne added numbers and clues to a diamond-shape grid, and the crossword was born.

The earliest-known word square is the SATOR square, which was discovered in the ruins of Pompeii, and thus was created no later than A.D. 79:

```
S A T O R
A R E P O
T E N E T
O P E R A
R O T A S
```

While it has the imperfection that *Arepo* seems to be a made-up proper name, this square is notable in that the five words, in order, form a palindromic Latin sentence; that is, it reads the same forward and backward. Much as English palindromes have somewhat tortured grammar, so does this one. Proposed translations include "The farmer Arepo works with the help of a wheel" and "The farmer Arepo holds the wheel with effort." (For more on palindromes, see page 310.)

The longer the words, the more difficult it is to make a word square. Seven-letter word squares aren't too tough, but beyond that you may need to turn to more obscure words or old-fashioned spellings. Here's a word square that uses eight words, all found in the dictionary:

```
L A T E R A L S
A X O N E M A L
T O E P L A T E
E N P L A N E D
R E L A N D E D
A M A N D I N E
L A T E E N E R
S L E D D E R S
```

What's That You Say?

Any word lover is familiar with the root dict-*, if for no other reason than it is at the heart of the word* dictionary.

✳   ✳   ✳   ✳

THE ROOT COMES from the Latin *dicere,* or "to speak." In English we have the verb *to dictate,* meaning "to put into words, utter," as well as "to order, command." The noun *dictate* is an authoritative decree, and a *dictator* is one who issues them, an absolute ruler. (There is also the little-used *dictatrix,* a female dictator.) A *dictum* is a saying or utterance.

Valediction, which comes from the Latin compound *valedictio* ("farewell saying"), denotes the action of bidding farewell or the utterance that accompanies a leave-taking. A *valedictory oration,* the speech given at graduations, comes from this usage. At this point, we're only one suffix away from the student who delivers this speech, a *valedictorian.* So, while convention stipulates that the valedictorian be chosen according to academic merits, there is nothing in the word itself that bars the class clown from the honor.

Make Sure You Enunciate

With or without good grades, it's important for valedictorians (or anyone engaged in public speaking) to practice good *diction. Diction* refers to a verbal style, either in one's choice of words or in one's elocution. Add the prefix *bene-* ("good") to it and you get a *benediction,* a blessing; add *mal-* ("bad") and you create a curse, or *malediction.*

Add the suffix *-ary* to form the word *dictionary,* which is from the Medieval Latin *dictionarius* or *dictionarium.* The suffix

-ary is the English form of the Latin ending and can mean "a place for, collection of." So a *dictionary* is "a collection of words." Modern dictionaries are, however, much more than a simple collection of words. In addition to cataloging a language's lexicon, today's dictionaries contain etymology information, pronunciation guides, alternate spellings, usage examples, and, of course, definitions.

Though *dictionary* and *dictator* share the same root, that doesn't mean dictionaries contain commandments on how to use words. Most modern dictionaries describe how words are used; they don't dictate.

---

* Although many people regard dictionaries as objective recordings of a language as it exists among its users, this hasn't always been the case—nor is it necessarily the case today. The 1961 publishing of *Webster's Third New International Dictionary*, which for the first time admitted words such as *ain't* without any qualifying statement about their "nonstandard" status, incited the fury of language mavens everywhere. Fifty years later, the debate surrounding the role of dictionaries rages on.

* As disturbed as logophiles were about *Webster's* decision to include "nonstandard" entries, just think how they must feel about UrbanDictionary.com. This website includes vulgarities, slang, street patois, and more. Anyone can submit an entry, and many do: There are more than 6 million entries, with many more being added every day.

Where Did It Come From?

Ain't: A widely used contraction of "am not," the term was first used in early-eighteenth-century England, where it was considered proper English by all classes.

If I'm Reading This Article Correctly, I Would Be Very Surprised

*A **paraprosdokian** is a kind of wordplay in which a sentence starts out seeming to say one thing, but then the end of the sentence changes the meaning of what's come before—for instance, Groucho Marx's line "She got her good looks from her father... he's a plastic surgeon."*

* * * *

THE WORD PARAPROSDOKIAN comes from two Greek roots meaning "beyond" and "expectation"; this makes sense, because it's not a paraprosdokian if it's not unexpected. Here are just a few samples.

* "Where there's a will, I want to be in it." (*unattributed*)

* "If I agreed with you, we'd both be wrong." (*unattributed*)

* "The last thing I'd want to do is hurt you. But it's still on my list." (*unattributed*)

* "The Commons, faithful to their system, remained in a wise and masterly inactivity." (*Sir James Mackintosh*)

* "If we do not hang together, we will surely hang separately." (*Benjamin Franklin*)

* "I belong to no organized party. I am a Democrat." (*Will Rogers*)

* "Take my wife... please." (*Henny Youngman*)

* "If you haven't got anything nice to say about anybody, sit right here by me." (*Alice Roosevelt Longworth*)

* "We are so fond of each other, because our ailments are the same." (*Jonathan Swift*)

* "I love good creditable acquaintance; I love to be the worst of the company." (*Jonathan Swift*)

* "An old tutor of a college said to one of his pupils: Read over your compositions, and wherever you meet with a passage which you think is particularly fine, strike it out." (*Samuel Johnson*)

* "Familiarity breeds contempt—and children." (*Mark Twain*)

Three's Company

Similar to the paraprosdokian is comedy's "rule of three," in which a pattern is set up by the first two parts of a series and broken by the third, as in this joke from *The Daily Show's* Jon Stewart: "I celebrated Thanksgiving in an old-fashioned way. I invited everyone in my neighborhood to my house, we had an enormous feast, and then I killed them and took their land."

Perhaps you'll be able to use your newfound knowledge of these techniques to work on your own jokes. Just remember: Comedy is harder than it looks, so don't bump your head on it.

Consonant Comments

If consonants are the building blocks of spoken language, then vowels are the mortar that goes between them.

* * * *

STREAMS OF CONSONANTS with no vowels to break them up are difficult to pronounce, so the English language sometimes avoids them by inserting vowels. For instance, *clutch* + *s* becomes *clutches*, and the silent *e* in *marked* becomes audible when an extra consonant is added in *markedly*. Even though the spelling of words doesn't always match their pronunciation, uninterrupted stretches of written consonants are still hard to find.

Czyk Your Spelling

The longest strings of consonants found in common words are six letters long. These stretches are found in compound words (*catchphrase, latchstring*) and words of foreign origin (*weltschmerz* and *borschts*, the latter of which is notable for having only one syllable). Seven consonants in a row can be achieved by stretching the definition of a word: *tsk-tsks* (also the longest word with no vowel at all). The longest common word with five consonants in a row and just one vowel is *strengths*.

There are many long words and phrases that feature only one consonant throughout—and a lot of them happen to be musical, like the Mary Wells hit "Bye Bye Baby," ABBA's "I Do, I Do, I Do, I Do, I Do" (featured in the musical *Mamma Mia!*), the classic rock standard "Louie Louie," and the Hall & Oates single "One on One." These examples achieve their length by repeating words; if that fact gives you palpitations, then call *nine-one-one* right away for a quick *tête-à-tête* with medical professionals (perhaps *Eli Lilly* will be available and you can see how he *assesses* the situation). Also call if you've been knocked out flat by boxer *Laila Ali*.

Famous First Lines

The first words of a novel can be enough to set the tone for the whole book. Here's a look at some memorable opening lines.

✳   ✳   ✳   ✳

"It is a truth universally acknowledged, that a single man in possession of a good fortune, must be in want of a wife."
—JANE AUSTEN, *PRIDE AND PREJUDICE* (1813)

"Call me Ishmael."
—HERMAN MELVILLE, *MOBY DICK* (1851)

"It was the best of times, it was the worst of times."
—CHARLES DICKENS, *A TALE OF TWO CITIES* (1859)

"Looking back to all that has occurred to me since that eventful day, I am scarcely able to believe in the reality of my adventures."
—JULES VERNE, *JOURNEY TO THE CENTER OF THE EARTH* (1864)

"'Christmas won't be Christmas without any presents,' grumbled Jo, lying on the rug."
—LOUISA MAY ALCOTT, *LITTLE WOMEN* (1868)

"Dorothy lived in the midst of the great Kansas prairies, with Uncle Henry, who was a farmer, and Aunt Em, who was the farmer's wife."
—L. FRANK BAUM, *THE WONDERFUL WIZARD OF OZ* (1900)

"This is the saddest story I have ever heard."
—FORD MADOX FORD, *THE GOOD SOLDIER* (1915)

An 👁 for an I

If you've ever seen the game show *Concentration* (or seen a lyric sheet by Prince), you know what a **rebus** is: a puzzle in which a word or phrase is represented by a combination of letters and symbols.

❋   ❋   ❋   ❋

REBUSES USE WORDS, pictures, letters, fonts, colors, and more juxtaposed in a way to reveal a common idiom, famous person, a movie or song title, or anything else. For instance, a picture of a water well, a supermarket aisle, and a bee could be a rebus for the phrase "Well, I'll be!" Many rebuses are phonetic (sometimes loosely so); a puzzle that begins with 10 + S and continues with L + a picture of an archer's bow would lead to the answer "tennis elbow." There are many common rebus substitutions—an eye for an *I* and 2 for *to*, of course, but many more as well, such as a sheep (that is, a ewe) or U for *you*, C for *see*, and 4 for…well, for *for*. The word *IOU* is essentially a rebus for "I owe you."

Some rebus puzzles get very elaborate, involving subtraction as well as addition. This sort of rebus is usually not pho-

S	S	S	S
B	B	B	B
A	A	A	A
R	R	R	R
G	G	G	G

netic, instead referring specifically to the spelling of the final answer. For instance, P + lantern - N + spear - R + nun - N + TS = Planters peanuts. (A crueler version might substitute a picture of T. S. Eliot for the TS.)

Other rebuses stick strictly to words and letters, relying on descriptions of the characters and their relationships to each other. Here's a fairly easy one:

COLLAR
HOT

That's "hot under the collar." Or try this harder one:

C
TR
SY

That's a C on TR over SY...or "controversy." And "5:00 5:00" would be "time after time." Some rebuses can be downright puzzling—take "DIGHIRA," for instance. By itself, it's hard to crack, but given the hint that it's the name of a famous political figure, you're likelier to figure out that the answer is Indira Gandhi ("in DIRA, G and HI"). Part of the fun of this kind of rebus is finding ways to minimize the amount of information necessary to produce a legitimate answer: "BA" could be a rebus for "bandana" ("B and an A") and "B" could be "abalone" ("a B alone").

Happy Rebus Solving 2 U

STEFRANKIN

ɔomǝ **kid**

Answers: Page 26, Up for grabs, Above top: Frankenstein, Bottom: Comeback kid

Cryptic Crosswords Made Easy (Well...Easier)

Many puzzle solvers have run across **cryptic crosswords,** *or* **cryptograms.** *And many of them have thought, "What the heck is this crazy thing?" and moved on. But cryptic crosswords needn't be intimidating. Solving them is just a matter of learning the rules.*

✳ ✳ ✳ ✳

Each clue in a cryptogram has two parts (a definition and some kind of wordplay) and a parenthetical number indicating the number of letters in the answer. Furthermore, solving is made easier—or maybe more complicated—by clues that signal the kind of wordplay.

Get a Clue

✳ Anagrams: Certain words, such as "broken" or "ruined," signal you to look for an anagram. (For more on anagrams, see page 316.) Take the clue "Damaged tapes are not in one place (8)," for example: If the phrase *tapes are* is "damaged" by rearranging the letters, you get *separate,* defined in the second half of the clue.

✳ Deletions: Clues about missing letters signal a deletion. A special kind of deletion is *curtailment,* in which the last letter of a word is deleted. Another special deletion is *beheadment,* or taking off the first letter: "Pirate, after losing his head, is angry (5)" leads to *irate,* after *pirate* literally loses its head.

✳ Reversals: If you see a word like "return," "invert," or "back," expect a word reversal: "Return

kingly brew (5)" tells you to reverse a word meaning "kingly."
Spell *regal* backward and you get *lager* ("brew"). Another way
to clue *lager* is with a homophone: "Lumberjack called for
beer (5)." A lumberjack is a *logger*, and *logger* "called" out loud
sounds like *lager*.

✳ Containers: Some clues signal containers, where one word
is put inside another. This is demonstrated in the clue
"Perfume magazine is in France (9)." A magazine may be
called a *rag*; put that inside *France* and you get *fragrance*.
Another way words can be inside each other is in a hidden
word clue: "Nudist emperor conceals anger (9)." The answer,
distemper ("anger"), is concealed inside *nuDIST EMPERor*.

✳ Charades: With charades, smaller words combine to make
a larger one, as in "Notice record ended (8)." (For more on
charades, turn to page 326.) The wordplay is in the second
half this time: A record is a *disc*, and something that's ended
is *over*; *disc* + *over* = *discover*, or "notice."

✳ Double definitions: One clue type—a double definition—
contains two definitions: "Small motorcycle was blue (5),"
for instance, contains two meanings of *moped*, though the
pronunciation changes.

✳ **The only person known to hold a college degree in enigmatol-
ogy (the study of puzzles) is Will Shortz, who designed his own
curriculum at Indiana University. He is also the founder of the
American Crossword Puzzle Tournament.**

Acrostics

The word **acrostic** *can refer to several different (but related) sorts of puzzles or wordplay. Those who do the puzzles in* The New York Times Magazine *will be familiar with one type, also known by various other names, including* anacrostic *and* double-crostic. *But this article focuses on another type of acrostic: the acrostic poem.*

✳ ✳ ✳ ✳

AN ACROSTIC POEM has a message hidden in its initial letters. Acrostics go back to biblical times; acrostics on the Hebrew alphabet can be found in Psalms and Lamentations (such as Psalm 119, which is divided into 22 stanzas of 8 lines each; each stanza—and each line within that stanza—starts with successive letters of the Hebrew alphabet). The fish symbol associated with Christianity also derives from an acrostic. The Greek translation of the phrase "Jesus Christ, God's Son, Savior" begins with the letters iota (I), chi (X, or *ch*), theta (Θ, or *th*), upsilon (Y, or *u/y*), and sigma (Σ, or *s*), spelling *ichthys*, Greek for "fish."

This acrostic poem by Lewis Carroll is the coda to *Through the Looking-Glass.* The poem's first letters spell the name of the real-life inspiration for Alice: Alice Pleasance Liddell.

A boat, beneath a sunny sky
Lingering onward dreamily
In an evening of July—

Children three that nestle near,
Eager eye and willing ear,
Pleased a simple tale to hear—

Long has paled that sunny sky:
Echoes fade and memories die.
Autumn frosts have slain July.

Still she haunts me, phantomwise,
Alice moving under skies
Never seen by waking eyes.

Children yet, the tale to hear,
Eager eye and willing ear,
Lovingly shall nestle near.

In a Wonderland they lie,
Dreaming as the days go by,
Dreaming as the summers die:

Ever drifting down the stream—
Lingering in the golden gleam—
Life, what is it but a dream?

It's a Wordapalooza!

*The -palooza suffix got its boost from alt-music festival
Lollapalooza, which began in 1991. The festival promoters took the
name from an American slang term dating to 1895, meaning "an
extraordinary example or specimen." Variously spelled* lallapalooza
or lollypaloozer, *the term is likely related to the more familiar* lulu.

✳   ✳   ✳   ✳

THE WORD LOLLAPALOOZA, which is now very much associated with the decade of the 1990s, has inspired a host
of *-palooza* words. Most are nonce words that were used only
once, or that have been independently coined multiple times:

✳ *drink-a-palooza*—an alcoholic binge

✳ *festapalooza*—a big party

✳ *party-palooza*—various meanings, all having to do with some
kind of celebration

✳ *pawn-a-palooza*—chess strategy aimed at taking all of the
opponent's pawns regardless of the cost, usually used more
for annoying the opponent than actually winning

✳ *Polar-Palooza*—a NASA-funded educational campaign
about Arctic and Antarctic climate science

✳ *Pope-a-palooza*—a 2005 papal trip around the world aimed
at connecting with youth

✳ *quote-a-palooza*—an academic paper filled with quotes so the
student doesn't have to write much

✳ *snooze-a-palooza*—remaining in bed all morning

And of course, it was only a matter of time before some wag
coined *paloozapalooza*, a word for the phenomenon of coining
words ending in *-palooza.*

Kangaroo Words

*Kangaroos: They're not just found in the Outback. Hop to it, and learn about **kangaroo words**.*

✳ ✳ ✳ ✳

SOME WORDS CONTAIN their own synonyms. Take the word *container*, for example. Looking over its letters from left to right (not consecutively), you can find the words *can* and *tin*, and both words are synonyms of the word *container*. This is a good example of a kangaroo word. (Some call the internal synonyms *joeys*.)

Particularly elegant kangaroo words have few leftover letters, and there is no etymological relationship between the outer and inner words— even though in the animal kingdom, one would assume that a mother kangaroo and her joey are, in fact, related. Only one letter is unused in the pair *amicable/amiable*, but since the words are both derived from the Latin *amicabilis* ("friendly"), it isn't surprising that they share so many letters. Other related pairs include *salvage/save, hostel/hotel, evacuate/vacate*, and *masculine/male*.

Jumping for Joey Joy

There are plenty of kangaroo words with etymologically unrelated joeys, though. For example, the kangaroo *indolent* comes from the Latin *in* ("not") + *dolentem* ("suffering"), but the joey *idle* is derived from a Germanic word, *idel* ("empty, worthless"). Independently of one another, both words later came to mean "lazy." Other examples: *encourage/urge, precipitation/rain, destruction/ruin, instructor/tutor, contaminate/taint, catacomb/tomb, unsightly/ugly, curtail/cut, falsities/lies, transgression/sin, scion/son, twitch/tic*, and *municipality/city*.

Some kangaroo words have joeys that appear in consecutive letter sequences, such as *crude/rude, perimeter/rim,* and *devilish/evil.* Because they don't reveal hidden letter patterns, some people don't count these as kangaroo/joey pairs. But while it's true they're less exciting, it seems unfair to discount them completely.

Kangaroo words lend themselves to a particular kind of puzzle, one in which solvers are given the kangaroo word with the letters of its joey removed and replaced with blanks or asterisks. Here are two examples (not already mentioned above) for you to solve:

pr*m*tu*e**   ob**rv*

Opposites Attract

While you're pondering those, also consider the interesting fact that some words contain their own opposite. There's no agreed-upon term for these words. Some such pairs are *stray/stay, covert/overt, animosity/amity, effective/effete, courteous/curt,* and *primordial/mod.* Some kangaroos contain both well-behaved and rebellious joeys, such as *feast,* which contains both *eat* and *fast,* and *fabrication,* which contains both *fact* and *fiction.*

As for the puzzles above, hopefully you didn't have to give up *prematurely,* or *early,* before skipping down to this paragraph to *observe,* or *see,* the answers.

"A symphony must be like the world. It must contain everything."

—GUSTAV MAHLER

"Do I contradict myself? Very well, then I contradict myself. I am large, I contain multitudes."

—WALT WHITMAN

Vowel Play

Four of the five most common letters in English are vowels (the fifth vowel, u, straggles in at #12). But they're not cliquish—they usually mingle freely with consonants.

✳ ✳ ✳ ✳

THE LONGEST STRETCH of uninterrupted vowels in a common word is five, in *queueing*. With proper names, you can get up to nine, as visitors to *Cauaiauaia*, Angola, or speakers of the Brazilian language *Uru-eu-uau-uau* know. Also including five vowels in a row, but more notably containing no consonants at all, is *aieee*, which is how the *Oxford English Dictionary* spells "an angst-filled interjection." There's also *aa*, a kind of lava, and *ai*, a sloth, both beloved by Scrabble players, and *IOU*, of course.

Eau is French but appears in many phrases assimilated into English. (Say *aye aye* if you agree that counts, or *aye-aye* if you see a nocturnal lemur of Madagascar.) The record for longest word containing no consonants is held by *Uoiauai*, a Brazilian language you probably won't run across unless you're in the habit of reading books like this one.

I'd Like to Buy a Vowel

The shortest common word with all five vowels is *sequoia*, followed by *dialogue*, *equation*, and *euphoria*. (The vowel-friendly French language offers *oiseau*, meaning "bird.") The shortest common words with all the vowels including *y* are ten letters long: *audiometry*, *buoyancies*, *coequality*, and *in-your-face*; we can get down to eight letters with the phrases *I dare you* and

I hear you. (For more words that include all the vowels, read up on abecedarian words on page 338.)

A, E, I, O, U ... and in this Case, Y

Sometimes one vowel does all the work, letting the others take a break. There's nothing but *a*'s in *handcraftsman, Ball Park franks, Sarah McLachlan, grasp at straws,* and *Graham Chapman,* for instance. *E* offers *strengthlessnesses, reentrenchment, effervescence, sweet-temperedness, deferred sentence,* Ellen DeGeneres, *letter-perfect, jeepers creepers, sleeveless dress,* Werner Klemperer, *"The defense rests,"* Renée Zellweger, *crème de menthe,* and *"Where's the beef?"*

There may be no *i* in *team,* but there's a team of *i*'s in *instinctivistic, disinhibiting, first things first, Miss Mississippi, pitching niblick, striking it rich, in high spirits,* and *missing link.* O takes the lead in *monophthong* (a diphthong's relative), *worst of both worlds, go from door to door, from top to bottom, follow protocol,* and *knock on wood.* O also has a religious bent, being the only vowel in *Song of Solomon, crown of thorns,* and *Book of Mormon.* U gets top billing in *dumbstruck, numbskulls, untruthful, unsunburnt, Crunch 'n Munch,* H. R. Pufnstuf, and *punch-drunk.* And even *y* has *rhythms, spryly, syzygy,* and *Spy vs. Spy.*

✳ *louea* is a genus of Cretaceous fossil sponges. It's also the only word in the English language that contains all five vowels once each with no consonants (making it a handy word to keep in mind if you're stuck with a bad Scrabble hand). Pronounced eye-o-yoo-EE-ah, it's the shortest four-syllable word in English.

✳ An *iotacist* is someone who makes excessive use of the letter *i*.

N-E Grammagrams 4 U?

Grammagrams *are 2 good 2 B 4-gotten.*

✳ ✳ ✳ ✳

WILLIAM STEIG, THE author of the children's book *Shrek!*, also wrote a book titled *C D B!* The illustration on the cover shows a child pointing out a bee to another child. The book (along with its sequel, *C D C?*) contains many examples of sentences formed by sounding out letters and numbers, from the accurately pronounced "I N-V U" ("I envy you") to the rather freewheeling "N-R-E S N T-S" ("Henry is in tears"), or "E-R S A M-R" ("Here is a hammer"). Other examples have appeared as punch lines to riddles ("What seven letters did the stranded motorist say to his gas tank?" "O, I C U R MT"). Noted linguist Richard Lederer coined a word to describe such sounded-out words: *grammagrams.*

While it's possible to find many examples by playing loose with phonetics, it's EZ to come up with a sizable list without resorting to such KG, arguably DVS (if not so bad as to be ODS) behavior. While there isn't an XS of grammagrams out there, there isn't NE dearth either—especially if you allow other characters to be used, which will LMN8 some obstacles and XLR8 your grammagram-finding XPDNC. You can even allow 4N letters, if you want to be a real QT.

Here are a few more grammagrams, in increasing order of length: 4A (*foray*), CD (*seedy*), DK (*decay*), IC (*icy*), IV (*ivy*), SA (*essay*), TP (*tepee*), XL (*excel*), ZT (*ziti*), 4N6 (*forensics*), AV8 (*aviate*), NME (*enemy*), NVS (*envious*), OPM (*opium*), SKP (*escapee*), TDS (*tedious*), XP8 (*expiate*), RKDN (*Arcadian*), VMNC (*vehemency*), XLNC (*excellency*), and OBDNC (*obediency*). As for phrases, a suspicious Cyclops might have a BD I, and you should be on the lookout for a C NMNE next time you're scuba diving.

Words of Wisdom from Thomas A. Edison

✳ ✳ ✳ ✳

✳ I have not failed. I have discovered twelve hundred materials that don't work.

✳ There is no substitute for hard work.

✳ To invent, you need a good imagination and a pile of junk.

✳ Genius is one percent inspiration and ninety-nine percent perspiration.

✳ Hell, there are no rules here—we're trying to accomplish something.

✳ I find my greatest pleasure, and so my reward, in the work that precedes what the world calls success.

✳ I have friends in overalls whose friendship I would not swap for the favor of the kings of the world.

✳ Many of life's failures are people who did not realize how close they were to success when they gave up.

✳ Nearly every man who develops an idea works it up to the point where it looks impossible, and then he gets discouraged. That's not the place to become discouraged.

✳ Restlessness is discontent, and discontent is the first necessity of progress. Show me a thoroughly satisfied man and I will show you a failure.

✳ To have a great idea, have a lot of them.

✳ We don't know a millionth of 1 percent about anything.

Chronograms: Timeless Wordplay

To commemorate a historic event, some people might build a monument. Others might compose a poem or write a scholarly essay. But those who are really up for a challenge might choose to produce a **chronogram.**

✳ ✳ ✳ ✳

THE WORD **CHRONOGRAM** literally means "time writing." It derives from the Greek words *chronos* and *gramma,* or "time" and "letter." So it makes sense that a chronogram is a sentence in which specific letters are converted to, or interpreted as, Roman numerals to stand for a particular date.

There are multiple ways to compose a chronogram. The most common (and easiest, as these things go) way is to compose a sentence in which all of the letters that can double as Roman numerals (I, V, X, L, C, D, M) are added together to achieve the desired sum. To do this you'll need to remember the value of each Roman numeral: I=1, V=5, X=10, L=50, C=100, D=500, and M=1,000. In this type of chronogram, all such letters *must* be used—no extraneous I's or V's left over at the end.

Here's an example of this type of chronogram: One might commemorate 2008 with the sentence ELECTION DAY CARRIES BARACK OBAMA TO OVAL OFFICE, which whittles down to L + C + I + D + C + I + C + M + V + L + I + C = 50 + 100 + 1 + 500 + 100 + 1 + 100 + 1,000 + 5 + 50 + 1 + 100 = 2008.

This sort of chronogram originated in the Roman Empire but became particularly common during the Renaissance in Europe, when it was often used to indicate the date of publication of books (with several common substitutions for Roman numerals—that is, a U was considered equivalent to a V, and likewise with I and J).

Because Roman Numerals Weren't Confusing Enough?

A less common and rather more difficult way to compose a chronogram is to maintain strict left-to-right order, using only the Roman numerals that appear in the date itself. A well-known example of this type is one that was composed in honor of Queen Elizabeth I's death in 1603: "My Day Closed Is In Immortality." In this slightly nonstandard chronogram we read only the initial letters, giving us MDCIII, or 1603.

A particularly noteworthy chronogram appeared on a medal commemorating a 1709 battle in which the French were defeated by the Duke of Marlborough. The inscription was LILICIDIVM—that is, "lilicidium"—which translates from the Latin as "the slaughter of the lily." (The lily, or fleur-de-lis, is a symbol of France.) Remarkably, this chronogram contains nothing *but* Roman numerals, and those Roman numerals indeed add up to 1709.

✳ **Chronograms were also composed with Hebraic numerals; in fact, a Hebrew chronogram dating from the year 1205 has been found, preceding the earliest known Latin chronogram by five years.**

The People's Prefix

The Greek demos *means "people" and is at the core of some popular words. Perhaps the most notable is* democracy, *or "rule by the people." In English use, the word is surprisingly recent, only making its appearance in the late sixteenth century. It's from the Medieval Latin* democratia, *which in turn is from Greek. So while we tend to think of the English-speaking world as being very democratic, in the great scheme of things this is a fairly recent development.*

✳   ✳   ✳   ✳

O F COURSE, DEMOCRATIC with a capital D is the name of a political party in the United States and other countries. Often it appears as part of a hyphenated party name. The modern American Democratic Party was once the *Democratic-Republicans* (no relation to the modern Republican Party). In the state of Minnesota, the Democratic party is officially known as the *Democratic-Farmer-Labor* party. In Europe, there are *Democratic-Socialist* parties.

Demos of *Demo-*

Another popular *demo-* word is *demographic. Demography* is the study of populations, and the word was coined in 1880. The use of *demographic* as a noun, naming a subset of the population that is a target for advertising, is even newer. It only dates to 1984.

Other *demo-* words include *demagogue,* a popular leader, especially one who plays to the base instincts and emotions of a population to further his or her own power. *To demagogue* is a verb meaning "to play the role of a demagogue." And in some religious and philosophical doctrines, the *Demiurge* is the creator of both the world and evil. The Demiurge is usually subordinate to the Supreme Being, and the word comes from the Greek meaning "public worker."

With its role as the key player in denoting self-government, *demo-* occupies a conspicuous place in the English lexicon. Perhaps surprisingly, though, English hasn't found much application for the root elsewhere; once you account for words formed from *democracy* and *demography*, there aren't many others left. Language is flexible, of course, and new words are being coined all the time.

So what would it take to see greater utilization of *demo-*? Why, nothing more than use by *the people* who speak the language.

"Democracy is the theory that the common people know what they want, and deserve to get it good and hard."

—H. L. Mencken

"The world is weary of statesmen whom democracy has degraded into politicians."

—Benjamin Disraeli

"If a man went simply by what he saw, he might be tempted to affirm that the essence of democracy is melodrama."

—Irving Babbitt

"Democracy cannot succeed unless those who express their choice are prepared to choose wisely. The real safeguard of democracy, then, is education."

—Franklin D. Roosevelt

"As I would not be a slave, so I would not be a master. This expresses my idea of democracy."

—Abraham Lincoln

Famous Last Words: Presidents

✳ ✳ ✳ ✳

"I am just going. Have me decently buried and do not let my body be put into the vault in less than three days after I am dead. Do you understand? Tis well."
—GEORGE WASHINGTON (1732–1799)

"Thomas Jefferson—still survives..."
—JOHN ADAMS (1735–1826) *(JEFFERSON DIED THAT SAME DAY, JULY 4, 1826)*

"Is it the Fourth?"
—THOMAS JEFFERSON (1743–1826) *(ON JULY 4, 1826)*

"The nourishment is palatable."
—MILLARD FILLMORE (1800–1874)

"I know that I am going where Lucy is."
—RUTHERFORD B. HAYES (1822–1893)

"I have tried so hard to do the right."
—GROVER CLEVELAND (1837–1908)

"Good-bye, good-bye, all. We are all going. It's God's way. His will be done, not ours. Nearer, my God, to Thee, nearer to Thee. We are all going. We are all going. We are all going. Oh, dear."
—WILLIAM MCKINLEY (1843–1901)

"Put out the light."
—THEODORE ROOSEVELT (1858–1919)

"I have a terrific headache."
—FRANKLIN D. ROOSEVELT (1882–1945)

"That's very obvious."
—JOHN F. KENNEDY (1917–1963)

M*ss*ng the Po*nt

It's time to turn to the thesaurus.

A LIPOGRAM IS A passage of text in which a letter of the alphabet is deliberately avoided. In general, the unused letter is a common one, since it's fairly easy to go on for a while without using a *q* or an *x*. But if you were to try to avoid the most common letter in the English language (*e*) while using all the other letters at least once (though this is not a requirement), you might get a paragraph like this next one:

> If a wordsmith thinks, "Today I'll draft a lipogram," a thing that hardy soul just won't want to do without is a book of synonyms. It's difficult to maintain clarity whilst choosing vocabulary that lacks such a common trait (to wit, that glyph lying twixt *d* and *f*). Only truly hard-working guys and gals won't quit, and will finally accomplish such a zany goal as this.

Entire lipogrammatic novels have been written, such as Ernest Vincent Wright's 50,000-word *e*-less *Gadsby* (1939) and Georges Perec's 300-plus-page *La Disparition* (1969). The latter was translated into English by Gilbert Adair as *A Void*; both it and the original contain no *e*'s. Perec later wrote a novella entitled *Les Revenentes* (1972) that omitted every vowel *except* the hard-working *e*. Ian Monk translated it in 1996 using the same constraint, with the title *The Exeter Text: Jewels, Secrets, Sex*. A 2002 epistolary novel, *Ella Minnow Pea*, by Mark Dunn, is not perfectly lipogrammatic, but it features a plot in which letters are banned one by one. The postal correspondence written by the characters in the book must avoid those letters by any means (including, in some cases, creative spelling). When the characters slip and use forbidden letters, they are punished. If *you* write any lipograms, hopefully it'll just be for the fun of it.

'Scuse Me While I Kiss This Guy

It's happened to everyone: You've known a song your entire life. You've got the lyrics memorized. You sing along to it in the car every time it plays on the radio. And then one fateful day, someone clues you in and you discover that, no, Jimi Hendrix is actually singing "'Scuse me while I kiss the sky" instead of what you thought he was singing, which was "'Scuse me while I kiss this guy."

✳ ✳ ✳ ✳

MISHEARD LYRICS ARE called *mondegreens,* a word that was coined by writer Sylvia Wright in 1954, inspired by her own mishearing of a line in the old Scottish ballad "The Bonnie Earl o' Moray." The first verse of the ballad goes, "Ye highlands and ye lowlands, O, where have ye been? They have slain the Earl o' Moray and laid him on the green," but she thought the second half went, "They have slain the Earl o' Moray and Lady Mondegreen." She wrote an article about her "enlightenment" in *Harper's* magazine in 1954, introducing the term. Columnist Jon Carroll of the *San Francisco Chronicle* brought it into the mainstream in the 1980s.

I Beg Your Pardon?

Other mondegreens include animals ("Olive, the other reindeer"—who used to call Rudolph names, apparently—and "Gladly, the cross-eyed bear," from the hymn "Gladly the Cross I'd Bear"); directions (Creedence Clearwater Revival's observation that "there's a bathroom on the right"—rather than a bad moon on the rise); food (the Crystal Gayle song "Donuts Make Your Brown Eyes Blue," mondegreened from "Don't It Make Your Brown Eyes Blue"; and the mysterious historical figure Richard Stans (made famous by the United States Pledge of Allegiance, which doesn't quite go, "and to the republic, for Richard Stans"). (Maybe he's the one who's responsible for making the nation "invisible.") Jingles don't escape unscathed, to the chagrin of the ad agencies who carefully craft them: The retail chain Sears sells many things, but, despite what you may think you've heard, computer software isn't one of them ("Come see the software side of Sears"—or "softer," as the case may be).

What causes mondegreens? Some words have similar phonetics, especially when the boundaries between words are unclear. When separating a stream of incoming sound into words and phrases, listeners normally rely on intonation and stress, which are often lost in song lyrics. Add some noise from other instruments and you've got a recipe for confusion. All of these are factors in the aural absorption of Jimi Hendrix's "Purple Haze." If you heard "'Scuse me while I kiss this guy," you're not alone: The editors of KissThisGuy.com, a database of mondegreens, claim it's the most common misheard lyric submitted to their site.

More Funny Mondegreens

* Dave Matthews, "Crash": "Hike up your skirt, little boy." (*Hike up your skirt a little more.*)

* Elton John, "Tiny Dancer": "Hold me closer. Tie me down, sir." (*Hold me closer, tiny dancer.*)

* Simon and Garfunkel, "Bridge Over Troubled Water": "Hello Douglas, my old friend." (*Hello darkness, my old friend.*)

* Steve Miller Band, "Fly Like an Eagle": "Shoot the children living on the street." (*Shoe the children living on the street.*)

* The Who, "Pinball Wizard": "Sure pleased to meet pinball." (*Sure plays a mean pinball.*)

---

* **The process of separating a stream of incoming sound into different words is called *parsing*. Errors in parsing can lead to changes in words: What we now call "an apron" used to be "a napron," and what we now call "a newt" used to be "an ewt."**

It All Adds Up

When is a word puzzle not a word puzzle? When it's actually a math puzzle.

✳ ✳ ✳ ✳

CRYPTARITHMS ARE A cross between cryptograms (see page 28) and arithmetical problems. Each number in an equation is replaced with a letter (with each letter always representing the same number in that equation). The solver has to use mathematical principles to decode each letter into a number, creating a true mathematical statement.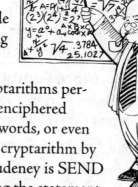

The wordplay component in cryptarithms pertains to the fact that, ideally, the enciphered version of the problem will spell words, or even a sentence. For instance, a classic cryptarithm by legendary puzzle writer H. E. Dudeney is SEND + MORE = MONEY: Decoding the statement yields the equation 9,567 + 1,085 = 10,652.

Other cryptarithms are formed with themed sets of words, such as YELLOW + YELLOW + RED = ORANGE (solution: 143,329 + 143,329 + 846 = 287,504) or the impressive SATURN + URANUS + NEPTUNE + PLUTO = PLANETS (solution: 127,503 + 502,351 + 3,947,539 + 46,578 = 4,623,971).

Your Math Teacher Would Be Proud

Some cryptarithms, when enciphered, produce new equations that are also correct. For instance:

✳ FORTY + TEN + TEN = SIXTY (with the solution 29,786 + 850 + 850 = 31,486)

* SIX + SIX + SIX = NINE + NINE (942 + 942 + 942 = 1,413 + 1,413)

* FIVE + FIVE + NINE + ELEVEN = THIRTY (4,027 + 4,027 + 5,057 + 797,275 = 810,386)

* In French, there's DEUX + SIX = HUIT (or 2 + 6 = 8; the solution is 7,601 + 451 = 8,052)

* In Italian, the same English sum comes out as DUE + SEI = OTTO (806 + 965 = 1,771)

Of course, one can also come up with verbal equations that are false to pair with correct mathematical statements, as with TWO × TWO = THREE (138 × 138 = 19,044). As perpetrators of creative accounting can tell you, numbers can't always be trusted!

---

* **Euler's Day Off is a pencil-and-paper word game. Letters are called out one at a time at random (by drawing Scrabble tiles, say), and as they are called out, players write them in a 5-by-5 square. The goal is to form as many words of three or more letters as possible going across and down; words may overlap. The winner is the player with the most words; in case of a tie, the player with the most five-letter words wins (then the most four-letter words).**

"Pure mathematics is, in its way, the poetry of logical ideas."

—ALBERT EINSTEIN

"Thus mathematics may be defined as the subject in which we never know what we are talking about, nor whether what we are saying is true."

—BERTRAND RUSSELL

Guessing Games: Botticelli

Twenty Questions isn't the only guessing game out there. Before you resort to singing "99 Bottles of Beer" to pass the time, why not try your hand at this fun word-guessing game?

* * * *

IN **BOTTICELLI,** ONE player thinks of a famous person or character and reveals the initial of their last name (or their only initial, if it's someone like Sting or Cher). Let's say it's L, for Jay Leno. Other players take turns asking questions to find the mystery figure, but they must have a person in mind. For instance, one might ask, "Were you a star of *Charlie's Angels?*" to which the answer might be, "No, I'm not Lucy Liu." Since the player being questioned named someone who fit the description (whether or not it was whom the guesser had in mind; perhaps they were thinking of Cheryl Ladd), the game continues with another question of the same type—such as, "Are you a talk show host?" If the player can't think of an alternative, he must answer, "Yes, I'm Jay Leno," and the game ends.

However, if the player thought to answer, "No, I'm not David Letterman," the game would have continued. What if the next question ("Are you a 1980s tennis pro?") stumps him? Then he simply answers "no." At this time the questioner reveals who they meant ("I guess you're not Ivan Lendl, then") and is now permitted to ask a single direct yes-or-no question, such as "Are you male?" or, if they are ready to attempt to win the game, an even more direct question, such as, "Are you Jay Leno?" (Some variants of the game allow direct questions to continue until one is answered "no.") If the identity hasn't been guessed, the guessers return to the original style of question.

Word Pluses and Minuses

Ditloid word puzzles are A. L. of F. (a lot of fun).

✳ ✳ ✳ ✳

A DITLOID IS A type of puzzle (also popularly known as an "equation analysis test") in which solvers are asked to guess what the initials stand for in a clue formatted to resemble a mathematical equation. For instance, the ditloid "26 = L. of the A." leads to the answer "26 = letters of the alphabet." Now that you know how it works, try solving the following: "88 = P.K."; "5 = D. in a Z.C."; and "200 = D. for P.G. in M." (Answers below.) Traditionally, short connecting words are spelled out, though in the case of the example that inspired the coinage *ditloid*, short words were abbreviated too, which led to the clue "1 = DitLoID" (referring to the novel *One Day in the Life of Ivan Denisovich* by Aleksandr Solzhenitsyn).

Ditloids as a form of wordplay really took off in 1981, after Will Shortz's "Equation Analysis Test" was published in *Games* magazine. The puzzle contained 24 ditloids (including the ones in the paragraph above). The puzzle spawned many sequels, both in *Games* magazine and written by enthusiastic solvers themselves. Shortz cited as his inspiration a similar puzzle by Morgan Worthy in the book *Aha! A Puzzle Approach to Creative Thinking*. Shortz made his puzzle more structurally rigid than Worthy's, which included such teasers as "N.N. = G.N." Some examples, such as "A. & E. were in the G. of E." weren't even written in equation form. (See answers below.) Shortz's *Games* version set the format as: number on the left, abbreviated text on the right. We'll revert to a less strict format, however, to say that "P. = S.S.S."

The answers to the puzzles above are: "88 = piano keys"; "5 = digits in a ZIP code"; "200 = dollars for passing Go in Monopoly"; "no news = good news"; "Adam and Eve were in the Garden of Eden"; and "parting = such sweet sorrow."

Looks Like...

When you hear the word bling-bling, *you may picture not only many pieces of flashy and gaudy jewelry, but also lots of light reflecting showily off it, accompanied by a sound effect similar to the one onomatopoeically rendered by the word itself. That's because* bling-bling *is an* **ideophone**—*that is, a word that makes a vivid sensory impression.*

✳   ✳   ✳   ✳

BLING-BLING IS PRIMARILY a visual *ideophone*, though it also has a sound component, with the word suggesting the sound of bracelets jingling against each other. The visual component comes from the initial sound of *bl-*, as in *blare, blast, blaze,* and *blam.* The suggestion is of something almost explosively bright.

Words like *flutter, flit, flurry, flip,* and *flicker* are also visual ideophones. All of these create images not just of flight, but of very specific kinds of movement.

Most people are familiar with the concept of onomatopoeic words, which are aural ideophones (see page 74 for more on onomatopoeia). Onomatopoeic words actually sound like what they represent, almost as if they were dictionary-sanctioned sound effects. Still, even with ideophones that are derived from sounds, the source of the sound may be so associated with the word that there is an associated visual component as well, as with the image of an accelerating car that might accompany *vroom,* or the gesture of hitting a key on a cash register to make a *ka-ching* noise.

Other non-aural ideophones include *zigzag* (try saying it *without* picturing someone or something moving back and forth), *heebie-jeebies* (evoking that shivering sensation), and *roly-poly* (perhaps calling to mind Violet Beauregarde's misadventure in *Charlie and the Chocolate Factory,* in which she turns into a giant blueberry).

Words of Wisdom: Silence

✳ ✳ ✳ ✳

"Silence is more eloquent than words."

—THOMAS CARLYLE

"Choose silence of all virtues, for by it you hear other men's imperfections, and conceal your own."

—GEORGE BERNARD SHAW

"He who does not understand your silence will probably not understand your words."

—ELBERT HUBBARD

"Nothing strengthens authority so much as silence."

— LEONARDO DA VINCI

"Everything has its wonders, even darkness and silence, and I learn, whatever state I may be in, therein to be content."

— HELEN KELLER

"Silence is a true friend who never betrays."

—CONFUCIUS

"Silence is a source of great strength."

—LAO TZU

"Silence is the best tactic for him who distrusts himself."

—FRANÇOIS, DUC DE LA ROCHEFOUCAULD

"It is tact that is golden, not silence."

—SAMUEL BUTLER

A Hodgepodge of Reduplications

One way that words are formed in English is by duplicating or echoing syllables. This is called **reduplication.** *Since this is reminiscent of baby talk—or, in some cases, is baby talk—the words thus formed tend to have a humorous tone.*

✳   ✳   ✳   ✳

SOMETIMES AN EXISTING word will have something appended after it (*teeny-weeny, lovey-dovey, super-duper, boogie-woogie, palsy-walsy*) or before it (*herky-jerky, chitchat, mishmash, razzle-dazzle, dillydally, wishy-washy*—yup, *washy* is a word; it means "overly diluted" or, by extension, "weak"). In some cases, both halves of the word are evocative but nonsensical on their own, as is the case with *heebie-jeebies, hocus-pocus, flimflam, namby-pamby, pell-mell, helter-skelter,* and *hodgepodge.*

Willy-Nilly, Shilly-Shally

Of course, things that seem nonsensical nowadays may have origins in forgotten words. *Hoity-toity* comes from the obsolete word *hoit,* which meant "to romp"; *hoity-toity* originally meant "acting giddy," only later coming to mean "pretentious and haughty." And the word *willy-nilly* is actually derived from the old phrase "will ye, nill ye" (which means, essentially, "whether you like it or not," as when Petruchio says to Katherina in *The Taming of the Shrew,* "And will you, nill you, I will marry you"). The same goes for *shilly-shally:* In the 1700s, some indecisive soul queried, "Shall I, shall I?" The phrase morphed into "Shill I? Shall I?" And later it became simply *shilly-shally,* a term to describe indecision.

> *"The truth must dazzle gradually*
> *Or every man be blind."*
> —EMILY DICKINSON

Don't Pooh-Pooh the Power of a Good Tautonym

Some reduplications are, in fact, exact reduplications (called **tautonyms**), such as *matchy-matchy, bling-bling, picky-picky, pooh-pooh, goody-goody, blah-blah, yada yada, choo-choo, tut-tut,* and *bye-bye.* From a wordplay standpoint, though, the most interesting tautonyms are the ones that aren't intentional, where the fact that the first and second halves of a word are identical, as with *tartar, hotshots,* and *wallawalla,* is just a happy coincidence.

Mapping It Out

Near-tautonyms can be found as well. *Intestines* merely shifts the *t* between halves, and *reappear* swaps the second *r* and second *p.* If you don't limit yourself to single words, you can construct reduplicated sentences like "Can we scan, Wes?" and the slightly ungrammatical "Let his uncle and I restyle this unclean, dire sty."

✳ The reduplication *razzle-dazzle* enjoyed some time in the spotlight as the title of a song in the hit Broadway production *Chicago.* Sung by the character Billy Flynn, the song is advice for Roxie, who is on trial for murder, to just "give 'em the old razzle-dazzle" to win sympathy from the jury.

✳ In biology, a tautonym is an informal zoological term that's made up of two identical words and indicates the scientific name of a species; for example, *Bison bison* or *Lynx lynx.* The first word indicates the animal's genus, and the second is the animal's specific name.

Siamese Twins

In rhetoric, **Siamese twins** *are pairs of words that appear together in a phrase connected by the word* and—*more specifically, the words in a given pair cannot switch places in the phrase without the meaning being lost. For instance, no one will bat an eye if you move* backward and forward *or* forward and backward, *but if you have to miss an all-night poker game because your* chain and ball *would disapprove, people will be confused.*

✳   ✳   ✳   ✳

SOME SIAMESE TWINS have their positions fixed because they represent things that happen in a logical order. Weight lifters might injure themselves performing a *jerk and clean,* for instance, and doing *tell and show* might make a child's classmates impatient to see the object being discussed. *Entering and breaking* is what a bull in a china shop might do, but that's not the sequence a jewel thief would use. Mostly, though, Siamese twins have the order they do because that's just how it worked out.

Together, for Worse or Better

Let's take a moment to enjoy the alternate universe in which these phrases are arranged the other way around. In that universe, kids inspired by the latest episode of *Order & Law* might fight *nail and tooth* while playing *robbers and cops* (which is all *games and fun* until someone loses an eye). After competing in *field and track* and studying *crafts and arts,* they might later graduate from high school wearing a *gown and cap.* Perhaps they go on to analyze *loss and profit* statements, or maybe their *butter and bread* is some other trade. Those who don't stick to the *narrow and straight* will find life to be not all *light and sweetness;* committing *battery and assault* will only lead to a game of *mouse and cat* with the authorities, and eventually being placed under *key and lock.* Not that we want to be too *mighty and high,* though; life is nothing but *error and trial,* and the *ends and odds* presented here are, like many things, only so much *mirrors and smoke.*

Words of Wisdom: Miracles

✳ ✳ ✳ ✳

"One miracle is just as easy to believe as another."
—WILLIAM JENNINGS BRYAN

"When we do the best we can, we never know what miracle is wrought in our life, or in the life of another."
—HELEN KELLER

"To me every hour of the light and dark is a miracle."
—WALT WHITMAN

"Whatever a man prays for, he prays for a miracle."
—IVAN SERGEYEVICH TURGENEV

"I have seen no more evident monstrosity and miracle in the world than myself."
—MICHEL DE MONTAIGNE

"This world . . . is still a miracle; wonderful, inscrutable, magical, and more, to whosoever will think of it."
—THOMAS CARLYLE

"All is a miracle. The stupendous order of nature, the revolution of a hundred millions of worlds around a million of stars, the activity of light, the life of all animals, all are grand and perpetual miracles."
—VOLTAIRE

"Miracles are propitious accidents, the natural causes of which are too complicated to be readily understood."
—GEORGE SANTAYANA

It's What's Inside that Counts

Many words carry more than one meaning, but some—called **containers**—*carry one meaning literally packed inside another. For instance,* eyesight *contains the word* yes *packed inside the word* eight, *and once you've finished the* lamb *at the* clambake, *there's still* cake *left over. This type of wordplay is also known as* word deletion, *since deleting the inner word leaves the outer word behind.*

✳   ✳   ✳   ✳

CONTAINER WORDS ARE abundant in English. Here are just a few of the longer ones (ten letters and up):

- *apparently = aren't* in *apply*
- *art gallery = gall* in *artery*
- *beleaguering = league* in *Bering*
- *borderland = order* in *bland*
- *centimeter = time* in *center*
- *chemotherapies = mother* in *cheapies*
- *chinchilla = chill* in *china*
- *churchiness = urchin* in *chess*
- *complexities = exit* in *complies*
- *disconcert = sconce* in *dirt*
- *grasshopper = shop* in *grasper*

- *guesthouses = thou* in *guesses*
- *heartrending = trend* in *hearing*
- *hithermost = thermos* in *hit*
- *impoverish = over* in *impish*
- *mind reader = dread* in *miner*
- *picaresque = cares* in *pique*
- *reconnaissance = con* in *renaissance*
- *reminiscent = minis* in *recent*
- *shaving cream = having* in *scream*
- *thundering = under* in *thing*
- *timberline = Berlin* in *time*

The word *warplanes* is an interesting specimen; it can be seen as *plan* inside *wares* or *lane* inside *warps* (as well as the trivial *plane* inside *wars*).

Variations are possible. For instance, two consecutive words may appear inside a longer word, as with *painfully*, which contains *in* + *full* inside *pay* (and moving the inner words to follow the outer word results in the phrase "pay in full"). Here are some other examples:

- *apartment = art + men in apt*
- *barefaced = ref + ace in bad*
- *bowlegged = owl + egg in bed*
- *propensity = open + sit in pry*
- *tournament = our + name in TNT*

Containers may also consist of nested words. If you read the words in *armaments* from the inside out, you get *men-at-arms*. Here are a few more:

- *basset hound = set in ash in bound*
- *collaborator = rat in boo in collar*
- *curmudgeon = mud in urge in con*
- *false alarm = sea in all in farm*
- *improvidently = Ovid in rent in imply*
- *mastermind = term in sin in mad*
- *nouveau riche = uvea in our in niche*
- *thistledown = led in stow in thin*

Foreshadowing has four nested words: *had* in *sow* in *rein* in *fog*.

Pilgrimages has two different sets of three nested words: *grim* in *lag* in *pies*, and *rim* in *gag* in *piles*.

Truly impressive, but try to contain yourself.

Chapter 2

Figures of Speech

Seeking Heaven's Aid

For the love of God, please read this article!

✳   ✳   ✳   ✳

SOME FIGURES OF SPEECH exist to provide a means to express strong emotion. Such a one is *deesis* (pronounced DEE-uh-sis or duh-EE-sis), Greek for "prayer" or "supplication." It is an expression of desire put in strong form by invoking some outward agency, usually the Supreme Being. It is also a call to witness an action or a situation.

Appealing to a Higher Power

Some standard invocations are "for God's sake," "for goodness' sake," and "for pity's sake." Similar statements—"as God is my witness," or the surviving English subjunctive in "would God that I had"—also call upon the heavens to take notice of a terrestrial situation.

The context requires strong emotion, but not necessarily reverence, as in John Donne's poem "The Canonization," which begins, "For God's sake hold your tongue, and let me love." Or, as a mother speaking to a teenage son on his way out the door might say, "For God's sake, put on a clean shirt"—an expression more of impatience or mild disgust than stronger emotion.

Deesis is also allied to *apostrophe*, the figure of speech in which God or the gods or a muse or some abstraction personified is addressed directly. When Perry White, Clark Kent's editor at the *Daily Planet*, encounters something startling, he blurts out "Great Caesar's ghost!" He isn't exactly talking to Caesar's shade, which would make this apostrophe, but rather invoking it as a mark of his surprise or as a witness to it.

More Earthly Appeals

Secular people may prefer to steer clear of divinities, and religious people may see casual mentions of the divine as profane. To satisfy both groups, the English language has developed euphemistic forms of deesis. For example, the Englishman's "By Jove!" invokes a deity not formally worshipped in Britain. People who say "Jeepers!" or "Jeez!" may or may not be aware that the words are euphemisms for *Jesus*. *Golly, gosh,* and *doggone* all avoid using *God* outright.

"The true object of all human life is play. Earth is a task garden; heaven is a playground."

—G. K. CHESTERTON

"Earth's crammed with heaven."

—ELIZABETH BARRETT BROWNING

"Earth has no sorrow that Heaven cannot heal."

—THOMAS MOORE

"As much of heaven is visible as we have eyes to see."

—WILLIAM WINTER

"In heaven, all the interesting people are missing."

—FRIEDRICH NIETZSCHE

From Little Eggcorns Grow...Great Jokes

If you've ever mistakenly written about a mute point, your doctor's bedside manor, or a handsome cab, then you've unwittingly contributed to a new category of language flub: the **eggcorn.**

✳   ✳   ✳   ✳

EGGCORNS ARE AKIN to malapropisms, but flavored with folk etymology. They occur when someone mishears or misremembers a phrase. Although they are incorrect, they often make more poetic or logical sense than the right expression or word. Linguist Geoffrey K. Pullum, who coined the term *eggcorn* in 2003, notes that no reference guide will help even the smartest person to correct this sort of "slip of the ear," because they've got nothing to look up in a dictionary.

Errors of the Intelligent Variety

When we hear an eggcorn we might be tempted to scoff or snicker. But linguists emphasize the logic and creativity behind them: Since *opposable thumbs* can be *posed* into many shapes, the spelling *a posable thumb* is an understandable invention. The meaning of *like a bull in a china shop* is inverted by *like a bowl in a china shop*, but the connection between china and bowls is strong. And because more people are familiar with chickens served on a plate than chickens sitting on a perch, the coining of *chickens come home to roast* was probably inevitable. So eggcorns are mistakes that show people are *smart*—kind of a refreshing concept!

Eggcorns are interesting to linguists because they provide insight into how people make meaning based on what they've heard and read. Eggcorns are interesting to the rest of us because they can be hilarious. Following is a list of some of the most preposterous.

* *After all is set and done* (after all is said and done)

* *Batter an eye* (bat an eye)

* *Cease the opportunity* (seize the opportunity)

* *Chuck it up to* (chalk it up to)

* *Cold slaw* (cole slaw)

* *Color-coated* (color-coded)

* *Curled up in the feeble position* (curled up in the fetal position)

* *Curve your enthusiasm* (curb your enthusiasm)

* *Cut to the cheese* (cut to the chase)

* *Front in center* (front and center)

* *Garbledygook* (gobbledygook)

* *Kill over and die* (keel over and die)

* *A new leash on life* (a new lease on life)

* *Mixmatch* (mismatch)

* *Physical year* (fiscal year)

* *Putting the car before the horse* (putting the cart before the horse)

* *Soaping wet* (soaking wet)

* *Up to stuff* (up to snuff)

* *Upmost* (utmost)

There are many others, but we'll end the list here *without further adieu.*

Words of Wisdom: Mistakes

✳   ✳   ✳   ✳

"A man should never be ashamed to own he has been in the wrong, which is but saying, in other words, that he is wiser today than he was yesterday."

—JONATHAN SWIFT

"Experience is the name that everyone gives to his mistakes."

—OSCAR WILDE

"A man of genius makes no mistakes. His errors are volitional and are the portals of discovery."

—JAMES JOYCE

"We lament the mistakes of a good man, and do not begin to detest him until he affects to renounce his principles."

—LETTERS OF JUNIUS

"All men are liable to error; and most men are, in many points, by passion or interest, under temptation to it."

—JOHN LOCKE

"Any man can make mistakes, but only an idiot persists in his error."

—MARCUS TULLIUS CICERO

"Tomorrow is always fresh, with no mistakes in it."

—LUCY MAUD MONTGOMERY

"Ignorance is preferable to error; and he is less remote from the truth who believes nothing, than he who believes what is wrong."

—THOMAS JEFFERSON

"In general, pride is at the bottom of all great mistakes."

—JOHN RUSKIN

Almost, but Not Quite

In Latin, the adverb quasi *means "as if, almost, practically."*
The adverb made its way into English with the Normans, first
appearing in print in 1485. The adverbial use of quasi *is now rare*
in English, but it survives as a rather productive prefix.

✳   ✳   ✳   ✳

THE FIRST *QUASI-* word to appear was *quasi-vacuity*, meaning "forgetfulness, empty-headedness." The word dates to 1643. The prefix remained rare until the nineteenth century, when it began to be used in earnest. Now, some 100 *quasi-* words can be found in the dictionary, including:

✳ *quasi-automatic*—not quite able to run on its own

✳ *quasi-divine*—highly respected but not sacred

✳ *quasi-eternal*—lasting for a long time, but not forever

✳ *quasi-legal*—of dubious legality

✳ *quasi-neutrality*—supporting one side in a conflict but staying just shy of belligerency

✳ *quasi-public*—characteristic of an institution that is partly run by the government and partly operated on free-market principles

✳ *quasi-stellar*—resembling a star; the word *quasar*, which names an immensely powerful source of light and radiation created by a supermassive black hole at the center of a distant galaxy, comes from *quasi-stellar*

✳ *quasi-universal*—a noun or adjective used to refer to something that is thought to be almost or virtually universal

✳ *quasi-war*—a cold war or an intense competition

Nothing is quasi- about *quasi-*; it's a very productive prefix.

Don't Have Anything Nice to Say? Use a Euphemism

Every culture has its taboos. In America today, many people are squeamish when it comes to talking about bodily functions, sex, and of course, death. That's where **euphemism** *comes in. People use euphemism—the replacement of negative or taboo terms with less-offensive or neutral ones—every day, often without even realizing it, to avoid using "bad" words and phrases.*

✳ ✳ ✳ ✳

THE ANCIENT GREEKS gave us the word (*eu*, "good" + *pheme*, "speech") and also made good use of the technique themselves. Because the Greeks believed that to speak ill of the gods was to invoke their wrath, they were careful not to draw attention to themselves by mentioning the gods by name. For example, they took to calling the Furies, a mythological trio of cruel, vengeful women, the *Eumenides*, or "Kindly Ones," even though in fact they were anything but kindly. Their true name, *Erinyes* ("Angry Ones"), was a far more accurate moniker.

Gee, gosh, and *jeepers* all developed as alternatives to *God* and *Jesus* so that speakers would not profane holy names. We still speak of "white meat" and "dark meat" as a heritage of the prudish Victorians' aversion to the words *breast* and *thigh*. *Casket* came into use in the mid-1800s to avoid the unpleasant associations of the word *coffin*. We teach children to say *number one* and *number two* instead of more explicit names for basic bodily functions.

Keeping Up with the Times

Over time, even some euphemisms come to be replaced with other euphemisms. After the euphemistic words work their way into everyday language as neutral terms, many eventually come to have the same connotations as the words they replaced. For example, *lame* gave way to *crippled*, which in turn yielded to *handicapped* or *disabled*. Today even those terms are less acceptable, and *physically challenged* or *differently abled* are now encouraged as alternatives.

Being Economical with the Truth

At its extreme, euphemism turns into *doublespeak*, in which language is used for political purposes to conceal, distort, or disguise meaning—in short, to prevaricate (okay, *lie*). The military and the corporate business world are prolific generators of euphemism. *Torture?* No way—this is just an *enhanced interrogation technique*. Are *layoffs* easier to swallow when they're called *reductions in force,* or *downsizing?* If you ask the "downsized" person, the answer is probably no.

Euphemistically Speaking

"True words are not beautiful; beautiful words are not true."

—LAO TZU

"Children and fools cannot lie."

—JOHN HEYWOOD

"... those comfortably padded lunatic asylums which are known, euphemistically, as the stately homes of England."

—VIRGINIA WOOLF

It's Not That Bad

While most people can identify a euphemism (the use of a less-offensive or neutral term in the place of a negative or taboo one), fewer people have heard of **dysphemism**.

* * * *

DYSPHEMISM IS THE opposite of euphemism: the use of a word or phrase that is more negative or objectionable than the term it replaces. The Greek prefix *dys-* ("impaired, bad") is the opposite of *eu-* ("good"), and is found in other English words such as *dyslexia* (a reading disorder) and *dystopia* (an anti-paradise, or the opposite of a *utopia*).

Dysphemism is often used as a conscious change of what linguists call *register*, the choice of vocabulary and grammar that is appropriate to a given social situation. The use of a negative or potentially offensive term—often slang terminology—can make a conversation more casual or serve as an in-joke to bring the listener or reader closer. It can also be used for shock value. In casual conversation among friends, it could be reasonable to describe a pal's skateboard wipeout by saying, "he ate dirt," but you would probably find a different way to describe the accident to the paramedics.

How 'Bout a Trip to the Greasy Spoon?

In general, use of dysphemism is intended to be humorous. Many of the expressions heard in diners, institutional cafeterias, the military, and other places where functional but unappealing food is served could be considered jocular dysphemisms. Army slang calls the ready-to-eat beef franks meal "the four fingers of death"; any drink made from powdered mix is called "bug juice"; and chipped beef on toast is often called "crap on a cracker" (or worse). Other examples in this vein include "axle grease" for butter, and "rabbit food" or "cow feed" for salad.

In the Army

Dysphemisms are common in everyday military parlance, where gallows humor may make outsiders wince but helps some soldiers deal with the unnerving awareness of the closeness of death. At the most macabre end of the spectrum, soldiers on the front line of an advance have been called "bullet stoppers" or "bullet sponges," and military helmets are known as "brain buckets."

Dysphemism adds spice, and often humor, to speech and makes an impact on listeners. But it can also be used as political statement, or a not-so-subtle way to show an objection to certain actions. Referring to cigarettes as "coffin nails," for instance, is a sarcastic way to convey an antismoking message without being openly preachy.

(For more on euphemism, turn to the previous page. Slang is discussed in greater detail on page 502.)

Where Did It Come From?

Slang: Nobody can say for certain where this word came from, but many believe it is derived from the Norwegian word *slengjakeften*, literally, "to sling the jaw" or "to abuse."

The Illusion of Allusion

Whether you are crossing the Rubicon, targeting someone's Achilles' heel, or enjoying your fifteen minutes of fame, having a shorthand way to evoke an image or emotion in your audience is quite helpful. An **allusion** *is just such a reference.*

✳ ✳ ✳ ✳

AN ALLUSION IS a literary device in which an indirect reference is made to a recognizable event in literature, film, mythology, or popular culture, evoking an idea or image in the audience's mind. The technique only works if the audience recognizes the reference, so you should probably refrain from alluding to hip-hop music at a convention of elderly classics scholars, or alluding to obscure biblical stories before an audience of fourth graders.

An *allusion* is not to be confused with an *illusion,* or something that is perceived falsely—such as a magician's card trick. An illusion *pretends to be* something else, while an allusion *refers to* something else. Both illusions and allusions can also be *elusive:* difficult to pin down or understand. An elusive illusion would be the mirage of an oasis in the desert—you can see it, but you can't reach it. Students are likely to encounter elusive allusions in literature written in an earlier era, when authors assumed that anyone reading their works would be completely familiar with the Bible and Greek and Roman mythology. John Milton's *Paradise Lost,* for example, published in 1667, is very difficult to appreciate fully without a thorough knowledge of both biblical stories and Greek mythology.

What? You Didn't Understand Our Allusions?

If you're wondering about the allusions in the first paragraph, they are useful ones to know. In 49 B.C., Julius Caesar took his army across the Rubicon River in northern Italy and put into motion his campaign to become the next Roman emperor. "Crossing the Rubicon" has therefore come to designate a major

decision point, or a point of no return. The Greek warrior Achilles considered himself to be invulnerable because when he was a baby his mother had dipped him into the River Styx. However, the one spot where her fingers had covered the skin—the heel—remained vulnerable. Despite his legendary strength and skill in battle, Achilles was killed by an arrow shot to the heel. An Achilles' heel, then, is a point of vulnerability. Twentieth-century artist and pop culture icon Andy Warhol once said, "In the future everybody will be world famous for fifteen minutes." So "fifteen minutes of fame" usually refers to the fleeting notoriety of someone or something that is briefly famous or in the news.

Where Did It Come From?

Cesarian: A 1903 shortened, Americanized version of the term *caesarian section* (first used in 1615), an operation that was supposedly named after Caius Julius Caesar, who had to be delivered of his mother surgically (legend traces his name to the Latin *caesus*, from *caedere*, which means "to cut"). This detail of Caesar's birth, however, may not be entirely accurate, as such operations in ancient times were inevitably fatal to the mother, and history shows that Caesar's mother did not die in childbirth. This is an awkward detail that everybody seems to have conveniently forgotten, as the name stuck.

Missing Word Puzzles

*A **crash blossom** is a poorly worded headline that is confusing or even misleading because it can be read two different ways. An Internet community called Testy Copyeditors created the name, inspired by an August 2009 headline in Japan Today that read: "Violinist Linked to JAL Crash Blossoms." Readers were left wondering, "What's a crash blossom?"*

✳   ✳   ✳   ✳

THOUGH YOU MIGHT suspect this awkward headline came about due to a low-budget translation from Japanese to English, that's not the case. The story was actually about a violinist who achieved professional success in the aftermath of a Japan Airlines crash that took her father's life. The headline was written with its subject (*violinist*) and verb (*blossoms*) separated by a clause that describes the subject. Unfortunately, most readers interpret the headline as a normal subject-verb-object sentence instead.

Sentences that have two grammatical interpretations are called *garden path* sentences. Like a forked trail, they can lead you in the wrong direction. They are common in headlines because important function words (like *is, are,* and *who*) or articles (like *a, an,* and *the*) are often omitted to save space.

Do You Want Grail with That?

Another example is this 2009 AP headline: "McDonald's Fries the Holy Grail for Potato Farmers." Because this headline is missing its verb (*are*), the natural tendency is to try to make *fries* the main verb of the sentence. The resulting image is both surreal and unappetizing.

While the term *crash blossom* is new, the phenomenon is most definitely not. For as long as there have been headlines, there have been badly constructed ones. The *Columbia Journalism Review* has been recording such flubs for years, and in

1980 they published a compilation of them: *Squad Helps Dog Bite Victim and Other Flubs from the Nation's Press*. Here are some choice examples from that book and other publications:

* "Lucky Man Sees Pals Die"

* "Genetic Engineering Splits Scientists"

* "Milk Drinkers Turn to Powder"

* "Kids Make Nutritious Snacks"

* "Juvenile Court to Try Shooting Defendant"

* "Greeks Fine Hookers"

* "Prostitutes Appeal to Pope"

* "Pastor Aghast at First Lady Sex Position"

* "Red Tape Holds Up New Bridges"

* "Drunk Gets Nine Months in Violin Case"

* "Hamlet Shaken by Murder Then Suicide"

* "Fried Chicken Cooked In Microwave Wins Trip"

* "Skywalkers in Korea Cross Han Solo"

* "Lawyer Says Client Is Not That Guilty"

* "Alzheimer's Center Prepares For an Affair to Remember"

* "Study Reveals Those Without Insurance Die More Often"

* "Harrisburg Postal Employees Gun Club Members Meet"

* "Typhoon Rips Through Cemetery—Hundreds Dead"

* "After Detour to California Shuttle Returns to Earth"

* "Woman Improving After Fatal Crash"

* "New Study of Obesity Looks for Larger Test Group"

* "A-Rod Goes Deep, Wang Hurt"

No Need to Be Nice

Sarcasm is a form of dry humor that relies on understatement rather than revealing emotion. It mocks as it amuses. It means to hurt, and it quite often succeeds.

✳   ✳   ✳   ✳

WORDS CAN STING, especially when they employ *sarcasm,* a form of irony (see page 304) used to express contempt of a person or situation. The word comes from the Greek *sarkazein,* meaning "to tear flesh," or later, "to bite the lips in anger" or "to speak bitterly."

The technique is very old, dating back even to biblical times. Although one might not expect to find sarcasm in the Bible, it's there. Check out the Book of Exodus, in which the Israelites, impatient with their trek through the wilderness and the lack of food, reproach Moses sarcastically: "Was it because there were no graves in Egypt that you brought us to the desert to die?" (14:11 NIV)

Yeah, Shakespeare—Like *He's* a Good Writer?

Shakespeare was a master of sarcasm—at times subtle, other times more overt. For example, in *Julius Caesar,* Mark Antony repeatedly refers to Brutus as "an honorable man" in his eulogy for the assassinated Caesar. With each reference, the ironic tone grows harsher and more deeply sarcastic. Antony knows that Brutus betrayed Caesar and is trying to publicly shame him. (Tone of voice often helps present sarcasm effectively. The sarcasm won't leap off the written page to someone unfamiliar with Caesar's fate, but one can just about hear the disdain in Antony's spoken words.)

Oooh, So Sophisticated!

Sarcasm is often considered a low form of humor, because often its form is simple. It doesn't take much wit for a basketball player to taunt an opponent who just missed the net with "Nice shot!"

However, sarcasm can also be more sophisticated; in fact, the more detailed the sarcastic comment, the more cutting it can be. Consider Han Solo's remark in *Star Wars*, after Princess Leia leads their fleeing group through a hatchway in the Death Star: "Garbage chute. Really wonderful idea. What an incredible smell you've discovered!" Short and to-the-point sarcasm can be equally effective, as in Jane Austen's *Pride and Prejudice*: "You have delighted us long enough."

Handle with Care

Sarcasm, like satire, must be handled carefully. It's important that the recipient be able to recognize a double message. If they can't, you risk hurting their feelings or confusing them. This is especially the case with written sarcasm, which lacks the intonation so often crucial to understanding. But then again, someone like you is certainly astute enough to figure that out.

✳ Sarcasm always comes from a person. People may be sarcastic, but situations are ironic.

Snap! Crackle! Pop!

Does your car zoom? Does your bacon sizzle in the skillet? Does the dishwater gurgle as the water drains? Zoom, sizzle, *and* gurgle *are all examples of one of the most playful qualities of the English language: the propensity for generating words that sound like the action they name.*

✳   ✳   ✳   ✳

THE TECHNICAL TERM for this is the Greek *onomatopoeia* (pronounced ah-nah-mah-tah-PEE-uh), or "word making." Onomatopoeic words have sounds that echo their meaning, and English has them by the bushel.

Many words representing common sounds are so widely in use that a reader might not immediately recognize them as being onomatopoeic. There's *buzz, giggle, hiccup, hiss, mumble, murmur, splash, sizzle, slurp, zip,* and *zoom,* to name a few.

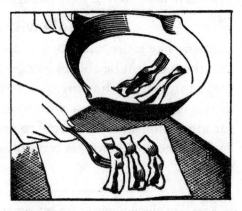

Words that represent animal sounds are favorites: *baa, cuckoo, hiss, meow, moo, neigh, oink, quack, woof,* and *yip.* A centuries-old example from classical Greek literature can be found in Aristophanes' *The Frogs,* in which the frogs are given a chorus: *brekehe—kesh, kodsh, kodsh* (which apparently sounded like croaking in classical Greek). Today, frogs just say *ribbit,* or perhaps *croak.*

Would a Gobble in Any Other Language Sound as Sweet?

As the previous example shows, onomatopoeia varies by language. For example, a turkey in Turkey goes *glu-glu* rather than *gobble-gobble*, as is heard in the United States. Roosters in Spain say *cocorico* instead of the English *cock-a-doodle-doo*, while Italian roosters say *chicchirichí* and Japanese roosters call *ko-ke-kok-ko-o*. Onomatopoeic words can even become the names of birds with distinctive calls, such as the whippoorwill and the cuckoo.

Many onomatopoeic words represent the sounds made by machinery: *Beep-beep* (also the call of the Road Runner in the Warner Bros. cartoons), *honk, vroom, whirr,* and *zap* are a few. You can clearly hear the *pocketa-pocketa* of heavy machinery as imagined by James Thurber in "The Secret Life of Walter Mitty." And of course comic books are known for employing words such as "Pow!" "Kablam!" and "Thwack!" to represent the sounds of fistfights and other action. But be careful using this device in your own writing: Used thoughtlessly, onomatopoeia can look intrusive, unintentionally humorous, or just tiresome. You don't want your writing to clatter or twang or blare cartoonishly.

Whoosh, There It Is

It's often possible to determine what an onomatopoeic word is describing based on the letter combinations that appear in it, whether at the beginning or the end. Onomatopoeic words related to liquid often begin with *dr-* or *sp-*: drip, drizzle, spray, sprinkle, splish, splash, sploosh. Those having to do with a crash or collision often begin with *cl-* (clank, clap, clatter, click, clink) or end with *-ng* (clang, ding, bang). An initial *th-* often signals a softer, duller sound: thump, thud. Sounds related to air may begin with the whispery *wh-* and/or end with the breathy *-sh*: whiff, whip, whizz, whoosh; swish, swoosh, fwoosh.

✳ Musician Todd Rundgren wrote a song made up almost entirely of onomatopoeia (titled, appropriately enough, "Onomatopoeia"). There are more than 50 different sounds represented in the lyrics, including "whack, whir, wheeze, whine" and "jingle, rattle, squeel, boing."

Words of Wisdom: Advertising

✳ ✳ ✳ ✳

"Advertising is a valuable economic factor because it is the cheapest way of selling goods, particularly if the goods are worthless."
—Sinclair Lewis

"Advertising is the art of convincing people to spend money they don't have for something they don't need."
—Will Rogers

"Many a small thing has been made large by the right kind of advertising."
—Mark Twain

"Nothing except the mint can make money without advertising."
—Thomas B. Macaulay

"You can tell the ideals of a nation by its advertisements."
—Norman Douglas

*"The codfish lays ten thousand eggs,
The homely hen lays one.
The codfish never cackles to tell you what she's done.
And so we scorn the codfish,
While the humble hen we prize,
Which only goes to show you
That is pays to advertise."*

—Anonymous

got snowclones?

If you've ever said, "What happens in <insert place name here>, stays in <same place>," or announced that you need a copy of <insert some task here> for Dummies, then congratulations! You've used a literary device called a **snowclone.**

✳ ✳ ✳ ✳

S NOWCLONES ARE LIKE mathematical expressions for language. They are fill-in-the-blank clichés, references, or patterns—such as "not your father's X," "X is the new Y," "I love the smell of X in the morning," and "have X, will travel."

The term *snowclone* was coined by linguist Glen Whitman in 2004, inspired by the frequently repeated formula, "If Eskimos have N words for snow, then X must have Y words for Z." By substituting new words in common clichés, a writer puts a new spin on a familiar turn of phrase.

Some snowclones are relatively simple and may have conventional "fillings." For example, the phrase "a few sandwiches short of a picnic" has typical variants like "a few bricks short of a load" and "a few beers short of a six-pack." But we can be as creative as we want, perhaps coming up with "a few feathers short of a chicken" or "a few aardvarks short of a zoo." The more unusual and unexpected the fillers, the funnier the snowclone is.

Not surprisingly, pop culture is a fertile source for snowclones. Do your best impression of Lieutenant Colonel Kilgore from *Apocalypse Now* while you say, "I love the smell of <*something nasty*> in the morning." And let's not forget advertising. The "got milk?" ads from the California Milk Processor Board have spawned phrases both divine ("got Jesus?") and ridiculous ("got polyester?"). The snowclone based on the tagline from the Las Vegas Convention and Visitors Authority works because of the humorous contrast between Sin City and someplace much more innocent. Did we really need reassuring that "What happens in Des Moines, stays in Des Moines"?

That's What They All Say

English boasts a wealth of common, pithy expressions conveying the collective wisdom of its speakers. An expression that contains some piece of practical wisdom or advice is known as an **adage.** *For example: "Don't count your chickens before they hatch."*

✳   ✳   ✳   ✳

ADAGES CAN BE warnings, as in Murphy's Law ("Anything that can go wrong, will go wrong"); "Haste makes waste"; "Look before you leap"; "Don't judge a book by its cover"; and "Don't look a gift horse in the mouth."

Adages may also offer encouragement: "Nothing ventured, nothing gained." Some are merely general advice, such as "Better late than never"; "Beggars can't be choosers"; "Make hay while the sun shines" (before it rains and brings the work to a premature halt); and "Strike while the iron is hot" (as a blacksmith does to shape the metal).

Aphorisms, Maxims, and Proverbs

Adages are often confused with *aphorisms, maxims,* or *proverbs.* The following descriptions should help you distinguish between them:

Aphorism: A trenchant or witty original thought, more identified with a specific author than with something handed down anonymously through generations. An example would be the following from Benjamin Franklin: "They who can give up essential liberty to obtain a little temporary safety, deserve neither liberty nor safety." A synonym of *aphorism* is *apothegm.*

Maxim: A general rule of conduct. The Golden Rule is perhaps the best known maxim: "Do unto others as you would have them do unto you." "Neither a borrower nor a lender be," spoken by Polonius in Shakespeare's *Hamlet*, has turned into a maxim through popular use. Other common maxims include "A lie told often enough becomes the truth"; "All's fair in love and war"; and "A little knowledge is a dangerous thing."

Proverb: A proverb is usually a folk expression of wisdom, truth, practical advice, and observation: "Hunger is the best sauce"; "A bird in the hand is worth two in the bush"; "Anger without power is folly"; and "A rolling stone gathers no moss." The distinction between an adage and a proverb is particularly blurry, though a proverb is often an observation, while an adage or maxim offers advice on how to do something.

There is a certain amount of overlap between these topics, so don't be shy about asking for help. After all, as the adage goes, "Two heads are better than one."

✳ What does "Don't look a gift horse in the mouth" mean, anyway? A horse's teeth are a good indication of its general health. If you look a gift horse in the mouth, you may discover that it is more a liability than a gift—but you risk appearing ungrateful and distrusting of the giver.

Ambiguous Amphibology

Here's a classic bit from Groucho Marx: "One morning I shot an elephant in my pajamas. How he got into my pajamas I'll never know." It's one of Marx's most famous jokes—but what makes it so funny?

✳ ✳ ✳ ✳

HE'S USING **AMPHIBOLOGY:** a grammatically ambiguous statement that appears to mean one thing at first but, upon rereading, could mean another—a bit like the verbal equivalent of an optical illusion. In the first sentence, the prepositional phrase "in my pajamas" could refer to the speaker or to the elephant— although of course no one automatically thinks this upon hearing it. So when the pajamas are unexpectedly assigned to the elephant, the laugh line turns the listener's expectations upside down.

Amphibology comes from the Greek word *amphibolos*, meaning "doubtful, ambiguous," which in turn comes from the prefix *amphi-*, meaning "on both sides," and from *ballein*, meaning "to throw." So an amphibolous statement is one with the ability "to throw on both sides"—or, in more modern terms, "to swing both ways" (grammatically).

But What Did They *Really* Mean?

Sometimes amphibology is deliberate, as when Benjamin Disraeli responded upon receiving an unsolicited manuscript, "Many thanks; I shall lose no time in reading it." When it's not deliberate, a copy editor somewhere is in trouble for not catching and correcting it. These two ill-advised signs, if they were ever actually posted in a restaurant, would provide fine examples of amphibology: "If you think our waiters are rude, you should see the manager" and "Try our food and you'll agree that nothing is better." Much of the humor of amphibology comes from leaving a phrase unexplained. There's a secret pleasure in being in on the joke of a sentence like this one, which could be used as a book blurb: "This novel will be read when Hemingway is forgotten." Adding "... and not until then" would clarify the meaning—but it would also ruin the joke.

To paraphrase Groucho Marx, "I never forget a joke. But in this case I'll make an exception."

Watch Out for the Flying Banana

But what about a sentence such as "Time flies like an arrow; fruit flies like a banana"? This could be considered a form of amphibology, but because it is based on confusing word usage rather than confusing grammar—*flies* is used as a verb in the first clause but as a noun in the second, and *like* is a preposition in the first but a verb in the second—it is more properly considered *equivocation*. The old joke about the panda who "eats shoots and leaves" falls somewhere in between, because the confusion comes not only from the word usage (is *shoots* a verb or a noun?), but also from the punctuation (a comma between *eats* and *shoots* would disambiguate). Whether equivocation or amphibology, such confusion is best avoided unless your humor is intentional.

✳ *The New York Times* said in Groucho Marx's obituary, "He developed the insult into an art form."

Why Bother?

*Did you know that a **rhetorical question** is not actually a question? And that no answer to it is expected? It is instead some other kind of statement—such as an assertion, request, denial, accusation, or implication—masquerading as a question. A rhetorical question could be answered, but an answer is not expected or necessary.*

✳   ✳   ✳   ✳

AQUESTION IS RHETORICAL if it is asked merely for effect; that is, if its purpose is not to elicit a response but rather to make a point. "Why me, God?" is a rhetorical question. It expresses feeling—distress, disappointment, anger—without expecting a reply from heaven. When a frustrated parent throws up his or her hands and asks their child, "Where did I go wrong?" they don't really expect a response. The question is intended to provoke feelings of guilt.

What's with All the Negativity?

The familiar "If you're so smart, why aren't you rich?" is actually an accusation that the person addressed is, in reality, not all that bright. In Shakespeare's *Julius Caesar*, Mark Antony proclaims, "Here was a Caesar! when comes such another?" It is clear in context that neither Antony nor his listeners expect that there will ever be another to match the slain ruler. In an old television commercial for Dial soap, the announcer says, "Aren't you glad you use Dial? Don't you wish everybody did?" The announcer is inviting you to feel superior while suggesting that other people are smelly.

Songwriters Love Rhetorical Questions . . . Or Do They?

The use of rhetorical questions has proven to hold great appeal for songwriters, from "Why do fools fall in love?" (umm, because they're fools) to "Who'll stop the rain?" (Mother Nature, presumably). In "Mrs. Robinson," Paul Simon asks,

"Where have you gone, Joe DiMaggio?" The question is a lament for something lost in American culture. Only the most literal-minded would say, "Holy Cross Catholic Cemetery in Colma, California."

Shall I Continue?

Some questions might be rhetorical or not, depending on the context. "Who left all those dirty dishes in the sink?" might or might not require an answer. In one context—that is, if the questioner knows exactly who left those dishes in the sink—the question carries the weight of accusation and is certainly rhetorical (and even an example of *epiplexis*— see page 274). On the other hand, perhaps the guilty party is unknown, and the question therefore requires an answer. Will the mystery slacker please step forward? (And no, that is *not* a rhetorical question.)

✳ A rhetorical question can be ended with either a question mark or an exclamation point, depending on what sort of emphasis the writer prefers to use.

This One's for You, Dear Reader

Sometimes writer and reader go face to face in **apostrophe**—*not the punctuation mark that indicates a contraction or possession, but the rhetorical device by which a writer addresses the reader directly, similar to the way an actor on the stage may break away from the action and speak to the audience in a soliloquy.*

✻ ✻ ✻ ✻

T HE TERM *APOSTROPHE* can also refer to a writer's address to an imaginary or absent person, or to an abstraction, as in the apostle Paul's "O death, where is thy sting? O grave, where is thy victory?" (1 Corinthians 15:55, KJV).

The Greek word means "turning away," and in apostrophe the writer or speaker turns away from the immediate situation, breaking off to say something that is often urgent or highly emotional. Apostrophe is also known as *turne tale, aversio,* and *aversion.*

Reader, I'm Talkin' to You

There are many famous apostrophes in literature. Charlotte Brontë opens the concluding chapter of *Jane Eyre* with "Reader, I married him," and nineteenth-century literature is so full of such addresses to the audience that "dear reader" has become an informal noun phrase among critics to identify the practice— and to dismiss it as dated and stagy.

But apostrophe is more often identified with drama, poetry, and song:

✻ The fifteenth-century verse known as "Western Wind" begins, "O Westron wind, when wilt thou blow?"

✻ Walt Whitman's "O Captain! My Captain!" apostrophizes the slain Abraham Lincoln.

✻ In *Frankenstein, Mary Shelley writes,* "Oh! Stars and clouds and winds, ye are all about to mock me; if ye really pity me, crush sensation and memory; let me become as nought; but if not, depart, depart, and leave me in darkness."

* Paul Simon's song "The Sounds of Silence" begins, "Hello, darkness, my old friend."

He's Gonna Sing, Folks

The device is also used for comic effect. In film, television, and on stage, this is often called "breaking the fourth wall." In 1952's *Road to Bali*, one of the Bob Hope and Bing Crosby *Road* movies, Bob Hope looks directly at the camera as Crosby is about to sing, saying, "He's gonna sing, folks. Now's the time to go out and get the popcorn."

The George Burns and Gracie Allen Show was famous for using this trope (George often turned to the audience and commented on what the other characters were doing), as was *Monty Python's Flying Circus*. More recent shows that broke the fourth wall include *Moonlighting* and *Boston Legal*.

In the most formal writing, addressing the reader as *you* is frowned upon, but in the conversational style of most contemporary writing it is increasingly acceptable. Just don't overdo it, okay?

Where Did It Come From?

Hello: Though it is one of the most commonly used words in the English language, the greeting didn't come into use until late in the nineteenth century. Its ancient predecessor *hallow* was used as early as the 1300s. "Hello" replaced the popular "hullo" after the invention of the telephone.

Acro- Is Tops!

After reading this article, you might want to move it to the top of your list; as you'll see, **acro-** *is of the highest importance.*

✻　✻　✻　✻

THE PREFIX ACRO- means "highest, topmost, peak" and comes from the Greek word *acro*. It's a fairly productive prefix in the English language, with quite a number of words formed from it, but most of these are rather technical and not particularly common. For instance, there is *acrolith*, from

acro- + *lith* ("stone"), meaning "a statue, the top part of which is stone and the lower part wood or some other material." Unless you happen to be an archaeologist or a curator of antiquities in a museum, you are unlikely to run across the word. But there are a handful of common *acro-* words with which you are probably familiar, including:

✻ The famed *Acropolis* is the hill in Athens on which the Parthenon stands. The name is from *acro-* + *polis* ("city").

✻ The word *acrobat* comes from *acro-* + *ba* (Greek for "to go, to step"), so an acrobat is someone skilled at "going" or working aloft on the high wire or trapeze.

✻ *Acrophobia*—fear of heights—is a technical term that has moved into common parlance. It comes from *acro-* + *phobia* ("fear").

✻ And of course all word lovers know about *acronyms*. An acronym is a word (*-nym*) formed from the first ("highest")

> *"The politician is an acrobat. He keeps his balance by doing the opposite of what he says."*
> —MAURICE BARRES

elements in the words that form a phrase. Three well-known examples are *radar*, which is an acronym for RAdio Detecting And Ranging; *scuba*, which comes from Self-Contained Underwater Breathing Apparatus; and *AIDS*, or Acquired Immune Deficiency Syndrome.

Some less-common *acro-* words include: *acrolect*, the most prestigious dialect of a language; *acrocarpous*, describing a plant where the fruit grows at the top; *acropetal*, meaning proceeding or developing from the base toward the apex, particularly in regard to a floral bud; and *acrophony*, the characteristic of certain hieroglyphic writing systems in which each hieroglyph represents the initial sound of the pictured word, as in *aleph*, or ox, representing the letter *a*, or those "A is for Apple" books that you are likely to remember from your childhood.

* *Acro-* often appears in words that describe body extremities such as the hands or feet. For example, there's *acromegaly*, a disease where the extremities become enlarged; *acrodermatitis*, a skin inflammation, especially of the hands and feet; and *acrodolichomelia*, abnormal or disproportionate length of hands and feet.

* The Acropolis was originally named Cecropia in honor of the legendary founder and first king of Athens, Cecrops, who was depicted as half man, half serpent. The word *cecrops* means "face with a tail." Athenians considered Cecrops a hero and referred to themselves as *Cecropidae* during his reign and throughout the reigns of the five following kings.

* The best Greek acrobats were called *neurobats*. Using a length of catgut that was comparable to modern fishing line in thinness, they appeared to be walking through the air.

X Marks the Spot

It's important to read this article to learn, not learn to read this article.

✳ ✳ ✳ ✳

IN **CHIASMUS,** THE second half of an expression is balanced against the first—but with the parts reversed. It is a form of **antithesis** (see page 646). In chiasmus, the grammatical structure in one phrase is reversed in a successive phrase: a + b, then b + a. The word, pronounced ky-AZ-mus, derives from the Greek letter *chi*, the equivalent of the Latin *X*, and means "crosswise arrangement."

Poet Alexander Pope was particularly fond of this device. In "Epistle to a Lady," he writes:

> *A fop their passion, but their prize a sot,*

The next line in the couplet reverts to strict parallelism, for contrast (for more on parallelism, see page 660):

> *Alive, ridiculous, and dead, forgot!*

No, That's Not a Compliment!

This is an example of chiasmus attributed to English poet Samuel Johnson:

> *Your manuscript is both good and original; but the part that is good is not original, and the part that is original is not good.*

Ouch.

Perhaps the most famous modern example of chiasmus comes from President John F. Kennedy's inaugural address in 1961, when he said:

> *And so, my fellow Americans, ask not what your country can do for you; ask what you can do for your country.*

> **"Science without religion is lame;**
> **religion without science is blind."**
> —ALBERT EINSTEIN

More recently, from President Barack Obama:

> *My job is not to represent Washington to you, but to*
> *represent you to Washington.*

The Kennedy and Obama quotations represent a subset of chiasmus called *antimetabole*, in which the exact words are inverted. But, as the quotation from Pope shows, chiasmus is not necessarily limited to reusing the same words.

An Ancient Device

The roots of chiasmus are deep. This literary technique shows up in ancient Sanskrit, Mesopotamian, and Egyptian writings. Consider this example from ancient Greece:

> *"Bad men live that they may eat and drink, whereas*
> *good men eat and drink that they may live."* (Socrates,
> fifth century B.C.)

Sorry, Charlie!

On the lighter side, the structure lends itself to punning, as in this line by Mae West:

> *It's better to be looked over than overlooked.*

And the tendency for chiasmus to stick in one's memory makes it useful in advertising, as in the long-running television commercials for StarKist tuna:

> *Sorry, Charlie. StarKist wants tuna that tastes good, not*
> *tuna with good taste.*

In Error, Sometimes Deliberately

When someone takes a word or phrase outside its usual context, using it in a sense other than the intended one, he or she is employing **catachresis** *(from a Greek word for "abuse"). Catachresis (cat-uh-KREE-sis) can be done deliberately, setting up an outlandish comparison for effect, or it may simply be a mistake. Because of this double nature of the term, the reader or listener has to decide whether the writer or speaker is original or merely inept.*

* * * *

WHEN HAMLET SAYS, "I will speak daggers to her," the reader understands immediately that he intends to be hostile, even violent, in his speech, though daggers cannot actually be spoken. In this case, although the word is logically misused, it is figuratively effective. The expression "to look daggers" at someone, meaning "to glare warningly," is also widely understood.

A catachresis can also be accidental, as in a malapropism such as "I resemble that remark" or (in the words of the original Mrs. Malaprop herself, in Richard Brinsley Sheridan's *The Rivals*) "she's as headstrong as an allegory on the banks of the Nile." (See page 16 for more on malapropisms.) But it is in mixed metaphors that readers most frequently and obviously encounter inadvertent catachresis.

Fight that Wave!

Sometimes a mixed metaphor serves a specific literary purpose: that of surprising the reader with an unexpected but vivid combination of disparate things. For example, again in *Hamlet*, the Danish prince questions in his famous soliloquy whether there is reason to "take arms against a sea of troubles." (How could a soldier wage an attack against a body of water?)

But more commonly, a mixed metaphor (catachresis) occurs when a writer (or a speaker) sets off in one direction before heading off in another within the same sentence or paragraph, without regard to consistency. Did you catch these catachreses?

* "So now what we are dealing with is the rubber meeting the road, and instead of biting the bullet on these issues, we just want to punt." (*Chicago Tribune*)

* "They counted the votes until the cows had literally gone to sleep." (Dan Rather)

* "Free societies will be allies against these hateful few who have no conscience, who kill at the whim of a hat." (George W. Bush)

---

* *Catachresis* also has a more specialized sense, as a term for a word being used to identify something for which no precise word exists, such as the *tooth* of a comb or the *leg* of a table.

It Would Be Superfluous to Say...

*It goes without saying that this article contains a wealth of information about the rhetorical device called **paralipsis**, not to mention the extreme technique of **prolepsis**.*

✳ ✳ ✳ ✳

ONE OF THE great things about rhetoric is that you can tell a reader or listener something by *not* telling it. Such is the utility of *paralipsis* (from the Greek for "passing over"), in which one emphasizes something by professing not to say much about it. In fact, the stock expressions "not to mention," "I don't mean to suggest," and "it goes without saying" are often used in paralipsis. The very act of calling attention to it while pretending to pass it over is a kind of irony.

Examples of paralipsis can be found in both literature and film. In *Moby-Dick*, Herman Melville writes, "We will not speak of all Queequeg's peculiarities here; how he eschewed coffee and hot rolls, and applied his undivided attention to beefsteaks, done rare."

Paralipsis can be sneaky, as when a political candidate says, "I intend to run a clean campaign, and I will not stoop to gutter politics by attempting to capitalize on my opponent's arrest for drunken driving." What will remain in the voters' minds, of course, is the phrase "my opponent's arrest for drunken driving." The opponent will likely not be sending a note of thanks for that purported omission.

It Only Counts If You Don't Say It

In *proslepsis*, the extreme form of paralipsis, the speaker or writer indulges in sharing great detail about the things he is pretending not to discuss: "I will not stoop to gutter politics by recounting my opponent's arrest for drunken driving after the car he was driving sideswiped six parked vehicles and collided with a police cruiser, after which he was found passed out at the wheel with an empty bottle on vodka on the seat beside him." Mission accomplished.

Paralipsis is a technique that can be quite handy in diplomacy, as when Charles Francis Adams, the U.S. minister to the Court of St. James in Great Britain during the Civil War, famously wrote to Lord John Russell about the possibility of Britain providing warships for the Confederacy: "It would be superfluous in me to point out to your Lordship that this is war." The phrasing allowed Adams to indeed point it out, while still avoiding a condescending tone.

Now that you understand the basics of paralipsis, I don't think we need to tell you that this article is done.

"Politics are almost as exciting as war, and quite as dangerous. In war you can only be killed once, but in politics many times."

—WINSTON CHURCHILL

"Politics ruins the character."

—OTTO VON BISMARCK

"Politics is the gentle art of getting votes from the poor and campaign funds from the rich by promising to protect each from the other."

—OSCAR AMERINGER

"I agree with you that in politics the middle way is none at all."

—JOHN ADAMS

"One of the penalties for refusing to participate in politics is that you end up being governed by your inferiors."

—PLATO

This Article Is as Good as Gold

Similes *are used to directly compare two things that are otherwise distinct. They're found in speech, song, and writing as often as the common cold.*

✳ ✳ ✳ ✳

USUALLY *LIKE* OR *AS* is used to introduce the comparison, though certain statements using *than* are also considered similes because the comparison is made explicit (for example, "stronger than an ox").

Similes abound in popular culture and in literature, poetry, and song:

✳ There is the signature quotation from the movie *Forrest Gump*: "Life [is] like a box of chocolates. You never know what you're gonna get."

✳ Superman is "faster than a speeding bullet, more powerful than a locomotive."

✳ William Faulkner wrote in *As I Lay Dying*, "He looks like right after the maul hits the steer and it's no longer alive and don't yet know that it is dead."

✳ The Beatles sang, "It's been a hard day's night / and I've been working like a dog."

✳ Simon and Garfunkel deemed friendship to be "like a bridge over troubled water."

Some Similes Are as Old as Dirt

Some similes are so common that they've become clichés in speech and writing. You're undoubtedly overfamiliar with: "as stubborn as a mule," "as big as a house," "as ugly as sin," "as good as gold," and "sings like an angel," to name a few. Clichéd similes often fail to adequately describe the object in question, but original, clever comparisons can make a tired subject seem fresh, as in this passage from Vladimir Nabokov's *Lolita*: "Elderly American ladies leaning on their canes listed toward me like towers of Pisa."

Similes aren't always as sweet as sugar. They can also be used to create less-than-favorable comparisons, as in the feminist mantra "A woman needs a man like a fish needs a bicycle," or Shakespeare's playful "My mistress' eyes are nothing like the sun."

I Never Met a Simile I Didn't "Like"

Similes often make use of irony or sarcasm. (See pages 304 and 72 for more on these literary tools.) It's pretty obvious when a simile is being employed in this way, for instance, in "as clear as mud" and "as enjoyable as a root canal."

The Similes Jump Off This Page Like Mexican Jumping Beans Out of a Sizzling Skillet

Overenthusiastic writers may get carried away. Not every comparison that emerges from the imagination is apt. The Internet is filled with examples of overwrought similes featuring all-too-vivid imagery, such as these (deliberately overwritten) examples submitted to *The Washington Post*: "She grew on him like she was a colony of E. coli and he was room-temperature Canadian beef"; "Her hair glistened in the rain like nose hair after a sneeze."

With simile, as with many figures of speech, questions of taste and discretion must be considered. Is the comparison apt or forced? Is it suitable for the subject, the audience, and the occasion? Does it reinforce the writer's point or distract from it? Determining the proper answer to these questions can be as difficult as finding a needle in a haystack.

The Music of Assonance

Spoken language and music use sounds and rhythms. But the reader can also "hear" the sounds of language in a text. Writers who understand this make use of devices that emphasize the sound that echoes in the reader's head.

✳ ✳ ✳ ✳

ONE OF THE most obvious of these is *alliteration* (see page 668), in which initial consonants are repeated. A related, but subtler, device, is **assonance,** in which vowel sounds are repeated. Unlike rhyme, which uses repeating vowel sounds at the ends of words, assonance uses repeating vowel sounds *within* words, in a manner that is often less obvious.

But that doesn't mean it's always subtle. Consider the riddle that begins, "As I was going to St. Ives, I met a man with seven wives." The four repetitions of the long *i* in 14 words build off each other and leap out; together, they seem to multiply into more *i* sounds than are actually present.

The lyrics of Pink Floyd's song "Grantchester Meadows," like many song lyrics and poems, are full of assonance: "Hear the lark and harken to the barking of the dog fox / Gone to ground" has two sets of words utilizing assonance in a single line—the *a* of *lark, harken,* and *barking,* and the *o* of *dog* and *gone.*

Though most often found in poetry, assonance also appears in prose writing. In Charles Dickens's *Bleak House*, Mr. Smallweed addresses his wife as a "... dancing, prancing, shambling, scrambling poll-parrot."

Words of Wisdom: Music

❋   ❋   ❋   ❋

"If music be the food of love, play on."

—WILLIAM SHAKESPEARE

"Music expresses that which cannot be said and on which it is impossible to be silent."

—VICTOR HUGO

"Music in the soul can be heard by the universe."

—LAO TZU

"Music is a higher revelation than all wisdom and philosophy."

—LUDWIG VAN BEETHOVEN

"Music is a moral law. It gives soul to the universe, wings to the mind, flight to the imagination, and charm and gaiety to life and to everything."

—PLATO

"Music is love in search of a word."

—SIDNEY LANIER

"Music is the shorthand of emotion."

—LEO TOLSTOY

"Who hears music feels his solitude peopled at once."

—ROBERT BROWNING

"When words leave off, music begins."

—HEINRICH HEINE

Chapter 3

Words on the Street

Cupertino Effect: The Corrections

Thank goodness for computer spell-checkers! They handily remove the need to actually know how to spell—right? Well... yes and no.

✳   ✳   ✳   ✳

IN THE EARLY 2000s, translators for the European Union noticed the word *Cupertino* (a city in northern California, headquarters of Apple Inc.) popping up in unexpected places in their documents. The source of the problem, they soon realized, were computer spell-checkers—along with human editors.

The word *cooperation,* a relatively new spelling for *co-operation,* was not programmed into the memory of their spell-checking programs. So, when these programs came across the word *cooperation* in a document, they balked. And, oddly enough, instead of listing *co-operation* first in the list of suggested alternate spellings, the first word suggested was *Cupertino.* Writers who weren't paying enough attention to the program absentmindedly clicked on the suggestion in the queue, and without a careful editorial eye double-checking the corrections (or, rather, "incorrections"), *Cupertino* made it into numerous published works, creating a new, and very bizarre, substitute for *cooperation.*

No, It Wasn't Just a New Euphemism

"The Cupertino with our Italian comrades proved to be very fruitful," read one report. Another proposal promised to "make international Cupertino easier"; yet another called for "regular review mechanisms and direct Cupertino."

Quirky chaos ensued in the most serious of sources, such as documents of the United Nations. "Incorrected" phrases included "teaching and learning methods that stress participation, Cupertino, problem-solving, and respect for differences" and "the strengthening of international peace and Cupertino should emanate from adults and be instilled in children."

Beyond *Cupertino*

Even as spell-checking programs were being updated to stop botching *cooperation,* other malapropisms gained notoriety as examples of "the Cupertino effect." (For more on malapropisms, see page 16.)

A police report read, "Police denitrified the youths"; in this case, the word *identified* was entered without the initial *i* and was consequently changed by a spell-checking program to a word for the removal of nitrogen. A lawyer filed a brief that contained the term *sea sponge*—a strange substitution for the Latin legal phrase *sua sponte.* Even the most respected newspapers aren't immune: When TV satirist Stephen Colbert coined the word *truthiness, The New York Times* rendered the word as *trustiness* (which means something very different). See page 595 for more on *truthiness.*

So let this be a lesson! Even though a spell-checker may just be the most wonderful, reliable writing tool there is—so much more accurate than programs that check grammar, for example—it still shouldn't be the final word.

A Devilish Dictionary

Today's veteran journalists have seen it all, metaphorically speaking, and it's not uncommon for them to become jaded and cynical. And online bloggers are even worse—without an editor to rein them in (or perhaps with an editor to egg them on!), their posts may become filled with sarcasm and cynicism.

✳   ✳   ✳   ✳

IMAGINE WHAT RENOWNED journalist Ambrose Bierce (1842–1913), author of 1911's *The Devil's Dictionary*, a satirical lexicon that "redefines" more than 1,000 words, would have to say today. Here is a sampling of some of the dark and sardonical entries in *The Devil's Dictionary*:

✳ **ABSURDITY,** *n.* A statement or belief manifestly inconsistent with one's own opinion.

✳ **ACADEMY,** *n.* A modern school where football is taught.

✳ **ALONE,** *adj.* In bad company.

✳ **AMNESTY,** *n.* The state's magnanimity to those offenders whom it would be too expensive to punish.

✳ **BRAIN,** *n.* An apparatus with which we think what we think. That which distinguishes the man who is content to be something from the man who wishes to do something.

✳ **BRIDE,** *n.* A woman with a fine prospect of happiness behind her.

✳ **CONGRATULATION,** *n.* The civility of envy.

✳ **CONGRESS,** *n.* A body of men who meet to repeal laws.

✳ **CONNOISSEUR,** *n.* A specialist who knows everything about something and nothing about anything else.

✳ **CONSULT,** *v.i.* To seek another's approval of a course already decided on.

* **DESTINY,** *n.* A tyrant's authority for crime and a fool's excuse for failure.

* **EDIBLE,** *n.* Good to eat, and wholesome to digest, as a worm to a toad, a toad to a snake, a snake to a pig, a pig to a man, and a man to a worm.

* **FAMOUS,** *adj.* Conspicuously miserable.

* **FUTURE,** *n.* That period of time in which our affairs prosper, our friends are true, and our happiness is assured.

* **GRAVE,** *n.* A place in which the dead are laid to await the coming of the medical student.

* **LOGIC,** *n.* The art of thinking and reasoning in strict accordance with the limitations and incapacities of human misunderstanding.

* **MONKEY,** *n.* An arboreal animal which makes itself at home in genealogical trees.

* **PHILOSOPHY,** *n.* A route of many roads leading from nowhere to nothing.

* **POLITENESS,** *n.* The most acceptable hypocrisy.

* **POLITICS,** *n.* A strife of interests masquerading as a contest of principles. The conduct of public affairs for private advantage.

* **QUOTATION,** *n.* The act of repeating erroneously the words of another. The words erroneously repeated.

* **RESPONSIBILITY,** *n.* A detachable burden easily shifted to the shoulders of God, Fate, Fortune, Luck or one's neighbor. In the days of astrology it was customary to unload it upon a star.

* **SELF-EVIDENT,** *adj.* Evident to one's self and to nobody else.

Positively Confounding

Prefixes such as un- *or* de- *create an antonym, or opposite, of the word they're attached to. But some words that appear to be negated with prefixes or suffixes have no positives. For instance, the opposite of* inane *is not* ane—*actually, there is no such word as* ane.

✳ ✳ ✳ ✳

Words with No Positive Forms

defenestrate	inchoate	misgivings
dejected	incognito	misnomer
disconsolate	incommunicado	nonchalant
disdain	indomitable	noncommittal
disgruntled	ineffable	nondescript
disheveled	inept	nonpareil
dismayed	inert	nonplussed
disrupt	infernal	unbeknownst
feckless	inhibited	ungainly
gormless	insidious	unswerving
impetuous	insipid	untold
impromptu	insouciant	untoward
inane	intact	
incessant	invert	

Words with Uncommon Positive Forms

disconcerting	inscrutable	unkempt
immaculate	insensate	unmitigated
impeccable	insufferable	unrequited
inadvertent	interminable	unruly
incapacitated	unbridled	unthinkable
incorrigible	unflappable	unwieldy
innocent	unfurl	

Doh! Homer vs. the Dictionary

When the Oxford English Dictionary *added* **doh** *to its list of entries in June 2001, the addition created a minor stir. The venerable dictionary, or so some said, was giving in to popular culture by adding the word (or perhaps more accurately, "annoyed grunt," as the screenwriters recorded it) made famous by animated TV character Homer Simpson.*

✳   ✳   ✳   ✳

BUT THE OED showed that the interjection had a history dating back to at least 1945, and even Dan Castellaneta, the actor who voices Homer Simpson, credited the actor James Finlayson as his inspiration. Finlayson, who played a recurring character in the 1930s Laurel and Hardy films, frequently said "do-o-o-o" as a euphemism for "damn!"

Simpsons trivia buffs may want to know that Homer's first use of *doh* (often spelled *d'oh*), is in the short "Punching Bag," which aired on *The Tracey Ullman Show* in November 1988. Homer's first use of it on *The Simpsons* is in the very first episode, "Simpsons Roasting on an Open Fire" (December 17, 1989).

Doh is not to be confused with *duh,* which is used to imply that another person has just said something blindingly obvious. *Duh* also has cartoon roots, this time in a 1943 *Merrie Melodies* cartoon in which a character says: "Duh . . . well, he can't outsmart me, 'cause I'm a moron!" As early as 1963, *The New York Times Magazine* was reporting on the word's use in children's slang:

> *A favorite expression is "duh." [. . .] For example, the first child says, "The Russians were first in space." Unimpressed, the second child replies (or rather grunts), "Duh."*

There are two lessons here. The first is that what seems like an inarticulate grunt can actually carry semantic meaning, and the second is that words come from all sorts of sources. When it comes to etymology, *The Simpsons* can be just as valuable as Shakespeare.

A Tantrum of Nuclear Proportions

The word **meltdown** *didn't have to be ominous. In fact, it started out deliciously.*

✳ ✳ ✳ ✳

THE *OXFORD ENGLISH DICTIONARY's* first example of the word *meltdown* comes from a 1937 review in the *Ice Cream Trade Journal:* "[This] ice cream melts down cleanly in the mouth . . . Due to the clean melt-down . . . a cooler sensation results in the mouth than with gelatin ice cream."

But with the dawn of the nuclear age came the threat that nuclear energy could blow up in our faces. In particular, there was the fear that the fuel of a nuclear reactor could overheat and melt the core—a meltdown.

A 1965 article in *New Scientist* still had the word in quotes: "Overheated fuel may result in 'meltdown' and general contamination of the reactor system." But soon our worst fears were realized: The meltdowns at Chernobyl and Three Mile Island showed us the danger of nuclear power, and the word became part of the general vocabulary.

I Liked the Ice Cream Usage Better

Those disasters probably helped make *meltdown* a more general synonym for *catastrophe*—particularly a catastrophe in which core components that are supposed to work together instead destroy themselves. So when the U.S. stock market collapsed in late 2008, it was widely described as a "market meltdown." The *OED* gives a definition of *meltdown* that matches this usage: "any uncontrolled and usually disastrous event with far-reaching consequences; a sudden and decisive collapse; (Finance) a rapid drop in the value of a currency, assets, shares, etc.; a crash."

A nuclear meltdown occurs when the cooling system fails and the material overheats. Once the tipping point is reached, the people who are supposed to keep such a thing from happening are powerless to stop it. The immense energy inside the reactor core fuels the inferno, which gets hotter and hotter. And it's dangerous. If the containment system is breached, the meltdown can destroy massive amounts of property in a matter of seconds.

Now, let's consider an overtired, hungry, bored toddler standing in line at the grocery store. She's already irritable, and a tempting-yet-forbidden display of candy stands beside her. Her temper boils over, and a minute later she's on the brink of a full-blown tantrum. What word other than *meltdown* could be more appropriate?

✳ It's hard to believe, but almost three million people in the United States live within ten miles of an operating nuclear power plant. U.S. power plants produce 2,000 metric tons of radioactive waste a year.

✳ *Nuclear fission* is the process of splitting of an atom in two, and and *nuclear fusion* is the process of combining atoms into one. (*Fission:* from Latin *findere,* "to split"; *fusion:* from Latin *fundere,* "to melt, pour.") Nuclear fusion has the potential to produce safer energy; however, the technology is not developed enough at this time to operate in a large power plant.

Where Did It Come From?

Aftermath: This derives from the 15th century term *after mowth,* which referred to the second harvest of hay cut every summer.

Demo- and Other -*Cracys*

No system of rule is perfect, but you can at the very least be grateful if you don't have to put up with one of the more bizarre forms of government named below.

✳   ✳   ✳   ✳

ALONG WITH -*ISM*, -*cracy* is the suffix most often used to denote a system of government, as in *democracy* ("rule by the people"). The suffix comes from the Latin -*cratia* and ultimately from the Greek -*kratia* ("power, rule") and -*kratos* ("strength, authority"). The suffix is also used to denote particular social classes, professions, or economic interests.

Yes, But Will You Raise Taxes?

So, among others, we get the following words for various systems of government, both real and imagined:

✳ *aristocracy*—rule by nobles; the noble class

✳ *bureaucracy*—rule by government officials; government officials as a class

✳ *gerontocracy*—rule by the elderly

✳ *gynecocracy*—rule by women

✳ *hierocracy*—rule by priests

✳ *kakistocracy*—rule by the worst citizens

✳ *meritocracy*—rule by the most able

✳ *mobocracy*—rule by the mob

✳ *narchocleptocracy*—rule by drug lords

✳ *plutocracy*—rule by the wealthy

✳ *pornocracy*—rule by prostitutes, especially in reference to Rome in the tenth century

Brewing a Beerocracy

Additionally, *-cracy* and *-ocracy* (with the additional *o* coming from the roots of words like *democracy*) have been used to coin nonce names for various groups, organized bodies, and governmental systems, often semiseriously or with outright ridicule:

* *adhocracy* (from *ad hoc*)—flexible and informal organization, or a bureaucracy characterized by inconsistency and lack of planning

* *barristerocracy*—lawyers

* *beerocracy*—brewers and beer sellers

* *cottonocracy*—the cotton trade (mainly used in the antebellum American South)

* *diabolocracy*—rule by the devil

* *Eurocracy*—originally, colonial rule by a European power; more recently, rule by European Union bureaucrats

* *foolocracy*—rule by fools

* *phallocracy*—rule by men (chiefly used in feminist writings)

And of course there is *logocracy*, "rule by words," which sounds good on paper but has never been used seriously.

Where Did It Come From?

Kowtow: Strictly meaning "to bow and touch your forehead to the floor," this verb has come to mean "to show deference to someone else." The origin is a bit harsher, deriving from the Chinese words *kou* ("head") and *tou* ("to knock"). Ouch.

As a Wise Man Once Said...

If you hear someone say, "Mark Twain once said...," there's a fair chance that what follows was never said by Twain.

✳ ✳ ✳ ✳

MARK TWAIN IS a *quote magnet,* a person to whom quotations are often falsely ascribed. And the process of ascribing quotations to such people is sometimes called *Churchillian drift,* a term coined by quotation maven Nigel Rees in reference to Winston Churchill, another powerful quote magnet. Churchill is probably the most common quote magnet in England, and Mark Twain takes the prize in the United States. Others who attract credit for a lot of quotes include Benjamin Franklin, Yogi Berra, Abraham Lincoln, Oscar Wilde, Satchel Paige, George Bernard Shaw, and, more recently, Sarah Palin.

Examples of falsely attributed quotations include:

✳ "The coldest winter I ever spent was a summer in San Francisco." Falsely attributed to Mark Twain. No one knows who first changed Twain's similar, but less eloquent, comment about Paris into this pithy form.

✳ "Donny Osmond has Van Gogh's ear for music." Falsely attributed to Orson Welles, but actually said by Billy Wilder in 1964 about actor Cliff Osmond (no relation): "Cliff has the musical ear of Van Gogh."

✳ "If you're not a liberal when you're 25, you have no heart. If you're not a conservative by the time you're 35, you have no brain." Falsely attributed to Winston Churchill; it's probably a paraphrase of a quote by historian François Guizot.

✳ "If they have no bread, let them eat cake." Falsely attributed to Marie Antoinette; actually taken from Jean-Jacques Rousseau's autobiography, *Confessions*, which was written 30 years before Antoinette arrived in Versailles. Another problem with this quote is that Rousseau actually wrote *brioche*, which is a kind of bread, not cake.

That's *Not* What He Said

Why are such people quote magnets? For one thing, it's easy to incorrectly attribute a brilliant saying to a particular great speaker who has already coined so many brilliant sayings. Also, a quote can be "improved," so to speak, and dignity and gravitas added to it, by attributing it to a famous person. People have a tendency to want to improve quotes, and a pithy bit of wisdom sounds better if it comes from Abraham Lincoln rather than your Uncle Henry. Even a quote from a famed director like Billy Wilder can be improved by attributing it to an even more famous director (and changing the subject to a more famous Osmond).

The problem has worsened in the age of the Internet, where myths and false attributions multiply like viruses until it's almost impossible to find the truth.

The lesson is to never trust a quotation unless the date and circumstances of its utterance are given. Perhaps the subject of quote magnets is best summed up by George Bernard Shaw: "I tell you I have been misquoted everywhere, and the inaccuracies are chasing me around the world."

Words of Wisdom from Mark Twain

※ ※ ※ ※

* "Let us live so that when we come to die even the undertaker will be sorry."

* "Life would be infinitely happier if we could only be born at the age of eighty and gradually approach eighteen."

* "Action speaks louder than words but not nearly as often."

* "All you need is ignorance and confidence and the success is sure."

* "Be careful about reading health books. You may die of a misprint."

* "Clothes make the man. Naked people have little or no influence on society."

* "Don't go around saying the world owes you a living. The world owes you nothing. It was here first."

* "Familiarity breeds contempt—and children."

* "Giving up smoking is the easiest thing in the world. I know because I've done it thousands of times."

* "Good breeding consists in concealing how much we think of ourselves and how little we think of the other person."

* "I don't like to commit myself about heaven and hell—you see, I have friends in both places."

* "It is better to deserve honors and not have them than to have them and not deserve them."

* "It is better to keep your mouth closed and let people think you are a fool than to open it and remove all doubt."

Aughts: There Oughta Be a Nickname

The year 2000 brought us a new millennium of possibilities, and a new round of questions about nicknaming decades. What should we call the first ten years of the twenty-first century?

✳   ✳   ✳   ✳

FOR EIGHT OUT of ten decades in any given century, we have a handy nickname ready. Just take the number of the decade's first year and pluralize it: *twenties, thirties,* and so on. As for the decade beginning with 1910, just call it *the teens* (even though, technically, 1913 was the first year of that decade with a name ending in *-teen.*)

That leaves a whole decade without a handy nickname: the first ten years of a century, beginning with the year ending in two zeros. You could use *the hundreds,* but that can also refer to the entire century—*the nineteen hundreds,* for example, usually refers to all of the twentieth century.

Among the nicknames bandied about for the 2000s were *the ohs, the double-ohs, the zeros,* and *the oughties.* One of the most popular suggestions was *the aughts,* stemming from an archaic name for zero, but it didn't really catch on. Nothing did. In fact, in the "least likely to succeed" category of the American Dialect Society's annual review of English, the winner for 2009 was "Any name of the decade 2000–2009."

At the outset of 2010, some people concluded that the previous decade—which brought the September 11 attacks, the war in Iraq, and a market meltdown—may as well remain nameless.

Don't Take Things So Literally

If, after you finish reading this article, you have the urge to literally jump for joy, please be careful not to hit your head on the ceiling fan.

✳ ✳ ✳ ✳

WE SOMETIMES TALK about the **literal** meaning of a word or phrase. For example, the literal meaning of *tropical* is "pertaining to the tropics," which is an exact geographical zone, located between the Tropic of Cancer and the Tropic of Capricorn. Although Florida may *feel* tropical—especially when you sizzle in Miami in August—it's not, if we take the word literally.

But what's the literal meaning of the word *literal*? It comes from the Latin *literalis,* meaning "of the letter." Originally, *literal* applied to biblical scripture and meant "a strict interpretation." Under a literal interpretation, "an eye for an eye," for instance, was taken at its word. Today, *literal* still means "not metaphorical." For example, suppose you take your car to the shop. The mechanic might say, "I think you've got a screw loose." If you take him literally, you should ask him to get a screwdriver. If you take him metaphorically, you'll probably be insulted!

Surely You Exaggerate

Metaphorical meanings are often exaggerations. For example, if someone "rubbed salt in your wounds," they probably made you feel worse about a bad situation. The metaphorical meaning is bad, but the literal one is almost physically torturous.

Because metaphors are often exaggerations, *literally* has also come to mean "not exaggerating." Someone might say, "I was literally up all night" or "My teenager can literally eat an entire pizza in 12 minutes." These aren't metaphors, but by using the word *literally*, such speakers are claiming that their statements are precisely true.

Wow, That's Intense

English speakers have combined these meanings. Now *literally* can be used to mean "metaphorical, but truthful," indicating that the metaphor in use expresses a true emotion or impact. Grammar guides will tell you not to confuse *literally* with *figuratively*. But when someone says that he is "literally dying of hunger," he's not confused. Instead, he's using *literally* as an intensifier. Like other words that show truthfulness—such as *honestly*, *really*, and *truly*—*literally* intensifies a statement by saying that the feeling behind it is genuine.

Metaphors and exaggeration have immense power to convey subjective meaning. Saying "I literally died laughing" might be the best way for someone to explain just how funny a situation was. Even if it makes the grammarians break out in a cold sweat. Literally.

"If we did all the things we are capable of, we would literally astound ourselves."

—THOMAS EDISON

"A man is literally what he thinks."

—JAMES ALLEN

Where Did It Come From?

Doubt: Distrust or suspicion that causes problems in decision making; an alternate of Middle English *douten*, which derives from Old French *douter* (to doubt), which in turn comes from Latin *dubitare*; akin to Latin *dubius* (dubious).

Jargon: How the Meaningless Can Mess with Your Mind

Mundane, inconsequential, impenetrable mumbo jumbo...yeah, that's about right.

✳ ✳ ✳ ✳

THE YEAR 1984 HAS come and gone, but George Orwell's fears in *Nineteen Eighty-Four*, the doomsday novel he published in 1949, still loom over us. In that masterpiece, Orwell imagined a totalitarian government—"Big Brother"—that was not only always watching, but always burying the truth by manipulating language.

In Orwell's timeless essay "Politics and the English Language," he defines *jargon* as a malicious tool "to make lies sound truthful and murder respectable, and to give an appearance of solidity to pure wind." He translates the poetry of Ecclesiastes—"the race is not to the swift, nor the battle to the strong...but time and chance happeneth to them all"—into this muddy pile of ugly jargon: "Objective considerations of contemporary phenomena compel the conclusion that success or failure in competitive activities exhibits no tendency to be commensurate with innate capacity, but that a considerable element of the unpredictable must invariably be taken into account."

Can You Repeat That?

Decades after the actual year 1984, government officials are still versed in doublespeak. During the first Gulf War of 1991, the U.S. military referred to civilian casualties as "collateral damage." During the second war in Iraq, the U.S. government put a tacit stamp of approval on the use of torture at Guantánamo Bay and elsewhere by calling it "enhanced interrogation techniques." In these instances, the jargon is *euphemistic*, or designed to make a bad thing sound more attractive. (See page 64 for more on euphemisms.) But most jargon is mundane: the inconsequential and impenetrable prose of instruction manuals, corporate memos, and academic journals. Such examples fit well with the word's etymology: *Jargon* is an Old French word for the incomprehensible and meaningless chattering of birds.

In a world awash with technical advancements that race faster than our capacity to understand them, our distaste for jargon deepens. And in a society whose wealth no longer comes from manufacturing products but from marketing them, we fear we'll forget just how unnatural and unnecessary the business jargon that surrounds us really is.

Translation, Please?	
What They Say	**What They Mean**
"Action item"	An item on your "to-do" list
"At this juncture"	Now
"Best practices"	Effective methods
"Bring to the table"	Contribute
"Buzzworthy"	Interesting
"Data-point"	Fact
"Fit for purpose"	Acceptable; working
"Path forward"	Business plan
"Populate"	Fill out (as paperwork)

-Calypse Now

An etymologist would not rate -calypse as a likely candidate for a productive suffix. It's not, after all, a "real" suffix or combining element. But that hasn't stopped wordsmiths from using the two syllables in a variety of humorous coinages.

✳   ✳   ✳   ✳

THE WOULD-BE SUFFIX comes from the word *apocalypse,* which comes from the Latin *apocalypsis* and is ultimately from the Greek *apokalypsis* (*apo,* "off" + *kalyptein,* "to cover"), meaning "disclosure" or "revelation." The *Apocalypsis Ioannis,* or the *Book of the Revelation of St. John,* is the final book of the Vulgate Latin Bible and provides a vision of the end of time. For centuries the word *apocalypse* was used in English to refer to this book, or as a general term for a disclosure or revelation.

But at the end of the nineteenth century, people began using *apocalypse* to describe the events in that biblical book or any cataclysm that necessitated the destruction of the earth or life as we know it. And much more recently, the element *-calypse* has become separated and applied to all sorts of calamitous or momentous events. The *-calypse* words are often followed by *Now,* in homage to the 1979 Francis Ford Coppola movie *Apocalypse Now.* A few examples include:

✳ *a-pop-calypse*—the destruction of Western civilization by the evils of popular culture; a segment on the television show *The Colbert Report*

✳ *aqua-calypse*—damage to the sea from overfishing

✳ *Grandma-calypse*—a visit from a relative who spoils the kids, and the attendant destruction of parental discipline

✳ *Ron-Paul-calypse Now*—derogatory term for the 2008 presidential campaign of Congressman Ron Paul

Excuse Me, Your Eminence

Royalty, politicians, and notable religious figures get many perks, including the right to be addressed in a particular fashion.

✳ ✳ ✳ ✳

THE PRESIDENT OF the United States is addressed simply as "Mr. President," the vice president as "Mr. Vice President," and the chief justice of the United States as "Mr. Chief Justice." (For now, anyway: Presumably someday soon Americans will add "Mrs." or "Ms." to this particular vernacular.)

✳ Mayors in the United States are addressed "Mr. (or Ms.) Mayor," but in Canada they are "Your Worship."

✳ U.S. senators are called "Senator," and representatives are "Congressman" or "Congresswoman" (plus a last name).

✳ Ambassadors and other foreign diplomats are addressed as "Your Excellency." Governors of states are also "Your Excellency," but only in writing (and not very often).

✳ Cardinals in the Roman Catholic Church are properly addressed as "Your Eminence," while an archbishop should hear "Your Grace," and the pope is called "Your Holiness."

✳ In Britain, a duke is also referred to as "Your Grace," an earl or a marquis as "Your Lordship," and the king or queen as "Your Majesty"—but only the first time. On subsequent references, you may say "Ma'am" or "Sir." Princes and princesses are addressed as "Your Royal Highness."

✳ **Forms of address and titles have simplified tremendously over the years. In the early 1500s, Fernando Cortés began a letter to Emperor Charles V with the address "Very High and Most Powerful Prince, Very Catholic and Invincible Emperor, King and Lord," and signed the letter "Most Powerful Lord, Your Caesarian Majesty's Very Humble Servant and Vassal who kisses the Royal Hands and Feet of Your Majesty."**

Snack Attack

Are you hungry for more on word origins? Feast your eyes on the etymological history of these delicacies.

✳ ✳ ✳ ✳

✳ **Bock beer:** From the German word for a male goat, because the beer's strength was said to make its drinkers behave just like the wild animal.

✳ **Cheeseburger:** Although you might think it has been around forever, the cheeseburger first became part of American culture in 1935, when Louis Ballast of the Humpty Dumpty Barrel Drive-In in St. Louis, Missouri, applied for a patent on the concept. (Although other places in California and Kentucky also claimed credit for the first cheeseburger, Ballast was the only one to finish the paperwork.) Alas for Ballast, the word *cheeseburger* remains in the public domain. No one can own it, and everyone can use it.

✳ **Coconut:** Of course, the coconut is not a nut at all, but it looked like one to the early Portuguese explorers as they sailed around Africa. They saw the fruit hanging from trees and thought they looked like small heads, grinning. *Coconut* resulted from a combination of *nut* and the Portuguese word *coco*, which means "a grinning face."

✳ **Ketchup:** This condiment would have been unrecognizable in its earlier incarnations, especially as a fish-based sauce. But as a matter of fact, that's how it got its name. Back in 1711, the Malay name for this sauce was *kichap*, from the Chinese Amoy dialect's *koechiap*, or "brine of fish." Early English versions of the condiment included mushrooms, walnuts, cucumbers, and oysters. The first modern form of ketchup began when New Englanders added tomatoes. *Catsup* (earlier, *catchup*) is a failed attempt at Anglicization but is still in use in some portions of the United States.

* **Lager beer:** Because it is aged in a storehouse before it is ready for consumption, this beer derives its name from the German word for "resting place."

* **Mushroom:** This name doesn't describe the fungus but probably resulted from the mispronunciation of the French word *mousseron*. Before the French word became popular, the mushroom was often known by its more descriptive name: toad's hat.

* **Mustard:** A food condiment; originated in 1190 from Old French *moustarde*, derived from *moust* (must) and the Latin *mustum* (new wine), so called because it was originally prepared by adding the substance *moust* to the ground seeds of the plant to make a paste.

* **Nachos:** The favorite midgame snack of millions—corn chips slathered in melted cheese and an assortment of toppings—was (at least according to the *Dallas Morning News*) named for the man who invented it in 1943. Ignacio Anaya was a cook in Piedras Negras, a Mexican town near the U.S. border. *Anayas*, presumably, didn't have quite the same ring as *nachos*.

* **Pretzel:** Though some have compared the twisted shape of these snacks to the arms of praying children, nobody knows for sure why pretzels are twisted—though the term itself is from the German word for "branch."

* **Sandwich:** Although John Montagu, consummate gambler, hasty eater, and the fourth Earl of Sandwich (1718–1792), is responsible for the name for this meal, people had eaten sandwiches long before the Earl made them trendy.

* **Snacks:** The tasty treats have been consumed since the 1600s, when the word was first used to describe small portions of food hastily snatched between meals.

The 411 on Texting

When u take out ur cell phone 2 send a quick txt, or when u hop online 2 IM with ur friends, u don't have 2 worry about perfect spelling and good grammar. JTLYK (just to let you know), there's a whole new language 2 learn. Here's a handy cheat sheet for those late 2 the party. OMG, u already know these terms? WTG (way to go)! If not, HTH (hope this helps).

❋ ❋ ❋ ❋

❋ 2MTH—Too much to handle

❋ 411—All the information

❋ 4COL—For crying out loud

❋ ADIH—Another day in hell

❋ ADIP—Another day in paradise

❋ BBIF—Be back in a few

❋ BFN—Bye for now

❋ BHL8—Be home late

❋ BISLY—But I still love you

❋ BRB—Be right back

❋ CWOT—Complete waste of time

❋ CYA—See ya

❋ FWIW—For what it's worth

❋ GFI—Go for it

❋ GJ—Good job

❋ GTG—Got to go; also, good to go

❋ HBU—How 'bout you?

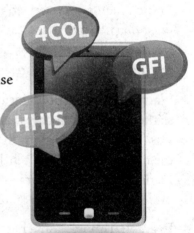

* HHIS—Hanging head in shame

* HMU—Hit me up

* IDC—I don't care

* IDK—I don't know

* IMHO—In my humble opinion

* IMSB—I'm so bored

* IRL—In real life

* JK—Just kidding

* JTLYK—Just to let you know

* KK—Okay

* LOL or LOLZ—Laugh out loud

* LTHTT—Laughing too hard to type

* LYLAB / LYLAS—Love you like a brother / Love you like a sister

* NP—No problem

* NTIM—Not that it matters

* NVM or NM—Never mind

* OMG—Oh my God/gosh!

* O RLY—Oh, really?

* OTOH—On the other hand

* ROFL—Rolling on the floor laughing

* SFSG—So far so good

* SUP—What's up?

* TBH—To be honest

* TTYL—Talk to you later (also TTYS—talk to you soon)

* TYVM—Thank you very much

* UOK—Are you okay?

* WB—Welcome back

* WDYMBT—What do you mean by that?

* WTG—Way to go

* WUT—What

---

* Here's a new word for the modern age: *intexticated.* It applies to people who are preoccupied with sending or receiving text messages, particularly while driving.

Parent Alert!

Want to know what your kids are saying to each other? Here are some common "parent alerts":

* CD9—Code 9, meaning "parents are around"

* KPC—Keeping parents clueless

* NP—Nosy parents (also used as "no problem")

* P911—Parents coming into room alert

* PAW—Parents are watching

* PIR—Parents in room

* POMS—Parent over my shoulder

* POS—Parent over shoulder

* PSOS—Parent standing over shoulder

Words of Wisdom: Family

✳   ✳   ✳   ✳

"The happiest moments of my life have been the few which I have passed at home in the bosom of my family."
—THOMAS JEFFERSON

"Nobody who has not been in the interior of a family can say what the difficulties of any individual of that family may be."
—JANE AUSTEN

"The best Christmas of all is the presence of a happy family all wrapped up with one another."
—ANONYMOUS

"He that raises a large family does, indeed, while he lives to observe them, stand a broader mark for sorrow; but then he stands a broader mark for pleasure too."
—BENJAMIN FRANKLIN

"Happy families are all alike; every unhappy family is unhappy in its own way."
—LEO TOLSTOY

"A brother offended is harder to be won than a strong city."
—PROVERBS 18:19, KJV

"For there is no friend like a sister in calm or stormy weather."
—CHRISTINA ROSSETTI

"You don't choose your family. They are God's gift to you, as you are to them."
—DESMOND TUTU

Word Roots and Branches
Counter- Points

As long as we're all on the same page (quite literally—this is a book, after all), let's stick together and discuss the history of a very oppositional prefix.

✳ ✳ ✳ ✳

THE PREFIX CONTRA- appears in words borrowed from Latin and the Romance languages. In Latin, *contra* is a preposition and adverb meaning "in opposition, against." With the exception of French, all the modern Romance languages retain the Latin spelling. But in French it has become *contre-*, from which the English *counter-* comes. Unlike *contra-*, the prefix *counter-* is extremely prolific, forming a large number of English words.

In English, *contra-/counter-* has several meanings. In the form *contra-*, it can mean "against," as in *contravene* (from the Latin *contra-* + *venire*, "to come") or *contradict* ("to speak against"). And *contrary* means "in opposition." It can also mean "against the law." *Contraband* comes from the Spanish *contrabanda*, or "smuggling," which in turn is from the Italian *contrabando*, or "unlawful dealing."

Some -*Counter* Words You May Encounter

As *counter-*, the prefix is extremely common and means "in opposition, against." Some examples:

✳ *counterbalance*—a weight used to balance another weight, or a power or force that balances the effects of another; also used as a verb

✳ *counterbattery*—artillery-on-artillery violence

✳ *countercharm*—something that neutralizes a charm

✳ *counterfeit*—an imitation or forgery; from the Old French *countrefet* and ultimately from the Latin *contra-* + *facere* ("to make in opposition")

* *counterintelligence*—prevention of espionage (spy vs. spy stuff)

* *countermand*—to revoke an order; from the Old French *contremander* and ultimately from the Medieval Latin *contramandare* ("to order against")

Further Opposition

Contra- can also be found in musical terms. Most of these come from Italian musical jargon, such as *contrapuncto* ("counterpoint"). Terms like *contrabasso* and *contralto* are musical voice parts in opposition to the *basso* or *alto* parts. And instruments like the *contrabass* have a pitch an octave below the regular bass.

The *con* in *pro and con* is a clipping of *contra*. And for those of you who remember international politics in the 1980s and the Iran-Contra scandal, the *Contras* were right-wing Nicaraguan guerillas, from the Spanish *contrarrevolucionario*, or "counter-revolutionary."

---

* A prefix similar in meaning to *contra-/counter-* is *anti-*. To learn more about *anti-*, turn to page 372.

Where Did It Come From?

Guy: Today the word *guy* is an accepted substitute for *man* or *boy*, but it came about in a less-than-positive manner. In the early seventeenth century, Guy Fawkes was instrumental in a plan to blow up England's Parliament. He was captured and hanged, but people celebrated the day by carrying effigies of Guy throughout the streets. Anyone resembling Guy or his manner of dress became known as a *guy*.

Janus Words

Words can have many different meanings. This is what linguists call **polysemy**, *from* poly *(meaning "many") and* sem, *the root of* semantic, *meaning "signification." With all these different senses, sometimes a word will develop meanings that are contradictory.*

✳ ✳ ✳ ✳

THESE WORDS ARE called *Janus words,* after the two-faced Roman god of gates/doors and beginnings/endings. (The month of *January* is named for him because in the Roman calendar it was the end of one year and the start of another.)

Janus words develop in two ways. First, sometimes two word roots that are unrelated to one another change over time to be very similar in pronunciation and spelling. The contradictory meanings can develop from different roots and, over time,

the words come to resemble one another in spelling and pronunciation. An example of this is the verb *to cleave,* which can mean both "to split asunder" and "to cling, adhere together." We now call it one word with two meanings, but in Old English there were two verbs: *cleofan,* meaning "to split," and *clifian,* "to adhere." Over the centuries, the descendants of these two words came to resemble one another; hence the contradictory meanings of the modern verb *to cleave.*

Don't Make a Habit of It

Or a pair of Janus words can start as a single root but develop slightly different senses that increasingly diverge over time until they mean the opposite of one another. An example of this is *custom*, which can mean both "habit" and "one of a kind, unique." The original sense of *custom* is that of "habit," which is preserved today. But it also came to mean "habitually frequenting a shop or establishment," as in *customer*. From there it came to refer to one-of-a-kind bespoke items created for a particular customer, as in *custom-made*.

Other examples of Janus words include:

* *bolt*, meaning "to secure in place" or "to dash away suddenly"

* *buckle*, meaning "to fasten, secure" or "to bend, break"

* *clip*, meaning "to fasten together; hold tightly" or "to cut apart; cut off"

* *cull*, meaning "to select" and "to reject"

* *fast*, meaning "quick" or "stationary"

* *fix*, meaning "a solution" or "a problem"

* *handicap*, meaning "an advantage" (as in sports) or "a disadvantage; disability"

* *put out*, meaning "to generate, produce" or "to extinguish; put an end to"

* *sanction*, meaning both "to bless" and "to ban"

* *screen*, meaning "to conceal" or "to show"

* *splice*, meaning "to join together" or "to cut in two"

* *stem*, meaning "to start or originate" or "to stop or contain"

* *trim*, meaning "to cut" and "to add to"

* *weather*, meaning "to endure, last" and "to erode"

---

* Janus words are also known as *autoantonyms*. Antonyms are two words with opposite meanings, so autoantonyms (*auto-*, "self") are words that are the opposite of themselves.

Translating Across the Galaxy

Hello? Is anybody out there?

✳ ✳ ✳ ✳

A PERSON WHO INVENTS a language may have lofty ambitions for it. L. L. Zamenhof, for example, invented Esperanto in the nineteenth century with the goal of giving all people of the world a common language in order to better understand each other and bring world peace. *Klingon,* on the other hand, was invented to be the language of the Klingons on *Star Trek*—the bronze, bulbous-headed adversaries of the starship *Enterprise.* The Klingons were named for Wilbur Clingan, a colleague of *Star Trek* creator Gene Roddenberry in the Los Angeles Police Department.

Actor James Doohan, who played Scotty, made up the basic sounds of Klingon for the 1979 release of *Star Trek: The Motion Picture.* Linguist Marc Okrand was hired to construct an actual language of Klingon for subsequent films based on Doohan's dialogue. Okrand told the *Los Angeles Times* that to help Klingon sound more alien, he tried to use sound combinations that do not occur in human languages. He also used a highly unusual sentence structure: object-verb-subject, as in "them defeated we" instead of "we defeated them." Okrand told the *Times,* "I looked at all those kinds of [linguistic] rules and then violated them on purpose."

Klingon Speak They

It's estimated that there are a few hundred Klingon speakers in the world—a record for a fictional language, according to *Guinness World Records*—though Okrand says only a dozen or so are actually fluent.

To learn Klingon's sparse vocabulary of less than 3,000 words, they rely on *The Klingon Dictionary*, first published in 1985 by Pocket Books, and innumerable fan websites, including the Klingon Language Institute (www.kli.org). The KLI has translated works of Shakespeare and the Bible into Klingon, and provides a list of everyday phrases and insults you can throw into casual conversation. So if you really want to disparage a Klingon, you could say, "Hab SoSlI' Quch!" This means, "Your mother has a smooth forehead!"

Na'vi 101

Na'vi is another language that was created for the entertainment industry. Developed by Paul Frommer, a linguist from the University of Southern California, for the 2009 film *Avatar*, Na'vi is more melodious than the guttural Klingon language and much easier to learn—and to speak.

At the time the film was released, Na'vi consisted of roughly 1,000 words, but Frommer has since expanded the language to more than 1,500 words. He has also published the grammar translation, meaning the language is accessible for anyone who wants to learn it.

✳ Klingon has no verb for "to be," so when the Klingons quote Shakespeare's "to be or not to be" in *Star Trek VI: The Undiscovered Country*, Okrand had them say "taH pagh, taHbe," or "whether to continue, or not to continue [living]."

Infixes: Getting into Words

A prefix attaches itself at the beginning of a word, and a suffix links up at the end. They both sit quietly to either side of a given word without disturbing it much. An **infix,** *however, barrels into the middle of a word with both arms swinging.*

✳   ✳   ✳   ✳

ONE EXAMPLE OF an infix is -*ma*- in *edumacation,* a playful botching of *education.* Urbandictionary.com defines *edumacation* as "an education that someone received at a crappy school, or a lack of education all together." Indeed, the -*ma*- infix makes you think the speaker is a bumpkin who needs a good education. Homer Simpson usually gets credit for coining *edumacation,* along with a slew of other words with infixes. When Bart asks, "Can I use the teleporter?" Homer replies, "Sorry, but this is a highly sophistimacated doowacky." In other episodes he uses *metabamalism, macamadamia nut,* and *hippomapotamus.* Linguist Alan Yu called this phenomenon "Homeric Infixation."

Infixes are also a trademark of hip-hop music, in which you'll often find -*izz*- inserted into the middle of a word. The Another Bad Creation song "Playground," for example, features the line "chillin' in the pizzark ... mother said be home by dizzark."

In some cases, entire words can be infixed. *The Simpsons'* Ned Flanders is known for infixing nonsense words, as in "I plead guilt-diddily-ildly as char-diddily-arged." We can also insert other words for emphasis and intensity, as in "abso-freaking-lutely!" Some linguists would insist that this usage be called *tmesis,* in which an entire word or phrase is inserted inside another for poetic effect (see page 291 for more on tmesis). And don't confuse an infix with an *interfix,* which is a particle without any meaning that is inserted between two halves of a compound word, as with the -*o*- in *fun-o-meter* or the *s* in *helmsman.* While an interfix is glue that holds two words together, an infix actually changes the meaning of a word.

Famous First Lines

The first words of a novel can be enough to set the tone for the whole book. Here's a look at some memorable opening lines.

✳   ✳   ✳   ✳

"All children, except one, grow up."
—J. M. BARRIE, *PETER AND WENDY* (1911)

"The director told me: 'I only keep you out of respect for your esteemed father, otherwise you would have been sent flying out of here long ago.'"
—ANTON CHEKHOV, *MY LIFE* (1896)

"The cold passed reluctantly from the earth, and the retiring fogs revealed an army stretched out on the hills, resting."
—STEPHEN CRANE, *THE RED BADGE OF COURAGE* (1895)

"You don't know about me without you have read a book called The Adventures of Tom Sawyer, *but that ain't no matter."*
—MARK TWAIN, *THE ADVENTURES OF HUCKLEBERRY FINN* (1885)

"Alice was beginning to get very tired of sitting by her sister on the bank, and of having nothing to do: once or twice she had peeped into the book her sister was reading, but it had no pictures or conversations in it, 'and what is the use of a book,' thought Alice, 'without pictures or conversation?'"
—LEWIS CARROLL, *ALICE'S ADVENTURES IN WONDERLAND* (1865

"Marley was dead, to begin with."
—CHARLES DICKENS, *A CHRISTMAS CAROL* (1843)

What Do You Mean by That? The Animal Edition

✳ ✳ ✳ ✳

Blind as a Bat

Actually, bats' vision isn't all that bad. They are color-blind (as are many humans), but they also have supersharp night vision and can find their way around very well by using echolocation, a form of natural sonar. While in flight, bats emit sounds that bounce off nearby surfaces, and they then use those echoes to judge distances.

Clean as a Hound's Tooth

Unlike other breeds of dogs, in earlier times a prized hound was allowed to live only if it was a specimen of perfect health—including its teeth. So something on par with a hound's tooth is judged to be perfectly clean. And that was before the time of toothpaste, let alone Sonicare brushes!

Crocodile Tears

When someone is said to be crying "crocodile tears," they are feigning sorrow. This phrase actually does come from crocodiles and specifically refers to a peculiarity in which crocodiles shed tears while eating. This is caused by food pressing against the roof of the animal's mouth, which activates the lachrymal glands that secrete tears, making crocodiles appear to be crying without really being sad at all.

Dirty as a Rat

Even before the Black Death in the fourteenth century, rats had a reputation for being filthy. Due to their lack of an assertive PR department, they haven't been able to point out that fleas were actually the responsible party. Rats, in fact, are quite clean and tidy. They spend 40 percent of their time washing themselves (more than the average house cat), searching out water for grooming, and compulsively cleaning their habitats.

Dog Days of Summer

The dog days of summer are the hottest, stickiest time of year—in the northern hemisphere, usually July and August; in the southern hemisphere, typically January and February. The nickname stems from ancient Rome, when people noticed that Sirius (the Dog Star) was visible in the sky during the summertime.

High on the Hog

The best cuts of meat on a pig come from its highest parts—steaks, chops, ribs. The less tasty, and less expensive, cuts are found lower on the hog—think pigs' feet. People living "high on the hog" are living extravagantly, spending their money on the finer things, including the best cuts of meat.

Monkey's Uncle

"Well, I'll be a monkey's uncle!" When noted biologist Charles Darwin outlined his evolutionary theory—that humans are descended from animals rather than brought into existence by God—there were plenty of people who thought the theory was a bunch of baloney. This exclamation of disbelief is used sarcastically; as in, there's absolutely no chance of that: "Yeah, right. If you're the queen of England, I'm a monkey's uncle."

Sweaty as a Pig

When humans get too hot, we sweat. We release perspiration through approximately 2.6 million (give or take a few) sweat glands in our skin, and that perspiration evaporates and cools us down. Pigs, however, have no sweat glands and can't sweat at all, which is why they attempt to lower their body temperature by wallowing in mud.

Slimy as a Snake

Although a snake's scales are shiny and often appear slimy, the reptile's body is dry to the touch. People may confuse snakes with amphibians such as frogs and salamanders, which have thin skins that are moist to the touch. Or maybe they're thinking of worms, which are definitely slimy.

The Talk of the Tracks: Hobo Slang

Has someone ever said to you: "I'm one John Hollow Legs. I don't even have an ace spot to my name, which is why I need to find a doughnut philosopher and beg him for a dukie." No? Then you've never conversed with a hobo.

✳   ✳   ✳   ✳

THE WORD *HOBO*, used to describe a wandering homeless person, became iconic during the Great Depression. Hoboes had a language all their own. The sentence at the top, for example, translates to: "I'm a hungry stiff. I don't even have one dollar to my name. I need to find a hobo who's satisfied with his coffee and food so I can beg him for something to eat."

First heard in the Pacific Northwest in the late 1800s, the term differentiates migrants, who are willing to work, from "bums" or "tramps," who will not. The term *hobo* itself is possibly slang for "Ho boy," "Hello Brother," or even "hoe-boy" (an itinerant farm worker). By the 1890s, hobo was an accepted term.

Some hobo terms are still common enough. A *cathouse* is still a brothel, while a *coffin nail* still describes a cigarette. A burial site for the destitute is called a *potter's field*, and *glad rags* means nice clothing. Other hobo jargon, however, is a bit more incomprehensible. For instance, *axle grease* means butter, and a *dog robber* is not someone who steals a pooch but rather a term for a boarding house keeper. *Flintstone kids* describes the latest generation of hoboes instead of the cartoon characters Pebbles and Bam-Bam, and a *town clown* means a policeman, not a municipal jester.

Hoboes have by and large faded from the American scene. However, that doesn't mean their lingo has, too. Who knows, maybe someday you'll get a request to hand out some *toadskins*. If you know that means paper money rather than the actual hide of a toad, you'll be much better off.

Not Even Close to *Non*-essential

Some people (but certainly none who are reading this book!)
nonchalantly dismiss the study of etymology and word roots as
nonsense. They are nonplussed over others' fascination with the
subject. But the popularity of the prefix non- shows us that even
non-logophiles use affixes and roots to create new vocabulary.
For non- is one of the most productive prefixes in English, and
has been for centuries.

✳   ✳   ✳   ✳

THE PREFIX NON- ultimately comes from the Latin adverb
non, meaning "no, not, by no means." It made its way into
English with the Normans. Many of the early *non-* words
were borrowed from French, including *nonage* (1400); *non-
payment* (1423); *nonresident* (1425); *nonpareil*, meaning
"peerless" (c. 1450); and *nonappearance* (1475). Other early
non- words were coined in English, such as *nonobservance*
(1453) and *nonability* (1477).

Non-'s productivity really picked up in the seventeenth century,
so much so that it would be almost *nonsensical* (1645) to list
all of the prefix's appearances. That and subsequent centuries
have given us some highlights, however: *nonconformist* (1618);
noncombatant (1811); *nonalcoholic* (1857); *nonsmoking* (1868);
nonfattening (1915); and *nonallergenic* (1949).

In addition to its function as a highly productive prefix, *non* also
shows up in wholesale Latin borrowings. A common example
is *non sequitur*, which literally means "does not follow." The term
refers to a conclusion that does not logically follow from its
premises or, less particularly, a response or remark that does not
logically follow from what has gone before. (For more on non
sequiturs, see page 664.) Other examples include *persona non
grata*, or "an unwelcome person," and *non compos mentis*, which
means "not of sound mind" and is often used in legal contexts.

Eponym: A Rose by Anyone Else's Name . . .

*Some words—namely, **eponyms**—have made their way into the English language courtesy of a special person.*

✳ ✳ ✳ ✳

T HE ENDING *-NYM* means "name," from the Greek. Put *-nym* together with different prefixes and you get words like *homonym* (*-hom*=same; "same name") *pseudonym* (*-pseudo*=false; "false name"), and *synonym* (*-syn*=together; "together name," or, two words that—together—name the same thing). And, more to the point of this article, the Greek *epo-* means "on, upon." So an *eponym* means having your "name on" something. For instance, in "Max's Restaurant," *Max* is an eponym.

Lasting Legacies

Eponyms mark the most enduring human accomplishments and afflictions. Astronomer Edmond Halley, a contemporary and friend of Isaac Newton, calculated the orbit period of the comet that is now eponymously called Halley's Comet. The element einsteinium wasn't actually discovered by Einstein, but the name is a tribute to the great thinker. Even the Fosbury Flop, the backward high jump technique introduced by jumper Dick Fosbury, honors a pioneer.

Have You Driven a Ford Lately?

How about a Chrysler, a Honda, a Dodge, or a Chevrolet? It was—and is—extremely common for automobile manufacturers to create a company in their own name, labeling their cars with their own surname. Many exotic makes are named after the company's founders as well: Think Ferrarri (Enzo), Bugatti (Ettore), and De Lorean (John). In fact, it's a common occurence for entrepreneurs everywhere to self-title their business. And why not? There's nothing wrong with broadcasting your success. Maybe that ex-girlfriend or ex-boyfriend will finally take notice.

A Legacy You'd Probably Rather Not Leave

Some eponyms are for distinctions no one aspires to. Lou Gehrig was a Hall of Fame baseball player, but his name might be best known for the disease he suffered from and ultimately succumbed to: amyotrophic lateral sclerosis (ALS), or Lou Gehrig's disease. The Lindbergh Law is an anti-kidnapping law. And design engineer Edward Murphy, who studied system failures, coined the term Murphy's Law ("Whatever can go wrong, will go wrong") to describe the results of his experiments.

Names That Will Live in Infamy

* Niccolò Machiavelli: Author of *The Art of War* and *The Prince*, considered a founder of political science, and known for his less-than-upstanding ethics, this Italian Renaissance politican lent his name to the adjective *machiavellian*, which means "cunning, scheming, and unscrupulous."

* Draco: The lawmaker from ancient Greece was known for his harsh and oppressive rule, and the adjective draconian means just that: harsh, oppressive, cruel, strict. (On a side note, *Harry Potter* fans will no doubt see how Draco Malfoy got his name.)

* Patrick Hooligan: An English criminal in the late nineteenth century, Hooligan, together with his family and friends, was known for troublemaking, crime sprees, and violence. Today, the *Oxford English Dictionary* defines *hooligan* as "a violent young troublemaker, typically one of a gang." The term is also often associated with violence in sports.

---

* Many recording artists debut with "self-titled" albums, or albums bearing just their name and no separate album title. The band R.E.M. had a little fun with this tradition and released a compilation album in 1988 with the title *Eponymous*.

* If you don't have a restaurant, comet, disease, or album to your name, you can always buy your eponymy. The International Star Registry is one of several services that will register a star with the name of you or your loved one. Prices start at about $50.

Words of Wisdom: Friendship

✳   ✳   ✳   ✳

"I find friendship to be like wine, raw when new, ripened with age..."

—THOMAS JEFFERSON

"The only way to have a friend is to be one."

—RALPH WALDO EMERSON

"A true friend is the greatest of all blessings."

—FRANÇOIS, DUC DE LA ROCHEFOUCAULD

"Life is nothing without friendship."

—MARCUS TULLIUS CICERO

"True friends stab you in the front."

—OSCAR WILDE

"There is no possession more valuable than a good and faithful friend."

—SOCRATES

"It is one of the blessings of old friends that you can afford to be stupid with them."

—RALPH WALDO EMERSON

"May the hinges of our friendship never grow rusty."

—OLD IRISH TOAST

"Friends cherish each other's hopes, they are kind to each other's dreams."

—HENRY DAVID THOREAU

"Friendship is the comfort, the inexpressible comfort of feeling safe with a person, having to neither weigh thoughts or measure words."

—DINAH MARIA MULOCK CRAIK

"My friends are my estate."

—EMILY DICKINSON

"Wherever you are, it is your own friends who make your world."

—WILLIAM JAMES

"Life is to be fortified by many friendships. To love and to be loved is the greatest happiness of existence."

—AESOP

"What is a friend? A single soul dwelling in two bodies."

—ARISTOTLE

"The best mirror is an old friend."

—GEORGE HERBERT

"If you have one true friend, you have more than your share."

—THOMAS FULLER

"Some people go to priests; others to poetry; I to my friends."

—VIRGINIA WOOLF

"I have friends in overalls whose friendship I would not swap for the favor of the kings of the world."

—THOMAS EDISON

"The one absolutely unselfish friend that man can have in this selfish world, the one that never deserts him, the one that never proves ungrateful or treacherous, is his dog."

—GEORGE GRAHAM VEST

"So long as we love we serve; so long as we are loved by others, I would almost say that we are indispensable; and no man is useless while he has a friend."

—ROBERT LOUIS STEVENSON

Sickening English Usage

It takes a serious lack of sympathy to hear someone say "I'm nauseous" and respond only by giggling and scolding their usage error. But it happens.

✳ ✳ ✳ ✳

NAUSEOUS, THE PEDANT will explain, is properly used to describe something that induces nausea. *Nauseated* is the correct term for suffering from nausea. So if you're "nauseous," the pedant insists, you're actually causing other people to throw up. (At which point you are free to puke on the pedant's shoes.)

In reality, the *-ous* ending in English often means "state of," as it does in *joyous* and *zealous*. The *Oxford English Dictionary* defines the suffix *-ous* as "forming adjectives with the sense 'abounding in, full of, characterized by, of the nature of.'" So using *nauseous* to mean "having nausea" is simply following this pattern. Reserving *nauseous* to describe "causing nausea," on the other hand, is a restriction on *-ous* that has little basis in current English usage.

Nor does history provide much argument for *nauseous* to mean only "causing nausea." The *OED*'s earliest attested meaning of *nauseous* is "inclined to sickness or nausea; squeamish." It quotes a 1651 example that reads, "It may be given ... to children or those that are of a nauseous stomach." While "causing nausea" was the most common meaning of *nauseous* in the seventeenth century, "having nausea" would soon follow (the *OED* says it originated in the United States). One 1885 newspaper report read, "I ... was bumped up and down and oscillated and see-sawed from side to side until I became nauseous."

By now *nauseous* is so commonly—and reasonably—used to describe the experience of nausea that you can properly tell pedants who insist otherwise, "You make me sick."

Seven Euphemisms for Infidelity

Birds do it, bees do it, even educated fleas do it... just don't let your significant other catch you doing it.

✳ ✳ ✳ ✳

1. **Having an Affair:** The term is straight to the point... but boring as can be!

2. **Cooking for Someone Else:** It's probably better to leave your utensils in your own drawer and out of someone else's pots and pans.

3. **Hiking the Appalachian Trail:** Thank you very much, South Carolina Governor Mark Sanford, for taking that excursion to Argentina and adding this priceless idiom to our vernacular in 2009!

4. **Open Marriage:** Welcome back to the 1970s! A popular phrase during the era of disco balls and leisure suits, the term does not "technically" describe infidelity, as both sides agree to have extramarital relations. Good luck dodging that frying pan, however, when one side "technically" has a change of heart.

5. **Parking the Car in Someone Else's Garage:** No further explanation necessary.

6. **Pinch the Cat in the Dark:** We have no idea what this means, but supposedly if you're Dutch, you're winking and laughing hysterically right now.

7. **Seven-Year Itch:** We can thank playwright George Axelrod for his 1952 play (and Marilyn Monroe for her 1955 film performance)—both of which led to this familiar phrase for infidelity. Statistically speaking, by the way, the U.S. Census Bureau maintains that most first marriages that fail do so after eight years. A case of life imitating art?

Read This Article? *Meh.*

It is with no lack of irony that a word expressing utter indifference and apathy is one of the hot words of this day and age. That word is **meh,** *an expression of indifference and absence of interest in the topic at hand, a sort of verbal shrug of the shoulders.*

✳ ✳ ✳ ✳

As of this writing, Urbandictionary.com has more than 280 user-supplied definitions of *meh.* Many of these definitions are duplicative, of course, but the fact that that many people took the time to write definitions and record examples is indicative of the fervor that *meh* generates.

Of course, not a little of *meh*'s popularity is due to its origin, which was on *The Simpsons*. In the episode "Sideshow Bob Roberts" (aired October 9, 1994), the following exchange takes place:

> Librarian: *Here are the results of last month's mayor election. All 48,000 voters and who they voted for.*
>
> Lisa: *I thought this was a secret ballot?*
>
> Librarian: *Meh.*

In a 2001 episode ("Hungry, Hungry Homer"), Homer's kids do not respond favorably to the possibility of a trip to Blockoland:

> Bart and Lisa: *Meh.*
>
> Homer: *But the TV gave me the impression that...*
>
> Bart: *We said, "meh"!*
>
> Lisa: *M-E-H, meh.*

Several writers—including Nathan Bierma of the *Chicago Tribune*—have suggested that *meh* has a Yiddish history, but there is no real evidence of this. Like *meh*'s more famous cousin, *doh* (see page 103 for more on *doh*), the word is far more likely to simply be a transcription of a grunt—and grunts can carry meanings.

Another reason for *meh*'s popularity is undoubtedly its utility in e-mail and texting. One of the troublesome aspects of some new media is the difficulty of conveying emotional tone in short, written exchanges. *Meh* is a perfect and pithy way of texting a response of indifference to a suggestion.

As *meh* has spread online, variations have included *mehish, mehitude, mehtastic, mehtacular,* and *mehalicious.* In 2008, the British *Collins English Dictionary* added *meh,* in what is sure to be the first of many such inclusions of a useful word.

"Those whom we can love, we can hate; to others we are indifferent."

—HENRY DAVID THOREAU

"The worst sin toward our fellow creatures is not to hate them, but to be indifferent to them: that's the essence of inhumanity."

—GEORGE BERNARD SHAW

"Men are by nature merely indifferent to one another; but women are by nature enemies."

—ARTHUR SCHOPENHAUER

"The true secret of giving advice is, after you have honestly given it, to be perfectly indifferent whether it is taken or not, and never persist in trying to set people right."

—HENRY WARD BEECHER

Indefinite Words Are Definitely Useful

Even the handiest person sometimes can't tell a doojigger from a hickeymadoodle.

✳ ✳ ✳ ✳

THE SUCCESS OF some fix-it jobs is measured in how many whatsits are left over once you have put the thingummy back together. Fortunately for those who like to tinker, putter, and dabble, English has a rich history of silly words for unidentifiable objects. Sometimes called *indefinite words,* these are often formed by joining parts of related words together.

✳ **Doo**—*Doo-* is a popular way to begin an indefinite word. *Doodad* was seen as early as 1905, and related words have included *doobob, doodaddle, doodibble, doodinkus, dooflicker, dooflunky, doofunny, doogadget, doojigger, doojumfunny,* and *doowhacker.* The *Historical Dictionary of American Slang* shows *doo-whanger* in action, circa 1927: "Whoever fired that doo-whanger at him's a poor shot."

✳ **Hickey**—*Hickeys* are better known as marks of love than objects of bafflement, but the "thingummy" meaning is older—at least as old as 1909, according to the *Oxford English Dictionary.* We've lost the usage of *hickey* by itself as an indefinite word, but we've still got its combined form with *doo-* to make *doohickey,* as well as several more obscure variations, such as *hickey-jigger* and *hickeymadoodle.*

✳ **Thing**—Few nouns are as unspecified as *thing,* making it the perfect stem for indefinite words. *Thingum,* meaning "something unimportant," was seen as early as 1672, but it was in 1870 that Mark Twain printed this tongue-in-cheek report: "In the case of the Queen vs. Whatshername, . . . it was distinctly laid down that a thingummyjig unable to come to a unanimous whatyoumaycallem might be lawfully discharged." Other variants include *thingy, thingummy, thing-amajig,* and *thingamabob.*

* *What*—Question words can be used to form indefinite nouns. In the 1600s, poets John Milton and John Dryden were saying "what d'ye call-him"; now we say "whats-her-name," or the even less polite "whats-her-face." Other words, like *whatsit* and *whosis,* may get the point across, but for sheer imprecision, nothing beats *whatchamacallit.*

Once you know the word parts, you can put them together creatively. Everyone will know what you mean if you ask for the hickeymathingum or the whatchamabob. Or no one will. But wasn't that the point?

A Kazillion and One, a Kazillion and Two, a Kazillion and . . .

Numbers give us another class of indefinite words. Through our familiarity with *million, billion,* etc., we can refer to impossibly large numbers as *zillion, bazillion, kazillion,* and more. At other times—say, around our birthdays—we might want to be deliberately vague about a known number. We may then be likely to mumble that we are "forty-ish" or "forty-something."

---

* **The Hershey Company introduced a candy bar called Whatchamacallit in 1978. In 2009 they debuted a variant of the peanut butter, chocolate, and caramel treat—named Thingamajig and featuring cocoa crisps instead of caramel. The snacks may be indefinitely named, but they are definitely delicious!**

Where Did It Come From?

Gadget: Originating in 1886 (although it may date back to the 1850s), gadget was sailors' slang for any small mechanical thing for which they had no name. It possibly originated much earlier than this time with the French *gâchette* ("trigger of a mechanism").

What's in a Name?

One hallmark of a great work of literature is that the characters seem to leap off the page. Or else they inhabit a world so realistic that the fictional setting becomes an avenue for speaking about the real world. In some cases, the author's name or perhaps the name of a character forms a word naming a concept or theme from the book.

✳ ✳ ✳ ✳

THESE NEW TERMS are called *eponymous adjectives* (from the Greek *epi,* "upon" + *onym,* "name"). (See page 136 for more on *eponyms.*) Many eponymous adjectives have come from mythological figures. A *Herculean* task is unusually difficult but possibly achievable; after all, Hercules did manage to slay the nine-headed Hydra and clean 30 years of filth from the Augean stables in one day. Less successful was Sisyphus, who was hurled into the Underworld by Zeus and forced to push a rock uphill for all eternity, only to have it roll back down each time. Therefore, a *Sisyphean* task takes great labor but is impossible to complete.

Investing in companies that profit from human suffering might be seen as a *Faustian* bargain. Faust, a character from German folklore (and later adapted to literary works by Christopher Marlowe and Johann Wolfgang von Goethe), sold his soul to the devil. By entering into a Faustian bargain, one might gain some benefit, but it will come at a great cost.

It's Elementary, My Dear

More-recent literary characters have also inspired adjectives based on their traits. *Holmesian* logic, for example, is deduction in the style of Sir Arthur Conan Doyle's Sherlock Holmes, who used miniscule clues to piece together the solutions to complex problems. And depending on the context, being called *quixotic*, after Miguel de Cervantes's Don Quixote, might or might not be a compliment. True, the term *quixotic* implies a restless romanticism and chivalry, but the reference also comes with the connotation of extreme impracticality and idealism.

In other cases it's the author's name that becomes associated with an abstract concept. For instance, an authoritarian, depersonalized, overly controlling, privacy-invading organization that reminds us of the frightening dystopian future in George Orwell's *Nineteen Eighty-Four* is considered *Orwellian*. Your bizarre or surreal experiences might not be as odd as turning into a giant cockroach, as Gregor Samsa does in Franz Kafka's *The Metamorphosis*, but they can still be deemed *Kafkaesque*.

If a situation gets truly terrible, it may become *Dantesque*. Even though Dante Alighieri wrote about paradise as well as hell in *The Divine Comedy*, the adjective *Dante-esque* usually suggests something as dark, somber, and inescapable as his nine circles of hell.

"The darkest places in hell are reserved for those who maintain their neutrality in times of moral crisis."

—DANTE ALIGHIERI

"Once you eliminate the impossible, whatever remains, no matter how improbable, must be the truth."

—SIR ARTHUR CONAN DOYLE

"Anyone who keeps the ability to see beauty never grows old."

—FRANZ KAFKA

"Never stand begging for that which you have the power to earn."

—MIGUEL DE CERVANTES

Chapter 4

In Other Words

-Philes, -Ists, and -Ologists

There's no limit to the types of items one might collect. But is there a limit to the names that exist for these collectors?

✳ ✳ ✳ ✳

CERTAIN WORDS FOCUS on a devotion to a subject: *-phile* words, from the Greek *-phile* ("lover of "); others stress the support of a certain specialist belief or study: *-ist* words, from the Latin *-ista*, from the Greek *-istes*; and others emphasize the study of a subject: *-ologist* words, from the Greek *-logia* ("study of "). Call them what you may; if you ever run across one of the following people at a cocktail party, you'll have an instant conversation starter.

–Philes

✳ *arctophile*—one who collects teddy bears (from the Greek *arktos*, "bear")

✳ *audiophile*—one who collects sound recordings and broadcasts (from the Latin *audire*, "to hear")

✳ *bibliophile*—collector of books (from the Greek *biblion*, "book")

✳ *cordatophile*—one who collects objects with a heart motif, or Valentine memorabilia (from the Latin *cord*, "heart-shaped")

✳ *oenophile*—one who enjoys wine; usually as a connoisseur (from the Greek *oinos*, "wine")

> *"Every passion borders on the chaotic, but the collector's passion borders on the chaos of memories."*
> —WALTER BENJAMIN

–Ists

❊ *cartophilist*—one who collects cigarette cards (from the French *carte*, "card")

❊ *coleopterist*—one who collects beetles (from the Greek *coleos*, "sheath," and *pteron*, "wing")

❊ *incunabulist*—one who collects books printed before 1501 (from the Latin *incunabula*, "swaddling clothes; beginning")

❊ *numismatist*—one who collects coins and medals (from the Latin *numisma*, "coin")

❊ *philatelist*—one who collects stamps (from the Greek *philein*, "to love," and *ateleia*, "exemption from charges"—as in, the person receiving a stamped letter does not have to pay charges)

❊ *phillumenist*—one who collects matchbooks or matchboxes (from the Greek *philein*, "to love," and the Latin *lumen*, "light")

❊ *vecturist*—one who collects transportation tokens (from the Latin *vectura*, "transport, money paid for transport, fare")

–Ologists

❊ *argyrothecologist*—one who collects money boxes (from the Greek *argyros*, "silver")

❊ *deltiologist*—one who collects postcards (from the Greek *deltion*, "writing tablet, letter")

❊ *tegestologist*—one who collects beer mats (from the Latin *teges*, "covering, material")

❊ *vexillologist*—one who collects flags (from the Latin *vexillum*, "flag")

Odd Jobs

At some point every kid is asked, "What do you want to be when you grow up?" Our language abounds in curious words denoting the occupations people have now or have had in historical times. In fact, many occupational terms are so strange that it's a real job figuring them all out.

✳ ✳ ✳ ✳

Unusual Occupational Terms

✳ *agonistarch*—a trainer of participants in games of combat

✳ *amanuensis*—a secretary or stenographer

✳ *boniface*—an innkeeper

✳ *dragoman*—an interpreter or guide for travelers, particularly where Arabic, Turkish, or Persian is spoken

✳ *famulus*—an assistant to a scholar or magician

✳ *funambulist*—a tightrope walker

✳ *hippotomist*—an expert dissector of horses

✳ *indagatrix*—a female investigator

✳ *moirologist*—a hired mourner

✳ *plongeur*—a dishwasher in a hotel or restaurant

✳ *pollinctor*—someone who prepares a body for cremation or embalming

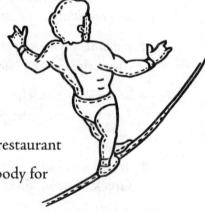

✳ *rhyparographer*—a painter of unpleasant or sordid subjects

✳ *scrivener*—a professional copyist or notary public

✳ *tragematopolist*—a seller of sweets

✳ *visagiste*—a makeup artist

✳ *yegg*—a burglar or safecracker

Words of Wisdom: Work

❋ ❋ ❋ ❋

"Ther nys no werkman, whatsoevere he be, that may bothe werke wel and hastily."

—GEOFFREY CHAUCER

"Choose a job you love, and you will never have to work a day in your life."

—CONFUCIUS

"All work is as seed sown; it grows and spreads, and sows itself anew."

—THOMAS CARLYLE

"Far and away the best prize that life has to offer is the chance to work hard at work worth doing."

—THEODORE ROOSEVELT

"The beginning is the most important part of the work."

—PLATO

"By the work one knows the workman."

—JEAN DE LA FONTAINE

"In order that people may be happy in their work, these three things are needed: They must be fit for it. They must not do too much of it. And they must have a sense of success at it."

—JOHN RUSKIN

"Work expands so as to fill the time available for its completion."

—CYRIL NORTHCOTE PARKINSON

"In the morning, when you are sluggish about getting up, let this thought be present: 'I am rising to a man's work.'"

—MARCUS AURELIUS

The Longest Words

*If you suffer from **hippopotomonstrosesquipedaliophobia,** or the fear of long words, avoid this article!*

✳ ✳ ✳ ✳

THE WORD FLOCCINAUCINIHILIPILIFICATION means "the act of deciding that something is completely worthless." It comes from four Latin words (*flocci, nauci, nihili,* and *pili*) that each mean "of little or no value." It is used mostly as an example of a funny word, rather than being used to actually express its supposed meaning. It was also the longest word in the first edition of the *Oxford English Dictionary*.

The longest word in the second edition of the *OED* is the 45-letter *pneumonoultramicroscopicsilicovolcanoconiosis,* which means "a lung disease caused by inhaling very fine ash and sand dust." The word seems to have been invented at a 1935 meeting of the National Puzzlers League, where Everett M. Smith, the league's president, called it the longest word in the English language.

Unfortunately, *pneumonoultramicroscopicsilicovolcanoconiosis* suffers from the same problem as *floccinaucinihilipilification,* in that it appears mainly as an example of a very long word . . . in fact, all evidence points to it being made up specifically to be a very long word, and nothing more.

That's Quite a Mouthful

Another long word that is used mostly as an example of a very long word is *antidisestablishmentarianism,* which means "the doctrine or political position that opposes the withdrawal of state recognition of an established church." (It's easy to see why this word isn't used very much for what it is supposed to mean.)

The longest word that appears in Shakespeare's works is *honorificabilitudinitatibus,* which appears in *Love's Labour's Lost* and means "the state of being able to achieve honors." The Bard didn't coin the term, however; it appears as early as the thirteenth century. It also happens to be the longest word in the English language that alternates vowels with consonants.

The Sound of It Is Something Quite Atrocious

One of the better-known long words in popular culture is *supercalifragilisticexpialidocious*. Looking for the meaning of this mouthful, which has 18 vowels and 16 consonants? While Mary Poppins defines the word as "something to say when you have nothing to say," the actual meaning, culled together from the different parts of the word (*super-* [above], *cali-* [beauty], *fragilistic-* [delicate], *expiali-* [to atone], and *docious* [educable]), would be closer to a definition such as "atoning for educability through delicate beauty"—not the most feminist of terms, to be sure.

And if *supercalifragilisticexpialidocious* isn't enough of a mouthful for you, you can try saying it backward, which, as one version of the song's lyrics points out, is *suoicodilaipxecitsiligarfilacrepus*.

If you want to know what to call the practice of using words that are really, really long, you can use *hippopotomonstrosesquipedalianism*. It comes from the word *sesquipedalian*, which means "a foot and a half long." Combined with "big" prefixes *hippo-* and *monstro-*, this makes a very big word indeed.

Going Green

Changing as often as a chameleon, the color green can't decide what to be.

✳ ✳ ✳ ✳

O<small>N THE ONE</small> hand, green is the color of money, and, by association, technology. Green can be as hard as emeralds and as polished as glass. It's a symbol for jealousy, treachery, and greed. But green also has its soft side: It's the color of nature—leaves, grass, moss, algae, and even, when the conditions are right, the sea. Soft greens bursting forth can beautify a landscape and herald the rebirth of spring. These days, the word *green* is synonymous with healthy living and environmental friendliness. It's also often used to signify youth and inexperience. With all these meanings, no wonder there are so many green words.

* *caesious*—bluish- or grayish-green

* *chrysochlorous*—of a greenish-gold color

* *citrine*—dark greenish-yellow

* *corbeau*—blackish-green

* *eau de nil*—pale green

* *glaucous*—sea green

* *lovat*—grayish-green; blue-green

* *olivaceous*—olive-colored

* *porraceous*—leek green (also *prasinous*)

* *smaragdine*—emerald green

* *tilleul*—pale yellowish-green

* *virescent*—becoming green or greenish

* *viridian*—chrome green (also *zinnober*)

Speaking of Tongues

"Tongue-lashing," "tongue-in-cheek," "tongue twister," "holding your tongue," "speaking with a forked tongue"... these are all turns of phrase that help give English its vitality and expressiveness.

✳ ✳ ✳ ✳

THERE'S A TREASURE TROVE of additional "tongue" words, most of which derive from the Greek *glot/gloss* and Latin *ling/lang*, both of which mean "tongue" or "language."

That's a Glotta Information

The *glottis* is the sound-producing apparatus between the vocal cords; when we speak, the vocal cords constrict and vibrate, producing speech sounds. The *epiglottis* is a protective flap that keeps food and liquids from entering the windpipe. *Monoglots* (*mono*, "one") and *polyglots* (*poly*, "many") speak one or several languages, respectively; similarly, *monolinguals* (also called *unilinguals*) know only their native tongue, while *bilinguals* (*bi*, "two") and *multilinguals* (*multi*, "many") know several. *Diglossia* (*di*, "two") is the community-wide use of both a nonstandard, colloquial language for speaking contexts and a standard, some-what archaic classical form for writing and formal oratory.

The Greek form *lalia/lalo*, meaning "talkative," refers to abnormal speech habits. *Tachylalia* (*tach*, "swift"), or extreme rapidity of speech, is often heard at the end of a television or radio advertisement. *Alalia* (*a-*, "not") and *dyslalia* (*dys*, "difficulty") refer to an inability to speak or difficulty in speaking. *Lalopathology* is the branch of medicine that deals with speech disorders. *Echolalia* is the habitual rapid repetition of words just spoken by another person. (*Echo* was the Greek nymph condemned to speak only by repeating what others had spoken.) *Coprolalia* (*copr*, "dung") is the involuntary shouting of obscenities, which can accompany Tourette's syndrome.

Tongue-tied? The English language is certainly not!

Does That Sound Wordish?

Like a lot of English suffixes, there is more than one -ish suffix. I'd say there are twoish, give or take.

❋   ❋   ❋   ❋

THE FIRST FORM of *-ish* represents the French *-iss-*, used in verbs. For example, the French *perer* ("to kill, destroy, die") had a past participle of *periscé* or *perissé*, which became the English *to perish*. Other English verbs formed this way include *accomplish, cherish, establish, garnish, languish, punish,* and *vanish*. This particular suffix ceased to form new English verbs all the way back in the Middle Ages.

Despite the fact that the Normans imported innumerable French words into England after 1066, English remains a Germanic language at heart. This Teutonic heritage shows through time and again. One example is the other *-ish* suffix, which is from the Old English *-isc*, meaning "belonging to, characteristic of." When you see *-ish* appended to a noun, it is almost certainly this Germanic suffix that is being used.

Do You Speak Anglish?

It can even be seen at work in the very name of our language, *English*, or *englisc* in Old English, originally meaning "characteristic of the Angles." The Angles were one of the Germanic tribes that drove the Celts out of England in the fifth and sixth centuries; the *Anglo* in *Anglo-Saxon* and the name *England* ("land of the Angles") came from them.

The -isc suffix was not all that common in Old English, but in later centuries it has produced many new words. In Old English the -isc suffix didn't carry with it any connotation, positive or negative—that is, it was *value neutral*—but over the centuries it acquired a deprecatory meaning. Words incorporating -ish tended to be used to denote unfavorable qualities, as in *apish, brutish, clownish, devilish, shrewish,* and *whorish.* More recently this has softened somewhat, but -ish still retains a slight deprecatory or playful quality in the words it appears in, like *geekish, nannyish* ("overprotective, fussy"), *nerdish, pubbish* ("like a pub"), *rockish* ("like rock music"), *slobbish, thuggish, wonkish,* and so on.

And there is the American dialectal use, found mainly in Minnesota and Wisconsin, of the stand-alone *ishy,* meaning "disagreeable, disgusting." This word could be a variant of *icky,* or it may come from an adjective like *squishy.*

Slang-ish

The suffix -ish has become incorporated into American slang to mean "kind of; sort of." For instance: "The cake was tasty-ish, but not worth the calories" or "I'm a size 6ish, but sometimes I can squeeze into a 4." It is also used as part of slang vocabulary to indicate an estimated time, as in "Let's meet in the library at noon-ish."

Where Did It Come From?

Churlish: The English had little respect for a *churl,* that is, a peasant or rude person. The word *churlish* takes that a step further, meaning someone who is vulgar or boorish.

Word Has It

Linguists, writers, and other language specialists love big words. See if you can wrap your mouth around these words pertaining to words and language.

* *antipriscianisticall*—ungrammatical

* *cacoepy*—the incorrect pronunciation of a word

* *carriwitchet*—a pun or conundrum

* *cruciverbalist*—a person adept at creating or solving cross-word puzzles

* *hellenomania*—the obsession with using either foreign or obscure wording

* *immram*—a kind of Irish sea story in which the hero and companions wander from island to island having adventures

* *lalochezia*—the use of foul or abusive language to relieve stress or ease pain

* *lethologica*—the inability to recall a precise word for something

* *linguipotence*—mastery of languages

* *loganamnosis*—the obsession with recalling a certain word

* *logocentrism*—excessive attention to the meanings of words or distinctions in their usage

* *logodaedaly*—wordplay, especially the playful invention of new words

* *logomachy*—fighting about words

* *maledictaphobia*—fear of bad words

* *monophrastic*—consisting of a single word or phrase

> *"Think like a wise man but communicate
> in the language of the people."*
> —WILLIAM BUTLER YEATS

* *notarikon*—the art of creating new words to represent entire sentences, or shorthand notation

* *oligosyllable*—a word of fewer than four syllables

* *parisologist*—a person who uses ambiguous language or evasive writing

* *pasilaly*—any universal language

* *pauciloquent*—using as few words as possible when speaking

* *philologist*—a person who loves literature and languages

* *polyonym*—a synonym of *synonym*

* *scholasms*—academic or pedantic expressions

* *semiopathy*—the tendency to read humorously inappropriate meanings into signs (e.g., "Slow Children Playing")

* *textome*—a word used to describe a body of literature, usually scientific research, that can be analyzed by software developed to find meaning and information

* *tropology*—use of metaphors in writing or speaking

* *verbigerate*—to repeat a word or sentence meaninglessly

In Vino Verbitas

The Latin phrase in vino veritas *("in wine [there is] truth")*
commonly translates to "drunks don't lie." In some ancient
civilizations, governing councils served wine supposedly in the
belief that a drunk man was more truthful than a sober one—
hence, in vino veritas. *Whether or not wine will lead you to any*
truth, it is true that English serves up a magnum-size selection
of wine words.

✳   ✳   ✳   ✳

BACCHUS, THE ROMAN GOD of wine and celebration, is now
the namesake behind wild, drunken *bacchanalian* gather-
ings. Today, *bacchanal* refers both to an alcohol-laced event such
as a Mardi Gras party and to each of its celebrants.

The science of wine is
called *enology* (from
the Greek *oinos,* mean-
ing "wine"; also spelled
oenology), and a wine
connoisseur is an *eno-*
phile (or *oenophile*). An
Italian restaurant might
call itself an *enoteca,* or
wine bar. Both *vini-*
culture and *viticulture*
(from the Latin for "wine" and "vine") refer to growing grapes
in vineyards for wine production; to *vinify* is to convert grapes
into wine through fermentation.

A Rosé by Any Other Name

Wines are typically classified as reds, whites, and rosés, which
range from dry to sweet. *Varietal* wines are produced principally from one variety of grape; chardonnays and reislings are
varietal wines. A wine with no bubbles is called a *still wine.*
Champagne, sparkling wine produced in France's Champagne

region, is a protected name that, under the terms of the Treaty of Madrid in 1891, can be used only for those sparkling wines produced in Champagne. Sparkling wine is called *prosecco, brachetto,* or *spumante* when it comes from Italy; it is *cava, Sekt, espumante,* and *Cap Classique* when it comes from Spain, Germany, Portugal, and South Africa, respectively.

The Nose Knows

Even if you're not a wine connoisseur, you may appreciate knowing these words if you want to impress your dinner companions. The term *bouquet* refers to the scent of the wine as a whole. The scent of the grapes is called the *aroma*. And when wine tasters want to describe the bouquet and aroma together, they use the term *nose*.

Does Size Matter?

A regular bottle of wine holds 0.75 liters, and bottle sizes go from the quarter-bottle *split* and *half* through the double-sized *magnum*, all the way up to the *jeroboam* (after Jeroboam I, tenth century B.C. king of the kingdom of Israel, referred to as the "mighty man of valor"), *methuselah* (after Methuselah, biblical patriarch represented as having lived 969 years), *salmanazar* (after Shalmaneser IV, eighth century B.C. king of Assyria), *balthazar* (after Balthazar, sixth century B.C. king of Babylon), and bacchanal-sized *nebuchadnezzar* (after Nebuchadnezzar II, sixth century B.C. king of Babylon), which respectively hold four, eight, twelve, sixteen, and twenty regular bottles of wine.

---

* If you consume too much wine of any variety, you might find yourself a bit *nimptopsical* (drunk).

* Corks seal most wine bottles, but a wine that's *corked* has gone bad. Today, screw caps are replacing cork on many wine bottles, and not just on the cheaper varieties. That leads to the question . . . if corked wine has gone bad, what does one call a bad wine from the other bottles?

* White wines gain color as they age; red wines lose color.

Words of Wisdom: Raise Your Glass

✴ ✴ ✴ ✴

"Let us have wine and women, mirth and laughter,
Sermons and soda water the day after."
—George Gordon, Lord Byron

"The discovery of wine is of greater moment than the discovery
of a constellation. The universe is too full of stars."
—Anthelme Brillat-Savarin

"If wine is taken in the right measure, it suits every age, every
time and every region."
—Arnaldus

"I rather like bad wine...one gets so bored with good wine."
—Benjamin Disraeli

"Wine is a peep-hole on a man."
—Alcaeus

"From wine what sudden friendship springs!"
—John Gay

"The best kind of wine is that which is most pleasant to him
who drinks it."
—Pliny the Elder

"It is better to hide ignorance, but it is hard to do this when we
relax over wine."
—Heraclitus

"Where there is no wine, love perishes, and everything else
that is pleasant to man."
—Euripides

"When it comes to eating without my glass of wine—I am
nowhere."
—Joseph Conrad

"Wine comes in at the mouth
And love comes in at the eye;.
That's all we shall know for truth
Before we grow old and die."

—WILLIAM BUTLER YEATS

"Wine, one sip of this will bathe the drooping spirits in delight
beyond the bliss of dreams. Be wise and taste."

—JOHN MILTON

"Joy is the best of wine."

—GEORGE ELIOT

"Wine gives great pleasure, and every pleasure is of itself
a good."

—SAMUEL JOHNSON

"What though youth gave love and roses,
Age still leaves us friends and wine."

—THOMAS MOORE

"Good company, good wine, good welcome
Can make good people."

—WILLIAM SHAKESPEARE

"He who clinks his cup with mine,
Adds a glory to the wine."

—GEORGE STERLING

"There are five reasons we should drink:
Good wine—a friend—or being dry—
Or lest we should be by and by—
Or any other reason why."

—HENRY ALDRICH

No Offense Intended

There's no shortage of uncomplimentary names to call unpleasant people, but if you really mean to insult someone, why not do it with an unusual word? For instance, you can try scobberlotcher, *which, in addition to meaning "an idler, a useless person," is very fun to say.*

✳ ✳ ✳ ✳

HERE ARE SOME other useful yet rude words to use for those who displease or disappoint you:

✳ *blatherskite*—a babbling, foolish person

✳ *dandisprat*—an insignificant or unimportant person

✳ *dawkin*—a fool

✳ *dowfart*—a stupid, dull person

✳ *gobemouche*—someone who believes everything he hears; a fool

✳ *hoddypeak*—a blockhead; a stupid person

✳ *jackeen*—a worthless person who thinks himself important

✳ *jaffler*—a lounger; a saunterer; an idler

✳ *naffin*—an idiot

✳ *ninnyhammer*—a simpleton

✳ *pettitoe*—a vile or worthless person

✳ *quakebuttock*—a coward

✳ *shabbaroon*—a mean-spirited person

✳ *slubberdegullion*—a contemptible person; a wretch

✳ *thimblerigger*—a dishonest person

✳ *wallydraigle*—a feeble person; a slovenly person, esp. a woman

Words of Wisdom from Oscar Wilde

✳ ✳ ✳ ✳

✳ "Always forgive your enemies. Nothing annoys them so much."

✳ "Every saint has a past and every sinner has a future."

✳ "I always pass on good advice. It is the only thing to do with it. It is never of any use to oneself.'"

✳ "I am not young enough to know everything."

✳ "There are only two tragedies in life: one is not getting what one wants, and the other is getting it."

✳ "I am so clever that sometimes I don't understand a word of what I am saying."

✳ "I can resist everything except temptation."

✳ "I sometimes think that God, in creating man, overestimated his ability."

✳ "It is what you read when you don't have to that determines what you will be when you can't help it."

✳ "Some cause happiness wherever they go; others whenever they go."

✳ "We are all in the gutter, but some of us are looking at the stars."

✳ "There is only one thing in life worse than being talked about, and that is not being talked about."

✳ "Keep love in your heart. A life without it is like a sunless garden when the flowers are dead."

The Color Purple

Are you ready for some purple prose? Some of these words may be as rare as a purple cow.

✳   ✳   ✳   ✳

SINCE ANCIENT TIMES, purple has been associated with wealth, royalty, and luxury. No wonder—the first purple dye (Tyrian purple) was more valuable than gold. Workers in Phoenicia (literally "the land of the purple") painstakingly extracted the pigment from a tiny gland in marine mollusks. Ten thousand mollusks might produce enough dye for a single garment. In modern times, purple still symbolizes royalty and divinity. It's the traditional liturgical color of Lent and Advent. What's your favorite hue?

* *amaranthine*—deep purplish-red

* *aubergine*—eggplant; dark purple

* *gridelin*—violet-gray

* *heliotrope*—a lighter shade of purple

* *hyacinthine*—of a blue or purple color

* *ianthine*—violet

* *mauve*—light bluish-purple

* *porphyrous*—purple

* *puce*—brownish-purple; purplish-pink

* *purpure*—heraldic purple

* *purpureal*—purple

* *solferino*—purplish-red

* *vinaceous*—wine-colored

* *violaceous*—violet-colored

Word Roots and Branches

A Lot of *Auto-*

The prefix auto- *is from the Greek* autos, *or "self," and is used to mean "by oneself, independently."*

❋ ❋ ❋ ❋

UNLIKE A LOT of Greek words and roots, *auto-* was not widely adopted by classical Latin. It did not become common in Latin, and by extension in other Western European languages, until medieval times. Some examples:

❋ An *autobiography* is one's own life story, inherently biased and often self-serving.

❋ *Autonomy* is independence, an *automaton* is a machine that operates on its own, and the *autonomic* nervous system controls those functions of our body that we don't think about, like breathing.

❋ Something that is *autochthonic* or *autochthonous* is indigenous, literally "sprung from the soil itself."

❋ An *autocrat* rules alone, sharing power with no one.

❋ The word *autograph* originally meant "in one's own handwriting" and only later developed the meaning of "signature."

❋ The *automatic* acts on its own, without outside intervention.

❋ At the end of a life, a doctor conducts an *autopsy* so he can see the cause of death with his own eyes.

❋ And an *autotheist* has delusions of godhood, while the more down-to-earth *autocentrist* merely has a big ego.

An *automobile*, of course, is a machine that moves under its own power, and that word has given rise to another, second-level prefix. Since the 1890s, *auto-* has also been used to form words relating to cars—*autoworker*, *automaker*, and the like.

Pardon Me? Words with No English Equivalent

English borrows freely from nearly every language it comes into contact with. There are still, however, many concepts and situations for which Anglophones lack le mot juste *(the perfect, precise word). Here are some suggested foreign words to add to your vocabulary, because you never know when you'll need them.*

✳ ✳ ✳ ✳

✳ *ashrag* (Hebrew)—a male animal that has testicles of unequal size

✳ *bakku-shan* (Japanese)—a girl who looks pretty from the back but not the front; this loanword would in fact be a loanword regifted, since it's already a combination of the English word *back* with the German word *schoen*, which means "beautiful"

✳ *bol* (Mayan)—for the Mayans of southern Mexico and Honduras, the word *bol* pulls double duty, meaning both "in-laws" and "stupidity"

✳ *dugnad* (Norwegian)—neighborly mutual aid; for instance, it is used to describe a party where the object is to help the host with something work-intensive, like painting the house or moving

✳ *gurfa* (Arabic)—the amount of water one can scoop up in one's hand

✳ *ilunga* (Tshiluba, Democratic Republic of the Congo)—a person who is ready to forgive any abuse for the first time, to tolerate it a second time, but never a third time

✳ *karelu* (Tulu, south of India)—the mark left on the skin by wearing anything tight

* *koev halev* (Hebrew)—identifying with the suffering of another person so closely that one (figuratively) hurts oneself

* *krevatomourmoura* (Greek)—when one keeps complaining about something late at night in bed while the other is trying to sleep; usually a wife to a husband

* *nakkele* (Tulu, south of India)—a person who licks the surface of the vessel or platter on which his food has been served

* *naz* (Urdu, southern Asia)—the pride or arrogance that comes from knowing that you will always be loved, no matter what you do

* *Nito-onna* (Japanese)—a woman who is so dedicated to her career that she has no time to iron blouses and so dresses only in knitted tops

* *Ølfrygt* (Viking Danish)—the fear of a lack of beer; often sets in during trips away from one's hometown, with its familiar watering holes

* *retrouvailles* (French)—the joy of meeting again after a long time apart

* *sgiomlaireachd* (Scottish Gaelic)—when you are rudely interrupted during a meal

* *swadge* (Orcadian, lower Scottich)—the pause between courses or during a meal to let your food digest and make room to continue eating

* *tingo* (Pascuense, eastern Polynesian)—to borrow from a friend until he or she has nothing left

* *uitwaaien* (Dutch)—walking in windy weather for the sheer fun of it

For German words that have no English translation, turn to page 174.

Kench and the World Kenches with You

Laughing—genuine laughter, that is—is probably one of the greatest experiences in life. As Charles Dickens wrote in A Christmas Carol, "There is nothing in the world so irresistibly contagious as laughter and good humor." Simply put, we love to laugh.

✳   ✳   ✳   ✳

EVERYONE HAS THEIR own sense of humor: Some people are silly, some are dry and sophisticated, and some can't help but snicker at locker-room jokes. But did you know that there are as many words for laughter as there are types of humor? Most people are familiar with *giggling, guffawing, chuckling, cracking up, howling with laughter, belly-laughing, tittering, hooting, snorting, sniggering, snickering, cackling, hee-heeing, tee-heeing, haw-hawing, ha-ha-ing, ho-ho-ing,* and *yukking it up.* But then there are the more obscure laugh-related words—like *kench,* which means "to laugh loudly." It was found a few times in the 1200s and seemingly disappeared, even though loud laughing has certainly stayed on the scene.

Here are some other obscure risorial words (that is, words that are related to laughter) that name specific varieties of laughter. Note: If you're gelophobic (afraid of laughter), you'd be best off avoiding this list!

* *cachinnate*—to laugh, usually loudly or convulsively

* *checkle* and *keckle*—two words reminiscent of *chuckle* and *heckle*

* *dacrygelosis*—the condition of alternately laughing and crying

* *fleer*—to laugh in a coarse, impudent, or unbecoming manner

* *gawf*—a loud, noisy laugh

* *nicker*—a sniggerlike or snickerlike laugh or a neighing sound

* *snarf*—the act of laughing while drinking and expelling the fluid through one's nose

* *snirt*—to snicker

* *snirtle*—the sound made by someone who is suppressing laughter

* *squirk*—a half-suppressed laugh

* *whicker*—another word that can name the whinnying of a horse or the snickering of a person, along with the half-suppressed sense of *squirk*

Buffoons, Jokers, and Jesters

Unsurprisingly, there are plenty of words that mean "a person who likes to play practical jokes; a clown." Here are a few of the more obscure:

* *goliard*—a monk who works as a jester

* *jack-pudding*—a jester

* *joculator*—a jester who also taught bears and apes to perform

* *merry-andrew*—a clown

* *Scaramouch*—a buffoonish character in pantomime

If any of these words made you squirk or snirt—and especially if you cachinnated or gawfed—well, then this article has done its job.

---

* **Abderian means "given to incessant or idiotic laughter." An agelast, on the other hand, is "someone who never laughs."**

* **Everyone knows what LOL means, but how about "ROFLSHCGU"? This unwieldy acronym stands for "Rolling On the Floor Laughing So Hard, Can't Get Up."**

Words of Wisdom: Laughter

✳   ✳   ✳   ✳

"A day without laughter is a day wasted."

—CHARLIE CHAPLIN

"Laugh then at any but at fools or foes;
These you but anger, and you mend not those."

—ALEXANDER POPE

"For what do we live, but to make sport for our neighbors, and laugh at them in our turn?"

—JANE AUSTEN

"We must laugh before we are happy, for fear we die before we laugh at all."

—JEAN DE LA BRUYÈRE

"If we may believe our logicians, man is distinguished from all other creatures by the faculty of laughter. He has a heart capable of mirth, and naturally disposed to it."

—JOSPEH ADDISON

"There is nothing more silly than a silly laugh."

—CATALLUS

"Laughter is the sun that drives winter from the human face."

—VICTOR HUGO

"Remember me with smiles and laughter, for that is how I will remember you all. If you can only remember me with tears, then don't remember me at all."

—LAURA INGALLS WILDER

"With mirth and laughter let old wrinkles come."

—WILLIAM SHAKESPEARE

Half and Half, and Half Again

There's nothing half-baked about the lexicon of English. If you run across any of these prefixes, please give them half a chance.

✳   ✳   ✳   ✳

THE WORD HEMIDEMISEMIQUAVER is a mouthful to say, but these eight syllables express hardly a peep of a sound because this improbable word contains *hemi* (meaning "half"), *demi* (again, "half"), *semi* (yet again, "half"), and *quaver* (a chiefly British English term for the musical eighth note): So a hemidemisemiquaver, or half of a half of a half of an eighth note, is...do the math!...a sixty-fourth note. There's also the *demisemiquaver*, or thirty-second note, and the *semiquaver*, a sixteenth note, plus the *semibreve*, or whole note (*breve*, "double note"). As far as we know, there's no fancy word for the half note, but the quarter note is sometimes called a *crotchet* (or "hook").

That's Not Even the Half of It

English has plenty of "half" words—that is, vocabulary items headed by the prefixes *hemi-*, *demi-*, or *semi-*. But the *semi-* prefix is by far the most productive, with more than 100 words containing this form. We're all familiar with *semiannual*, *semifinals*, and *semisweet*, but *semi-* gives us many lesser-known words as well: Semilunar (*lun*, "moon") means "crescent-shaped"; *semipalmate* (*palm*, "palm of the hand") describes the feet of some web-toed birds; and a *semidiurnal* (*diurn*, "day") event, such as the ocean's high and low tides, occurs every 12 hours.

The *hemi-* prefix occurs mainly in scientific and technical vocabulary. Besides the well-known *hemisphere*, English has *hemicycle*, a semicircular shape or structure, and *hemiplegic* (*pleg*, "paralysis"), a person who, usually from injury or stroke, has no muscle control or movement on one side of the body (compare to *paraplegic* and *quadriplegic*). Demi- is found in *demitasse* (*tasse*, "cup"), a small cup in which espresso is served, and in *demimonde* (*monde*, "world"), which denotes the world and culture of prostitution.

The Germans Have a Word for It (and Now We Do Too)

Many everyday words in the English language come from German. In fact, they're so familiar that we rarely think of their German roots. Some such words include blitz, bratwurst, delicatessen, diesel, kindergarten, pretzel, poltergeist, pumpernickel, rucksack, *and* zeitgeist, *among others.*

✳ ✳ ✳ ✳

YOU MAY ALSO recognize *schadenfreude*, which is the pleasure one feels when something bad happens to someone we dislike. (There's a related word, *freudenschade*, which was modeled after the German word but doesn't exist in German. It names the feeling of being miserable because of someone else's success.)

But there are plenty of funny-sounding words borrowed into English from German. These may bring pause to a conversation because they're not exactly words you hear every day: *Torschlusspanik* is a such a word, for example. It means "a sense of anxiety, especially in middle age, caused by feeling that one no longer has the same opportunities as one did when younger." It comes from German words that literally mean "gate-shut panic," as if you were seeing a door close on you.

English has also taken from German such words as *zugzwang*, a situation in a chess game where a player must make an undesirable move; *zugunruhe*, the urge, especially in captive birds, to migrate; and *treppenwitz* (what the French call *l'esprit d'escalier*, or "staircase wit"), which is the witty, funny, or cutting thing you think of to say after you've left the conversation (or the party).

A couple lesser-known German words that have been adopted by English speakers are *schlimmbesserung*, which is the act of making something worse while trying to make it better, and *fingerspitzengefühl*, which names a good sense or intuition about how things (usually delicate or difficult things) ought to be done.

Still Can't Find the Right Word? Try One of These

* *backpfeifengesicht* (German)—a face that's just begging for someone to slap it (a familiar concept to anyone fond of daytime television)

* *blechlawine*—literally "sheet metal avalanche": the endless line of cars stuck in a traffic jam on the highway

* *drachenfutter*—literally "dragon fodder": a makeup gift bought in advance; traditionally used to denote offerings made by a man to his wife when he knows he's guilty of something

* *fremdscham*—embarrassment felt on behalf of someone else (often someone who doesn't know that they should be embarrassed for themselves)

* *kummerspeck*—literally "grief bacon": excess weight gained from overeating during emotionally trying times

* *neidbau*—a building of little value, erected for the sole purpose of annoying one's neighbor

* *putzfimmel*—a mania for cleaning; indispensable for people with neat-freak significant others or roommates

* *trennungsagentur*—a person hired by a woman to tell her boyfriend that she is dumping him

* *übermorgen*—the day after yesterday

* *vorgestern*—the day before yesterday

After reading this book and learning thousands of new words, it might not be a stretch to say you have *sprachgefühl*, which literally means "a feeling for language" and knows what sounds correct or appropriate.

For more foreign-language words with no English equivalent, turn to page 168.

Don't Let These Words Confuse You

Who am I? How did I get here? What does it all mean? I think I was looking for something. Oh, yes, I had a word in mind...if only I could remember....

✳ ✳ ✳ ✳

IF YOU EXPERIENCE a bout of confusion but can't quite put your finger on what you're feeling, these words may come in handy:

✳ *baffound*—to stun or perplex

✳ *blutterbunged*—to be confused, surprised, taken aback

✳ *cabobble*—to confuse (verb); a mistake (noun)

✳ *captious*—calculated to confuse

✳ *disoccident*—to confuse as to direction

✳ *dwaal*—a state of befuddlement

✳ *flummocky*—in a confused disarray

✳ *flurry*—to confuse

✳ *galimatias*—garbled or nonsense talk

✳ *imbroglio*—an almost impossibly complicated situation

✳ *inaniloquent*—speaking foolishly or saying silly things

✳ *jargogle*—to mix up or garble something

✳ *malnoia*—a vague feeling of mental discomfort

✳ *maze*—to confuse

✳ *mazily*—confusedly, as in a maze

✳ *moidered*—confused, muddled, or stupefied

* *morologist*—a boring fool who speaks nonsense

* *muffled*—confused or muddled

* *muzzed*—confused, especially from drink

* *nebulochaotic*—a state of being hazy and confused

* *obfuscate*—to make something obscure or difficult to understand

* *obnubilate*—to cloud or obscure

* *obreptitious*—done or obtained by trickery

* *paralogia*—pathologically incoherent or illogical speech or thinking

* *phlyarologist*—one who constantly speaks nonsense

* *pitch-kettled*—puzzled, confused

* *pixilated*—bewildered or confused, often through drink

* *synchysis*—confusion or disarray, especially of the words in a sentence

* *tzimmes*—a fuss, a confused affair (from Yiddish; also the name of a stew)

* *welter*—a state of turmoil

* *winx*—to speak foolishly

W-I-N-N-I-N-G W-O-R-D-S

In 1925, the Louisville Courier-Journal *sponsored the first national spelling bee. More than eighty-five years later, and now known as the Scripps National Spelling Bee, it's still going strong.*

❋   ❋   ❋   ❋

IN THE EARLY years of the bee, students managed to win the competition by spelling difficult but still commonplace words such as *knack* (1932), *intelligible* (1935), *initials* (1941), and *psychiatry* (1948). However, as the event became more competitive and entrants studied ever-longer and harder word lists, the winning words became more challenging, esoteric, and outright bizarre. Here are the winning words (and their language of origin) from 1990 through 2013:

❋ *fibranne* (1990)—a fabric made of spun-rayon yarn (French)

❋ *antipyretic* (1991)—an agent that reduces fever (Greek)

❋ *lyceum* (1992)—a hall for public lectures or discussions (Latin, from Greek)

❋ *kamikaze* (1993)—an airplane containing explosives to be flown in a suicide crash on a target (Japanese)

❋ *antediluvian* (1994)—made, evolved, or developed a long time ago (Latin)

❋ *xanthosis* (1995)—yellow discoloration of the skin (Latin, from Greek)

❋ *vivisepulture* (1996)—the act of burying something alive (Latin)

❋ *euonym* (1997)—a well-suited or well-chosen name (Greek)

❋ *chiaroscurist* (1998)—an artist in chiaroscuro (Italian)

❋ *logorrhea* (1999)—excessive talkativeness (Greek)

* *demarche* (2000)—course of action, countermove, maneuver (French)

* *succedaneum* (2001)—a substitute or successor (Latin)

* *prospicience* (2002)—the act of looking forward (Latin)

* *pococurante* (2003)—not concerned, indifferent (Italian)

* *autochthonous* (2004)—indigenous to a region, native (Greek)

* *appoggiatura* (2005)—in music, an embellishing note (Italian)

* *Ursprache* (2006)—a parent or ancestral language (German)

* *serrefine* (2007)—a small forceps for clamping a blood vessel (French)

* *guerdon* (2008)—reward or compensation (Middle English and Old French)

* *Laodicean* (2009)—pertaining to Laodicea, an ancient city in Asia Minor (Latin)

* *stromuhr* (2010)—an instrument for measuring blood flow (German)

* *cymotrichus* (2011)—having wavy hair (Greek)

* *guetapens* (2012)—ambush, snare, or trap (French)

* *knaidel* (2013)—a dumpling (Yiddish)

---

* **The winning word in the inaugural national spelling bee was *gladiolus*.**

* **In the bee's history there have been 89 national champs. (There were no bees during World War II from 1943 to 1945.) Female champions outnumber male champions 47 to 42 as of 2013.**

Fear and Loathing

In his 1933 inaugural address, President Franklin Delano Roosevelt sought to calm a country in the throes of the Great Depression with these words: "The only thing we have to fear is fear itself." And fear not, dear reader, for no matter what fear you may possess, the English language has a term that covers it.

✳   ✳   ✳   ✳

THE PHOB WORDS come from the Greek *phobos* ("fear"), and the following are a few of the more obscure members of the fear family.

✳ *ablutophobia*—fear of bathing

✳ *agyiophobia*—fear of street or crossing the street

✳ *aichmorhabdophobia*—fear of being beaten by a pointed stick

✳ *alektorophobia*—fear of chickens

✳ *allodoxaphobia*—fear of other people's opinions

✳ *apeirophobia*—fear of infinity

✳ *arachibutyrophobia*—fear of peanut butter sticking to the roof of the mouth

✳ *basophobia*—fear of standing, walking, or falling over

✳ *blennophobia*—fear of slime

✳ *cacophobia*—fear of ugliness

✳ *catagelophobia*—fear of being ridiculed

✳ *chorophobia*—fear of dancing

✳ *deipnophobia*—fear of dinner conversation

✳ *didaskaleinophobia*—fear of going to school

* *doxophobia*—fear of expressing opinions or of receiving praise

* *elurophobia*—fear of cats

* *ergophobia*—fear of work

* *gamophobia*—fear of marriage

* *geliophobia*—fear of laughter

* *gnosiophobia*—fear of knowledge

* *hypophobia*—fear of not being afraid

* *iatrophobia*—fear of doctors or going to the doctor

* *kakorrhaphiophobia*—fear of failure

* *linonophobia*—fear of string

* *nyctohylophobia*—fear of dark wooded areas or of forests at night

* *ochlophobia*—fear of crowds or mobs

* *omphalophobia*—fear of belly buttons

* *panophobia*—fear of everything

* *paralipophobia*—fear of neglecting duty or responsibility

* *phengophobia*—fear of daylight or sunshine

* *scolionophobia*—fear of school

* *soceraphobia*—fear of parents-in-law

* *sophophobia*—fear of learning

* *xanthophobia*—fear of the color yellow or the word *yellow*

---

* **If you suffer from *hippopotomonstrosesquippedaliophobia* (fear of long words), you'd best put this book away!**

Love and Marriage

Is love, as London councilman (and whisky distiller) Sir Thomas Dewar said, merely "an ocean of emotions entirely surrounded by expenses"? Or is it—as Sophocles is reported to have said—the word that "frees us of all the weight and pain in life"?

✳ ✳ ✳ ✳

WHETHER CYNICAL OR romantic, perhaps we can agree with actress Pearl Bailey that love is "the sweetest joy, the wildest woe." These little-known words demonstrate the complexity of love and marriage:

* *ambilocal*—in anthropology, a system of marital relationships in which a couple may live in either the husband's or wife's home

* *anagapesis*—the feeling when one no longer loves someone like they once did

* *anaxiphillia*—the act of falling in love with the wrong person

* *banns*—a public notice of an intended marriage

* *bashert*—a predestined partner; soul mate

* *belgard*—a loving look

* *billet-doux*—a love letter

* *cagamosis*—marital unhappiness

* *cariad*—a sweetheart or lover

* *deuterogamy*—a second marriage

* *eleutherophilist*—advocate of free love

* *heterogamosis*—marriage of mismatched partners

* *hypnerotomachia*—the struggle to decide between sleeping and making love

* *geneclaxis*—marriage entered into only due to physical attraction

* *inamorate*—enamored, in love

* *incalescence*—growing lusty with love

* *indissolublist*—one who opposes divorced people being remarried in church

* *lebensabschnittsgefahrte*—the person who shares your life and your love for a little while before moving on

* *libidocoria*—uncontrollable and insatiable sexual desire

* *limerence*—a state of obsessive infatuation; the initial thrill of falling in love

* *mahr*—in Islamic law, a gift given by a bridegroom to his intended bride

* *miai*—in Japan, the first formal meeting of a couple in an arranged marriage

* *noeclexis*—the act of selecting a spouse or lover based on intelligence rather than beauty

* *opsigamy*—marriage late in life

* *passade*—a brief love affair or romance

* *philophobia*—fear of falling in love

* *philter*—a love potion

* *prothalamion*—a song or poem written in honor of an upcoming wedding

* *proxenete*—a marriage negotiator or matchmaker

* *uxoricide*—murder of a wife by a husband

* *wittol*—man who tacitly accepts his wife's adultery

Words of Wisdom: Marriage

✳   ✳   ✳   ✳

"A good marriage is that in which each appoints the other guardian of his solitude."
—RAINER MARIA RILKE

"Marriage is popular because it combines the maximum of temptation with the maximum of opportunity."
—GEORGE BERNARD SHAW

"Marriage is like life in this—that it is a field of battle, and not a bed of roses."
—ROBERT LOUIS STEVENSON

"Hasty marriage seldom proveth well."
—WILLIAM SHAKESPEARE

"Keep your eyes wide open before marriage, half shut afterwards."
—BENJAMIN FRANKLIN

"There is no more lovely, friendly and charming relationship, communion or company than a good marriage."
—MARTIN LUTHER

"Saw a wedding in the church. It was strange to see what delight we married people have to see these poor fools decoyed into our condition."
—SAMUEL PEPYS

"Come, let's be a comfortable couple and take care of each other! How glad we shall be, that we have somebody we are fond of always, to talk to and sit with."
—CHARLES DICKENS

Amerce the Abject's Conversation (or, Punish the Outcast's Conduct)

Bible study takes on a new meaning when you factor in that over time, the meanings of many words have shifted.

✳ ✳ ✳ ✳

THE KING JAMES VERSION of the Bible was published in 1611, and over the past 400 years the English language has changed significantly. Although many of the words that were used in that edition are still in use in modern language, some now mean something else entirely, and readers might be hard-pressed to figure out the original context. Below are examples of such words from the King James Version.

✳ *abjects*—outcasts; attackers (Psalm 35:15)

✳ *amerce*—to fine; impose a penalty (Deuteronomy 22:19)

✳ *armholes*—armpits; wrists (Jeremiah 38:12)

✳ *bowels*—feelings or emotions; heart (Philippians 1:8)

✳ *chimney*—a window (Hosea 13:3)

✳ *conversation*—way of life; behavior or conduct; citizenship (Philippians 3:20)

✳ *leasing*—lying, deception, or falsehood (Psalm 4:2)

✳ *matrix*—womb (Exodus 13:12)

✳ *prevent*—to go before, anticipate, or precede (Psalm 88:13)

✳ *reins*—innermost being; heart, mind, or spirit; kidneys (Psalm 7:9)

✳ *shambles*—a meat market (1 Corinthians 10:25)

✳ *tell*—to count (Genesis 15:5)

✳ *unicorn*—a wild ox (Job 39:9)

Don't Diss *Dis-*

Despite sounding the same, the two prefixes dis- *and* dys- *are quite different, both etymologically and semantically. Dis-* is *Latin, while* dys- *is from Greek.*

✳ ✳ ✳ ✳

DIS- HAS A number of different uses, most of which are no longer productive (i.e., not used to produce new words). These are:

✳ Meaning "apart, asunder, away," as in *discern* ("to separate, make distinct"), *discord* ("absence of harmony"), or *dispute* ("argue, contend"). Frequently, *dis-* words in this sense are in opposition to words beginning with *con-* or *com-* ("with"), as in *concern*, *concord*, or *compute*.

✳ Meaning "removal, negation." *Discard, discredit, dislocate, disrespect*, and *dissociate* are good examples.

✳ Adding emphasis in verbs that already imply separation or negation, as in *distend* and *disannul*.

✳ Meaning "between." This use is pretty rare in English. An example is *dijudicate*, "to judge." (In Latin, the *dis-* was sometimes clipped to just *di-* before certain consonants, such as *j*.)

"The function of wisdom is to discriminate between good and evil."
—MARCUS TULLIUS CICERO

Dis- has a sense that is currently productive in forming new English verbs. This is the sense of undoing or reversing the action of the verb. So *to disown* is "to cast away, reject ownership of," *to disestablish* is "to take apart," and to *disavow* is "to deny knowledge of or refuse to accept responsibility for."

Dys-, on the other hand, has a meaning in Greek of "hard, bad, unlucky." In English, it is found in words borrowed from Greek, and, as an active, productive prefix, it is chiefly found in scientific and technical jargon, like *dysfunctional* ("with aberrant or abnormal function"). Sometimes *dys-* words are in opposition to *eu-* (Greek for "good") words. (See page 422 for more on words that begin with *eu-*.) Other *dys-* words include:

* *dysentery*—disease of the bowels

* *dysgenic*—tending to promote the survival of the weak at the expense of the strong (the opposite of *eugenic*)

* *dyspepsia*—indigestion

* *dysphoria*—unease, mental discomfort (the opposite of *euphoria*)

* *dystopia*—a bad imaginary place (the opposite of *utopia*)

Finally, *to diss* is modern American urban slang meaning "to show no respect or regard for." It's a clipping of *disrespect* that dates to at least 1982. While the clipping is relatively new, the use of *disrespect* as a verb is not. It's been used this way since at least 1614.

Chapter 5

Word Origins

Chauvinism: Blame the French

Though we're used to hearing about male chauvinism these days, the term **chauvinism** *originally stood for pig-headed nationalism. It is an eponym stemming from legendary French soldier Nicolas Chauvin, one of Napoleon's staunchest supporters. As the* Oxford English Dictionary *says, Chauvin's "demonstrative patriotism and loyalty were celebrated, and at length ridiculed, by his comrades."*

✳ ✳ ✳ ✳

ACCORDING TO THE (perhaps apocryphal) Chauvin legend, there was nothing this zealous patriot wouldn't withstand for the benefit of his country and his leader. It is said that during his tenure as a soldier in the French Revolution and Napoleonic Wars, Chauvin sustained wounds on 17 separate occasions, lost fingers, and had his face disfigured, all the while maintaining his commitment to a cause that was becoming increasingly unpopular. In recognition of his unfailing loyalty, Napoleon awarded Chauvin a ceremonial sword and a monetary prize.

Satirical Support

Just as today terms gain footing by their appearance in TV shows or movies—like *dark side* and *regifting* were launched by *Star Wars* and *Seinfeld*, respectively—so did the French *chauvinisme* get a boost from its appearance in *La Cocarde Tricolore*

("The Tricolor Cockade"), a French vaudeville production that satirized Chauvin.

Upon its entrance into the English lexicon, which the *Oxford English Dictionary* dates to 1870, the word *chauvinism* bore a definition directly attributable to Chauvin and his legendary exploits: "Exaggerated patriotism of a bellicose sort; blind enthusiasm for national glory or military ascendancy; the French quality which finds its parallel in British 'Jingoism.'"

Patriotic Pork?

Today, however, *chauvinism* has acquired a more generic sense, that of blind loyalty to one's own kind or cause. Consequently, there are now many kinds of chauvinism, including cultural chauvinism, scientific chauvinism, and national chauvinism, to name just a few. Surely you've encountered several additional varieties this week alone.

As is often the case with eponyms (words that come from a person's name—see page 136), *chauvinism*'s connection with its historical source has all but disappeared for those who make use of the word in our current day and age. What's more, the word's strong association with male chauvinism—as in the phrase "male chauvinist pig"—

has shifted *chauvinism*'s popular meaning from bellicose nationalism to pompous sexism, a change that begs the question: Was Chauvin a chauvinist?

Words of Wisdom: Patriotism

✳   ✳   ✳   ✳

"No cause is utterly lost so long as it can inspire heroic devotion. No country is hopelessly vanquished whose sons love her better than their lives."

—ABBE MAC-GEOGHEGAN, CHAPLAIN OF THE IRISH BRIGADE

"When I die I desire no better winding sheet than the Stars and Stripes, and no softer pillow than the Constitution of my country."

—ANDREW JOHNSON

"[The American flag] means the rising up of a valiant young people against an old tyranny, to establish the most momentous doctrine that the world has ever known, or has since known—the right of men to their own selves and to their liberties."

—HENRY WARD BEECHER

"It is my living sentiment, and by the blessing of God it shall be my dying sentiment—Independence now and Independence forever!"

—JOHN ADAMS

"What we need are critical lovers of America—patriots who express their faith in their country by working to improve it."

—HUBERT HUMPHREY

"He loves his country best who strives to make it best."

—ROBERT G. INGERSOLL

"And so, my fellow Americans: ask not what your country can do for you—ask what you can do for your country."

—JOHN F. KENNEDY

"Break out the flag, strike up the band, light up the sky."

—GERALD R. FORD

Who's That Girl?

At first glance, the word **girl** *might seem uninteresting, a term perhaps unworthy of a word nerd's attention. Girl: a young female. Simple. Right? Au contraire: The story of this seemingly straightforward word has all sorts of complexities.*

✳   ✳   ✳   ✳

THE JURY IS still out regarding where the English word *girl* comes from, but the most popular theory points to the Old English *gyrela* ("dress, apparel"). What is known, though, is that *girl* originally referred to a child of either sex, and through Middle English, *knave girl* and *gay girl* were used as gender-specific terms for *boy* and *girl*, respectively. The *Oxford English Dictionary* suggests the word's meaning narrowed to denote a female child by the 1530s, but this date is up for debate.

Although *girl* is still used to refer to a female child, the word wears a number of semantic hats. Over the centuries it has been used to denote a sweetheart, servant, prostitute, homosexual man, and even cocaine. Why such versatility? Part of the answer lies with *pejoration*, or the process by which a word acquires a negative or less elevated meaning over time. This accounts for *girl*'s senses of "servant" and "prostitute"; this change in meaning is comparable to paths taken by *maid(en)* and *wench*, both of which originally denoted a young girl.

The use of *girl* in reference to adult females has proved a source of indignation for those interested in equal rights between the sexes. Feminists contend that calling women *girls*, especially in the workplace, is offensive because the word—with its association with servants and prostitutes—brings with it connotations of social inferiority. Moreover, the male counterpart to *girl*, *boy*, is not applied to men in the same way. This sort of semantic asymmetry is pervasive in English (take the difference between the once parallel terms *master* and *mistress*), and it's a topic that could fill up an entire book.

Don't Go Viking on Me

When you consider the Vikings, chances are that horned hats, wooden ships, or maybe Minnesota football are among the first things that come to mind. "Linguistic innovation" probably doesn't even crack the top 10—though perhaps it should, at least for their contribution toward one fairly common term of today.

✳ ✳ ✳ ✳

TODAY, TO BE or to go **berserk** is to be frenzied, out of one's mind, with a connotation of violent behavior. That violent connotation was once the word's primary meaning.

Nordic Nomenclature

The word comes from the Icelandic *berserkr,* a word for a powerful Norse warrior who displayed a wild and uncontrolled fury on the battlefield. In other words, a typical Viking warrior. (Or at least this is the popular image of what a typical Viking was like. In reality, the typical Viking was more likely to be a peaceful merchant than the ransacking and pillaging barbarian of lore. But, evidently, there were enough of the pillaging barbarians among the Norse nation to give them all a bad name.) The ultimate origin of the Icelandic word is somewhat uncertain, but it probably comes from *bear + sark,* a type of shirt or tunic. So a *berserk* or *berserker* was literally a bearskin-clad warrior. Yikes—powerful, indeed!

The word made its English appearance as early as 1814 in the original Icelandic sense of "a fierce warrior." By the middle of the nineteenth century, however, the word was being used as an adjective in English, meaning "violent or frenzied."

Kipling Goes Berserk

One of the first writers to use the verb phrase *go berserk* was Rudyard Kipling, who used it in his *A Diversity of Creatures*, published in 1917 (but written in 1908):

> *"You went Berserk. I've read all about it in* Hypatia.*"*

> *"What's 'going Berserk'?" Winston asked.*

> *"Never you mind," was the reply....* *"You've gone Berserk and pretty soon you'll go to sleep. But you'll probably be liable to fits of it all your life."*

It's clear that Kipling was aware that "going berserk" wasn't common terminology and there was a good chance his readers would not understand its meaning. The popularity of the phrase did not take off until the 1930s, when it became popular not only among newspaper beat reporters writing about violent criminals, but also among sportswriters and teens. Since then, *to go berserk* has entered into our everyday parlance.

Where Did It Come From?

Madcap: Back in the 1500s, the word *cap* was often used to refer to a person's head, and *mad*, of course, meant "crazy." So *madcap*, then and as now, describes someone (or something) who is a little bit silly or reckless.

Word Roots and Branches

Scandal-gates

Not all prefixes and suffixes come from Greek and Latin. Some are quite modern. Perhaps one of the most famous and productive of these suffixes is -gate, coined as a result, of course, of the Watergate scandal of the early 1970s. While the incident inspired other names as well—Watergater, Watergoof, Watergative, Watergatology, Watergaffe, and Waterfallout, among others— it's the -gate suffix that became entrenched in the language of politics and scandal.

✳   ✳   ✳   ✳

O N JUNE 17, 1972, five men working for Richard Nixon's Committee to Re-elect the President (a poor choice of names, as the committee inevitably and aptly became known as "CREEP") were arrested for breaking into the Democratic National Committee headquarters in the Watergate office-hotel complex in Washington, D.C. Nixon and his White House staff subsequently tried to cover up the connection to the president and impede the investigation.

This led to further investigations, which revealed a host of related and unrelated criminal activities perpetrated by the Nixon administration, and Nixon was forced to resign the presidency on August 9, 1974. Ironically, Nixon defeated Democratic candidate George McGovern in '72 in one of the biggest landslides in American electoral history, and CREEP had little to gain by such ham-handed activities as the break-in.

Suffix-gate

Subsequent to the Watergate scandal, the suffix *-gate* begin to, well, creep into the language as a way to denote various scandals. In 1976, the influence-peddling scandal in Washington that centered around the government of South Korea was dubbed *Koreagate*. The connections of Billy Carter, brother of President Jimmy Carter, to the Qaddafi regime in Libya became known as *Billygate*. The Reagan-era Iran-Contra arms-for-hostages deal was also known as *Irangate*. In 1992, the revelation of U.S. representatives kiting bad checks became *Rubbergate*. The list goes on.

Watergate was a Republican scandal, but the *-gate* suffix knows no political affiliation, and subsequent scandals have afflicted Democrats and Republicans alike.

✳ The first known post-Watergate coinage using the *-gate* suffix was run in *National Lampoon* in 1973. In a satire of the Watergate scandal, the humor magazine ran an article about a fictional Russian scandal known as *Volgagate*.

"Certainly in the next 50 years we shall see a woman president, perhaps sooner than you think. A woman can and should be able to do any political job that a man can do."

—RICHARD NIXON

"Don't get the impression that you arouse my anger. You see, one can only be angry with those he respects."

—RICHARD NIXON

"I believe in the battle—whether it's the battle of a campaign or the battle of this office, which is a continuing battle."

—RICHARD NIXON

"I brought myself down. I impeached myself by resigning."

—RICHARD NIXON

"I can see clearly now . . . that I was wrong in not acting more decisively and more forthrightly in dealing with Watergate."

—RICHARD NIXON

Where Did It Come From?

"Expletive Deleted": This phrase came into popular usage following the Nixon-era Watergate imbroglio, in which court transcripts used the phrase in place of profane utterances.

Gargoyles, Chimeras, and Grotesques, Oh My!

From gargoyles to grotesques to Valley Girls—what a wild and meandering path the English language takes us along!

✳   ✳   ✳   ✳

MOST WOULD AGREE that *gargoyle* is not the prettiest word in English, which is fitting, as gargoyles are grotesque carvings of people or animals, usually attached to gutters to carry rainwater away from buildings. (Gargoyles were originally used in the thirteenth century to keep water from running down the walls of buildings and eroding the mortar holding the stones together.)

Gargoyle comes from the Old French *gargouille* ("throat"), and most gargoyles spout water through their throats. (Other words related to *gargoyle* are *gargle, gurgle,* and *gullet*—they all ultimately originated from a Greek word meaning "to gargle.") Because the functionality of gargoyles requires that they extend a good length from the building in order for the water to drain prop-erly, they are usually exaggerated and bizarre representations of people and animals—typically monkeys, dogs, lions, snakes, wolves, or eagles. It's common for one gargoyle to combine several different creatures—you'll see harpies, griffins, and mer-maids featured. These gargoyles are called *chimeras.*

Simply Grotesque

A carving that does not spout water is not strictly a gargoyle, no matter how frightening it looks. The proper name is *grotesque*, a word that comes from the Italian *grottesca*, which literally means "grotto-esque" and refers to the paintings found in some excavated Roman buildings. This artwork was highly fanciful and included depictions of people, animals, plants, and flowers. Sprung from this origin, the meaning of the word *grotesque* changed over time from "imaginative" to "absurd, ludicrous" or "bizarre."

The word *grotty*, meaning "nasty, dirty," is a shortened form of *grotesque*, and dates from the 1960s. From this clipped term, which is used primarily in the United Kingdom, came the word *grody*, a variation favored in the United States. It is suspected that *grody* arose from the pronunciation differences between a British *t* and an American *t* when it occurs between two vowels. (Think how a Brit would say the word *writer* versus how an American would say it; in American English, the word sounds more like *rider*.) In the 1980s, *grody* became a staple of "Valley Girl" speak, as epitomized in the phrase "grody to the max."

---

* *Hunky Punk* is an English dialect term for an ornamental carving on a building (often grotesque, like a gargoyle) that serves no structural purpose.

* A grotesque human face (often looking like a fawn or satyr) found in Roman architecture is called a *mascaron*.

Where Did It Come From?

Ugly: This word was derived from the original *uglike* (c. 1250, to be "frightful or horrible in appearance"), which in turn came from the Old Norse *uggligr* ("dreadful, fearful"). The meaning was slightly softened (if you can call it that) to "very unpleasant to look at" around 1375.

Boycott This Article

*The word **boycott** names a refusal to buy goods or otherwise engage in commerce with a person or organization, usually as a means of political or social protest.*

✳ ✳ ✳ ✳

BOYCOTT IS AN *eponym*, or a word that comes from a person's name.* In this case, the namesake is Captain Charles Boycott, the agent of Charles Crichton, the Earl of Erne, an absentee landlord in County Mayo, Ireland. In 1880, Boycott evicted tenants who were demanding reduced rents. In response, the Irish Land League organized an effort to ostracize Boycott. He was unable to hire workers, buy goods, or even get his mail delivered. With the help of Irish Protestants and the protection of government troops, Boycott managed to get the autumn crop harvested, but it cost him more than the crop was worth. At the end of 1880, Boycott resigned his post and returned to England, the action against him having worked beyond the wildest imaginings of its organizers.

The astonishing thing about *boycott* is the rapidity with which the word caught on. Boycott evicted the tenants at the end of September; the response was organized by the beginning of November; by the middle of that month, the word *boycott* was in common use across Ireland and England; and in the beginning of December, Boycott had fled Ireland. The word even made it into French vocabulary before the end of the year.

Very often a term that arises this quickly dies just as quickly, but *boycott* managed to stick. Its place in the English lexicon is so solidified that it has all but lost its association with Charles Boycott. That is, we can know what a boycott is—and even participate in one—without knowing a thing about the man to whom we owe the name.

*See page 136 for more on eponyms.

Worldly Wisdom: Proverbs of the British Isles

✳ ✳ ✳ ✳

✳ The older the fiddler, the sweeter the tune. (*English*)

✳ A joy that's shared is a joy made double. (*English*)

✳ A little knowledge is a dangerous thing. (*English*)

✳ A poor workman always blames his tools. (*English*)

✳ A stumble may prevent a fall. (*English*)

✳ A deaf husband and a blind wife are always a happy couple. (*English*)

✳ A mother's love never ages. (*English*)

✳ Better to bend than break. (*Scottish*)

✳ False friends are worse than bitter enemies. (*Scottish*)

✳ What may be done at any time will be done at no time. (*Scottish*)

✳ A bad wound may heal, but a bad name will kill. (*Scottish*)

✳ A liar should have a good memory. (*Scottish*)

✳ A great sin can enter by a small door. (*Welsh*)

✳ Perfect love sometimes does not come until the first grand-child. (*Welsh*)

✳ A sword's honor is its idleness. (*Welsh*)

✳ A wise wolf hides his fangs. (*Welsh*)

✳ Scatter with one hand, gather with two. (*Welsh*)

Puttin' on the Blitz

Blitzing *is as inherent to football as goalposts and concussions, but the word itself didn't originate with the game. Like many commonly used terms—*deadline *and* AWOL, *to name a couple—it has a résumé of war.*

* * * *

THE WORD IS derived from the German *blitzkrieg* (literally "lightning war"), defined by the *Oxford English Dictionary* as "an attack or offensive launched suddenly with great violence with the object of reducing the defenses immediately." Hitler's forces first employed this ruthless war tactic in the early stages of World War II, marking a dramatic shift in a conflict that until then had been characterized more by propaganda than by violent military attacks.

Pigskin Parlance

It wasn't long before the shortened version of the term found its way into the lexicon of America's favorite rough-and-tumble pastime. By the early 1960s it was ubiquitous enough to be codified in 1963's *Defensive Football*. And for anyone familiar with the goings-on of the gridiron, it's not difficult to see why the word was adopted to denote an aggressive play in which all or part of the defensive line, which typically remains along the line of scrimmage, rushes the opposing team's vulnerable quarterback. The play, if successful, results in a damaging loss of yardage for the offense.

All's Fair In Language and War

While war buffs and sports fans might most readily associate the word *blitz* with a literal exertion of force, the term has enjoyed what linguists call *semantic broadening*, making it useful for those of us who occupy ourselves with more civil diversions. Like other sports terms—*home run* and *slam dunk*, for example—*blitz* can be used in a figurative sense. Consequently, we might refer to a new ad campaign as a marketing blitz, or

complain about being blitzed by an overzealous sales team at a particular mall kiosk.

Though its origins are grave indeed, *blitz*, thanks in part to the visibility gained through its association with football, is available as a colorfully descriptive resource in our everyday vocabulary.

✴ *Blitzkrieg* has also left a lingering legacy in the world of rock music. The Ramones released their song "Blitzkrieg Bop" in 1976. It's still one of their best-known tracks. Chances are, just the mere mention of this classic has gotten it stuck playing in your head, likely on repeat.

✴ As mentioned, another word with military roots is *deadline*. Although you might dramatically pronounce, "If I don't make this 5:00 deadline my boss will kill me," Civil War POWs were quite literally forced to adhere to their "dead-line"—a line around a military prison beyond which guards were authorized to shoot escaping prisoners.

Be Gentle

A gentle touch... a gentle word... a gentle rain falling. The current meaning of **gentle** *is pretty clear, conveying softness, care, consideration, quiet. While this sense has been around at least since the time of Shakespeare, the word had a more genteel beginning.*

✳   ✳   ✳   ✳

Yes, this word has a bit of a snooty résumé. It comes from the Old French *gentil*, meaning "high-born, noble," and when it entered Middle English in the thirteenth century it bore this same meaning. The *Oxford English Dictionary* expounds on this original sense, explaining that *gentle* was "originally used synonymously with *noble*, but afterwards distinguished from it, either as a wider term, or as designating a lower degree of rank."

The broadening in the meaning of *gentle* to refer to things— from wind and rivers to voices, words, and caresses—rather than just people is likely a function of old notions about the temperaments of the "gentle" classes. Wealth allows a person to be understated and calm, to eschew excitement and coarseness.

For Gentlemen Only

Knowing that *noble* and *gentle* used to mean the same thing, it isn't surprising that *nobleman* and *gentleman* were once synonyms. Speaking of *gentleman*, that's a word that has been doing quite a job as a euphemism (see page 64). A few recognizable phrases:

✳ *gentleman cow*—a bull

✳ *gentleman in black*—the devil

✳ *gentleman in black velvet*—a mole

✳ *gentleman in brown*—a bedbug

* *gentleman in red*—a soldier

* *gentleman of fortune*—a pirate

* *gentleman of the first staff*—a constable

* *gentleman of the road*—a highwayman

* *gentleman of the three outs*—a fellow "without money, without wit, and without manners"

* *gentleman who pays the rent*—a pig

Judging by this list, *Gentlemen's Quarterly* magazine has a much broader demographic than one might expect. Perhaps they should seek out additional subscriptions from members of the pirate community?

---

* Curiously, *gentle* has another identity, one quite apart from its highfalutin origins. Since at least the sixteenth century, the noun *gentle* has denoted "a maggot, the larva of the flesh-fly or bluebottle employed by anglers as bait." From the upper crust to the creepy-crawly, *gentle* runs the semantic gambit.

Where Did It Come From?

Magazine: The original meaning (from the Arabic *makhzan*, or "storehouse") was altered by 1583 to that of a "place where goods, particularly military ammunition and supplies, are stored." In fact, the word is still used to denote a metal receptacle for bullets inserted into certain types of automatic weapons. The most common current definition of *magazine*, though, that of a "periodical journal," dates back to the publication of the very first example of such a printed work, 1731's *Gentleman's Magazine*. The name was probably derived from the publication's being a "storehouse" of information.

Watch Out for the Juggernaut!

*The word **juggernaut**, used to characterize a literal or metaphorical force that is regarded as unstoppable, is quite versatile. Television shows with huge ratings are referred to as juggernauts. Successful sports teams are juggernauts. Hollywood director James Cameron is a juggernaut. You get the idea....*

✳ ✳ ✳ ✳

DESPITE—OR, PERHAPS, because of—its versatility, the origin of this word is rather opaque. It evolved from the Hindi word *Jagannath*, a combination of *jagat* ("world") and *natha* ("lord, protector"). In Hinduism, the word refers to Krishna, the eighth incarnation—or avatar—of the religion's supreme deity, Vishnu. Every year in the Indian city of Puri, an idol of this deity is hauled in a procession on a huge, elaborately decorated chariot or car. Countless fervent worshippers are said to have thrown themselves in sacrifice under the wheels of the moving idol. This combination of mass suicide, religious devotion, and public spectacle sounds so memorable, impressive, and terrifying that it's no wonder *juggernaut*, the English word it spawned, stayed firmly planted in the lexicon.

The word has semantically broadened to become a bit less fatal, but *juggernaut's* two subtly different figurative senses each nod to the aforementioned parade mayhem. In reference to the vehicle, there is *juggernaut* as inexorable force. Another sense, that of something—an institution, movement, campaign, notion, or practice—that elicits blind and often destructive devotion, relies more heavily on the word's idol-worshipping lineage.

While recent uses have mostly taken the wanton destruction and loss of life out of the concept, some modern applications—to a football team, for instance—are in the spirit of the original. Given the violent, concussion-causing collisions of the NFL, one could say the whole sport of football is a juggernaut, as the players are willingly ground under its wheels.

A Galoot in a Navy Suit

*The word **galoot** refers to a clumsy and not-too-intelligent person. The term is often used in affectionate deprecation; you might call a friend a "big galoot." But most people would be surprised to find that the word has an origin in Royal Navy slang.*

✳ ✳ ✳ ✳

GALOOT WAS ORIGINALLY a mildly offensive term for a marine or soldier onboard a ship, much like a modern marine might use *jarhead*. The word first appears in 1812 in James Hardy Vaux's *A New and Comprehensive Vocabulary of the Flash Language*, a glossary of slang ("flash language") used by convicts and criminals in Australia and the British Isles.

Vaux, a former sailor, was convicted in England of stealing a handkerchief and sentenced to seven years in the penal colony of Australia, arriving in 1801. He returned to England in 1807, but two years later was convicted of stealing and sent again to Australia. He was pardoned in 1820, but, proving to be a true galoot, in 1830 he was convicted of passing forged banknotes and was banished to Australia yet again, making him the only person known to have been exiled to Australia three times. Vaux was released from prison in 1841 and disappeared.

In the 1860s, *galoot* gained a foothold in America, where it became a popular epithet among soldiers fighting the Civil War. It gradually shed its association with the navy and marines and acquired the current, general sense that we know today.

It has been suggested that the etymology of *galoot* derived from the Krio adjective *galut*, which is applied to people and means "large." (Krio is an English-based Creole language spoken in Sierra Leone.) It is possible that the Royal Navy picked up the term during its operations combating the Atlantic slave trade in the first half of the nineteenth century, but it is more likely that the similarity is mere coincidence.

Be Aware of -*Ware*

Tupperware, the brand of airtight plastic containers famous for their "burping seal," has been a steady presence in the kitchen since its introduction in 1946. Though the name Tupperware has only been in use for just over half a century, it has origins that date back a millennium.

✳ ✳ ✳ ✳

LONG BEFORE THE advent of Tupperware parties, Old English had the feminine noun *waru*, which modern English has retained as *ware*, or "articles of merchandise or manufacture." Over the centuries, the word has also gained traction as a suffix, tacked on to words to denote specific types of products. So *hardware* names goods made from metal (c. 1515), *earthenware* denotes goods from clay (1673), and *ovenware* represents pots that can be used in an oven (1921). Patented in 1946, *Tupperware* gets its name from the clever marrying of *ware* with the name of company founder Earl Silas Tupper.

The dawn of the computer age in the mid-twentieth century ushered in a new class of *wares*. Starting in 1947, computer scientists and engineers began referring to their equipment as *hardware*, an extension of the old meaning of goods made of metal. A counterpart, *software*, didn't come along for another decade, making its appearance in 1958. And *software* created a new class of *-ware* words, denoting various types of computer programs. Some of these are:

* *firmware* (1968)—permanent read-only software that controls the basic functions of computer hardware

* *middleware* (1970)—software that acts as a bridge between a computer's operating system and applications

* *courseware* (1978)—software programs for training and education

* *groupware* (1981)—software that facilitates collaboration between workers

* *freeware* (1982)—software distributed at no cost

* *shareware* (1983)—software distributed for free, but for which habitual users are expected to make a payment to the creators

* *vaporware* (1984)—software offered for sale or advertised that does not actually exist or is only in an early stage of development

* *malware* (1990)—software that contains damaging algorithms

* *adware* (1992)—software that is distributed for free and displays advertising to generate revenue for its creators

* *spyware* (1994)—software that surreptitiously monitors computer use

Ware Are You From?

Old English also had another *ware*—a homonym to the *ware* above—that functioned as a suffix. It denoted a citizen or resident of a place. Thus *burgwaran* were the residents of a city, *eorwaru* was humanity (earth-dwellers), *Romwaran* were Romans, and *hellwaran* were demons and the damned.

Skedaddle Skedaddles into the Lexicon

How exactly can this silly-sounding word have a history that involves the Civil War, modern goofball Jack Black, and the seemingly arbitrary number 23?

* * * *

THE WORD **SKEDADDLE** is a delightfully fun collection of letters, with sound symbolism both ahead and behind. The *sk-* reminds us of *skip, scoot, scram, scuttle,* and *scatter.* And the verb *to addle* means "to make confused or disoriented"; the same final sound is found in *muddle* and *befuddle.* Put the meanings together, and we understand *skedaddle:* "to flee, especially in a chaotic or unplanned manner."

The word's origin is murky at best. According to Michael Quinion of weekly e-magazine World Wide Words, *skedaddle* became popular during the Civil War. The original usage specifically pointed

to a sudden retreat from battle, but it quickly made its way into civilian speech and print. Its first appearance in print, in the *New York Tribune* (1861), suggests not just retreat but a cowardly one at that: "No sooner did the traitors discover their approach than they 'skiddaddled,' (a phrase the Union boys up here apply to the good use the seceshers make of their legs in time of danger)."

How Many Times Must I Scram, Exactly?

In the early part of the twentieth century, the classic and now charmingly old-fashioned American catchphrase *twenty-three skiddoo* was suddenly seen and heard everywhere. It too meant "get lost!" or "let's get out of here."

Why twenty-three? (Why not, say, thirty-seven?) No one knows for sure, but as early as 1899, George Ade of *The Washington Post* noted that *twenty-three* was used as slang for "scram." Around the same time, the word *skiddoo* became popular, almost certainly derived from *skedaddle* and with the same meaning as *twenty-three*. The two words were soon married into an inextricably linked phrase.

Linguistic Kung Fu

More recently, *skedaddle* has been credited with influencing the creation of another hot catchword: *skadoosh*. Actor Jack Black improvised the word during the making of *Kung Fu Panda*. In case you missed the movie, it's the sound a warrior makes as he or she incinerates enemies in a display of kung fu awesomeness called the Mushi Finger Hold. But it can be used during any display of superiority.

You might vanquish your opponent in a video game, or perhaps you so clearly out-skate, out-brag, or out-argue him that he slinks away in chagrin. Either way, "Skadoosh!" is an appropriate victory cry, suggesting that the winner has gained the upper hand, and it's time for the loser to clear out. The loser may be befuddled, muddled, or addled, but he's certainly got to skedaddle.

Where Did It Come From?

Zap: This word comes to the English language courtesy of sci-fi writer Philip Francis Nowlan, who first used it in 1929 in connection with the "paralysis gun" wielded by his most famous creation, Buck Rogers.

The Man Behind *Gerrymander*

*The word **gerrymander** leaves a legacy that is somewhat unfair to its namesake, Elbridge Gerry (1744–1814), a signer of the Declaration of Independence, governor of Massachusetts, and vice president of the United States.*

✳ ✳ ✳ ✳

THE U.S. CONSTITUTION requires that a census be taken every ten years and that state legislatures redraw the districts of the House of Representatives to reflect changes in population. Of course, this creates plenty of opportunity for political mischief, as each political party seeks to redraw the district boundaries to favor its own electoral chances.

One of the early egregious examples of this practice occurred in 1812 in Essex County, Massachusetts. The Massachusetts legislature, dominated by Democratic-Republicans (the forerunner of the modern Democratic Party), drew one district so that it snaked around the borders of the county, favoring their party. Gerry, who was the Democratic-Republican governor at the time, did not support the plan and only reluctantly signed it into law because of his party's wishes—but as the party's leader, he was given credit for the plan in the popular imagination.

The district's serpentine shape inspired painter and sometime political cartoonist Gilbert Stuart to sketch a head, feet, and wings on the drawing of the district and label it a "salamander." (Salamanders don't have wings, but the legendary salamanders in medieval bestiaries are sometimes depicted as having wings; this is undoubtedly where Stuart got his inspiration.) Stuart submitted the cartoon to the Federalist-leaning paper the *Boston Centinel*, whose editor, Benjamin Russell, captioned it with the name "Gerrymander." Thus a political term was born. The word became a Federalist rallying cry in the 1812 election, and Gerry lost his gubernatorial reelection bid because of it (but he was elected the country's vice president later that year).

Words of Wisdom: Peace

❋ ❋ ❋ ❋

"We shall find peace. We shall hear the angels, we shall see the sky sparkling with diamonds."

—ANTON CHEKHOV

"We look forward to the time when the power to love will replace the love of power. Then will our world know the blessings of peace."

—WILLIAM E. GLADSTONE

"Five enemies of peace inhabit with us—avarice, ambition, envy, anger, and pride; if these were to be banished, we should infallibly enjoy perpetual peace."

—PETRARCH

"Only a peace between equals can last."

—WOODROW WILSON

"Never be in a hurry; do everything quietly in a calm spirit. Do not lose your inner peace for anything whatsoever, even if your whole world seems upset."

—ST. FRANCIS DE SALES

"Peace puts forth her olive everywhere."

—WILLIAM SHAKESPEARE

"First keep the peace within yourself, then you can also bring peace to others."

—THOMAS À KEMPIS

"Peace is always beautiful."

—WALT WHITMAN

"A crust eaten in peace is better than a banquet partaken in anxiety."

—AESOP

Making the Case for *Basket Case*

*Today we use the term **basket case** pretty casually, without giving much thought to its application—or origins. The source of this strange-when-you-think-about-it term, however, is more macabre than you might guess.*

✳ ✳ ✳ ✳

A s the term is commonly used today, a *basket case* is someone who is under physical or—more usually—mental distress to the point where he or she can no longer function. It may also refer to a dysfunctional situation or organization, frequently a country, as demonstrated in this quote from a 2010 article in Canada's *National Post:* "Once the bread basket of southern Africa, Zimbabwe became a basket case."

You Mean It's Not a Picnic?

Although its contemporary definition may not suggest it, the term has a rather grisly origin on the battlefields of the First World War. But while the origins of the term *basket case* are beyond doubt, the existence of literal basket cases from that war appears to be an urban legend.

During World War I, the term *basket case* was purportedly used to describe a quadruple amputee—a soldier who had lost both legs and both arms—who couldn't be carried on a stretcher and had to be transported in, yes, a basket. The idea of basket cases arose despite the fact that no soldiers in such a condition actually existed. The following is from the Official U.S. Bulletin by the U.S. Committee on Public Information of March 28, 1919:

> *The Surgeon General of the Army, Maj. Gen. Merritte W. Ireland, denies emphatically that there is any foundation for the stories that have been circulated in all parts of the country of the existence of "basket cases" in our hospitals.*

True or false (and these tales were undoubtedly false), sensational stories like this do not die, and during World War II the army's surgeon general had to issue the same denial. In the May 12, 1944, issue of *Yank* magazine, Surgeon General Norman T. Kirk stated that there was nothing to the rumors of the so-called "basket cases."

A Better *Basket Case*

Over time, the term gradually lost its grisly association and began being used figuratively. (This process by which words and phrases lose their negative connotation is common, by the way. Linguists call it *amelioration*.)

By the early 1950s, the term was extended to include mental and emotional distress. In the following decade it was extended to politics. On March 25, 1967, the *Saturday Review* said of the Ghanaian president who had been deposed in a coup the previous year:

> Kwame Nkrumah should not be written off as a political basket case.

(The magazine was wrong, by the way; Nkrumah spent his remaining years in exile.)

Where Did It Come From?

World War I: One would think that they would wait for the second one to start before referring to the first as such, but some forward-thinking commentators were calling the European conflict of 1914 to 1918 the "First World War" before it was even over.

Oh, the Humanitarian!

In an era of ubiquitous, round-the-clock media, we have become accustomed to encountering the word **humanitarian.** *It's used variously to describe people—do-gooder philanthropists operating on an epic scale—as well as events, tragedies, and disasters on the level of hurricanes and genocides. Today,* humanitarian *is a multipurpose word, and its history reveals even more versatility.*

✳ ✳ ✳ ✳

As with so many others, the word *humanitarian* has come a long way from its original meaning, which, as the *Oxford English Dictionary* puts it, was "a person believing that Christ's nature was human only and not divine." The first known use dates to about 1792. The term was also a synonym for *anthropomorphite,* or "one ascribing (as an article of religious belief) a human form to God"—a word that existed centuries before *humanitarian* and applied to fourth-century Egyptians as well as tenth-century Westerners.

The word was also used to name adherents of humanistic religions before settling into its current meaning in the late nineteenth century. Interestingly, to be called a *humanitarian* was not a compliment at first. The word was synonymous with *humanity-monger,* and it was reserved for those then-considered "deplorable" people interested in promoting reform in the treatment of criminals and the poor. Note the disapproval in this 1843 quote: "Such is the argument used by modern humanitarians, to the great scandal of justice and common sense."

The word has undergone the process of *amelioration,* and this deprecatory connotation has disappeared. Today, being a humanitarian just might earn you a Nobel Peace Prize. If language is a reflection of the people who use it, this shift in connotation might be seen as an indicator of our collective movement toward a more empathetic society.

Words of Wisdom: Hope

"It is good to embrace a hope."

—OVID

"Hope is like the sun, which, as we journey toward it, casts the shadow of our burden behind us."

—SAMUEL SMILES

"Ah, Hope! what would life be, stripped of thy encouraging smiles, that teach us to look behind the dark clouds of to-day, for the golden beams that are to gild the morrow."

—SUSANNA MOODIE

"Hope is a waking dream."

—ARISTOTLE

"Hope conquers cowardice, joy grief."

—ARTHUR HUGH CLOUGH

"Hope deferred maketh the heart sick."

—PROVERBS 13:12, KJV

"Fear cannot be without hope nor hope without fear."

—BENEDICT SPINOZA

"Hope is the best possession. None are completely wretched but those who are without it."

—WILLIAM HAZLITT

"Take short views, hope for the best, and trust in God."

—SYDNEY SMITH

"If youth is the season of hope, it is often so only in the sense that our elders are hopeful about us."

—GEORGE ELIOT

Idiot-Proof (or Not)

*In some ways, the word **idiot** has stayed remarkably consistent. The earliest meaning in the Oxford English Dictionary—"a person without learning; an ignorant, uneducated man; a simple man; a clown"—is not far from its contemporary sense as "a term of reprobation for one who speaks or acts in what the speaker considers an irrational way, or with extreme stupidity or folly; a blockhead, an utter fool." A new idiot would not surprise observers of old idiots, and vice versa.*

✳   ✳   ✳   ✳

THE WORD HAS its origins in the Greek *idiotes*, meaning "commoner" or "layman" and, hence, one who is ignorant or ill-informed. It came to English from the French *idiot* by way of the Latin *idiota*, which, similar to the Greek, means "an uneducated, ignorant person."

While staying on the same general thoroughfare, the term has gone down some interesting alleyways over the years. In some cases, it has named a profession, similar to a clown, fool, or jester (this sense inspired the term *idiot's hood*, a predecessor of *dunce cap*). There have been variations such as *idiot boy, idiot fool,* and *idiot man*. Other *idiot* uses include:

✳ *idiot asylum*—an unkind term for a mental asylum

✳ *idiot box*—a TV set

✳ *idiotize*—to become, let us say, closer in intelligence to a brick

✳ *idiot stick*—a shovel

Diagnosis: Idiot

Although *idiot* is now more or less interchangeable with any of the innumerable dummy-denoting descriptors, it was once a quasi-technical medical term. In the not-so-distant past, the word functioned as part of an IQ-based intelligence classification system. Up until the early 1970s, psychologists used the terms *moron, imbecile,* and *idiot* to distinguish between different levels of intellectual disability. This system was eventually recognized as insensitive, and the terms were replaced by less pejorative labels—and factors other than IQ are now considered in diagnoses.

Low Culture

In addition to its tenure as a "technical" psychological classifier, *idiot* boasts some high-profile appearances in classic literature as well as in pop culture. Originally written in Russian, the title of Fyodor Dostoyevsky's 1868 novel is translated as *The Idiot* in English. It is said that *The Idiot's* idiot, Prince Lev Nikolayevich Myshkin, represents Dostoyevsky's desire to depict "a positively good man"—not quite the sort of idiot we're used to. The title of Iggy Pop and David Bowie's album *The Idiot* is supposedly inspired by the novel.

More recent plugs for *idiot* come from rock band Green Day's album *American Idiot,* as well as the Broadway play it inspired. An amusing variation of the word is *Idiocracy,* coined as the title of a 2006 Mike Judge movie that portrayed a vision of a future America that makes our current population seem like a collection of Einsteins and Rembrandts.

Where Did It Come From?

Vacuous: This adjective means "stupid or lacking in intelligence." In Latin it is *vacuus* ("empty"), which pretty much says it all, doesn't it?

Words of Wisdom: Nature

✳ ✳ ✳ ✳

"Surely there is something in the unruffled calm of nature that overawes our little anxieties and doubts: the sight of the deep-blue sky, and the clustering stars above, seem to impart a quiet to the mind."

—Jonathan Edwards

"The indescribable innocence and beneficence of Nature—of sun and wind and rain, of summer and winter—such health, such cheer, they afford forever! and such sympathy have they ever with our race, that all nature would be affected, and the sun's brightness fade, and the winds would sigh humanely, and the clouds rain tears, and the woods shed their leaves and put on mourning in midsummer, if any man should ever for a just cause grieve."

—Henry David Thoreau

"In spring, all nature is beautiful and glad . . ."

—Llywarch, a Celtic bard

"All Nature wears one universal grin."

—Henry Fielding

"Nature makes nothing incomplete, and nothing in vain."

—Aristotle

"What is man in nature? A nothing compared to the infinite, an everything compared to nothing, a midpoint between nothing and everything."

—Blaise Pascal

"No sooner are we supplied with every thing that nature can demand, than we sit down to contrive artificial appetites."

—Samuel Johnson

Don't Get Cute with Me

We are living in an era of cataclysmic cuteness. Evidence of this can be found in innumerable websites, movies, products, and phenomena. Although we may be in the midst of a media- and technology-driven cute explosion, humanity's affinity for cuteness did not arise with the advent of the YouTube video.

✳   ✳   ✳   ✳

SCIENTISTS SUGGEST THAT our affinity for cuteness is actually an evolutionary trait, a biological assurance that we take a liking to our round-headed and big-eyed—in a word, cute—offspring and, consequently, keep the species going.

But even though our love for cuteness is probably hardwired into us, and we've probably been wired that way since Noah sailed boats in the bathtub, the word *cute* hasn't been so consistent. *Cute* is actually the child (the puppy, if you will) of *acute*. It comes to us through the process of *aphesis*, or the loss of an initial vowel, and it originally meant the same thing as its progenitor—"clever, keen-witted, sharp, shrewd."

A century or so after its appearance, *cute* had become a substitute for the word *cunning* in the sense of "quaintly interesting or pretty, attractive, taking." While this variation gets us closer to today's connotations of cute, it doesn't quite apply to our kitten-coddling culture. In fact, the *Oxford English Dictionary* entry on *cute*, which lists the contemporary colloquial sense as "attractive, pretty, charming," might need an update, since this definition seems a little too cunning and not cutesy enough.

By the way, *cutesy* started appearing in the 1960s, along with the variation *cutesy-poo*. There probably isn't a more "cute" suffix than *-poo*. Whether we're having a *drinky-poo*, giving a *kissy-poo*, or adopting a *Jack-a-poo*, the connotation is clear.

A Buried Etymology

Some words that we use today without much thought have long and complex histories that, when dug up and revealed, offer glimpses into worlds we likely never expected to find. So grab your shovel (and maybe a notebook, too): We're off to take part in an etymological excavation.

✳ ✳ ✳ ✳

ONE SUCH WORD with a hidden history, used fairly commonly today, is **undermine.** To undermine something is "to destroy it through some surreptitious means, to subvert it."

Militaristic Mining

The etymology of *undermine* becomes readily apparent when examining its constituent elements: *under + mine.* The two elements are from different sources: *Under* is Old English, and *mine* is from the Anglo-Norman verb *miner,* meaning "to excavate beneath a wall or structure in order to collapse it." The Anglo-Norman *miner* comes from the Medieval Latin *minare,* meaning "to mine, to undermine."

The original senses of the English, French, and Latin verbs are all military in nature, in that the act denoted by the word indicated belligerent purposes, with the sense of *mine* meaning "to extract minerals from the earth" coming shortly afterward. The English verb *to undermine* appears in the fourteenth century with the same meaning as the Anglo-Norman *miner,* and it is somewhat redundant in the sense that all *mines* are *under.*

Unearthing Modern Usage

In English, the military senses of both *undermine* and *mine* existed throughout the medieval period. In the early seventeenth century, however, the verb *to mine* ceased being used in the military sense and came to mean only "to dig, to excavate." And in the fifteenth century, *undermine* began to be used figuratively to mean "to destroy by surreptitious means." This is the chief sense in use today, since military mining isn't as important a tactic as it once was.

The modern *land mine* also comes from the same linguistic root. Often, once a tunnel was dug underneath a castle's walls, explosives, or *mines*, would be placed inside it and detonated, bringing the walls down. The "breach" in the walls of Harfleur that Shakespeare's Henry V charged "once more into" was created by just such a mine. This sense of *mine* eventually evolved into any buried or submerged explosive.

Knowing the etymology of this word has one additional advantage. If you've ever played the old board game Stratego and wondered what the *miner* was doing on the battlefield—well, now you know!

✳ When used as a prefix, *under-* has some historically interesting habits. In Old English, there are about 80 words with *under-* as a prefix—about 50 are verbs, 25 are nouns, and adjectives are few and far between. A few of the more unusual words in Old English utilizing *under-* are: *underburn* ("to burn too little"), *undercry* ("to cry aloud"), and *underheave* ("to heave or lift from below").

Where Did It Come From?

Explode: Though the term now refers to a destructive force, its original meaning was from the Latin *ex-* and *plaudere* ("to applaud"). It referred to the clapping and heckling that poor actors received from their disgruntled audiences.

The History of *Hag*

Like the old woman it denotes, the word **hag** *has been around for a long time. And while today* hag *simply names an ugly old woman, the history of the word conjures up images of spells and spirits, of witches and black magic, and other things you definitely don't want to mess with. You can't say we didn't warn you....*

❋　❋　❋　❋

THE WORD HAG originally existed in Old English (the language spoken in England before the Norman Conquest of 1066) as *hægtesse*, which referred to a witch, a fury, or an evil female spirit. Sometime during the Middle English period (c. 1100–1500) it was clipped to *hagge*, getting us closer to the word as we know it today, and throughout subsequent centuries the word has borne a number of different, though related, meanings.

A Spirited History

From its earliest days, *hag* has had the meaning of "an evil spirit, a female demon." The word was used to refer to the furies and harpies of classical mythology, as well as various female spirits of the Germanic mythos. The word was also used to refer to female ghosts and spirits believed to visit men at night—the succubi of nightmares—and it survives in this sense in *night-hag*, the name for the psychological phenomenon of imagined paralysis and hallucination that occurs in some people as they fall asleep.

Hag has also been used as a synonym for *witch*, or for a woman who is otherwise associated with the devil. It can be applied to any feminine personification of evil or vice. And, of course, it can simply name an ugly, old woman—but there's almost always the connotation of evil or malice.

Other Terms of Endearment

There are plenty of other words that mean "an old woman" or "a mean woman," including *beldam*, which comes from French words meaning "fine lady"; *crone*, which comes from an Old French word meaning "cantankerous woman"; and *harridan*, which may come from a French word meaning "a worn-out horse." Yep, that's a weird one.

Without a similarly haunting history, however, these epithets don't hold a hat to *hag*.

✳ In folklore, the Old Hag is a nightmare spirit who sits on sleepers' chests and transmits nightmares into their sleep, making them *hagridden*—afflicted by nightmares. Interestingly, this is essentially the same creature as the Anglo-Saxon *mæra*, or Scandinavian *mara*. Knowing this, the history of the word *nightmare* is a bit more transparent. *Nightmare* originally referred less to the concept of a scary dream and more to the mythical female spirit—the Old Hag—that would produce feelings of suffocation in a sleeping person.

Where Did It Come From?

Spinster: Originally the word *spinster* simply described a woman who spins wool. But the meaning has done some spinning of its own, eventually coming to mean a woman with little else to do but spin, as in a dried-up old woman or unmarried old maid.

Chapter 6

Words to the Wise

In Plain Sight

The triple whammy of homophones **cite**, **site**, *and* **sight** *has the potential to cause a great deal of confusion. The words have identical pronunciations but different spellings and—here's the kicker—more than one meaning each.*

✳ ✳ ✳ ✳

CITE IS A verb derived from the Latin *citare*, meaning "to put in motion, summon." Usually we cite people or the fruits of their intellectual labor. *To cite* can mean "to quote someone, or someone's work, as an authoritative source to support an argument." Scholarly papers require *citations*, so scholars do a lot of *citing*. We can cite facts to support an argument or proposal. *To cite* also means "to name someone formally in a commendation, a court summons, or a parking ticket." So scholars like to be cited, but drivers usually don't.

A Building *Sits* on a *Site*

Site is usually a noun, but it has a derivative use as a verb. A site is a location, and to site something is to locate it. *Site* comes from the Latin *situs*, which also means "location." But a site isn't a

> ### *"The only thing worse than being blind is having sight but no vision."*
> —Helen Keller

location for just any old thing, like where you left your wallet, for example, or where you parked your car at the mall. Rather, a site is a place where a significant event happened or is happening (as in "the site of a major battle" or "the site of an archaeological dig"), or a place occupied by an important structure ("the site where the Taj Mahal is located").

And, in keeping with the spatial metaphor people employ when talking about "navigating" the web, a collection of web pages at a particular web domain is known as a *website*, which we can "visit."

Eye See You

While *cite* and *site* came to us from Latin, *sight* is a good Old English word. *Sight* is a noun for the visual sense itself (you can have a "good sense of sight"); for the content of visual perception ("the sight of poison ivy makes me itch"); or even for something worth looking at ("the Corn Palace is a sight that should not be missed"). Having *foresight* (Old English *fore*, "before in time, rank, position" + *gesiht*, "thing seen") means the ability to look forward, or a view to the future.

A sight is also a device to aid with vision, as in a rifle sight. Lastly, *sight* is also a verb, meaning "to catch sight of" ("a mountain lion was sighted in Discovery Park").

Oh, I See!

Here's a mnemonic you can employ to help keep these words straight: A building *sits* on a *site*; *sight* is difficult at *night*; and *cite* is related to the noun *citation*.

Words of Wisdom: Education

✳   ✳   ✳   ✳

"Education makes us what we are."
—CLAUDE ADRIEN HELVETIUS

"Don't let schooling interfere with your education."
—MARK TWAIN

"Education is an admirable thing, but it is well to remember from time to time that nothing that is worth knowing can be taught."
—OSCAR WILDE

"Genius without education is like silver in the mine."
—BENJAMIN FRANKLIN

"An investment in knowledge pays the best interest."
—BENJAMIN FRANKLIN

"The secret of education lies in respecting the pupil."
—RALPH WALDO EMERSON

"The roots of education are bitter, but the fruit is sweet."
—ARISTOTLE

"Nothing in education is so astonishing as the amount of ignorance it accumulates in the form of inert facts."
—HENRY BROOKS ADAMS

"What sculpture is to a block of marble, education is to a human soul."
—JOSEPH ADDISON

"A good education changes your judgment and conduct."
—MICHEL DE MONTAIGNE

Take a Hint

When your birthday comes around and someone gives you a present to open, you understand the situation clearly: One person has put something into a box, and another person is going to take that something out of the box. Assuming you can keep that distinction in your mind, there is no reason for you to have any difficulty with the words **imply** *and* **infer.**

✳ ✳ ✳ ✳

To IMPLY SOMETHING is to suggest or hint at a meaning without making it explicit. The verb has a history linked to the word *ply*. A ply is a fold of cloth, and when a speaker or writer implies something, he or she metaphorically folds the meaning inside their words. (Think of this speaker or writer as placing their meaning inside a loosely sealed box.)

To *infer* something is to reason or deduce what such a speaker or writer is hinting at, what they are implying. The verb goes back to the Latin *ferre*, meaning "to bring." Inferring brings the concealed meaning into the open. (The listener or reader doing the inferring is the one who opens the box again and pulls out the meaning.)

The same distinction separates the related nouns. An *implication* is a suggestion, often with the sense that something improper is being hinted at. An *inference* is a conclusion drawn from the evidence of a suggestive statement. Political rhetoric is heavily laden with implications, usually that a candidate's opponent is a crook and a rascal and maybe worse. Advertising is also rife with implications. And everyone but the most naive picks up on such meaning—they are able to make inferences as to what the speech or advertisement means to imply.

✳ The noun *ply* comes from the French verb *plier*, meaning "to fold." But the verb *to ply*, like the verb *to apply*, comes from a slightly different root—the Latin *applicare*, meaning "to fasten."

Laying Out the Facts About *Lay* and *Lie*

There's no need to lie about it: The difference between **lay** *and* **lie** *can be hard to remember.*

✳ ✳ ✳ ✳

T HE WORDS LAY and *lie* differ only in their vowel sounds and their grammatical contexts, and they have almost identical meanings. Other word pairs like that include *rise/raise* and *sit/set*.

Lie is an intransitive verb. That means it's not followed by a direct object. In one of its senses, the verb *to lie* means "to occupy a place on the ground or some other horizontal surface in a horizontal position." A person can lie on a bed or a book can lie on a table. There's also a noun form of *lie* that refers to the position in which something lies: If you hit a golf ball close to the green, you have a good lie. The verb *to lie* also means "to say something untrue with the intention to deceive someone," and the noun *lie* refers to the untrue statement itself.

Laying It on the Line

The verb *to lay* is transitive—it occurs with a direct object. It means "to place something somewhere so that it's lying." In other words, *to lay* means "to cause to lie." For that reason, it's known to grammarians as a *causative verb*. With *lay*, as with other causative verbs, the subject of the verb is the causer of the action, and the direct object is the entity that's changed or affected in some way. So, you can lay a book on the table, or a nurse can lay a patient on an operating table. A book, being an inanimate object, can't *lay* anything. *Lay* also has special uses that involve more specific ways of placing things, as in "lay tile," "lay cement," and "lay an egg."

To keep *lie* and *lay* straight, remember that the first vowel in *lie* is *i*, for "intransitive."

"When it comes to my own turn to lay my weapons down, I shall do so with thankfulness and fatigue, and whatever be my destiny afterward, I shall be glad to lie down with my fathers in honor. It is human at least, if not divine."
—ROBERT LOUIS STEVENSON

What Is It with Songwriters?

The distinction between *lay* and *lie* seems to be losing ground in English. Many people use *lay* intransitively. Bob Dylan, for instance, on his 1969 album *Nashville Skyline*, sang, "Lay, lady, lay... lay across my big brass bed." Eric Clapton made the same error when he sang "Lay down Sally." Unless he wanted someone to lift Sally up and lay her on the ground (or a bed, or a sofa, or anywhere else), he should have sung "Lie down, Sally." And Bonnie Raitt fell prey to the same grammatical bugaboo, in "I Can't Make You Love Me." Rather than "Lay down with me, tell me no lies," she should be asking you to lie down with her.

Remember the Past

As if matters weren't already a bit confusing, *lay* is also the past tense form of *lie*. The past tense of *lay* is *laid*. So you might say: "Last night I laid my book on the table and turned out the light. But then I lay in bed thinking about today." The perfect form of *lie* is *lain*: "The book has lain on the table for two weeks." The perfect form of *lay* is *laid*: "I have laid many books in that exact spot."

---

* *"Now I lay me down to sleep. / I pray the Lord my soul to keep. / If I shall die before I wake / I pray the Lord my soul to take."* You probably know this classic children's bedtime prayer from the eighteenth century. But you may not recognize it in its first incarnation, written by Joseph Addison in 1711: *"When I lay me down to Sleep / I recommend my self to his care / when I awake, I give my self up to his Direction."* This is a great example of how rhyming can help make something easier to memorize.

This Suffix Makes Me Sick!

Hypochondriacs, pop a Dramamine and pay attention: You're really going to love this suffix.

✳ ✳ ✳ ✳

T HE SUFFIX -*ITIS* comes from Greek, where it denoted the feminine form of some adjectives, but it is also used to denote a disease or ailment. The names of numerous diseases come, via Latin, from classical Greek names for the ailments:

* *arthritis: arthro-* ("joint") + -*itis*, 1543

* *nephritis: nephro-* ("kidney") + -*itis*, 1566

* *peritonitis: peritoneum* (lining of the abdominal cavity) + -*itis*, 1771

In English, -*itis* became a suffix for all sorts of diseases, particularly those involving inflammation or infection of a particular body part:

* *tonsillitis*—inflammation of the tonsils, 1801

* *gastritis*—inflammation of the stomach, 1806

* *bronchitis*—inflammation of the bronchial mucous membrane, 1814

* *laryngitis*—inflammation of the larynx, 1822

-*Itis* Obsession

Starting in the early twentieth century, -*itis* started to be used jocularly to indicate something with which people are obsessed.

It's now often used to describe any abnormality, not simply an inflammatory one. Such terms include:

* *fiscalitis*—among politicians, excessive concern over the costs of social reform, 1903

* *suffragitis*—fear of women's right to vote, 1906

* *testitis*—in cricket, inability to perform in test matches (aka, "choking in the big match"), 1912 (not to be confused with the medical term for inflammation of the testes)

* *electionitis*—excessive fervor over an upcoming election, 1945

* *senioritis*—disease that causes apathy, lack of focus and concentration, drop in academic performance, and absenteeism on balmy spring days among students in their final year of school, from at least 1967

What is lovely about this suffix is its versatility. Indecision can cause a case of *maybe-itis*. Dissatisfaction with a business can cause a diagnosis of *overpriced-junk-itis*. Overstuffing yourself at Thanksgiving can lead to *pumpkin-pie-itis*. It is perhaps the most contagious suffix of all.

---

* According to UrbanDictionary.com, *itis* is the feeling of sleepiness or drowsiness that often overwhelms a person after a heavy meal—post-Thanksgiving dinner, for example, perhaps due to a case of pumpin-pie-itis.

Where Did It Come From?

Quarantine: This word comes from the French *quarante,* which means "forty," and *-aine,* which adds a degree of approximation (equivalent to "-ish" in English). This is because sailors whose ships were suspected of carrying disease were restricted from shore contact for about 40 days upon arriving in a port.

Pouring Out or Poring Over?

Pour your heart out to me, you poor thing!

✳ ✳ ✳ ✳

THE VERBS **PORE** and *pour* may sound the same, but they have different meanings. In some areas of the United States, the regional pronunciation of *poor* adds it into the mix as well. But *poor* is a common adjective meaning "not having much (usually money)," and it is not as easily confused with the more similar verbs. There is also the noun *pore*, which names a tiny opening in the skin of a person or animal, but it is entirely unrelated to the verb.

Pour is primarily a transitive verb (a verb that takes a direct object), and the object—the thing that is poured—is usually a liquid or something acting like a liquid. You can pour water, wine, or tea, for example, but also sand or gravel. Rain pours from the sky during particularly bad storms. Metaphorically, a woman might attempt to pour herself into a dress that's a smidge too tight. *Pour* is sometimes used with the preposition *out*.

The less common *pore*, on the other hand, is an intransitive verb (a verb that does not take a direct object), and it is almost always used with the preposition *over*. To pore over something (such as a book or manuscript) is to read or study it carefully and thoroughly. This verb is often used to suggest scholarly or even arcane pursuits, calling up images of dusty libraries and bespectacled scholars.

To remember which is which, try this mnemonic: One might pore over a book (all *o*'s) or pour soup (both contain *ou*). You can pour soup over something (preferably not a book), but you wouldn't pore over soup—unless it's alphabet soup, perhaps? And you certainly wouldn't want to do so in a library! That would be evidence of poor judgment indeed.

Keep Your Hands to Yourself, Bud

Come on, people, keep it clean. We're trying to maintain a level of decorum here, trying to sort out the phrases **nip it in the bud** *and* **nip it in the butt.** *The former is a traditional idiomatic expression, the latter an error.*

✳ ✳ ✳ ✳

IF YOU HAVE done any gardening or tending to houseplants, you know that a bud is a little knobby growth on a plant that will develop into a leaf or a flower or a shoot. If you want to stop the plant from producing that leaf, flower, or shoot, you pinch off the bud, or nip it. You *nip it in the bud* before it can grow into something you don't want.

Metaphorically, this stock expression means "to halt something at its early stages." (Those who prefer Westerns to gardening may choose to think of this as "heading it off at the pass"; in other words, "stop it before it gets to where it wants to go.")

When you see your child emerge from the kitchen with a pair of scissors in his or her hand, heading purposefully toward the cat, you recognize that some nefarious plan is being put into action—a plan you have to nip in the bud. If you're lucky, you confiscate those scissors and return them to the kitchen drawer before any damage is done.

People's tendency to slur pronunciations leads to a tendency in others to mishear words, which is probably what leads to constructions like *nip it in the butt*. If to nip something in the butt means anything at all, it probably means "to pinch or poke someone's behind," an action traditionally known as *goosing*. But unless you are sure that the recipient of the goose will be receptive to the gesture, nipping in the butt is even less advisable than barbering the cat.

It's Time to Think About *Its*

*Many people—even some writers, teachers, and, often, sign makers—get particularly confused by the difference between **it's** and **its**. One is a possessive pronoun, and the other means "it is"—but which is which?*

✳ ✳ ✳ ✳

THE INTERNET IS teeming with photos of road, business, and handwritten signs featuring misplaced apostrophes, and such photos are often accompanied by sneering commentary about how incorrect apostrophe usage is leading to the decline of civilization. Yet somehow there are many more complaints than there are explanations of just how to use an apostrophe correctly. More explanation and less sneering would go a long way, because correct apostrophe usage is often tricky.

There are two general apostrophe rules that you're taught when you're learning English punctuation.

1. An apostrophe shows possession (that it "owns" the noun that follows): for example, the teacher's book, Johnny's dog, the book's chewed pages, Johnny's detention.

2. An apostrophe takes the place of a missing letter (or letters) in a contraction: I can't bear it / You don't love me anymore / Can't we still be friends?

Rule #3: Don't Assume Rule #1

The confusion lies in understanding (or not understanding) which of these rules governs the apostrophe in *it's*. Many people assume that the first rule is in play and the word is the possessive form of *it*, but in fact *it's* is the exception to the general rule that one should use an apostrophe to indicate possession, and the second rule holds sway here: *It's* is a contraction of *it is,* not a possessive pronoun.

There's an easy way to determine if you're using the right form: Read the sentence in question aloud to yourself, substituting *it is* (or *it has*) when you get to *its* or *it's.* If the substitution works, *it's* is a contraction and requires an apostrophe. For example, try "You can't judge a book by *it's* cover." Read it aloud with the substitution: "You can't judge a book by *it is* cover." Nope, doesn't make sense; therefore, the construction must be "You can't judge a book by *its* cover."

Another way to remember this is to keep in mind that *its,* a possessive pronoun, works in the same apostrophe-free way of its possessive pronoun pals. There are no apostrophes in *his, hers, ours,* or *theirs,* and there should be no apostrophe in *its,* either.

And it's worth pointing out that there is absolutely, positively, no such word as *its'.*

✳ **Jeff Deck and Benjamin Herson (authors of** *The Great Typo Hunt: Two Friends Changing the World, One Correction at a Time***) have traveled the country looking for typos, misplaced apostrophes, and spelling mistakes on signs and billboards. The misuse of** *its* **and** *it's* **is a common error.**

✳ **In 2008 the Chicago Cubs unveiled a 7-foot statue of Hall of Famer Ernie Banks. It was a well-deserved tribute to "Mr. Cub"—however, the execution fell a bit short. The granite base of the sculpture proudly proclaimed Banks's trademark phrase: "Lets play two!" Fortunately, nothing is written in stone (as the old adage goes), and an engraver was able to chisel in the needed apostrophe.**

It Has Come *To* This

The identical pronunciation of **to, too,** *and* **two** *leads to frequent errors when they are used in writing. So of course we find not one, not two, but three homophones to mess us up.*

✳ ✳ ✳ ✳

THE WORDS *TOO* and *too* have a common etymology from Old English. Both senses, adverb and preposition, were originally spelled *to*, but they split into two separate words in the sixteenth century. *Two* comes from the Old English feminine form *twa* and shares an etymology with the masculine *twain*, which survives in the expression "never the twain shall meet."

Two is simply the number 2: "The animals boarded the ark two by two." It has one meaning only. *Too* and *to*, however, are decidedly more flexible, and each has multiple meanings.

To is a preposition, and among prepositions, *to* is a workhorse. It works to show motion in a direction ("I'm going to the hardware store"), location ("Cereal can be found to the left of the canned goods"), identification of a person ("She was rude to her mother"), identification of a relationship ("Jeff is now serving as assistant to the president"), and many other things. Used with a verb, it indicates the infinitive: "My goal is to swim the English Channel before I turn 30."

Too is an adverb. It can mean "excessive" or "more than one wants" ("He put too much turkey on his plate"); "very" ("Her mother was too kind"); or "in addition to, also" ("The Johnsons are staying the night too").

In the "also" sense, it is okay to set off *too* with a comma in written English, and it's also okay not to. "I like pizza too" is fine. Adding a comma puts a bit more bounce on *too*, so it should not be used unless you want to be emphatic: "I'll get you, my pretty, and your little dog, too!" Beginning a sentence with *too*—"Too, there are serious consequences to consider"—sounds pompous. Avoid it.

Worldly Wisdom: Chinese Proverbs

✳   ✳   ✳   ✳

✳ I hear and I forget.
I see and remember.
I do and I understand.

✳ A journey of a thousand miles begins with one step.

✳ The fire you kindle for your enemy often burns you more than him.

✳ Learning is a treasure that accompanies its owner everywhere.

✳ All the flowers of all the tomorrows are in the seeds of today.

✳ One may desert one's father, though he be a high official, but not one's mother, though she be a beggar.

✳ One should be just as careful in choosing one's pleasures as in avoiding calamities.

✳ To understand your parents' love, you must raise children yourself.

✳ He who asks a question is a fool for five minutes; he who does not ask a question remains a fool forever.

✳ You cannot prevent the birds of sadness from flying over your head, but you can prevent them from nesting in your hair.

✳ A bird does not sing because it has an answer. It sings because it has a song.

✳ A bit of fragrance clings to the hand that gives flowers.

✳ A book tightly shut is but a block of paper.

✳ Be not afraid of growing slowly, be afraid only of standing still.

Precede Precedes *Proceed* in the Dictionary

There's no need to dilly-dally over this article. Let's proceed as planned, everybody.

✳ ✳ ✳ ✳

THE WORDS **PRECEDE** and *proceed* are both etymologically related to the Latin word *cedere*, which means "to go." *Precede* comes from *praecedere* ("to go before"), while *proceed* comes from *procedere* ("to go forward"). Both of these verbs relate to motion along a path, a concept that has far-reaching metaphorical applications.

Precede (also meaning "to go before") deals with the relative positions of two bodies moving on a path, and focuses on the one that's in front. This basic idea applies metaphorically to time, so that *precede* can mean "to happen before something else" (as in "my birthday precedes yours"). It also applies to any type of *precedence* or ranking system: *To precede* means "to outrank or to be more important than." To express this idea, you can also say one thing "takes precedence" over another. Because *precede* has a meaning involving two entities or events, it's typically used transitively, with the thing that's in front or that comes first expressed as the grammatical subject, and the thing that follows or comes second expressed as the direct object.

Setting a Precedent

Precedent is a related adjective that means "prior to" in all literal and metaphorical senses. *Precedent* is also a noun used for a prior instance of something that serves as a model or sets a convention for later instances. It's often used for a legal decision that establishes a conventional interpretation of a law that applies to subsequent cases.

Proceed ("to go forward") is an intransitive verb that describes the motion of an individual entity. That idea of forward motion can be applied metaphorically to other purposeful action; we can proceed with any kind of activity, not just actual motion.

Proceedings and *procession* are related nouns that stem from the same root as *procede*. *Proceedings* is used to refer to the totality of what happens in a situation. It's typically used in a legal context—we speak of divorce proceedings, for example. *Proceedings* can also be used to label  a kind of written record: Conference proceedings, for example, are a collection of papers presented at a conference. A *procession* is "a marching onward."

Now that you've read and understood the preceding information, you can proceed with your study of other words!

"Practice yourself, for heaven's sake in little things, and then proceed to greater."

—Epictetus

"It is our duty as men and women to proceed as though the limits of our abilities do not exist."

—Pierre Teilhard de Chardin

"If the headache would only precede the intoxication, alcoholism would be a virtue."

—Samuel Butler

"Intelligence must follow faith, never precede it, and never destroy it."

—Thomas à Kempis

What a Difference an *A* Makes

As they're pronounced in casual speech, the words **than** *and* **then** *sound pretty much the same, so it's easy to get them mixed up in writing.*

❋   ❋   ❋   ❋

THE WORD *THEN* has its roots in Old English. Its most basic function is to talk about time. When someone asks you if it's okay to move a 12:00 lunch date to 12:30, you might say, "I'd be happy to join you then." In this case, *then* is "pointing" to the mentioned time (in the same fashion, the word *that* points to an object that's already been mentioned or that's known from context). *Then* can also be used to introduce a clause or sentence that describes the next step in a narrative: "First we found a place to park, and then we ran to the restaurant." In a related use, *then* marks the second part of a conditional statement: "If you eat all your veggies, then you can have dessert." Conditional sentences can also be used to describe evidence and a conclusion drawn from it: "If his fingerprints are on the gun, then he must be the killer."

Than is etymologically derived from *then*. The two words have only been distinguished in spelling for a few centuries. *Than* is a word of comparison; it's about differences. When it occurs after a comparative adjective, it introduces the standard of comparison from which something differs in a particular way: "That fish was longer than the boat!" In this example, *than* is acting as a preposition, because it is introducing a noun phrase. *Than* can also introduce shortened clauses: "I ate much more than you did." In combination with words such as *other* and *rather*, *than* can be used to talk about unspecified difference: "Let's eat somewhere other than here" or "I'd rather eat there than here."

A good way to remember the difference between *then* and *than* is to keep in mind that *then*, a time word, has the same ending as another time word: *when*.

There You Have It

*Three homophones—***there, their,** *and* **they're**—*have traditionally bedeviled writers, but it's easy enough to sort out the adverb from the pronoun from the contraction in order to avoid looking sloppy or uneducated.*

✳ ✳ ✳ ✳

FIRST, THERE IS an adverb that indicates "at a place or position": "Your glasses are right there on the table in front of you." When *there* is used at the beginning of a sentence in a *there is/there are* construction, it may look like the subject, but it is actually still an adverb, not a noun. In such a sentence, *there* merely indicates the existence of whatever noun follows the verb. Because it is not really the subject, it's necessary to look at what comes after the verb to find the subject and decide whether *is* or *are, was* or *were* is appropriate: "There is more than one way to skin a cat" or "There are three homophones in this article."

There can also act as a mild exclamation, as in the title of this article or "There, I told you so."

Their is a possessive pronoun, meaning "belonging to them." It works as an adjective: "They left their clothes piled in heaps on the floor of their room, and their dirty glasses were left without coasters on the good coffee table." The variant *theirs* is also a possessive pronoun. It indicates something belonging to two or more people: "They act as if the family car is theirs to use whenever it suits them."

The use of *they're* is much more straightforward. The word is simply a contraction of *they are.* If you have the slightest doubt about which of the *there/their/they're* spellings to use, try using *they are* and see if the sentence makes any sense. If it doesn't, *they're* is not the right choice, and you must try one of the other two homophones.

Principal Principles

*If precision in using language is one of your principal aims, you will observe these distinctions between the words **principal** and **principle**.*

✳   ✳   ✳   ✳

I F YOU WERE ever summoned to the principal's office back in your school days—easy now, nothing is going to happen to you here—you were facing the person in charge. This is one of the meanings of the noun *principal*. As an adjective, *principal* usually means "foremost." The Latin root word of both is the adjective *principalis*, which means "first" or "original." That in turn comes from *princeps*, meaning "chief." The English word *prince* derives from the same root, as does *principality*, a state ruled by a prince.

Who's Your Pal?

At one time, before the position became a specialized administrative one, the principal of a school was the head teacher: the first among equals, the *principal* teacher. In a law firm, the principal is the person with the most authority; in opera or ballet, the principal is the main performer. These are the  *foremost* people. An agent or representative who conducts business on behalf of other people may also be called a principal in the transactions.

As an adjective, *principal* means "having first place in importance" or "for the most part." Your principal reason for reading this book may be an intention to improve your knowledge of the English language. As an adverb, *principally* means "mainly."

A grammarian is principally concerned with the functions of words in syntax.

A Princely Sum

Another noun sense of *principal*, which everyone who has a college loan or a mortgage knows all too well, is the original sum of money borrowed in such an arrangement, on which the interest is calculated. It is the first, or the original, sum of money in the transaction.

It's the Principle of the Thing

A slightly different word, often confused with *principal*, is *principle*, which also comes to us from the Latin *princeps* ("first" or "chief"), but by a slightly different route—through *principium*, meaning "source," and *principia*, meaning "foundations." The words are pronounced the same, but *principle* is always a noun and means "a fundamental thing, a foundational truth or proposition for beliefs or behavior." In the plural form, one's *principles* are one's fundamental beliefs and guides to behavior. *Principled* behavior is that which conforms to one's basic moral beliefs.

"All animals, except man, know that the principal business of life is to enjoy it."

—SAMUEL BUTLER

"The principal act of courage is to endure and withstand dangers doggedly rather than to attack them."

—THOMAS AQUINAS

"She owes her success in practice to her inconsistencies in principle."

—THOMAS HARDY

"Moderation in temper is always a virtue; but moderation in principle is always a vice."

—THOMAS PAINE

Hold Your Horses

*The difference between **rein** and **reign** would seem to be clear and unmistakable. After all, kings have reigns, and horses have reins, right? Unless kings and queens start wearing saddles and eating hay, or a palomino issues a decree raising taxes, the two concepts seem diametrically opposed. But as with so many aspects of language, the reality is far less simple.*

✳   ✳   ✳   ✳

REINS ARE PHYSICAL tools, a means by which a rider steers a horse or controls its behavior. If the rider lets the reins go slack, the horse goes wherever it chooses to go; it has been given *free rein*. However, people often substitute the spelling *free reign*, even though *reign*, a noun meaning "the period of a monarch's rule," makes no sense in this context. *Reign* also frequently and incorrectly appears in the expressions *reign in* and *reigns of power*.

So why do these errors appear so often? No doubt *rein* has shrunk in prominence because few people commute to work or school via the equine these days. There are few reminders of reins for anyone not spending a lot of time at the horse track. And while we don't have a king in the United States, either, we do have a president, congresspeople, sports champions, CEOs, celebrities, and other folks who are said to have reigns of authority, power, influence, or popularity. If the expression "reins of government" were still commonly used—it faded away after the nineteenth century—the two terms might be even more confused, if that is possible.

In fact, *reign* is used in place of *rein* so often that it's debatable whether or not this is even an error anymore—it's looking like an evolution. This kind of organic, from-the-bottom, spontaneous-yet-gradual change is how language has always evolved. Like it or not, the people ultimately have free reign over language.

Bartender, Don't Be Slow

*Inexperienced drinkers sometimes think that **sloe gin** is slow gin. They are mistaken on three counts.*

❋ ❋ ❋ ❋

FIRST, THEY HAVE fallen for a homophone. Homophones are words with identical or similar pronunciations but different meanings and different spellings.

Second, sloe gin is not actually a gin but a liqueur, made from the sloe berry from the blackthorn tree. (The sloe berry is bluish-black and responsible for the term *sloe-eyed*, applied to those having attractive dark eyes, usually almond-shaped.) The berries are infused with gin or grain spirits and sugar to produce a beverage that some find a bit cloying. Gin, however, is made with neutral spirits and juniper berries, in addition to spices such as cloves and cinnamon. The name *gin* comes from the French *genièvre* or the Dutch *jenever*, both of which mean *juniper*.

Third, sloe gin is not slow-acting. It registers 30- to 60-proof and can be mixed with other alcoholic and nonalcoholic beverages to make gin fizzes and other cocktails of varying lethality.

The word *slow* has varying senses:

❋ Lacking in speed: "Traffic on the interstate was very slow on the Sunday after Thanksgiving."

❋ Taking a long time: "The class fidgeted while waiting for the slow readers to finish."

❋ Sluggish in understanding: "You'll have to explain that one more time; I'm a little slow until I've had my morning coffee."

❋ Boring: "I don't know why I chose to go to college in this slow little backwater; there's nothing to do."

That third category of *slow* is perhaps linked to the consumption of too much sloe gin the night before.

Words of Wisdom from Benjamin Franklin

* * * *

* "All mankind is divided into three classes: those that are immovable, those that are movable, and those that move."

* "Anger is never without a reason, but seldom with a good one."

* "Any fool can criticize, condemn and complain and most fools do."

* "At twenty years of age the will reigns; at thirty, the wit; and at forty, the judgment."

* "Beware of little expenses. A small leak will sink a great ship."

* "By failing to prepare, you are preparing to fail."

* "Creditors have better memories than debtors."

* "He that lives upon hope will die fasting."

* "He that rises late must trot all day."

* "Lost time is never found again."

* "Life's tragedy is that we get old too soon and wise too late."

* "The Constitution only gives people the right to pursue happiness. You have to catch it yourself."

* "Beauty and folly are old companions."

* "We are all born ignorant, but one must work hard to remain stupid."

* "Three can keep a secret, if two of them are dead."

* "Guests, like fish, begin to smell after three days."

First Things First

The Romans gave us so much, and we hardly ever thank them.

✳   ✳   ✳   ✳

TAKE, FOR EXAMPLE, the Latin word *primarius*, meaning "principal" or "foremost." From it we get our English word *primary*, as in primary school (often a child's first formal period of schooling) and primary election (a preliminary vote). *Primarius* itself derives from *primus*, meaning "first," which led to the English *prime*, meaning "of first importance" and having many other allied meanings. A prime minister is the chief or foremost minister in government. When you go to the meat counter at the grocery, you know that prime steak is the highest grade. *Primus* also led in Latin to *princeps*, which gave us *prince* and *principal* (the chief, or the main thing).

Filtered through France, *primarius* gave us the frequently confused *premier* and *premiere*. Let's sort them out.

Premier, as an adjective, means "having first place in importance," or "foremost." In winemaking, a *premier cru*, literally "first growth," is a wine of superior quality. People still argue about whether the Beatles or The Rolling Stones were the premier rock band of the 1960s. As a noun, *premier* is a synonym for *prime minister*, the head of government in Britain, Canada, and other countries.

Premiere relates to performing a play or musical or showing a film for the first time. It can indicate the first performance ever; in that case, the term *world premiere* is sometimes used. Or it can simply be the first performance in a particular country or city. As a transitive verb, *premiere* means "to give the first performance": "After out-of-town tryouts, the producers premiered the show on Broadway." As an intransitive verb, it means "to have a first performance": "The musical premiered on Broadway." *Premiere* can also be an adjective, as in "the premiere showing" of a film.

A Peek at *Pique* and *Peak*

Homophones are the source of many errors in written English. The more meanings each homophone has, the more difficult it can be to distinguish between them. Such is the case with **peek, peak,** *and* **pique.** *Each of these words has at least three meanings, and* peak *alone has around two dozen! How, then, do we distinguish between them?*

❋ ❋ ❋ ❋

THE CENTRAL MEANING of *peek,* the simplest of the three words, is "to look quickly or furtively," and it is only used when the context has something to do with sight. A handy mnemonic: You p*ee*k with your *ee*yes (remember the two *e*'s). *Peak,* despite the number of different senses listed in a dictionary, is not that much more complicated. The central meaning is one of height or a maximum amount: A mountain peak is the very top of the mountain, peak traffic is the time when the most traffic is on the road, and the peak of someone's career is the time when he or she is most successful. Some people remember that the capital A in PEAK looks a little like a mountain, so if you're talking about a mountain (real or metaphorical), use *peak.*

Peaked is also an adjective. In one sense it means just what one would expect: "pointed," or "having a peak." But it also means "sickly," or "having a pale or wan appearance."

How Irritating—Ergh, I Mean Exciting

Pique is the rarest of these words, so it is the most often confused. It is pronounced the same as *peak* and *peek* and, as a noun, it is used to describe an emotional state of some sort. In the phrase "a fit of pique," it means "irritation" or "resentment": "After 30 minutes of listening to sleep-inducing hold music, she finally hung up the phone in a fit of pique." (That's probably a polite phrase to describe her state of mind.) In the phrase "to pique one's interest," *pique* functions as a verb meaning "to excite or arouse": "The enchanting voice repeating 'All our representatives are currently busy' piqued his interest, and he stayed on hold for hours just to listen to it."

Is Your Interest Piqued or Peaked?

Probably the most common *pique/peak* error is the use of *peak one's interest* instead of *pique one's interest*. Using *peak* makes some sense, because the user is probably thinking of someone's interest moving toward its maximum point; but the phrase really indicates the initiation of an emotional response, and not the maximizing of one.

Pique comes to us from French, which people have called "the language of love." Perhaps remembering that *pique* is French will help you to remember that if you're talking about curiosity, frustration, interest, or another emotion, use *pique*.

"One sees great things from the valley; only little things from the peak."

—G. K. CHESTERTON

"We should not judge people by their peak of excellence; but by the distance they have traveled from the point where they started."

—HENRY WARD BEECHER

"Zeal is a volcano, the peak of which the grass of indecisiveness does not grow."

—KHALIL GIBRAN

Where Did It Come From?

Peekaboo: A children's game found as early as the 1590s. Also an adjective meaning "see-through," dating from 1895. From *piken,* meaning "look quickly and slyly" (fourteenth century, origin unknown) and *boh,* "an expression meant to startle" (early fifteenth century). Also *peek-a-boo.*

Lost in Space

What a difference a space can make!

✱ ✱ ✱ ✱

THERE ARE MANY words in English that can be spelled either as two words with a space between them (an open compound) or as one word with no space (a closed compound). *Any way* ("in any manner") and *anyway* ("regardless") are one example, as are *under way* ("in motion") and *underway* ("occurring while in motion"), as well as *any one* ("any single one") and *anyone* ("anybody").

An Other Instance of Evolving Language

And then there are words that seem like they should be two words, but they really aren't. For some people, *another* is just such a word. It does, in fact, come from (and mean) *an other*, and instances of both spellings are found in Middle English and in early modern English.

Citations in the *Oxford English Dictionary* include Chaucer writing *an other*, and his contemporary William Langland writing *another* (both around 1380). By about the sixteenth century, however, the spelling had been standardized, and it is now considered correct when it is spelled as a closed compound: *another*.

You've Got A Nother Think Coming

During the time when *another* was spelled as an open compound, some writers split it as *a nother*. In some dialects of English, this gave rise to a variant pronoun, *nother*, meaning "a second or additional (thing that is being referred to)" and leading to such other (now obsolete) forms as *no nother* ("none other") and *no notherwise* ("not otherwise").

Linguists call the process of reinterpreting a word based on a misunderstanding of meanings or segment boundaries *metanalysis*, and it shows up in several other English words, such as *apron*, originally *a napron* but misunderstood as *an apron*, and *newt* (a type of amphibian), originally *an ewt* but misunderstood as *a newt*.

A Whole Nother Usage

In the United States it is not uncommon to hear the dialectal or informal phrase "a whole nother," which may come from *nother* as explained above. It is slightly more likely, however, to be an example of *tmesis*, the process of inserting an intensifying word into the middle of another word. (See page 291 for more on tmesis.) In that case, the odd split is probably for a different reason: One would never say "an whole other" (because *whole* takes *a*, not *an*), so in order to make the phrase still recognizable as *another*, you have to put the *whole* in what seems like the wrong place.

"I believe that every human mind feels pleasure in doing good to another."

—THOMAS JEFFERSON

"When we do the best that we can, we never know what miracle is wrought in our life, or in the life of another."

—HELEN KELLER

"We must be our own before we can be another's."

—RALPH WALDO EMERSON

"We are all dependent on one another, every soul of us on earth."

—GEORGE BERNARD SHAW

"Any man may easily do harm, but not every man can do good to another."

—PLATO

✳ Pink Floyd's song "Another Brick in the Wall" is actually the title of not one but three songs from the band's 1979 rock opera, *The Wall*. The trio is subtitled Part 1 ("Reminiscing"), Part 2 ("Education"), and Part 3 ("Drugs").

The Tortuous Truth About *Torturous*

*Would you rather undergo a **tortuous** interrogation or a **torturous** one? While neither would be pleasant, you'd be better served opting for the tortuous one.*

✳   ✳   ✳   ✳

A TORTUOUS INTERROGATION WOULD probably involve abrupt changes in topic and tone. One moment the detective might be shining a light in your eyes and grilling you about your alibi, and the next moment she might be offering you a cold drink and chatting about the weather. *Tortuous* is derived from the Latin *torquere*, meaning "to twist," and is etymologically related to the word *torque* ("a turning or twisting force"). Something that's tortuous has many unexpected twists and turns.

Winding roads and other physical paths can be literally tortuous. Also, because paths are often used as metaphors for communication, it follows that stories and conversations are often described as tortuous (the opposite of direct and straightforward). Paths may be used as metaphors for behavior. So, if you don't keep on the straight and narrow, you might end up on a tortuous moral path.

On the other hand, something *torturous* is something that inflicts pain, either literally or metaphorically, as when you have a "torturous day at the office." *Torture* is also derived from the Latin *torquere*, perhaps because some methods of torture involve twisting. An interrogation might be torturous figuratively as well as literally, involving both physical discomfort and the mental stress that results from a difficult line of questioning. *Torturous* can also mean "slow and difficult" (as in "The summit brought days of torturous negotiations"), and here it's especially close in meaning to *tortuous*. Negotiations, like interrogations, might be torturous (slow and difficult) precisely because they're tortuous (filled with lots of twists and turns).

A Piece on *Peace*

*If you get angry, you might give someone a **piece** of your mind in order to achieve a little **peace** of mind.*

❋   ❋   ❋   ❋

PEACE IS A state of quiet or harmony or nonconflict. "Peace" is what the hippies said when they flashed two fingers. Peace is what John Lennon asked us to give a chance. Peace is what you get a little bit of when your kids are finally in bed.

A *piece* is a bit or a chunk: It's a part of something, usually separated from the whole. You can have a piece of pie, a piece of chicken, or even a piece of history. A piece can also be one of a number of more-or-less interchangeable items, as with a piece of fruit. A piece can be a creative product such as a sculpture, a musical composition, or an essay. Pieces often make their appearance metaphorically in idioms. You can "go to pieces," "pick up the pieces," and then finally "get your piece of the pie." *Piece* is occasionally a verb as well, as when you "piece things together."

Pieces are countable. You can have a piece or several pieces or a million pieces. Peace, on the other hand, is an abstract state that isn't countable. You usually don't use an article with the word *peace*, unless it's in a phrase like "a lasting peace," in which you're emphasizing a particular property, or "a little peace," in which the article is part of a measure expression.

Remembering how to spell the two soundalike words *piece* and *peace* is enough to drive a person to pieces. To keep them straight, remember that it is correct to ask for a piece (not peace) of pie; *piece*, helpfully, contains the word *pie*.

Peace and *piece* are classified as true homonyms—words that are pronounced the same but have different meanings and different origins. The noun *piece* comes from the postclassical Latin word *pecia* ("fragment"), whereas the word *peace* comes from the Latin word *pax*, which means "safety, welfare, and prosperity."

Swans Are Mute, Points Are Moot

Some phrases in the English language are particularly difficult to understand because they incorporate words that have otherwise dropped out of the English vernacular. One such phrase is **moot point.** *To further confuse the issue, the phrase has two almost opposing meanings: "a point that is debatable" and "a point that is not worth debating."*

✻　✻　✻　✻

To sort out the meanings, we need to start with the word *moot,* a very old Germanic word meaning "a meeting place." During the Anglo-Saxon period of English history (from the fifth century A.D. to the Norman Conquest in 1066), *moot* (or, often, *mot*) was used to mean "a legislative or judicial assembly, a place where decisions are made." From this arose the first meaning of *moot point:* a point of law or justice that was to be debated at a moot.

But *moot* was also used in the study of law to describe the practice of arguing hypothetical legal cases, and this leads to the easily confusable second meaning. Because arguing hypothetical cases is still a part of legal studies, speakers of modern English are far more likely to be familiar with the concept of a *moot court* than with a *moot* as an assembly. And because the cases argued in a moot court have no legal standing, the points brought up there—the *moot points*—could be considered not worth debating. In American English especially, "a point that is irrelevant or not worth arguing" has become the primary meaning of *moot point.*

Shhhh...

Mute is not as old a word in English as *moot,* but it is far more common in modern English, so it's likely to be the word that comes most easily to mind for many people. It primarily means "not able to speak," but it can also mean "not speaking," so it's perfectly reasonable that one might extend that to "not worth speaking (about)." In modern-day vernacular, *mute* has also morphed into a verb; that is, "When the telephone rang, Sam muted the TV so he could answer the call."

That's What *Friends* Is For

A point that is not worth *arguing* about could easily be considered a point not worth *speaking* about, which may be what gave rise to the common miswording *mute point*. (*Mute point* can be considered an *eggcorn*; for more on eggcorns, see page 60.) And, while not quite an eggcorn, this conversation between Rachel and Joey on TV's *Friends* demonstrates a perfect misunderstanding of the phrase.

> Joey: *It's just a moo point.*
>
> Rachel: *A moo point?*
>
> Joey: *Yeah. It's like a cow's opinion. It just doesn't matter. It's moo.*

So while *mute point* is a perfectly logical construction, it's also an incorrect one, and many people consider the usage ignorant—so it may be better to remain mute than to utter this phrase. *Moot point*, on the other hand, has a long and intriguing history that connects us to the first speakers of what came to be called English and is worth preserving for the future.

"My greatest weapon is mute prayer."

—MAHATMA GANDHI

"Law stands mute in the midst of arms."

—MARCUS TULLIUS CICERO

You Can't Wring a Bell

*A **ring**, whether it's a circle or a sound, is a simple thing, and it has a simple spelling. The spelling of **wring**, like its meaning, is a little twisted.*

❋   ❋   ❋   ❋

THE WORD RING is a noun that refers to a variety of objects with a circular shape, such as the piece of jewelry you wear on your finger or the toy an infant chews on to soothe sore gums. In some cases, *ring* refers to an area enclosed on all sides, even if it's not circular, such as a boxing ring. The word can also be used metaphorically to refer to a closed group of people engaged in a (usually) nefarious pursuit, as with a ring of smugglers, a ring of counterfeiters, or a ring of thieves. A ring can also be a sound: Don't call people early in the morning, because the ring of the phone might wake them up.

Ring can also be used as a verb. A phone can ring, ears can ring, trees can ring a pond, and a story can ring true. You can ring a bell literally, and something that seems faintly familiar can "ring a bell" figuratively.

Wring is a verb that means "to twist and squeeze something," usually to get liquid out of it. What you typically wring is something made of cloth. You might occasionally be tempted to wring someone's neck, but you must of course resist, lest their loved ones wring justice from you. That last usage ("wring justice") points to a figurative sense, "to extract something with effort," as when you "wring meaning" from a difficult text.

Wring is one of those odd words, like *wrong, wreck,* and *wrestle,* that has a silent *w* before the *r*. This is a case of fossilized spelling. Several centuries ago, the *w* was pronounced. The pronunciation has changed over time, but the spelling, preserved in written records, remains the same.

Party On

Are you a party animal? If you are, read on!

✳ ✳ ✳ ✳

THE WORD PARTY has only recently developed a sense as a verb meaning "to have an exuberant good time," reflected in the colloquial pronunciation "pahr-TAY." Since *partying* in this sense carries some vigorous associations—large crowds, loud music, freely flowing alcohol—partiers have looked for an expression to convey both the enthusiasm and the stamina required to sustain it. They have often turned to **party hearty.**

Hearty, when describing a person, means "loud," "vigorous," or "cheerful," all apt adjectives for the kind of informal celebration the term *party hearty* suggests (though the downstairs neighbors attempting to sleep may use terms other than *hearty* or *vigorous* when they pound on the door to complain). *Hearty* is an adjective, so the phrase is technically grammatically incorrect, but coupling the verb with an adverbial form, resulting in *party heartily,* would look (and sound) pedantic. Using the adjective retains a rhyme and the double-syllable rhythm.

Party hardy, which some people use mistakenly, suggests something quite different from boisterous celebration. *Hardy,* from an Old French root meaning "bold," means "robust" or "vigorous." A hardy camper can endure the cold of winter as well as the heat of summer. *Party hardy* suggests something like an endurance contest, perhaps involving drinking games leading to excess or dangerous physical feats. Steer clear of this expression, as you would of such occasions.

Hearty, in the senses of "enthusiastic," "healthy," "nourishing," or "satisfying," is related etymologically to *heart.* ("She gave him a big hug and a hearty hello." "He has been hale and hearty since recovering from surgery.")

Words of Wisdom: Dancing

✳ ✳ ✳ ✳

"And those who were seen dancing were thought to be insane by those who could not hear the music."

—FRIEDRICH NIETZSCHE

"O body swayed to music, O brightening glance, How can we know the dancer from the dance?."

—WILLIAM BUTLER YEATS

"Will you, won't you, will you, won't you, will you join the dance?"

—LEWIS CARROLL

"Common sense and a sense of humor are the same thing, moving at different speeds. A sense of humor is just common sense, dancing."

—WILLIAM JAMES

"We're fools whether we dance or not, so we might as well dance."

—ANONYMOUS

"True ease in writing comes from art, not chance, as those move easiest who have learned to dance."

—ALEXANDER POPE

"All the ills of mankind, all the tragic misfortunes that fill the history books, all the political blunders, all the failures of the great leaders have arisen merely from a lack of skill at dancing."

—MOLIÈRE

Threw and Through

The words **threw** *and* **through** *sound alike, but they could hardly be more different.*

✳   ✳   ✳   ✳

THE PAST TENSE of the verb *to throw* is *threw*, and it can be used in many senses. You might say that you threw a ball, threw a javelin, or threw a fit, or that something threw you off balance or threw you for a loop. Maybe the purple walls of your old apartment threw your canary yellow couch into stark relief.

Through is more complicated. Usually it's a preposition, as in the phrase "through the tunnel." But it can also be an adjective meaning "finished," as in "I'm through with all that." In some instances, such as "see it through to the end," *through* functions as an adverb.

Now, about the spelling of *through*. What are those silent letters doing in there? Well, they're an odd little reminder of the historically based strangeness of English spelling. (The *-ough* ending is especially strange. Think of all the different ways it gets pronounced: *bough, dough, through, rough, cough*).

Pronunciations are ephemeral and change rapidly, by historical standards. Spellings don't change as quickly. The word *through* derives from the Old English *thurh*. The *h* on the end of the Old English word represents a consonant sound that English doesn't have anymore, one similar to the final sound in the name *Bach*, as it's pronounced in German. The *-gh* at the end of our modern word *through* is a remnant of that old pronunciation.

Here are a couple tips to keep the spelling of these two words straight: First, the more complicated spelling belongs to the more complicated word. Second, remember the sentence "The child threw the ball through the window." This sentence features both *threw* and *through* in simple, exemplary usage; furthermore, the words appear in alphabetical order, so you can easily check which spelling goes with which word.

Word Roots and Branches
Here We Go *A*-prefixing

Knowing the meanings of prefixes, suffixes, and roots can be very helpful when trying to puzzle out a word's meaning. But sometimes a root or affix will have more than one meaning, and the multiple meanings can cause confusion and error. The a-prefix is atop this list.

✳   ✳   ✳   ✳

PREFIXES A- AND *an-* are among those that have multiple meanings. In fact, the *Oxford English Dictionary* has six different entries for *a-* and two different entries for *an-*. If you don't know which one is being used in a given word, you can easily misconstrue the word's meaning. Read on to learn the differences.

"Without"/"Not"

Perhaps the most obvious and productive (i.e., used to form new words) use of *a-/an-* is in forming nouns and adjectives where the prefix means "without" or "not." Examples include *atheist*, *asexual*, and *anarchy*. The *a-* is generally used when the root begins with a consonant, and *an-* when it begins with a vowel. *A-/an-* is found in older words borrowed from Greek, Latin, or French, and since the seventeenth century it has also been used to form new words within English.

"On"/"Onto"

Another use for *a-/an-* is to create verbs, adverbs, and prepositions with the sense "on" or "on to." So we have *abed*, *aboard*, *adrift*, *among* and *awaken*. This use is no longer productive, but it is helpful to know this meaning in order to avoid misinterpreting such words.

Creating Adverbs

The prefix *a-* is also added to nouns to create adverbs regarding time, place, or manner. Hence we have *atop*, *abeam*, *alive*, and *asleep*. This adverbial use is still occasionally productive, chiefly in poetic diction.

Clipped Prefixes

The prefix *a-* is also found where speakers have clipped other prefixes over the centuries. It appears as a shortened form of *or-*, *at-*, and *of-*, and in some words borrowed from Old French and derived from the Latin *ad-*. These have never been used productively in English, but some of the borrowed words using them are quite common, including *accurse*, *abandon*, *akin*, and *achieve*.

New Forms

Finally, in some dialects, the *a-* prefix is informally added to a verb to create a new form of the verb or change it into an adjective. Someone might go *a-hunting*, or be *a-tired* after a long day's work, or be *a-fixing* to make supper, for example. This use is chiefly found in the southern United States and in southwestern England.

So, when encountering an unfamiliar word that begins with *a-* or *an-*, it's reasonable to guess that the prefix means "without, not." Just be aware it is not necessarily so.

Where Did It Come From?

Ahoy: First recorded in Tobias Smollett's *The Adventures of Peregrine Pickle* (1751), the word was by then a common greeting among sailors—though it originated with hog farmers who used it to call to their animals. Alexander Graham Bell wanted the term to be the standard greeting for telephone calls.

Who Cares?

For at least a couple of generations, students of the English language have been saying that **whom** *is on its way out. Any minute now it will be, like Charles Dickens's Jacob Marley, "dead as a door-nail." And yet it comes back to us, rattling its chains as it shuffles through our texts, refusing to go quietly into the night.*

✳   ✳   ✳   ✳

THE WORD WHOM may not be dead yet, but it looks increasingly moribund. According to proper usage, *whom* should be used in place of *who* when acting as the object of a verb or preposition. But *who*, at least in American speech, has been doing double duty as subject and object for some time now, and its dominance has been spilling over into written English as well.

The schoolteacher's advice for deciding whether *who* or *whom* is appropriate in a given instance is to try substituting *he, she,* or *they,* or *him, her,* or *them* into the sentence in question. If the first word group works, *who* is the appropriate choice. If the second group would be grammatically correct, use *whom.* That process works pretty well, but it opens up a question: If native speakers can easily distinguish *she* and *her,* why should they have trouble with the parallel pronouns *who* and *whom?* The fact that so many native speakers appear to have lost the ability to distinguish *who* from *whom* suggests that the battle is lost and it is time to retire from the field.

Who Wants Whom?

Still, until the word has officially breathed its last, it's important to maintain proper usage. Especially on those occasions when you are writing formally, or if you have reason to think that your audience will be finicky, make the *he/who, him/whom* substitutions in an effort to use the correct word. If the pronoun is embedded in a question, which usually inverts normal sentence order, you may have to reverse the order of the sentence to make the determination: *Whom do you want to give the first answer? Do you want* him/her/them (whom) *to give the first answer?*

There is one particularly tricky point to watch out for. If the pronoun is the subject of a clause, it must *always* be *who*. This is true even if the clause itself is the object of a verb or a preposition. One of the most common errors in current writing is to use *whom* when the pronoun is the subject of a subordinate clause. Here's an example of correct usage: "I'll outplay whoever tries to challenge me." In this case, *whoever* is the subject of *tries* and therefore cannot appear in the sentence as *whomever*—even though *whoever tries to challenge me* is the direct object of *outplay*.

But when in doubt, maybe you should just use *who*. That may be the way of the future. Who knows?

✳ **Who's on first?** Abbott and Costello's most famous bit, the comedy sketch "Who's on First," was not a concept original to them. It is a direct decendent of common burlesque sketches from the turn of the twentieth century, including "Who's the Boss?" and "Who Dyed?" The 1930 movie *Cracked Nuts* featured a similar bit, with dialogue such as, "What is next to Which. What is the name of the town next to Which? Yes."

✳ The classic rock band The Who briefly changed their name to The High Numbers in 1964, releasing only one single ("Zoot Suit/I'm the Face") before reverting back to The Who.

Where Would You Be If You Were Stationery?

*People get the words **stationary** and **stationery** mixed up so often that stationery stores often include the key word stationary on their websites just to get the traffic.*

✳   ✳   ✳   ✳

STATIONARY IS AN adjective that means "motionless." It's related to the word *station*, which counts among its meanings "a place where one is assigned to stand or remain" and "a way of standing." So, to be stationary means to remain in or at your station, or just to stand still. *Stationary* also means "unchanging," following a common metaphor that treats change as motion. A stationary population, for instance, is one in which the birth rate and death rate are equal, resulting in an unchanging overall number of people.

Stationery is an umbrella term for the paper, cards, envelopes, and even pens and ink that people use for correspondence—in other words, for writing letters. Writing letters used to be serious business back in the days before telephones and e-mail. There's actually a word, *stationer*, which used to mean "bookseller" and came to mean "someone who sells tools for writing." These tools then came to be known as *stationery*.

It's no accident that *stationary* and *stationery* are so similar. The word *stationer*, noted above, came from the Latin *stationarius*, which was used in medieval times to distinguish a stationary seller from a peddler who moved around with a cart. *Stationarius* was used in Latin to describe things related to a military station, and it was the etymological source for *stationary* as well.

There are two handy mnemonics to help you distinguish between these words: First, people write letters on stationery (note the *e*'s in both words). Also, stationary with an *a* is an adjective, and *adjective* begins with *a*.

Word Roots and Branches
An Easy *Mis-* Mistake to Make

The prefix mis- *is actually two different prefixes, but since they both mean "badly, wrongly, mistakenly," you wouldn't know it to look at them. They both came into English from the same Germanic root, but by very different routes. With this indiscriminate prefix attaching itself to so many English words, it certainly is hard to* mis-*!*

✳ ✳ ✳ ✳

THE LESS COMMON *mis-* comes from Old French, brought across the English Channel by the Normans. There are only a handful of words using this form of the prefix, including:

✳ *misadventure*—an ill-conceived, misguided, or regrettable enterprise

✳ *mischief*—evildoing

✳ *miscreant*—a heretic, infidel, or villain

✳ *misnomer*—a wrong or misleading name

The more common *mis-* is older, dating back to the Old English of the Anglo-Saxons. It is one of the most productive prefixes, with more than 1,000 *mis-* words in the *Oxford English Dictionary*. A few of these are:

✳ *misconduct*—improper behavior

✳ *misconstrue*—to interpret badly, to mistake the meaning of something

✳ *misfire*—of ammunition: to fail to discharge

✳ *misinformation*—wrong or misleading data

✳ *misprint*—to print incorrectly; a printing error

✳ *mistake*—to err; an error

✳ *misuse*—to use wrongly or improperly

No Need to Torture Yourself

Of the best-known medieval instruments of torture—the thumbscrew, the iron maiden, the stake, and so on—none has established itself as firmly in the English language as the rack. The victim was forced to lay on a frame, and their hands and feet were attached to rollers. As the torturers cranked these rollers, stretching the frame, the victim's limbs were stretched out until his or her joints dislocated.

✳ ✳ ✳ ✳

THE INSTRUMENT YIELDED a verb, **to rack,** meaning "to cause severe physical or mental pain." The phrase "racked with guilt" is a stock expression that describes an extreme emotional state. To "rack one's brains," in the sense of "stretching," is to torment oneself (metaphorically) in the effort to come up with an answer.

The expression "to rack up," meaning "to accumulate something," as in "the varsity squad racked up a high score," comes from the original sense of *rack* as a horizontal bar from which things that have been collected are hung, or a shelf on which they are stored. Figuratively, when you have accumulated enough information on a topic, you can account for it or "rack it up" to a reason.

Sounds the Same, with Much Less Pain

The noun *wrack*—same pronunciation as *rack*—identifies wreckage. The detritus left floating in the sea or that washes up

> *"Of all the icy blasts that blow on love, a request for money is the most chilling and havoc wreaking."*
> —GUSTAVE FLAUBERT

on the shore when a ship sinks could be considered wrack. The word gives us the familiar expression *wrack and ruin*. *Wrack* is also a verb; we see the past participle in use in *storm-wracked*. (This leads to the obvious eggcorn, or error, of *storm-wrecked*. For more on eggcorns, see page 60.)

People who like things to be tidy and logical prefer to restrict *rack* to that sense of being tortured or tormented, and *wrack* to wreckage. However, because the English language is a vast, fluid language, it is often neither tidy nor logical. *Wrack* has been in use as a variant spelling of *rack* since the middle of the sixteenth century, and this interchangeability continues into the present. People are about as likely to write *wrack one's brains* as *rack one's brains*, a tense situation may be called *nerve-wracking* or *nerve-racking*, and, although pundits might consider this to be wrecking the English language, no one is likely to misunderstand the meaning and intent of these usages.

Wreaking Havoc

Wreck (or *wrack*) may also be confused with *wreak*, which means "to cause (extensive damage or harm)." *Havoc*, or "great destruction or confusion," is what is most commonly *wreaked*, or *wrought*. In this case, unlike with *rack* and *wrack*, the issue is clear-cut: To *wreck havoc* is simply wrong. (This is not to say that one should really go around *wreaking* havoc, either; while it may be grammatically correct, it's certainly not good manners.)

Never Lean on the Podium

One of the most common fears that people will admit to is apprehension about speaking in public. And one of the most common errors involved with public speaking is mischaracterizing the structure from which it is done.

✳ ✳ ✳ ✳

A N E-ZINE ARTICLE titled "Ten Points on Poor Podium Use by Presenters" could use a few pointers itself; namely, regarding the definition of **podium.** According to this article, it's best for presenters to stand behind or to the side of a podium rather than use the podium to support their body. It cautions that leaning on the podium might make a presenter look too relaxed, or as if they need a crutch to keep from falling. In fact, leaning on the podium will indeed make a speaker look quite relaxed—considering that a podium is actually a platform from which someone is speaking. The word comes from the Greek *podion,* a diminutive of the word for "foot."

Don't Lean on the Lectern, Either

What a speaker does present from is a *lectern*—a stand with a slanted top on which books or papers can be rested. The word derives from the Latin *lectrum,* itself a derivative of the verb *legere,* or "to read." Lecterns were set up in churches as places from which a reader, or *lector,* could read from Scripture. The English *lecture,* a formal address of instruction, often defined as a reading from a prepared text, also derives from *legere.*

Preaching may be done from a **pulpit,** a raised platform with a lectern—the word coming from the Latin *pulpitum,* meaning "scaffold" or "platform." Some speakers declaim from a **rostrum,** also a raised platform, and usually an elaborate one. This word comes from the Latin *rostra,* a plural form of the Latin word for "beak." The Romans took the rams of ships captured in war and used them to create a platform for public speakers in Rome.

Can You Make Less Mistakes?

*Do you wish there were **less** rules of grammar and usage to worry about? Or do you wish there were **fewer**?*

❋　❋　❋　❋

Less and fewer are both comparative adjectives of quantity that come to us from Old English. A traditional view is that *fewer* should be used to describe a smaller quantity of countable things, and *less* should be reserved for measurable but non-countable amounts. So, sticklers might call for *less* carelessness and *fewer* mistakes; however, *less* has actually been used in both ways since Old English.

Less is more . . . than just an adjective. It indicates "a lower value on a scale of quantity, degree, or frequency" in a variety of grammatical contexts. It can be used as a noun ("I'll have a little less than that"), an adverb that modifies verbs ("I've been driving less since I moved to the city"), an adverb that modifies adjectives ("The server was less friendly than last time"), and a preposition ("Five less three is two"). As a representation of an abstract quantity, *less* lends itself to philosophical abstractions. Ludwig Mies van der Rohe, a pioneer of twentieth-century architecture, adopted the slogan "Less is more" to describe his minimalist design philosophy, and the phrase has entered popular usage.

Fewer is restricted to a counting context. Unlike *less*, *fewer* is an explicitly marked comparative form of another word: *few*. *Fewer* can be used as a noun and an adjective, but it's a bit more complicated: With many words that quantify nouns, the noun can be left out when its meaning is understood, so the quantifying word seems to perform the function of the noun. For example, you can say, "I'll have two spring rolls, please," or you can say, "I'll have two." *Less* and *fewer* both work this way. When planning an office holiday party, for example, you could say, "Inviting fewer managers would be best." But you could also just use "Fewer would be best" if one happens to walk into the room while you're speaking.

Parental Discretion Advised

*If you've never been able to put your finger on the difference between **discrete** and **discreet**, here's your chance to figure it out—discreetly, of course.*

✳   ✳   ✳   ✳

MANY ENGLISH HOMONYMS (words that sound the same but are different in meaning and, sometimes, spelling) occur because the words in question have come into English from different languages, and the spellings reflect the unique histories of each word. But this is not true of all homonyms: Sometimes the words are derived from the same source but have been passed down through different routes—such as a  Latin word that has been passed down through both German and French languages. Such words are called *doublets* by linguists. *Discreet* and *discrete* form an example of this process.

Developing Discrete Discretion

Both *discreet* and *discrete* are derived from the Latin word *discretus*, meaning "separate" or "distinct." *Discrete* took the more direct route and retains the original meaning. Things that are discrete are separate from each other or easily distinguishable—the notes played on a piano, for example, in contrast to the notes played with the slide on a trombone or a penny whistle. *Discrete* is also used as a mathematical or scientific term: Discrete numbers include integers (1, 2, 3, etc.) that are distinct from each other and are not part of a continuum of numbers.

Discreet, on the other hand, came into Middle English via Old French, where it had acquired the meaning "with discernment, circumspectly." In current English it is often used to describe someone who has the ability to keep a secret, or to describe a behavior executed without other people noticing. A discreet person, then, is one who keeps his or her mouth shut instead of telling other people's secrets. A discreet action is one that is subtle or not easily noticed, like a parent slipping a coin surreptiously under a sleeping child's pillow when acting on behalf of the tooth fairy.

The simplest way to remember which of these terms is which is to notice that while they both have two e's in the final syllable, in *discreet* they are placed together, while in *discrete* they are separated by the *t* and, therefore, are discrete from one another.

---

* Homonyms are a popular source of lexical humor in the English language, especially when put into use as phonological puns in jokes—meaning that the humor works best when heard and not read. Some well-known jokes that employ this technique are: What's black and white and read all over? (a newspaper); and Why did Dracula go to the doctor? (because of the coughin').

"Every man has his dignity. I'm willing to forget mine, but at my own discretion and not when someone else tells me to."

—Denis Diderot

"Great is our admiration of the orator who speaks with fluency and discretion."

—Marcus Tullius Cicero

"Judgment is not upon all occasions required, but discretion always is."

—Philip Stanhope

"Philosophy is nothing but discretion."

—John Selden

"Depart from discretion when it interferes with duty."

—Hannah More

Chapter 7

Figuratively Speaking

It Looked So Nice, They Used It Twice

In most cases—both in literature and in life—it is considered inelegant or sloppy to repeat oneself. Use of the same word, term, or phrase over and over is usually (at best) unnecessary, and often (at worst) distracting, pulling listeners out of a conversation or written passage. However, did you know there is an artful figure of speech entirely based upon repeating oneself? That's right. Perhaps the next time you find yourself retreading the same verbal ground, you can remember this article and finesse a fumbling faux pas into a refined figure of speech.

✳ ✳ ✳ ✳

THE WORD **DIAPHORA,** from a Greek word for "distinction" or "variance," names a figure of speech in which a word is repeated to serve two distinct purposes. The first purpose is to identify an individual person or group of persons, and the second purpose is to indicate qualities associated with the person or persons.

Diaphora Will Be Diaphora . . .

"Boys will be boys" is a common expression that illustrates the term, telling us that individual boys display the characteristics common to all boys. (Those characteristics will vary depending on whom you ask, but usually this phrase is used when some sort of mischief has been perpetrated by a male figure—and not always a young one.)

When the devout proclaim "our God is a mighty God," they are making use of a diaphora. They are saying that their god has particular characteristics ascribed generally to all deities—and, though it may not be explicitly stated, that their god is the mightiest (or most godly) of all.

Robert Burns's "A Man's a Man for a' That" is another example of diaphora. The title says it all: An individual man has the qualities of masculine identity despite all other circumstances ("a' That").

A crushing instance of diaphora occurred in the 1988 vice-presidential debate between Republican Dan Quayle and Democrat Lloyd Bentsen. In response to a comment in which Quayle compared himself with John F. Kennedy, Bentsen countered, "Senator, I served with Jack Kennedy. I knew Jack Kennedy. Jack Kennedy was a friend of mine. Senator, you are no Jack Kennedy."

... Except When It's Antanaclasis

A closely allied figure of speech is *antanaclasis,* in which a word is repeated—but in a different sense the second time. The great football coach Vince Lombardi's succinct "If you aren't fired with enthusiasm, you'll be fired with enthusiasm" is a classic example. *Fired,* meaning "motivated," is followed by *fired,* meaning "discharged." Benjamin Franklin's "Your argument is sound—all sound" is another example. *Sound,* meaning "solid, substantial, persuasive," is followed by *sound,* meaning "noise, wind."

✳ A related term is *amphibology,* in which an ambiguous grammatical structure carries the potential for more than one meaning. For more on amphibology, see page 80.

You're Better Than That

The art of rhetoric is the art of persuasion, and its strategies and terms are numerous. A particularly tricky tool is **epiplexis,** *in which the speaker tries to persuade an audience by chiding them.*

✳ ✳ ✳ ✳

EPIPLEXIS (FROM THE Greek root *plessein,* "to strike") often takes the form of a rhetorical question, in which a speaker or writer suggests something in the form of a question for which no answer is expected. With epiplexis, the speaker reproaches the audience not to plunge them into shame but to provoke them into action.

Writing in 1798 about sectional frictions in the new republic, Thomas Jefferson asked:

> *If to rid ourselves of the present rule of Massachusetts and Connecticut, we break the Union, will the evil stop there? Suppose the New England States alone cut off, will our nature be changed? Are we not men still to the south of that, and with all the passions of men?*

Epiplexis is perhaps not so gentle in all cases. "How could you have been so stupid?" is obviously not uttered to get an answer to the literal question, but instead to goad the listener into agreeing with the speaker rather than appear dim-witted.

Epiplexis can also be used to express strong emotion, such as grief or distress, rather than a more or less direct call to action. In the "O what a rogue" soliloquy in Shakespeare's *Hamlet,* the young prince berates himself for being too cowardly to avenge his father's murder. He calls himself a "peasant slave," an "ass," and "a dull and muddy-mettled rascal." After 40 lines of self-reproach, he finally bucks up and commits himself to action. Note that these barbs are not delivered through rhetorical questioning—which, though common, is not necessary for epiplexis. (See page 82 for more on rhetorical questions.)

Words of Wisdom: Failure

✳ ✳ ✳ ✳

"There is the greatest practical benefit in making a few failures early in life."
—Thomas Henry Huxley

"Far better it is to dare mighty things, to win glorious triumphs, even though checkered by failure, than to take rank with those poor spirits who neither enjoy much nor suffer much, because they live in the gray twilight that knows not victory or defeat."
—Theodore Roosevelt

"Those who dare to fail miserably can achieve greatly."
—Robert F. Kennedy

"Act as though it were impossible to fail."
—Ralph Waldo Emerson

"It is better to fail in originality than to succeed in imitation."
—Herman Melville

"My great concern is not whether you have failed, but whether you are content with your failure."
—Abraham Lincoln

"Of all failures, to fail in a witticism is the worst."
—Walter Savage Landor

"Failure is simply the opportunity to begin again, this time more intelligently."
—Henry Ford

"A person who doubts himself is like a man who would enlist in the ranks of his enemies and bear arms against himself. He makes his failure certain by himself being the first person to be convinced of it."
—Ambrose Bierce

Similar Opposites

Oxymorons *are combinations of words that contradict each other. But maybe that's, um, old news to you.*

❊   ❊   ❊   ❊

FROM JOHN DRYDEN'S great satire on bad poetry, "Mac Flecknoe," comes this gorgeous couplet:

> *His Brows thick Fogs, instead of Glories, grace,*
> *And lambent Dulness play'd around his Face.*

"Lambent Dulness," or glowing dimness, is an *oxymoron*, a combination for effect of two terms that are ordinarily contradictory. The word comes from the Greek *oxus*, meaning "sharp," and *moros*, "foolish"—so the word itself is oxymoronic.

Opposites Attract

In examples such as Dryden's, the oxymoron is an arresting figure of speech, demonstrating the power of the imaginative mind to discover similarities and correspondences even among opposites. Traditionally, the term refers to that discovery of similarities, of something surprisingly true, and not to a mere contradiction.

For example, the computer term *fuzzy logic* is a deliberate oxymoron. It refers to logical reasoning about conditions that can be "sort of" true or false. The oxymoron is used to highlight how different this is from traditional computer logic, which works in black and white, not shades of gray.

Many oxymorons have become commonplace, most commonly in adjective-noun combinations: *silent scream, deafening silence, sweet sorrow, open secret, jumbo shrimp*—even *bittersweet.*

Oxymoronic on Another Level

Sometimes apparent oxymorons can be made with one word that has two meanings—in such cases, one of those meanings will contrast with a second word. For example, *burn* usually refers to damage by heat, but can also refer to any damage from the elements. Hence the apparent oxymoron *freezer burn*.

Seriously can be a synonym for *very* as well as the opposite of *funny*, which leads us to the oxymoron *seriously funny*. James Thurber used this technique when he wrote, "That building is a little bit big and pretty ugly." Often, oxymorons are used deliberately and ironically, as in "that's a definite maybe," or "I think she did it accidentally on purpose."

In some cases, oxymorons show subtle distinctions of meaning. Someone may ask for an *original copy*, meaning a copy of an original, as opposed to a copy of a copy. Proposing to offer an *objective opinion* may cause some head-scratching, but the offer really promises an opinion without a specifically biased agenda behind it.

Here are some additional examples of oxymorons:

* act natural
* exact estimate
* rolling stop
* civil war
* living dead
* sound of silence
* clever fool
* only choice
* virtual reality
* constant variable
* paid volunteers

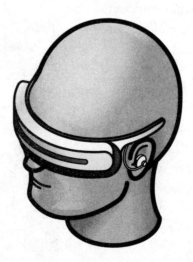

The Whole Enchilada

We're often told these days to be concise, to "keep it brief," to avoid wasting anyone else's time or energy by writing or blabbing on about anything more than is absolutely necessary. Brevity may indeed oftentimes be applaudable, but there is still a time and a place for those who enjoy being a bit more verbose with their vernacular.

* * * *

IN THE LATE twentieth century and early twenty-first century, prose has gotten leaner and leaner. Many writers model themselves on the kind of spare, understated writing favored by E. B. White and *The New Yorker*. To keep the fat off, they compress. For this purpose, authors commonly use two literary devices closely related to metaphor: *metonymy* (using one attribute to stand for the whole thing—e.g., *crown* for *royalty*) and *synecdoche* (using one part to stand in for the whole—e.g., *bread* for *food*). (See pages 658, 652, and 671 for more on metaphor, metonymy, and synecdoche, respectively.)

The Long Version

But sometimes writers want to be expansive rather than compact. A writer might prefer, for some purpose, to refer not to *Queen Elizabeth II*, but rather to *Her Britannic Majesty Elizabeth II, Queen of Great Britain and Northern Ireland, Defender of the Faith.* The latter description illustrates **merismus,** or **merism,** in which rather than mentioning the part for the whole, the parts of the whole are separated and enumerated.

A more common example is the expression "lock, stock, and barrel," used to mean "the entire entity." Some might think the expression has something to do with warehousing—imagining the lock on the door, all the stock inside, and even the barrels containing the stock. But the expression actually describes the parts of a rifle: the lock, or firing mechanism (as in a *flintlock*); the stock, or butt; and the barrel. The separation and enumeration of the parts, not the concept of a rifle, is what represents "absolutely everything." A similar example (with a similar meaning) is "body and soul."

I'll Love You More than Always

Another commonly encountered type of merismus is the use of polar-opposite words to signify "... and everything in between." A traditional wedding vow, for example, includes the words "for better or for worse, for richer, for poorer, in sickness and in health." It's true that "always" or "no matter what" might say the same thing more efficiently, but those are hardly words to bring a tear to the eye.

Merismus—from the Greek *merismos*, "a dividing," and *merizo*, "to divide into parts"—was a popular literary tool in the sixteenth and seventeenth centuries, when English writers reveled in being expansive and elaborate. In modern times, authors favor brevity over elaboration. Even so, sometimes it's important to draw attention to a concept through its details. When used appropriately, such tactics can sometimes help a reader (or listener) get to know a given topic quite thoroughly—or, as some might choose to put it, backwards and forwards.

✳ **The British monarch's title "Defender of the Faith" was originally conferred upon King Henry VIII by Pope Leo X in 1521, in thanks for Henry's treatise condemning Martin Luther's reformist views. When Henry later broke with Rome and made the Church of England autonomous, Pope Paul III retracted the title. English Parliament later "granted" the title to the king, and his successors continue to use it to this day.**

Words of Wisdom: Magic

✳ ✳ ✳ ✳

"Make no little plans; they have no magic to stir men's blood."
—DANIEL BURNHAM

"Any sufficiently advanced technology is indistinguishable from magic."
—ARTHUR C. CLARKE

"O magic sleep! O comfortable bird,
That broodest o'er the troubled sea of the mind
Till it is hushed and smooth."
—JOHN KEATS

"All that mankind has done, thought, gained or been: it is lying as in magic preservation in the pages of books."
—THOMAS CARLYLE

"Magicians can do more by means of faith than phyisicians by the truth."
—GIORDANO BRUNO

"Magic is believing in yourself, if you can do that, you can make anything happen."
—JOHANN WOLFGANG VON GOETHE

What If?

A **hypothetical** is a "what if…?" Hypotheticals are valuable
because they allow people to explore different possibilities before
committing themselves to action.

✳   ✳   ✳   ✳

STEMMING FROM THE Greek *hypo-* ("under") + *thesis* ("a
placing, proposition"), a hypothetical question asks what
the consequences of a particular action or course of action
might be. In science, a *hypothesis* is a provisional explanation
of some phenomenon to be tested.

Job applicants may be required to field some hypothetical questions, with the specific answer being less important than what
the answer reveals about him or her: *What would you do if you
discovered that a colleague had plagiarized material for an article?*
A candidate's answer will reveal something about their attitude
toward the ethics of plagiarism, of course, but also about how
they might address a touchy workplace situation.

In science and philosophy, specialized "what if" questions called
thought experiments are a legitimate form of research. Thought
experiments can't always be tested scientifically, but they allow
researchers to speculate on how a principle might function in a
given situation. For example, one famous thought experiment
poses the question of whether an infinite number of monkeys
typing for an infinite amount of time would eventually produce
the complete works of Shakespeare.

Some hypothetical questions are unanswerable because they
pose paradoxes: *If God is all-powerful, could he create a stone so
heavy that he could not lift it himself? Which came first, the chicken
or the egg?* (For more on paradoxes, see page 666.) These questions engage our minds, prompting discussion of complex
topics that yield no easy answers. People will continue to
discuss such topics as long as the monkeys keep typing.

Coulda, Shoulda, Woulda

It's usually best to try to use the established pronunciation of a given word in order to make sure that the given word is understood properly by your intended audience. But changes in standard or common pronunciation do occur over time, sometimes due to the loss of a letter or syllable from a word.

✳   ✳   ✳   ✳

IF YOU FAINT, a doctor will diagnose your problem as *syncope,* a temporary interruption of adequate blood flow to the brain. The word comes from a Greek word meaning "to cut short." Similarly, if you drop a letter or syllable from a word, altering its pronunciation and perhaps its spelling as well, a linguist will call *that* syncope. Syncope is one variety of *metaplasm* (see page 290).

Progressive Pronunciation

This practice is actually quite common in speech, due to people's common tendency to swallow letters or whole syllables as they speak, as well as the pattern over time of detaching pronunciation of words from their spellings. The word *interesting,* for example, is usually pronounced "IN-trest-ing" in standard speech.

Similarly, *extraordinary* often comes out "ex-TROR-din-ayr-ee." People who sound out all the syllables ("IN-tur-est-ing," "ex-truh-OR-din-ayr-ee") may seem as if they're trying too hard to sound intelligent.

Several, diaper, and *vacuum* have all gradually come to be pronounced as two-syllable words in standard English. *Family, grocery, chocolate,* and *conference* appear to be headed in the same direction, though there are pockets of resistance, and *omelet* is all over the place, sometimes pronounced with two syllables, sometimes with three. But the tendency in English is that once a letter or syllable drops out of a word in speech, it stays gone.

If You've Ever Wondered How Exactly to Pronounce *Worcestershire*...

If you have a bottle of Worcestershire sauce in the kitchen cabinet, you (might) know that syncope dictates that it is pronounced "WUHS-ti-shur." In England, *Gloucester* is "GLAHS-tur," and *Cholmondeley*, mystifyingly, is "CHUM-lee."

Writers who try to reproduce the sounds of everyday speech will write *gonna* for *going to* and *wanna* for *want to*, though these usages have yet to make their way into formal writing. Many instances of syncope, however, have become standard. For example, *boatswain* (a petty officer on a merchant ship who is in charge of hull maintenance) long ago came to be pronounced as "BO-sun," not "BOT-swayn," and the variant spelling *bos'n* followed suit.

More formal examples of syncope can be found in poetry, with *o'er* used for *over* in places where a single syllable fits the rhythm better than two. *Heaven* similarly becomes *heav'n*, *never* becomes *ne'er*, and *every* becomes *ev'ry*.

✳ *Apocope* **is the term for omitting a syllable at the end of a word.** *Oft* **for** *often* **and** *morn* **for** *morning* **are among the poetic examples.** *Photo* **for** *photograph* **is one you will certainly recognize from common usage.** *Aphaeresis* **is the term for dropping an initial vowel, as in** *'cept* (*accept* **or** *except*), *'tention* (*attention*), **and** *'bout* (*about*)**.**

If A and B, Then C

Those who struggle with logical reasoning should read this article. Are you one who struggles with logical reasoning? If so, it then follows that you should read this article. See what we did there? If not, read on.

❊   ❊   ❊   ❊

I T WAS ARISTOTLE who invented the *syllogism*—from the Greek word *sullogismos*, or "reasoning"—as a device to try out deductive reasoning. A syllogism has three propositions (two premises and a conclusion), and it operates like this: If premise A (the major premise) is true, and premise B (the minor premise) is true, then the conclusion C must also be true.

Here's a common example:

> *All men are mortal.*
> *Socrates is a man.*
> *Socrates is mortal.*

Some Syllogistic Basics

As you can see, the conclusion of the syllogism above has terms in common with both its major and minor premises.

A syllogism's premises and conclusions are either affirmative or negative, and either universal or particular. This allows only four types of statement: universal affirmative ("All dogs have fleas"), universal negative ("No dogs have fleas"), particular affirmative ("My dog has fleas"), and particular negative ("My dog does not have fleas"). These can be combined in patterns that have been taught in logic classes since the Middle Ages. Simple, right?

Spurious Syllogisms

Unfortunately, no. Syllogisms can go wrong quite easily. For example, be careful which term from the major premise you repeat. You can easily—and quickly—arrive at a nonsensical, invalid syllogism. For example, to make the syllogism below work, what we really needed was a minor premise about trees, not about green things:

All trees are green. (major premise)
Peas are green. (minor premise)
Peas are trees. (conclusion)

When one of the terms has more than one meaning—a real hazard in English—watch out:

All tables have legs.
A set of data organized into rows and columns is a table.
A set of data organized into rows and columns has legs.

If the major premise is false, the conclusion will therefore also be false:

Louisville is the capital of Kentucky. (Actually, it's Frankfort.)
Judy lives in Louisville.
Judy lives in the state capital.

Attempting to make a single instance a generalization results in the same kind of trouble:

Alice's cat does not like chicken.
Scout and Graymalkin are cats.
Scout and Graymalkin do not like chicken.

It may be true that Scout and Graymalkin do not like chicken, but this has not been demonstrated logically.

In fact, if you are not careful, you are as likely to go wrong with a syllogism as to go right.

This Device Is Not Unheard Of

Imagine that you've spent hours carefully preparing a meal for a dinner guest. You watch as your guest takes their first bite, and then proclaims the dish to be..."surprisingly undisgusting."*

✻   ✻   ✻   ✻

Is THIS A compliment? Well, sort of. Your guest has expressed an opinion by negating its opposite. This device, which is not at all uncommon, is called **litotes** (pronounced LY-tuh-teez or, less commonly, ly-TO-teez).

It is not rare to find litotes, a form of understatement, in literature as well as in casual speech. Sometimes it is used to "damn with faint praise," as the saying goes. To say that someone is "not unkind" could mean that the person is, in fact, kind—or it could mean that the person is just on the edge of being unkind, but you don't actually want to come out and say that. In the same fashion, one might describe a suitor as "not unattractive," meaning, usually, that their appearance is unremarkable.

In speech, it is not hard to tell when litotes is being used in this way. If the emphasis is on the *un-* in "not unattractive," it is not unlikely that the person has average looks. If the emphasis is on the *not*, however, it could mean that the person is very far from unattractive—in fact, maybe quite attractive.

Litotes, then, can also be used to intensify a statement. Queen Victoria's famous line, "We are not amused," would not be nearly so quotable had she just said, "We are really annoyed!" In this case, the negation exaggerates her feelings so that it is clear that she is far beyond amusement and well into irritation or anger. In an example not dissimilar to the previous one, a writer who claims "the rising tide of mediocrity is no small problem" is emphasizing just how not small (i.e., large) the problem is.

By the way, there are not a few instances of litotes on this page. Can you find them all?

Word Roots and Branches
An (In)Famous Prefix

We live in a celebrity-obsessed society, and thanks to "reality" television and star-making competitions, many of us dream of becoming celebrities ourselves, if only for a moment.

✳ ✳ ✳ ✳

WITH ALL THIS celebrity worship, one might think that the root *celeb-* would produce many words. But surprisingly, there are only a handful of *celeb-* words.

Celebrity, from the Latin *celebritatem*, meaning "fame, renown, crowded conditions," has been in English use since at least 1600. It originally meant "fame, notoriety," a meaning it still holds. The sense of "a famous person," however, is relatively recent, having been with us only since the mid-nineteenth century. The short form, *celeb*, has been around since at least 1913.

Of course, there is the verb *to celebrate*, meaning "to perform a rite or ceremony" as well as "to proclaim, extol." And there are the *celebrants* who perform the rites and proclamations in question. A bride and groom may *celebrate* their marriage, but it is the priest, minister, rabbi, or other officiant who is the *celebrant*.

Other celebrated words include:

✳ *celebutante*—a blend of *celebrity* and *debutante*, an Americanism from 1939 denoting a famous socialite

✳ *célèbre*—from the French, is chiefly known in the phrase *cause célèbre*, meaning a "famous legal case" or a "notorious thing, incident, or episode"

✳ *celebrable*—the granddaddy of them all. Meaning "worthy of being famous," it was coined by Geoffrey Chaucer back around 1380. But evidently the word was not in itself very celebrable—as no other writer has used it since.

Just for the Pun of It

Puns have been described as "a short quip followed by a long groan." **Puns** *are plays on words, based either on different meanings of the same word or on similar meanings or sounds of different words.*

✳ ✳ ✳ ✳

CHILDREN DELIGHT IN discovering that one word can be confused with another because of similar sounds, which makes punning popular in juvenile circles. Take a typical knock-knock joke as an example:

> Knock, knock. *Who's there?*
> Doris. *Doris who?*
> Doris locked; that's why I had to knock.

Not All Pun and Games

Because punning can be simple and is often mined for an easy laugh, some call it a low form of humor. However, punning can be elevated to a more clever form of wordplay. Shakespeare was notoriously given to punning, as evidenced in this exchange in Act III of *Othello:*

> CLOWN: Are these, I pray you, wind instruments?
> FIRST MUSICIAN: Ay, marry, they are, sir.
> CLOWN: O, thereby hangs a tale.
> FIRST MUSICIAN: Whereby hangs a tale, sir?
> CLOWN: Marry, sir, by many a wind instrument that I know.

"Thereby hangs a tale," meaning "there's a story in that," first gives an opportunity to pun on *tail*. Then there's the joke of treating *wind instrument* both as a musical instrument and as the source of flatulence.

Literary Pundamentals

When punning grows up and gets serious, it is called *paronomasia.* One of the most famous examples comes from the

Gospel of Matthew, which quotes Jesus as saying, "And I tell you that you are Peter, and on this rock I will build my church" (16:18 NIV). In the Greek of the New Testament, the pun is clear: *Peter* is *petros,* and *rock* is *petra.*

Lewis Carroll delighted in wordplay, and the Alice books are full of puns. When Alice tries to explain to the Duchess, "You see the earth takes twenty-four hours to turn round on its axis," the Duchess mishears *axis,* interrupts Alice, and proclaims, "Talking of axes . . . chop off her head!"

In twentieth-century literature, mighty wielders of the pun include James Joyce, whose *Finnegans Wake* is virtually an alternate world built on multiple plays on words. Vladimir Nabokov also indulges in the practice. There's a reference in *Lolita* to "The Bustle—A Deceitful Seatful," in which the author adds the double rhyme to the play on *seat* and *full.*

Thus one can see that the pun links both the lowest and the highest writing.

Where Did It Come From?

IOU: Believe it or not, it's nothing more than the obvious pun on "I owe you," but it goes all the way back to 1618.

Putting Something In, Taking Something Out

We've all come to the realization at one point or another: Change is inevitable. This holds true in most areas of life, and the world of words and language is no exception to the rule.

✳   ✳   ✳   ✳

A METAPLASM (from the Greek *metap-lasso*, meaning "to mold differently, remodel") is a change in the spelling, and therefore pronuncia-tion, of a word. In English, letters and syllables are added, omitted, inverted, and substituted all the time—sometimes by design, sometimes by chance or ignorance. In poetry or lyrics, metaplasm can help words fit nicely into a metrical pattern or rhythm.

The Gang's All Here

What follows is a list of specific terms for different types of metaplasm. A familiarity with these metaplasm varieties is certainly nice, but thorough knowledge of them is not essential for the purposes of most writers or language users. You can, however, use these terms to stun your friends at parties.

✳ *antisthecon*—the substitution of a sound: *dawg* for *dog*

✳ *aphaeresis*—the subtraction of a syllable from the beginning of a word: "reading, writing, and 'rithmetic"

✳ *apocope*—the subtraction of a syllable from the end of a word: "And when I ope my lips, let no dog bark!" (Shakespeare, *The Merchant of Venice*)

* *epenthesis*—the addition of a syllable to the middle of a word: *umbrella* pronounced as *umberella*, *athlete* as *athalete*, *realtor* as *realator*

* *metathesis*—the transposition of letters in the middle of a word: mistaking *cavalry* (troops on horseback) for *Calvary* (site of Jesus' crucifixion), saying *revelant* for *relevant*, or the (unfortunately) ever-popular mispronunciation of *nuclear* as *nucular*

* *proparalepsis*—the addition of a syllable to the end of a word: "Thanks muchly"

* *prosthesis*—the addition of a syllable before a word: *beloved* for *loved* (You probably already know *prosthesis* for its use naming an artificial body part added to replace one that is missing.)

* *syncope*—the subtraction or reduction of a letter or syllable from the middle of a word: *over* becomes *o'er*, *heaven* becomes *heav'n*, etc. In the musical *Cats*, the word *memory* in the song of the same name is pronounced *mem'ry*. (In music, *syncopation* is an unexpected movement of stressed and unstressed beats.) Turn to page 282 to read more about syncope and see many additional examples.

---

* A related term is *tmesis,* in which a word or phrase is inserted into the middle of another word. It usually carries some emphasis or comic effect, as when an Englishman says, "abso-bloody-lutely," or when *The Simpsons'* Ned Flanders proclaims, "Ned Flanders at your ser-diddily-ervice."

* Poet e. e. cummings is perhaps best known for ignoring the conventional rules of grammar and spelling. In doing so, he made a name for himself as one of the great innovators of language. His famous poem "r-p-o-p-h-e-s-s-a-g-r" (a play on the word *grasshopper*) uses the misspelling to imitate the lively movement of the insect itself.

Cran-tastic!

If you're a wordaholic who loves the funtastic challenge of forming new language, well, this vocab-rific article is for you.

✳ ✳ ✳ ✳

THE PREFIX CRAN- is an example of, and the inspiration for, what linguists like to call **cranberry morphemes**. A *morpheme* (from *morph*, meaning "shape") is a structural element of a word, root, prefix, or suffix. It is in opposition to a *phoneme*, which is a distinct sound.

Cran- is not a traditional prefix, of course, but that hasn't stopped Ocean Spray and other cranberry producers from using it as a prefix in compounds like *cranapple*, *crangrape*, *cranraspberry*, and *crantastic*.

This *cran-morphing* is not restricted to the tart red berries. There are other "cranberry" morphemes used to form new words. The morpheme *-licious*, from *delicious*, is popular in forming words having to do with food. We get *veganlicious* for tasty vegan food, for example. The morpheme *-rific*, from *terrific*, is also popular. *Tea-rific* is used in advertising tea, and it's a particularly deft coinage. Another favorite morpheme is *-tastic*, as in *fantastic*. *Funtastic* is a classic, and *shoe-tastic*, *carpet-tastic*, and *swim-tastic* have all been used to sell products. (For more on the suffix *-licious*, see page 580.)

There is also *-aholic*, used to semiseriously denote addiction. It's from *alcoholic*, of course, but is used in words like *shopaholic* and *chocoholic*, which name those in conditions a bit less dire.

For the ultimate in cranberry morpheme goodness, you have to look at *blog-*. This prefix denoting an Internet journal is used in many compounds, such as *blogosphere*. But it is also combined with other cranberry morphemes to provide 100-percent cranmorphtastic goodness. We've got *blogorific*, *bloglicious*, and *blogtastic*, of course. But there's *bloggerific* and *blognoscenti* too.

Words of Wisdom: Science

❋ ❋ ❋ ❋

"Learn the ABC of science before you try to ascend to its summit."

—IVAN PAVLOV

"Whoever, in the pursuit of science, seeks after immediate practical utility, may generally rest assured that he will seek in vain."

—HERMANN VON HELMHOLTZ

"Science is built up with facts, as a house is with stones. But a collection of facts is no more a science than a heap of stones is a house."

—JULES POINCARÉ

"I am sorry to say that there is too much point to the wisecrack that life is extinct on other planets because their scientists were more advanced than ours."

—JOHN F. KENNEDY

"There are in fact two things, science and opinion; the former begets knowledge, the latter ignorance."

—HIPPOCRATES

"It has become appallingly obvious that our technology has exceeded our humanity."

—ALBERT EINSTEIN

"Men have become the tools of their tools."

—HENRY DAVID THOREAU

"One machine can do the work of fifty ordinary men. No machine can do the work of one extraordinary man."

—ELBERT HUBBARD

The Smallest Prefix?

The prefix nano- *has a very specific technical sense of "one billionth," or 10^{-9}, but in general it just denotes something that is very, very small.*

✳ ✳ ✳ ✳

WHILE NANO- HAS its roots in the Latin and Greek of antiquity, it's a very recent addition to the English language. *Nano-* is from the Latin *nanus*, or "dwarf," and ultimately the Greek *nanos*, also meaning "dwarf."

There were a couple of *nano-* words borrowed from French at the beginning of the twentieth century, but for the most part, *nano-* has only been in English use since the middle of the last century. *Nanoid* ("resembling a dwarf; dwarfish") is one of the few *nano-* words that date to the mid-nineteenth century.

At present there aren't many *nano-* words in the dictionary— only 50 or so in the *Oxford English Dictionary*—but this is changing: The prefix is becoming more and more productive as technology enables us to create things that are smaller and smaller. Some of the *nano-* words are:

✳ *nanoampere*—a billionth of an ampere of electrical current

✳ *nanodevice*—a tiny machine

✳ *nanoelectronics*—nanoscale electronic devices

✳ *nanofabrication*—methods for producing nanoscale devices

✳ *nanogram*—one billionth of a gram

✳ *nanosecond*—a billionth of a second; more generally, a very short period of time

✳ *nanotechnology*—technology that deals in dimensions of a

billion of a meter, or manipulates individual atoms and molecules

* *nanowire*—a wire with a diameter of a few nanometers

Nano- is a useful prefix for coining new words. Here are some nonce words that are making their way into the common hipster vernacular:

* *nanobabble*—the ultimate in small talk

* *nanomanage*—to try to control someone's every action—a nanomanager is even worse than a micromanager!

* *nano nap*—a seconds-long nap that you accidently take during a boring lecture or meeting. It's usually so short no one but you notices—thank goodness.

You might notice that the *nano-* prefix typically attaches itself to a whole, stand-alone word—what's known as a *free morph*. There's at least one exception, however: *nanobot*, a contracted form of *nano-* and *robot*, referring to a nanoscale machine, usually capable of reproducing itself. It may sound like science fiction, but nanobots appear to be a very real part of the technology of the future. There's even talk of the development of nanobots that can enter the human body to perform various medical procedures. Now that's no small feat.

---

* Now you know how the Apple Nano got its name! Conceived as a replacement for the iPod Mini, it was half as thick as its predecessor and 25 percent narrower.

* On the other end of the spectrum from the *nano-* prefix: Physicists at the University of California-Davis are trying to have the popular slang term *hella* introduced into the English language as the official word for 10 to the 27th power (10^{27}, or 1,000,000,000,000,000,000,000,000,000). The word actually makes an appearance in the *Oxford English Dictionary*, though not as a scientific term. Rather, it was first entered in 1987, with the meaning of "very," or "a lot" (as in, "We had a hella good time at the party").

Department of Redundancy Department

Many people find redundant phrases irritating—free gift, safe haven, and advance planning, for example. Generally speaking, using more words than are required to say what you want to say, repeating the same idea in only slightly different words, going round and round the barn without forward progress, and fatiguing readers by inflicting on them incessant and unrelenting repetitions is thought to be a bad thing. (See how it works?) **Tautology** *is the repetition of the same idea in different words.*

✳ ✳ ✳ ✳

AUTOLOGY COMES FROM the Greek *tautologos*, or "repeating what has been said." In *A Dictionary of Modern English Usage*, H. W. Fowler called it "saying the same thing; i.e., as one has already said," and he did not admire it.

Intentional, Deliberate Tautologies

Repetitions that appear to be unintentional, or are performed clumsily, are labeled tautologies, but it is certainly possible for someone to make limited intentional use of tautology to increase the impact of an idea by driving it home—just as a carpenter's carefully aimed blows with a hammer fasten the nail with a minimum of repeated strokes.

Take, for example, the familiar phrase from Abraham Lincoln's second inaugural address: "with malice toward none, with charity for all." The phrase expresses the same sense of generosity of spirit twice, in similar words, but carries its effect by stating the idea first in the negative, then in the positive.

It's a Tautological, Tautological World

Many geographical features and locales bear tautological names. For instance, the Sahara Desert literally means "Desert Desert," since *sahara* means "desert" in Arabic. Similarly, Lake Tahoe means "Lake Lake" in Washo, and the Mississippi River is "Big River River" in Algonquin. The world's most extreme example of a tautological place name is probably Torpenhow Hill of west England (locally pronounced "TRUHP-en-hah"). *Tor*, *pen*, and *how* all mean "hill" in different languages, the first two being Celtic and the last being Anglo-Saxon. Therefore, Torpenhow Hill literally means "Hillhillhill Hill."

✳ *Pleonasm* is a subtly different form of tautology in which unnecessary or redundant words are used to convey a particular meaning. For example, in the phrase "Could you please reiterate that again?" *again* is already implicit because the definition of *to reiterate* is "to say or do again." Similarly, there's no need to say "a round circle," because by definition all circles are perfectly round.

✳ If you really enjoy repeating yourself, turn to page 272 to read up on *diaphora*, a figure of speech in which the same word is used twice to serve two different purposes. With both diaphora and tautology in your bag of linguistic tricks, who knows what verbal acrobatics you'll be able to pull off—again and again! And again...

Where Did It Come From?

Chestnut: Other than the nut itself, this word is also used to describe an oft-repeated joke or story. It came about as part of *The Broken Sword,* a popular play in 1816. In it, two characters banter back and forth, ending with one saying the answer is "chestnut"—that is, he knows because he's heard the story 27 times. By the 1880s, *chestnut* came to mean that very thing: a story told over and over again.

What's Missing?

Let's face it . . . there's just not enough time in the day. With so many emails to send and text messages to fire off . . . who has time to compose entire sentences anymore? Thankfully, we do have a few tricks to save us from such a tedious fate. Among them . . . the **ellipsis***! There's so much we could say about this useful piece of punctuation . . . but we'll just let the next paragraph take over.*

✳ ✳ ✳ ✳

Most people are familiar with the punctuation mark that stands in for text that has been left out of a quoted statement. The mark is composed of three spaced periods, and many people know that it is called an ellipsis (the plural form being *ellipses*).

Ellipsis Logistics

The ellipsis is used to conserve space and to clarify meaning by deleting unnecessary or irrelevant parts of quoted text. It is typographically acceptable to use three periods in a row (...) or with spaces between them (. . .), but standards can vary. (Consistency of spacing in a given work is most important.)

Ellipses should be used judiciously when quoting a source, as they can lead to confusion or outright deception. If a poster or commercial for a new movie quotes a review as saying, "This was the best . . . movie I've seen all year!" you would not be out of line to translate that as "the best [darn] movie" or "the best [action] movie." But if the original review actually said, "This was the best [example of a poorly conceived, acted, and directed] movie I've seen all year," you might leave the theater feeling sorely disappointed. Meanwhile, the movie's PR team cherish their own wit—and the studio counts its millions.

No Sense in Repeating Oneself!

Ellipsis has another definition, however. It also appears in linguistics with a meaning closely related to the function of the punctuation mark. Especially in casual speech and writing, there are many instances where technically necessary words can be dropped from a sentence without detracting from the listener's understanding—that dropping is called *ellipsis*.

This happens most often when a word is being repeated in a series of phrases or clauses. One can just as well say, "I have my faults, and he, his" as "I have my faults and he has his," because the repetition of the verb *to have* can be inferred by the listener. Nouns can undergo ellipsis too: "I have my faults, and he has his." Here, the noun *fault* is left out of the second clause because the listener will easily understand that *fault* is the object of both clauses.

Even entire phrases can be subtracted using ellipsis, and in these cases the dropped words usually don't appear elsewhere in the sentence. You could ask, "What's going to happen if I don't finish my homework?" or, just as easily, "What if I don't finish my homework?" Even though the "is going to happen" has been omitted in the second statement, the sense of the sentence remains the same.

In any case, ellipsis is best avoided if confusion could result, but when used appropriately, it is perfectly acceptable even in formal speech or writing.

Where Did It Come From?

Polka Dot: Back in the 1830s, a new dance from Bohemia (the *polka*, or "Polish woman") was all the rage. People rushed to combine the name with everyday items. When a new fabric came out in the United States that featured round, evenly spaced dots, it was dubbed the polka dot. Connecting the fabric with the fad worked, and the name stuck.

Words of Wisdom: Language

✳ ✳ ✳ ✳

"Kindness is the language which the deaf can hear and the blind can see."

—MARK TWAIN

"If you talk to a man in a language he understands, that goes to his head. If you talk to him in his language, that goes to his heart."

—NELSON MANDELA

"The best part of human language, properly so called, is derived from reflection on the acts of the mind itself."

—SAMUEL TAYLOR COLERIDGE

"England and America are two countries separated by the same language."

—GEORGE BERNARD SHAW

"If you don't say anything, you won't be called on to repeat it."

—CALVIN COOLIDGE

"The limits of my language means the limits of my world."

—LUDWIG WITTGENSTEIN

"The language of friendship is not words but meanings."

—HENRY DAVID THOREAU

"Language gradually varies, and with it fade away the writings of authors who have flourished their allotted time."

—WASHINGTON IRVING

"To have another language is to possess a second soul."

—CHARLEMAGNE

"All speech, written or spoken, is a dead language, until it finds a willing and prepared hearer."

—ROBERT LOUIS STEVENSON

"The poetical language of an age should be the current language heightened, to any degree heightened and unlike itself, but not...an obsolete one."

—GERARD MANLEY HOPKINS

"High thoughts must have high language."

—ARISTOPHANES

"A well-written Life is almost as rare as a well-spent one."

—THOMAS CARLYLE

"When one man dies, one chapter is not torn out of the book, but translated into a better language."

—JOHN DONNE

"I wish he would explain his explanation."

—GEORGE GORDON, LORD BYRON

"Words should be employed as the means, not the end; language is the instrument, conviction is the work."

—JOSHUA REYNOLDS

"You taught me language; and my profit on 't is, I know how to curse: the red plague rid you, for learning me your language."

—WILLIAM SHAKESPEARE, *THE TEMPEST*

"Money speaks sense in a language all nations understood."

—APHRA BEHN

"Language is the archives of history...Language is fossil poetry."

—RALPH WALDO EMERSON

Human Eyes Humanize

Call it poetry or call it arrogance, but human beings have a definite history of looking for the humanness in anything and everything that surrounds them.

❋　❋　❋　❋

THE ACT OF ascribing human characteristics to nonhumans, particularly gods and animals, is called **anthropomorphism.** It surely has its origins in the prescientific era, when our distant ancestors explained the world by seeing natural objects and phenomena as akin to themselves.

Anthropomorphism is common in the figures of Greek and Roman mythology. Deities are not human, but in human form they exhibit human qualities: The goddess Aphrodite is an embodiment of love, for example; the goddess Athena, wisdom. Natural forces such as fire, thunder, the ocean, and even death itself are symbolized by powerful gods that possess human characteristics and motivations such as jealousy, anger, and affection for favored humans.

I Want YOU to Understand Personification

Personification is a closely allied technique, and the distinction between the two is subtle. While both ascribe human traits to nonhumans, personification designates an inanimate object or abstraction as the embodiment of something else, endowing it with human qualities or representing it as possessing human form. For example, we might personify the weather as Mother Nature or the United States of America in the figure of Uncle Sam. Personification is also known as *prosopopoeia.*

Although anthropomorphism and personification are often found in nature (think angry thunderclouds, waving branches, and the man in the moon), it's also common for people to see human qualities in artificial objects. We often ascribe motivations and emotions to our technological gadgets. One might say, "My car is being stubborn today," or "My computer really hates me."

Bringing Death to Life

Personification is a favorite form of metaphor in literature and in poetry. For example, Emily Dickinson portrays Death as the driver of a carriage, taking her toward eternity:

Because I could not stop for Death—
He kindly stopped for me—
The carriage held but just ourselves—
And Immortality.

Even everyone's favorite everyman, Homer Simpson, has been known to use personification:

The only monster here is the gambling monster that has enslaved your mother! I call him Gamblor, and it's time to snatch your mother from his neon claws!

Simply put, it's human nature to want to make things more like us. Look back to the 1970s, when pet rocks were a popular fad: People were able to envision personality in something as simple as a rock.

✳ Uncle Sam has been used as a personification of the United States since the War of 1812. The most familiar image of Uncle Sam—as an elderly, goateed man in a dark blue suit, white shirt, and red tie—comes from a 1917 army recruiting poster. His stern look, pointing finger, and slogan ("I Want YOU for U.S. Army") create the sense of authority needed to bring in new soldiers.

You Can't Be Serious

*It's a safe bet to say that most of us hear the word **irony** or the phrase "that's ironic" used all the time, in all kinds of situations—some proper, some not. Some of us even put the word through such use—and abuse—ourselves. But despite these current woes, there is a rich history behind irony that can help us to illuminate proper use of the word today.*

❋   ❋   ❋   ❋

IN CURRENT USAGE, the words *irony* and *sarcasm* are often used interchangeably. That's too bad, because irony has a long history as not just one, but several related philosophical and literary techniques.

Here's the Breakdown

❋ *Socratic irony*, in which a speaker feigned ignorance for the purpose of interrogating an interlocutor's beliefs, was fundamental to the Socratic method.

❋ *Dramatic irony* is when the audience understands a meaning the character doesn't; one of the most famous examples occurs in Sophocles' *Oedipus the King*, in which the audience knows that Oedipus is pushing forward to solve a murder only to discover that he has killed his father and married his mother.

❋ *Situational irony* is when an action has unintended or unexpected results. Dorothy's companions in *The Wizard of Oz* seek to acquire a brain, a heart, and courage, only to discover in the end that they already possessed what they were looking for.

⁎ And *verbal irony* occurs when a character's meaning is different from what she says.

These were Shakespeare's favorite tools. Critics should treat them with care, and not flatter snarky teenagers saying "whatever" by calling them ironic. Instead, call them detached, or at least call them sarcastic.

Irony vs. Sarcasm

Sarcasm is similar to irony in that both can mean a distinction between what is said and what is meant. However, sarcasm is meant to wound rather than to entertain or inform. In fact, the word *sarcasm* comes from the Greek *sarkazein*, meaning "to tear the flesh." (For more on sarcasm, see page 72.)

The real story behind the blurring of *ironic* and *sarcastic*, writes linguist Geoffrey Nunberg in *The Way We Talk Now*, is that irony used to be considered lighthearted and has gotten meaner, while sarcasm used to be considered nasty and is getting nicer. It used to be, says Nunberg, that "with irony you're winking at your listener, whereas with sarcasm you're sticking out your tongue. Irony is a private joke, sarcasm is public ridicule."

Now that irony has gotten darker, and sarcasm more lighthearted, it's hard to tell the difference. But, as they say: whatever.

⁎ Mere *coincidence* is sometimes mislabeled as irony. "Both students failed the examination; ironically, both had eaten a hearty breakfast that morning" is a statement of coincidence, not irony.

Chapter 8

A Play on Words

Caesar Shifts

As a child, did you ever use codes to write secret messages to your friends, or even just to write something in your diary that you wanted no one else to be able to read? If so, you may have used methods similar to those discussed in this article—and it turns out such methods predated you by more than a few years.

✳   ✳   ✳   ✳

CAESAR SHIFTS ARE a type of wordplay derived from an old enciphering method in which letters are moved a given distance ahead in the alphabet. A Caesar cipher is a simple substitution cipher: If letters move ten spaces ahead in the alphabet, *ghost* becomes *qrycd* (the alphabet wraps around from *z* to *a* when counting). Caesar himself used the cipher to send secret messages, but since it's easy to break, it's not actually very useful for keeping things secret.

Et Tu, Vigenère?

A variation that's trickier (although still vulnerable to expert cryptanalysts) is the Vigenère cipher, in which a keyword is chosen—say, *chew*. Each letter of the keyword represents a different Caesar cipher alphabet; *c* is the alphabet in which *a* is encoded as *c* (that is, the cipher in which every letter is shifted two letters ahead). Each letter of each word in a message is encoded by the different cipher alphabets in sequence, so *know* would become *muss* ($k + 2$, $n + 7$, $o + 4$, $w + 22$).

Of course, most words won't accidentally become other words in a Vigenère cipher, but that helps bring us back to the wordplay meaning of *Caesar shift*: a word that makes another word when its letters shift the same number of steps forward in the alphabet.

Let's Shift into Some Examples...

For example, *irk* shifted 13 steps ahead makes its synonym, *vex*, and applying the same shift to *tang* makes *gnat*, its semordnilap (see page 311). The French *oui* can be translated into the English *yes* by shifting it ten letters ahead. A *cold* may cause a *frog* (three ahead) in one's throat, and someone of good *cheer* is clearly *jolly* (seven ahead). *HAL*, the computer from Stanley Kubrick's *2001: A Space Odyssey*, is just one letter from *IBM*. Many have assumed this to be intentional, but it was a coincidence.

Long Caesar shift pairs are rare, but here are some:

✳ *adder/beefs* (1)

✳ *banjo/ferns, pecan/tiger* (4)

✳ *fizzy/kneed* (5)

✳ *chain/ingot, jimmy/posse, mocha/suing, munch/satin, fusion/layout* (6)

✳ *timer/aptly, nonet/uvula, wheel/dolls, manful/thumbs* (7)

✳ *river/arena, sleep/bunny* (9)

✳ *cubed/melon* (10)

✳ *spots/dazed* (11)

✳ *purely/Cheryl, nowhere/abjurer* (13)

Larger sets exist as well. Listening to *ABBA* is a *deed* (three ahead) you might perform at *noon* (ten further ahead). And *god* + 8 = *owl*; *owl* + 4 = *sap*; *sap* + 4 = *wet*. To create your own Caesar shifts, give it a *try* and see if you can make anything *gel* (13).

Highly Unusual Endings

Can you name more than two English words ending in -gry?

❋ ❋ ❋ ❋

BEYOND *HUNGRY* AND *ANGRY*, words ending in *-gry* are rare indeed. The list includes *aggry* (a multicolored glass bead), *puggry* (a cloth strip worn around a pith helmet to shade the back of the neck), and *iggry* (an Egyptian interjection meaning "hurry up!"), among other obscurities.

However, *-gry* is hardly the only rare word ending out there. Can you think of the one common word ending with *-mt*? No? Perhaps after some rest you'll have *dreamt* of it. There's also only one common English word ending in *-onse* and just one ending in *-sede*. If you're thinking of some close-but-no-cigar answers, hopefully the correct *response* will *supersede* them. Other endings with only one common word to match are *-cay*, *-hany*, *-iph*, *-ln*, *-mth*, *-nen*, and *-wth* (*decay, epiphany, caliph, kiln, warmth, linen, growth*). The ending *-ov* just has *improv*—unless you include phrases, in which case, *mazel tov*! There's one other word that ends in *-pth* besides *depth*, but it might take you until the *umpty-umpth* try to think of it.

When a few words share a rare ending, coming up with all of them may be complicated by the fact that pronunciations can vary. For instance, four common words end in *-vous*; three are *grievous, nervous,* and *mischievous*. You'll need to think laterally to come up with the fourth, *rendezvous*. Or, given that two common English words end with *-cht* and one of them is *yacht*, can you think of the other? (It's *borscht*.) Two of the three words ending in *-anse* are *manse* and *expanse*. Name the other! Stuck? Here's another puzzle to *cleanse* your palate: Many words end with *-pse*, such as *ellipse* and *synapse*, but in only two does a consonant precede the *-pse*. Hopefully you won't need to catch a *glimpse* of a *corpse* to think of the answer.

Famous Last Lines

Every beginning needs an ending, and a really great ending will resonate long after we turn the final page.

✳   ✳   ✳   ✳

"But I reckon I got to light out for the Territory ahead of the rest, because Aunt Sally she's going to adopt me and sivilize me and I can't stand it. I been there before."
—MARK TWAIN, *THE ADVENTURES OF HUCKLEBERRY FINN* (1885)

" 'God's in His heaven, all's right with the world,' whispered Anne softly."
—L. M. MONTGOMERY, *ANNE OF GREEN GABLES* (1908)

" 'All that is very well,' answered Candide, 'but let us cultivate our garden.' "
—VOLTAIRE (TRANS. ROBERT M. MCADAMS), *CANDIDE* (1759)

"I took her hand in mine, and we went out of the ruined place; and, as the morning mists had risen long ago when I first left the forge, so the evening mists were rising now, and in all the broad expanse of tranquil light they showed to me, I saw no shadow of another parting from her."
—CHARLES DICKENS, *GREAT EXPECTATIONS* (1863 EDITION)

"But that is the beginning of a new story—the story of the gradual renewal of a man, the story of his gradual regeneration, of his passing from one world into another, of his initiation into a new unknown life. That might be the subject of a new story, but our present story is ended."
—FYODOR DOSTOYEVSKY, *CRIME AND PUNISHMENT* (1866)

"Yes I said yes I will Yes."
—JAMES JOYCE, *ULYSSES* (1922)

Huh, Yay, Wow!

*If you're already familiar with **palindromes,** then you'll catch the joke at the end of the next sentence. If you don't know much about palindromes, we suggest studying this article until you understand them backward and forward.*

✳ ✳ ✳ ✳

A PALINDROME IS A series of letters that reads the same backward and forward. It can be a single word (such as *mom, peep, kayak, level, Hannah, redder, deified,* or *racecar*) or something a bit longer, such as a phrase, a sentence, or even a paragraph—or, if you're an ambitious author like Lawrence Levine, a nearly 32,000-word novel (*Dr. Awkward & Olson in Oslo,* in case you're wondering).

A Pack of Palindromes

Famous palindromes include the introduction "Madam, I'm Adam"; the story of human ingenuity briefly summed up in "A man, a plan, a canal—Panama!"; and Napoleon's lament about how exile destroyed his potency, "Able was I ere I saw Elba." Songwriter "Weird Al" Yankovic composed a Bob Dylan parody in which every line is a palindrome, including many well-known examples such as "If I had a hi-fi," "Too bad I hid a boot," and "Do geese see God?"

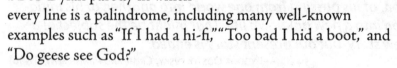

Here's a list of some other great palindromes:

✳ Was it Eliot's toilet I saw?

✳ Are we not drawn onward, we few, drawn onward to new era?

✳ A nut for a jar of tuna.

* Dennis and Edna sinned.

* Oozy rat in a sanitary zoo.

* Ana, nab a banana!

* Borrow or rob?

* Vanna, wanna V?

* We panic in a pew.

* Never odd or even.

* Murder for a jar of red rum.

Meet the Extended Family

Semordnilaps are words that, when reversed, spell a word—but not the word you started with. (The word *semordnilap*, of course, is *palindromes* reversed.) *Desserts* is a semordnilap of *stressed*, for instance. Some other pairs are *wolf* and *flow*, *warts* and *straw*, *stink* and *knits*, and *reviled* and *deliver*.

Palindromes tend to have a certain characteristic cadence—especially the longer ones—and a lot of words (including many semordnilaps) tend to recur in them frequently. That brings us to *plaindromes*, sentences that sound like they surely ought to be palindromes but aren't (or are near misses), such as "Stella, Edna, and Otis deified Satan" and "A man, a plan, a canal—Suez!"

---

* *Palindrome* comes from the Greek *palinodia*, which means "recantation," from *palin* ("over again") and *odia* ("an ode or song"). The word has spun off several other words. There's the adjective *palindromic*, designating the quality of reading the same forward and backward; an adverb, *palindromically*, as in "a palindromically presented sequence of events"; and even a noun, *palindromist*, naming someone who writes or invents palindromes.

The Devil Finds Work for Idle Clues

Had your fill of standard crosswords, word searches, and anagrams? If you're a real word-puzzle pro, you may want to use your puzzling prowess to tackle the formidable wordplay challenge discussed in this article: Are you ready to find words that have vanished from their sentences without a trace?

✳   ✳   ✳   ✳

PRINTER'S DEVILRY IS a type of wordplay used in some cryptic crosswords. It's considered nonstandard and generally only appears in a puzzle consisting of nothing but printer's devilry clues (indicated as such in the instructions). The first printer's devilry puzzle was composed in 1937 by the British puzzle constructor Alistair Ferguson Ritchie, known by the pseudonym Afrit. It has remained a popular type—mostly in the UK, although it periodically appears in American publications. The clue type is similar to a traditional cryptic "hidden word" clue, but much trickier.

Time to Find a New Printer

A printer's devilry clue starts out with a normal-sounding sentence that contains a hidden word inside it, in consecutive letters. The hidden word is then deleted from the sentence— perhaps by a mischievous printer, hence the name—and what remains is left in the same order but respaced (and perhaps repunctuated) to make something that hopefully still looks like a normal sentence but probably makes less sense.

The solver is then required to determine what word has been deleted. Unlike traditional cryptic clues, there is no definition of the answer; it must be determined from context only. Here's an example: Say we start with the sentence "Superman entitled his biography *All the Way to Earth*." We could then delete the word *permanent* (Su**permanent**itled) and change the spacing and formatting to leave the clue "Suit led his biography all the way to earth."

On Second Thought, I'll Keep the Fiat

See if you can solve these examples before reading ahead for the solutions. The answer to this first one is ten letters: "It's a Fiat, but I still miss the old fireplace." Correct *fiat* to *fine thermostat* and you'll see the answer, *nethermost*. This next one has a seven-letter answer (and if you want a clue, think *pasta*): "Whenever I, he, and reams of gypsies come to mind." There's a lot of repunctuating and respacing here; the sentence started out as "Whenever I hear a violin, dreams of gypsies come to mind," giving the answer *ravioli*.

Getting the hang of it? Here's one last example, with an eight-letter answer: "I didn't cheat when I hosted that game show; I need the answer for the contestants." Replace *need* with *never mouthed* and you've found *vermouth*. And feel free to toast yourself with it if you found all of those hidden words—you deserve it!

✴ Speaking of game-show cheaters: The 1994 film *Quiz Show* is based on the TV quiz show scandals of the 1950s. In 1956, a producer for the show *Twenty-One* coached a contestant to lose the show. When this information was made public, it caused a huge scandal and forced networks to cancel their quiz shows. In 1960, Congress passed a law preventing anyone from fixing quiz shows.

✴ Arthur Wynne is frequently cited as the inventor of the cross-word for his "word-cross" puzzle that was printed in the *New York World* in 1913.

Where Did It Come From?

Martini: Though you can use Martini & Rossi brand vermouth to make this cocktail, its name actually derives from the place where it was allegedly invented: Martinez, California. The drink was originally called a "Martinez cocktail."

Working Together with *Syn-*

Ever wondered where the ubiquitous term synergy *comes from?*

❋   ❋   ❋   ❋

THE PREFIX SYN- comes from the Greek preposition meaning "with." So *synthesis*, for example, is a combination of the Greek elements *syn-* ("with"), *the* ("to place"), and *-sys* ("action of") to form "the action of placing with." But the prefix can be a bit confusing due to sound changes when combined with some roots. While *syn-* is usually attached to a root as is, it can undergo a change before certain consonants. Before the letter *l*, for instance, *syn-* becomes *syl-*, as in *syllable* (*syn-* + *-lab-*), literally "a taking with." And before an *s* or a *z*, it is clipped to just *sy-*, as in *system* (*syn-* + *-sta-*), literally meaning "set up with."

Some other examples of *syn*-ful words are:

❋ *synagogue* (*syn-* + *agein*, "to bring")—literally "a bringing together, assembly," used to refer to Jewish congregations

❋ *synchronous* (*syn-* + *kronos*, "time")—happening at the same time

❋ *syndactyl* (*syn-* + *dactyl*, "finger")—web-footed, where two or more digits of foot or hand are fused

❋ *synergy* (*syn-* + *erg*, "work")—cooperation producing increased output

❋ *synod* (*syn-* + *odos*, "way, travel")—literally "a journey together," used to refer to an assembly of clergy

❋ *syntax* (*syn-* + *tak*, "to arrange")—an arrangement, especially the arrangement of words in a sentence

❋ *syzygy* (*syn-* + *suzugia*, "yoke, pair")—an astronomical conjunction of celestial bodies, famous for being the last *s* word in many dictionaries

This Title Is *Autological*

It can be impolite to draw attention to oneself, but in the case of these words and sentences, it's actually pretty cool.

✳ ✳ ✳ ✳

A N **AUTOLOGICAL WORD** is one that is self-describing. For example, on this page the word *printed* is printed, so in this case it is autological—although it wouldn't be if it were spoken out loud (but the word *oral* would be, as would the word *loud* if spoken at a high volume, or *wealthy* if said by Bill Gates). The word *red* isn't autological here, but if you got yourself a red pen and wrote it in the margin, then it would be autological, as would be the word *read*, unless you stopped reading it halfway through. Some words are autological no matter what, such as *polysyllabic, unhyphenated, adjectival, pronounceable,* and others. *Mispelled* is autological, though it's arguable whether a misspelled word counts as a word.

It doesn't have to stop at words. An autological sentence also describes itself (is "self-referential"); for instance, "This sentence has five words." Some self-referential sentences are quite elaborate, such as "This sentence includes two *a*'s, one *b*, three *c*'s, three *d*'s, thirty-one *e*'s, six *f*'s, three *g*'s, nine *h*'s, ten *i*'s, one *j*, one *k*, two *l*'s, one *m*, twenty *n*'s, fifteen *o*'s, one *p*, one *q*, eight *r*'s, twenty-four *s*'s, twenty-three *t*'s, four *u*'s, two *v*'s, eight *w*'s, two *x*'s, five *y*'s, and one *z*." (Count them if you don't believe it!) And yet a word or a sentence can be self-referential without being autological, because it's only autological if it's true—and self-referential sentences can easily lie about themselves ("This sentence is in French") or create irresolvable paradoxes ("This sentence is false").

And, of course, some words are autological based on one's perspective. Is the word *autological* self-descriptive? If you think it is, then it is. But if you think it isn't, then it isn't. It's entirely up to you.

Anagrams

You've surely played around with scrambled words before, but this article will take you one step further.

✳   ✳   ✳   ✳

IN MOST SITUATIONS, when someone refers to **anagrams,** they simply mean words that can have their letters rearranged to make other words—like *alignment* and *lamenting, Eric Clapton* and *narcoleptic,* or *involuntariness* and *nonuniversalist.* In the world of recreational wordplay, though, the aforementioned pairs are known as *transposals.*

An anagram, rather, is a rearrangement of the letters in a word, phrase, or sentence to make a new word, phrase, or sentence that refers to or defines the original in some way—for instance, *dormitory* and *dirty room,* or *greyhound* and "*Hey, dog—run!*"

An Assembly of Anagrams

Here's a list of some particularly nice ones; you'll notice that one handy trick anagrammatists use is adding little words like *the* to their starting phrases, which gives them more letters to work with (and common ones to boot), offering more flexibility.

✳ *adios amigos = I go so I am sad*

✳ *angered = enraged*

✳ *astronomers = moon starers*

✳ *Clint Eastwood = Old West action*

✳ *computer station meltdown = we lost important document*

✳ *the countryside = no city dust here*

✳ *the eyes = they see*

✳ *the famous painter Pablo Ruiz Picasso = popularizes cubism into a phase of art*

* *inconsistent* = "n is," "n is not," etc.

* *the Morse code* = *here come dots*

* *the nudist colony* = *no untidy clothes*

* *the piano bench* = *beneath Chopin*

* *slot machines* = *cash lost in 'em*

* *snooze alarms* = *alas, no more z's*

Normally, it's considered inelegant for an anagram to repeat a word from the original phrase, but sometimes it really is necessary, as when anagramming *eleven plus two* into the mathematically equivalent *twelve plus one.*

Antigrams Beg to Differ

A phrase that has been anagrammed into something that means or implies its opposite is called an **antigram**—for instance, the aforementioned *astronomers* can be changed into *no more stars.* Here are a few more:

* *funeral* ≠ *real fun*

* *filled* ≠ *ill-fed*

* *protectionism* ≠ *nice to imports*

* *diplomacy* ≠ *mad policy*

* *the Boston Strangler* ≠ *grabs, throttles none*

Some anagrams might be considered antigrams depending on one's opinions. For instance, some people might feel that *Ronald Wilson Reagan* was an *insane Anglo warlord,* but people on the other side of the political fence would probably disagree; fans of *The Towering Inferno* might have a beef with the negative review "*Not worth fire engine.*" These ambiguous anagrams are called *ambigrams* (a word that has more than one wordplay meaning—see page 345 for the other).

Letter Pairs

The fate of these words hangs in the balance.

✳   ✳   ✳   ✳

ONE DEFINITION OF a *balanced word* involves assigning a numeric value to each letter based on its position in the alphabet (1 for *a*, 2 for *b*, and so on to 26 for *z*). A word is balanced if you can add up the values of each of its letters, compute the average, and get a result of 13.5—the average of the full alphabet, or the midway point between *m* and *n* if the alphabet is imagined as a number line. *Dopily* is one example: d (4) + o (15) + p (16) + i (9) + l (12) + y (25) = 81, which, divided by 6 (the number of letters in the word), averages to 13.5.

But the term *balanced word* is more commonly used to refer to words in which letters are paired with their symmetrical counterpart in the alphabet (*a-z*, *b-y*, *c-x*, and so on). Examples of balanced words in which every letter's counterpart is located in the exact opposite position in the word are *bevy*, *hovels*, *Polk*, *vole*, and *wizard*. Some variant examples include *love* and *shrive* (in which pairs are adjacent), *valorize* (pairs are adjacent or in opposite positions), and *overslight* (pairs are mixed).

Akin to balanced words are **vicinals,** which are words composed only of letters that are adjacent in the alphabet—such as *blacksmith*, which contains *a*, *b*, and *c*; *h* and *i*; *k*, *l*, and *m*; and *s* and *t*. *Unreconstructed* is another example, which contains *c*, *d*, and *e*; *n* and *o*; and *r*, *s*, *t*, and *u*. A more constrained sort of vicinal is one in which the letters can all be separated into alphabetically adjacent pairs—such as *fights*, which contains *f* and *g*, *h* and *i*, and *s* and *t*. Others include *horridness* (*de*, *hi*, *no*, *rs*, *rs*), *finest hour* (*ef*, *hi*, *no*, *rs*, *tu*), *spinsterhood* (*de*, *hi*, *no*, *op*, *rs*, *st*), and, if the alphabet is considered a continual loop, *Zebadiah* (*ab*, *de*, *hi*, *za*). Some vicinals in which all the pairs remain adjacent are *feed*, *pout*, *stab*, *debars*, and *stoned*; vicinals in which the pairs are symmetrical include *this* and (aptly enough) *done*.

Word Games

Gather a group of friends: Here are two great word games.

✳   ✳   ✳   ✳

THE GAME *INITIALS* begins when you create a list of...yes, initials. The list can be as long as you like, using any criteria. Once you have a list, pick a time limit. (Five minutes works well, but be flexible if players want more time.) Then start the clock and try to think of celebrities who have those initials—say, Frederick Douglass, Fran Drescher, or Francis Drake for F.D.; or Marilyn Monroe, Mike Mussina, or Matthew Modine for M.M. When time's up, players read their lists. A celebrity someone else also thought of scores one point; a celebrity nobody else came up with scores two points; and if you're the only player who found any celebrity at all for one of the pairs of initials, you score three points for it.

If you don't like limiting yourself to celebrities, there's **Cool Game,** in which a pair of letters is picked, and players think of as many names and phrases that start with those letters as possible. For instance, the starting letters *t* and *d* might suggest *tap dancing, Ted Danson, test drive, Teapot Dome, ten dollars,* and many more. Compound words, hyphenated words, and phrases with short connecting words are also acceptable, such as *touchdown, tie-dye, Torvill and Dean, take a dive,* and *truth or dare.* The scoring system is opposite that of Initials: In Cool Game, the object is to match as many of the other answers as possible. When time is up, players read their lists and score points for items appearing on multiple lists (related phrases, like *tap dance, tap dancer,* and *tap dancing,* count as matches). If no one else thought of a phrase, no points are scored for it. Matches score points equal to the number of other lists they appear on; if you and one other person thought of *tofu dog,* you each get one point, but if you and four other people had *three of diamonds,* you each get four points.

Clerihews: Poetic Views

If you like the idea of composing a piece of poetry, but are put off by all those perplexing considerations of word rhythm, line length, etc., then the **clerihew** *might be right up your alley. It'll help if you have a few "facts" on hand about some famous folks.*

✳ ✳ ✳ ✳

THE CLERIHEW IS a short, humorous poetic form invented by English novelist and humorist Edmund Clerihew Bentley. It consists of four lines of no fixed length or rhythm, with the rhyme scheme AABB, and tells a mini story about a famous person (whose name typically appears as, or in, the first line of the poem).

The Worse It Is, the Better

This poem is not expected to be necessarily factual or informative in any way, and the clunkier and more awkward the rhythm, the better. For instance, here is a famous one by Bentley himself:

> *Sir Christopher Wren*
> *Said, "I am going to dine with some men.*
> *If anybody calls,*
> *Say I am designing St. Paul's."*

The rhymes are often strained for humorous effect, as in these examples, also by Bentley:

> *The people of Spain think Cervantes*
> *Equal to half-a-dozen Dantes:*
> *An opinion resented most bitterly*
> *By the people of Italy.*

> *Edgar Allan Poe*
> *Was passionately fond of roe.*
> *He always liked to chew some*
> *When writing anything gruesome.*

A Clerihew Revue

The style is evocative of Ogden Nash, though the form predates his work. Bentley's first collection of light verse, *Biography for Beginners*, was published in 1905, when Nash was only three years old. It's unknown whether Ogden Nash took any inspiration from clerihews; he never wrote any, as far as anyone knows. But others did—for instance, the eminent poet W. H. Auden.

This one is by Bentley's son, Nicolas:

> Cecil B. DeMille,
> Rather against his will,
> Was persuaded to leave Moses
> Out of the War of the Roses.

This verse is no less amusing for being anonymous:

> William the Bastard
> Frequently got plastered
> In a manner unbecoming to the successor
> Of Edward the Confessor.

Still, of the people who've written clerihews—well, perhaps it's best said in verse:

> Edmund discovered the clerihew
> And although there were a few
> Who waded into its waters gently,
> Its best-known explorer is still Bentley.

Where Did It Come From?

Wacky: Denoting "crazy" or "eccentric," this word made its debut in 1935 as a variant on the late-1800s British slang term *whacky*, which came from the idea of being struck sharply—or *whacked*—on the head once too often. *Wacko* came into being around 1975, whereas *wack*, urban slang for "worthless" or "stupid," arrived in the late 1990s.

Taking the Good with the Bad

Can a prefix have an evil twin? What about a nemesis? Sworn enemy, at least? The answer to these questions is almost surely a firm no, but such issues do easily come to mind when discussing the prefixes mal- *and* bene-.

✳   ✳   ✳   ✳

SOMETIMES PREFIXES APPEAR in pairs that are in opposition to each other. Such is the case with *mal-* ("badly") and *bene-* ("well"). Both are from Latin, introduced into English when the Normans invaded and conquered England in 1066. Both *mal-* and *bene-* are widely used in Latin as prefixes.

Try to Get Along, You Two

In English, we get contrasting pairs of *mal-* and *bene-* words, such as:

✳ *malediction* (1447), "a curse," and *benediction* (c. 1440), "a blessing"; literally "bad word" and "good word"

✳ *malefactor* (c. 1438), "wrongdoer, criminal," and *benefactor* (1532), "one who renders aid"

✳ *malefit* (1755), "misfortune, disadvantage," and *benefit* (1377), "good deed, gift"; *malefit* appears to have been deliberately coined twice as the antithesis of *benefit*, once in the eighteenth century and again in the twentieth after it fell out of use

✳ *malevolence* (c. 1454), "ill will," and *benevolence* (c. 1384), "good will"

✳ *malice* (c. 1325), "bad intent," and *benefice* (1340), "good deed, gift, means of living"

> **"It is absurd to divide people into good and bad. People are either charming or tedious."**
> —OSCAR WILDE

* *malign* (c. 1350), "evil, injurious," and *benign* (c. 1320), "good, kindly, harmless"

Bad Language

Sometimes *mal-* is used but *bene-* is not, particularly when a root itself carries a good connotation and *mal-'s* function as a prefix is to reverse the meaning, as in:

* *maladroit*—clumsy (1685)

* *malady*—disease, sickness (c. 1275)

* *malaria*—a parasitic blood disease carried by mosquitoes (1740); literally "bad air," from the belief that the atmosphere in swamps and marshlands (mosquito breeding grounds) was the cause of the disease

* *malcontent*—discontented, or a discontented person (1581)

* *malinger*—to feign illness (1820)

* *malpractice*—injurious action on the part of a professional, especially a physician (1671)

Curiously, there are few *bene-* words that do not have a *mal-* counterpart. Presumably it's easier to do bad than good.

---

* Ever wonder why exactly English uses *good-better-best* and *bad-worse-worst* instead of *good-gooder-goodest* and *bad-badder-baddest*? If so, turn to page 538 for an explanation.

Another Humdrum Conundrum

Today, **conundrum** *is just a fancy word to describe a perplexing problem, but the word started out with a more academic and literary meaning.*

✳ ✳ ✳ ✳

ENGLISH MAJORS AND self-proclaimed grammarians find the word *conundrum* deliciously vexing. Most people use it to mean any difficult problem, paradox, or dilemma, but the "grammarati" hold that it can only mean a riddle that involves wordplay.

The word first appeared in print in 1596, and it was spelled *quonundrum*, reflecting the then-fashionable academic humor of inventing Latin words to poke fun at current events and situations. It initially described someone who was overly pedantic or fussy about a seemingly unimportant point.

By 1646, *conundrum* had evolved to mean any bit of confusing wordplay, especially an insulting one. In the 1700s, it began to refer specifically to a riddle based on a pun or verbal trickery. A modern example of this kind of conundrum is "What occurs once in a minute, twice in a moment, but never in a thousand years?" (The letter *m.*)

By the end of the eighteenth century, *conundrum* was commonly used in reference to any mind-bending puzzle, especially one without an easy answer. Can you come up with an answer to these burning questions? If nothing sticks to Teflon, then how do they make Teflon stick to the pan? If you try to fail but you succeed, which have you done?

✳ **The riddle of the Sphinx, from Sophocles's play *Oedipus the King,* is a famous conundrum. The Sphinx asks Oedipus, "What walks on four legs in the morning, two in the afternoon, and three in the evening?" The answer is "a person": crawling as a child, walking as an adult, and using a cane in old age.**

Words of Wisdom: Home

✳   ✳   ✳   ✳

"A child was asked, 'Where is your home?'
The little fellow replied, 'Where Mother is.'
Ah, that is home—'Where Mother is.'"

—HENRY VAN DYKE

"Where we love is home, home that our feet may leave, but not our hearts. The chain may lengthen, but it never parts."

—OLIVER WENDELL HOLMES

"This is the true nature of home—it is the place of Peace; the shelter, not only from injury, but from all terror, doubt, and division."

—JOHN RUSKIN

"He is happiest, be he king or peasant, who finds peace in his home."

—JOHANN WOLFGANG VON GOETHE

"A house is no home unless it contains food and fire for the mind as well as for the body."

—MARGARET FULLER

"Something like a home that is not home is to be desired; it is found in the house of a friend."

—SIR WILLIAM TEMPLE

"A man travels the world over in search of what he needs and returns home to find it."

—GEORGE MOORE

"I do hate to be unquiet at home."

—SAMUEL PEPYS

Sounds Like...Charades!

*You're probably familiar with **charades** from the parlor game in which words and phrases are acted out piecemeal, using mimed actions and gestures. But the game is actually descended from an earlier pastime of the same name. So don't worry, we're not going to make you act out anything embarrassing in front of your friends and family... at least not for this article.*

✳ ✳ ✳ ✳

CHARADES WERE ORIGINALLY riddles in verse in which a word was clued in more than one part, like this one, from an 1883 collection:

> *My first is coarse and homely food,*
> *The cotter's fare, but still 'tis good.*
> *My second you may quick define,*
> *The place in which we dance or dine.*
> *My whole when fresh, and nicely cooked*
> *No epicure e'er overlooked.*

Is That Portobello or Porcini?

The first couplet clues the first part of the word, *mush*, and likewise the second couplet hints at the second part of the word, *room*. Combining the halves gives the answer to the clue in the final couplet: *mushroom*.

This type of puzzle evolved into the parlor game of charades, but the earlier sense of the word *charade* still exists in reference to a word that can be broken into smaller words. The earliest verse charades broke words between syllables, which meant that most charades were based upon compound words, such as *fire + place*, *blue + bell*, or the one clued here:

> *My first makes all nature appear of one face;*
> *At the next we find music, and beauty and grace;*
> *And if this Charade is most easily read,*
> *I think that the third should be thrown at my head.*

Charade Parade

The answer is *snow + ball = snowball*. Nowadays that wouldn't be considered noteworthy, as wordplay goes. Modern charades preferably form words unrelated to the original word, often splitting the word somewhere other than the syllable breaks or causing the pronunciation to change, or both. Some examples include:

* *bra + very = bravery*

* *cab + leg + ram = cablegram*

* *chart + reuse = chartreuse*

* *feat + herbed = feather bed*

* *Incan + descent = incandescent*

* *mead + owl + ark = meadowlark*

* *must + ache = mustache*

* *pronoun + cement = pronouncement*

* *spa + retire = spare tire*

* *tapes + tries = tapestries*

* *teaser + vice = tea service*

* *warp + ain't = war paint*

Charades in verse still exist, though you won't find them on the newsstand, as you might have 100 years ago. You might, however, find charades sharing the page with the Sunday crossword, among the clues of the cryptic crossword. (For more on cryptic crosswords, see page 28.)

---

* When two separate words are combined to form a new word, like *ulterior* and *alternative* to form *alterior,* it is referred to as *lexical blending*. In most cases both words are still recognizable in the newly formed lexeme, as in *brunch,* which is a combination of *breakfast* and *lunch*. *Brunch* is also a portmanteau word—see page 586 for more details.

Secret Languages

It's very common for children to want to use secret languages so that grown-ups can't understand what they're saying. Of course, there are multiple reasons why this is silly. First among them is the fact that grown-ups were kids once too, and so they probably knew the same secret languages and can still understand them.

✳ ✳ ✳ ✳

Tʜᴇ ᴍᴏsᴛ ᴄᴏᴍᴍᴏɴ "secret" language is **Pig Latin,** in which the initial consonant sound of a word is moved to the end, with the sound "ay" added after it, so "Pig Latin" becomes "igpay atinlay." Words that begin with vowel sounds usually have "way" added at the end (though there are regional variations that use "day," "hay," or "yay" instead). Many words make new words when translated into Pig Latin; for instance, *be* becomes *eBay,* *trash* becomes *ashtray,* *stout* becomes *outstay,* *trice* becomes *ice tray,* *beast* becomes *East Bay,* *dearth* becomes *Earth Day,* and *plunder* becomes *underplay.* And since Pig Latin is a spoken language, we can include words with spelling changes in the list as well, such as *wear* and *airway* or *wonder* and *underway.*

Another secret language is **Ubbi Dubbi** (also called Pig Greek), in which the sounds of each word remain in order, but the syllable "ub" is added before each vowel sound (the *u* is pronounced as a schwa). So, in this language, "Pig Latin" becomes "pubig Lubatubin" (puh-BIG luh-BAT-uh-bin), and "SpongeBob SquarePants" becomes "SpubongeBubob SqubarePubants" (you're on your own pronouncing that one). Other variations of the language use other syllables, including some multisyllabic options.

Hip-hop lyrics sometimes include "izz" as an inserted syllable before a vowel—"chillin' in the pizzark" instead of "chillin' in the park," say—which led to Snoop Dogg's "Izzle" language (but that doesn't have many rules except "add or substitute *izzle* when desired").

Climbing the Word Ladder

*In a **word ladder,** a word is changed to another word (usually a related one) by changing one letter at a time, like so: LOVE, LONE, LANE, LATE, HATE.*

✳ ✳ ✳ ✳

SOMETIMES THE PATH from one word to the other can be quite circuitous, especially if you start with longer words. For instance, one way to get from CLEAN to SLATE takes 11 steps: CLEAN, CLEAT, CLEFT, CLEFS, CHEFS, CHEWS, CREWS, CRAWS, CLAWS, SLAWS, SLATS, SLATE. Generally, pairs of words that don't have the same consonant/vowel pattern are harder to connect. Particularly elegant ladders change every letter exactly once, requiring no extra steps, as in MICE, RICE, RACE, RATE, RATS. (That one even changes its letters in order from left to right.)

The word ladder was invented by Lewis Carroll in 1877; he originally called the puzzle "Word Links," and later published it as "Doublets" in *Vanity Fair*, where his example was HEAD, HEAL, TEAL, TELL, TALL, TAIL. The starting and ending words are, in his terminology, a "doublet," the words between are "links," and the whole series is a "chain." He adds, "It is, perhaps, needless to state that it is *de rigueur* that the links should be English words, such as might be used in good society."

A variant (proposed by Carroll himself) allows anagramming as a step. Carroll pointed out in a letter that while it had once been impossible to change IRON to LEAD, adding the ability to anagram allowed this chain: IRON, ICON, COIN, CORN, CORD, LORD, LOAD, LEAD. Utilizing this and/or other possible variants opens up a head-spinning amount of possibilities. There's nothing wrong with sticking to the traditional rules, though, which have stood the test of time and are as GOOD as GOLD.

Word Roots and Branches
The History of -*Ist*

Is a **galactophagist** *some kind of sci-fi villain? Read to find out.*

✳   ✳   ✳   ✳

THE SUFFIX *-IST* comes to English from the French *-iste*, the Latin *-ista*, and the Greek *-istes*, where it forms the agent of a verb—that is, the "doer" of the action. The suffix performs the same function in English, especially for verbs that end in *-ize*, including *antagonize/antagonist*, *baptize/baptist*, and *plagiarize/plagiarist*. This function is extended to include people who practice a particular art or profession, as with *archaeologist*, *botanist*, *dentist*, *etymologist*, *humorist*, *phlebotomist*, and *satirist*.

This suffix can also be used to denote a devotee or practitioner of a religion or theoretical doctrine, especially one that ends in *-ism*, as in *atheist*, *Buddhist*, *communist*, *Darwinist*, *fascist*, *humanist*, and *polytheist*. It can additionally be used to designate someone with a general philosophy or method for engaging with the world, as with *egotist*, *materialist*, and *opportunist*.

There is a relatively recent use of the suffix denoting someone who discriminates for or against people based on a socially objectionable criterion. This use comes from words like *racist* and *sexist*, but includes terms like *ageist*, *classist*, and *sizeist*.

There are thousands of *-ist* words in English, including:

✳ *agriolist*—one who studies primitive peoples

✳ *dromedarist*—a camel rider

✳ *galactophagist*—a milk drinker

✳ *magirist*—a cook

✳ *nemophilist*—a lover of the woods

✳ *oneiropolist*—an interpreter of dreams

Isolano and Onalosi

What and who, now? If these two titular terms leave you scratching your head, read on for a full explanation.

✳   ✳   ✳   ✳

A**N ISOLANO IS** a word that cannot possibly be transformed into another word by changing one of its letters. For instance, take the word *ecru:* There's no other word with any of the letter patterns *?cru, e?ru, ec?u,* or *ecr?.* Therefore, *ecru* is an isolano—and the shortest one. Arguably, *emu* is a shorter isolano, depending on what words one considers allowable. *EMT* can be made by changing the last letter (but that only counts if we permit acronyms), or *eau* by changing the middle letter (and while *eau* is not a stand-alone word in English, it is part of many English phrases).

The isolano's counterpart is the **onalosi**—a word in which *every* letter can be changed (one at a time) to make a new word. An example is *shore,* which can be changed to *chore, snore, share, shove,* and *short* (among other words). The longest known onalosi is *pasters,* which can be changed to *masters, posters, patters, passers, pastors, pastels,* and *pastern* (among others).

Other restrictions can be added. For instance, here's an onalosi with only one common word that can be made at each letter position: *chase* (making *phase, cease, chose, chafe,* and *chasm*). There are also onalosis in which the changed letters, read in order, spell a new word. For instance, if you change the letters in *pine* to *mine, pane, pile,* and *pint,* the new letters spell *malt.* The word *crimp* is quite unusual; not only does it have only one common word for each letter position, but the new letters also spell a word (*primp, chimp, cramp, crisp,* and *crime,* spelling *phase*). Another rarity is an onalosi in which the same letter can be used in every position, such as *goad,* which requires only the letter *l* to change to *load, glad, gold,* and *goal;* and *team,* which can become *ream, tram, term,* or *tear* with the letter *r.*

Luck of the Irish Bull

An **Irish bull** *is a statement that seems to make sense, but is paradoxical or logically inconsistent upon closer inspection.*

✳   ✳   ✳   ✳

WHAT IS PERHAPS the canonical example was provided by Professor John Pentland Mahaffey of Dublin University in the late nineteenth century. When asked to explain the difference between an Irish bull and any other bull of unspecified nationality, he said, "An Irish bull is always pregnant." Another well-known explanation of an Irish bull (this one of unknown origin) says, "Supposing there were 13 cows lying down in a field and one of them was standing up; that would be a bull."

The purest form of an Irish bull is spoken unwittingly (or, even more appropriately, accidentally on purpose). Clearly, Irish bulls are not limited to the Irish. Baseball's Yogi Berra was a master of them, making such remarks as "Ninety percent of this game is half mental"; "It gets late early out there"; and "I never said most of the things I said!" Movie mogul Samuel Goldwyn was another, providing the first known citation of one famous phrase when he said, "I'm giving you a definite maybe." Other bulls attributed to Goldwyn include "Anybody who goes to a psychiatrist should have his head examined" and "We're overpaying him, but he's worth it." Gerald Ford, mocked on *Saturday Night Live* for being clumsy, also stumbled over his words sometimes—as when he said, "If Lincoln were alive today, he'd roll over in his grave."

Oscar Wilde, who *was* an Irishman, probably thought he was merely being witty when he said, "I can resist everything except temptation," but he was also creating a homegrown Irish bull. Examples abound as well in Irish proverbs ("It's better to be a coward for a minute than dead for the rest of your life"). Hundreds of Irish bulls exist, but we'll proceed to stop here.

Worldly Wisdom: Irish Proverbs

✳ ✳ ✳ ✳

* Better today than tomorrow morning.

* Where the tongue slips, it speaks the truth.

* The older the fiddle the sweeter the tune.

* An old broom knows the dirty corners the best.

* Though there is no bone in the tongue, it has frequently broken a man's head.

* When death comes, it will not go away empty.

* A good word never broke a tooth.

* It's easy to halve the potato when there's love.

* If you are lucky enough to be Irish, you are lucky enough.

* Your feet will bring you to where your heart is.

* No man ever gave advice but himself were the better for it.

* Let your anger set with the sun and not rise again with it.

* Wisdom makes a poor man a king.

* Thirst is the end of drinking and sorrow the end of drunkenness.

* Time is a good storyteller.

* Every terrier is bold in his own doorway.

* Long as the day is, night comes.

* Two shorten the road.

* The only cure for love is marriage.

* He who lies down with dogs will get up with fleas.

Alternades

Words hidden within other words? That's a lot of bang for your buck. For a true word lover, it's hard to imagine anything better.

✳   ✳   ✳   ✳

A**N ALTERNADE IS** a word in which each set of alternate letters (the letters in odd-numbered positions and the letters in even-numbered positions) also spells a word. For example, in the word *spoiled*, the odd letters spell *sold* and the even letters spell *pie*. (Hopefully you won't often find those three words in the same sentence; if someone sold spoiled pie, that would be an unfortunate occurrence.)

The Short and Long of It

Short alternades are not hard to find, and some examples are listed here:

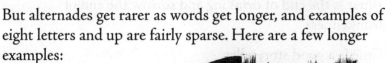

✳ *allied = ale + lid*

✳ *chains = can + his*

✳ *friend = fin + red*

✳ *lounge = lug + one*

✳ *parrot = pro + art*

But alternades get rarer as words get longer, and examples of eight letters and up are fairly sparse. Here are a few longer examples:

✳ *Ariadne = aide + ran*

✳ *collude = clue + old*

✳ *diaries = dais + ire*

✳ *throaty = tray + hot*

✳ *calliope = clip + aloe*

* schooled = shoe + cold

* ballooned = blond + aloe

* fleetness = fetes + lens

* triennially = tinily + renal

Alternative Alternades

If phrases are allowed as well as words, then *alternation*, appropriately enough, becomes an alternade, making the phrase *A Train* (as in "take the A Train") and the musical direction *lento*. Reverse alternades are made by reading the letters backward, such as *tea leaf* becoming *feat* and *ale* or *thickest* turning into *tech* and *skit*.

Three-word alternades are also possible, where each of the smaller words uses each third letter of the long word, such as:

* lacerated = let + are + cad

* safe water = set + awe + far

* similarly = sir + ill + may

* tabulated = tut + ale + bad

* washrooms = who + arm + SOS

* benevolentness = belts + evens + none

If letters are considered in pairs or triplets instead of singly, then bigram or trigram alternades are possible, including:

* savagery = sage + vary

* legal tenders = legend + alters

Of course, if this sort of wordplay isn't your cup of tea, there are many other alternatives.

What Rhymes with *Unrhymable?*

You can stop banging your head against the wall: There really is no English rhyme for orange—as well as a good number of other words. That doesn't mean we can't have a good time getting creative in our efforts to rhyme such words, however. But really, banging your head against the wall just won't help things.

✳ ✳ ✳ ✳

IF YOU'VE EVER tried writing a poem, you know that one thing you don't want to do is write yourself into a corner. For instance, if you start your sonnet with the line "My mistress' eyes are nothing like the sun," then you've got lots of rhyming possibilities: *one, fun, run, shun, pun, stun,* or—if you're Shakespeare and actually writing the poem in question—*dun,* among many others. But if you make the mistake of starting with "My mistress' eyes are speckled bright with silver"... well, then you're in trouble.

An Unrhymable Rainbow

That's because there are no common English words that rhyme with *silver.* (There's *chilver,* a word for a female lamb, but you may find *silver/chilver* is a less useful pairing than, say, *life/wife.*) While there are many unrhymable words in the English language, it seems that an awful lot of them are colors. In addition to *silver,* there's *orange, purple,* and *olive.* Some other unrhymable words include *month, rhythm, angst, chimney,* and *penguin...* and there are many more.

Colorful Rhymes (via Poetic License)

Never say never, though. Wordplay expert Willard R. Espy composed this rhyme using the word *orange:*

> *The four eng-*
> *Ineers*
> *Wore orange*
> *Brassieres.*

And satirist Tom Lehrer wrote this one, using a different pronunciation of *orange*:

> *Eating an orange*
> *While making love*
> *Makes for bizarre enj-*
> *oyment thereof.*

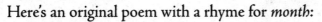

Here's an original poem with a rhyme for *month*:

> *Assuming, then,*
> *The last attempt to find a rhyme for* month
> *Was numbered* n,
> *The one I'm writing is the* n-*plus-oneth.*

If you want to write a poem that includes a rhyme for *purple*, you may wish to talk about feeling too full after a meal, and how a *burp'll* relieve the discomfort.

As you can surely begin to see by now, with creativity, almost anything is possible. As musical theater legend Stephen Sondheim put it:

> *To find a rhyme for* silver
> *Or any "rhymeless" rhyme,*
> *Requires only will, ver-*
> *Bosity, and time.*

SILVER

✳ **Speaking of words that sound the same:** *True homonyms* are words that are pronounced the same but carry different meanings and come from different origins. *Peace* and *piece* would be classified as true homonyms. *Polysemous homonyms,* on the other hand, are words that stem from the same root, such as *head* (of an organization) and *head* (on top of your neck).

In Alphabetical Order, Please

If you're the sort of person who likes to have your books alphabetized, you'll probably appreciate **abecedarian** *(pronounced ay-bee-see-DAYR-ee-an) words, which come presorted alphabetically. That is to say, their letters all appear in alphabetical order, as in* begins *or* first *(which seem like good words to start with).*

✳ ✳ ✳ ✳

THE LONGEST ABECEDARIAN word is *aegilops*, a kind of grass. Five- and six-letter examples include the words *abhors, abort, adept, adopt, aglow, almost, befit, below, bijoux* (the plural of *bijou*), *biopsy, chimps, chinos, chintz, deity, dirty, empty, filmy,* and *ghost*. If we allow repeated letters, the words *abbess, accent, accept, access, accost, adders, beefily, bellow, billowy, chilly, choosy, choppy, effort, floors, floppy, glossy,* and *knotty* can be added to the list. The only abecedarian number is *forty*, and there is also exactly one reverse abecedarian number, with its letters in reverse alphabetical order—*one*, appropriately enough.

As for other reverse abecedarian words, the longest is *spoon-feed*, the longest unhyphenated example is *trollied*, and the longest without repeated letters are *sponged* and *wronged*. Others include *polka, solid, sonic, spied, spoke, tonic, urged, yoked,* and *zoned* (five letters), and *sniffed, spoofed, spooked, spooled, trolled, wolfed* (as in "wolfed down"), and *zonked* (six letters).

Counting only vowels, the words *facetiously* and *abstemiously* (among others) include all five of them once each in alphabetical order (or all six if you count *y*). *Subcontinental* has the canonical five vowels in reverse order, as does *uncomplimentary* (if you *don't* count *y*). To get all six vowels reversed with the *y* included, you need to use the phrase *syrup of ipecac*. And with any luck that's the only thing you'll ever need syrup of ipecac for.

Tri, Tri Again

What do the words carrot, vanish, *and* planet *have in common? The word game* **Tri, Tri Again** *will help you figure it out.*

✳ ✳ ✳ ✳

IN THE COMMERCIAL game of TriBond, players are given sets of three words and must figure out what they have in common. For instance, if a set contains *potato, needle,* and *Cyclops,* the category would be "things with eyes." A more freewheeling and improvisational version of the same concept is the party game *Tri, Tri Again,* which begins with one player thinking of a category and three words that belong to it. He or she announces the three words to the rest of the players, who raise their hands when they think they know the category. The third person to raise his or her hand is called upon to give their answer. (Why not the first? Because guessing the category is part of the fun, and this way more people get a chance to do so before it's blurted out.) If that person is correct, they think of a new set, with one constraint: The first word in the new set must belong to the category of the previous set.

For example: Say the first set is a simple one, like *broccoli, artichoke,* and *asparagus.* After correctly naming the category ("vegetables"), the guesser must come up with the next set. He or she might brainstorm by thinking of other vegetables, eventually arriving at a new set composed of *carrot, vanish,* and *planet.* If no one can guess the category, the player must add more words to the set as hints. In this case, they might add *taxing.* The category here is "words that begin with vehicles" (CARrot, VANish, PLANEt, and TAXIng). The player to correctly guess this might then think of words that start with *bus* to come up with the next set, possibly arriving at *bust, stand,* and *split* (blackjack terms). And the game continues from there, as long as people think it's a *hit.*

Unusual Beginnings

It's important to start strong. Whether we're talking about an athletic competition, a day filled with things to do, or a complex work project, a solid and effortful start to the proceedings can go a long way toward helping the end result stand out. The same can be true with language. In the cases below, however, you'll find that words sometimes stand out in the end because they simply have no rivals in the beginning.

✳ ✳ ✳ ✳

WITH SOME WORDS, once you see the first few letters, you can predict the rest. For instance, a word that begins with *zyd-* must be *zydeco* (Cajun dance music), since it's the only English word that begins with that sequence of letters. Other unusual beginning letter sequences are:

✳ *bdellium (bd-):* a gum resin

✳ *gjetost (gj-):* a caramel-colored cheese

✳ *nth (nt-):* last in an infinite series

✳ *oeuvre (oeu-):* body of work

✳ *pschent (psc-):* double crown worn by Egyptian kings

✳ *ptarmigan (pta-):* a bird

✳ *sfumato (sfu-):* gradation of color in a painting

✳ *sjambok (sj-):* a whip made of rhinoceros hide

✳ *tmesis (tm-):* a figure of speech in which a word is internally interpolated in another word, as in "any-old-how" (see page 291)

✳ *zugzwang* (*zug-*): a chess situation in which, on your turn, any move weakens your position

Sometimes there are a few (or many) words that share a letter sequence in their language of origin, but only one of these words has made its way into English.

Some Other Strong Starters

With some beginnings, you don't have a 100-percent shot at guessing correctly, but your odds are still pretty good: *zw-* only leads into *zwieback* (a cracker) and *zwitterion* (an ion with both positive and negative charges). The letters *cz-* lead into *czardas* (a Hungarian folkdance) and *czar* (and related words such as *czarina*). Lowercase *sv-* only begins *svelte* and its comparatives, but capitalize it and you'll find *Svengali*, *Sven*, and *Svetlana*.

Thanks to the Greek goddess of memory, Mnemosyne, we get *mneme*, *mnemonic*, and *mnemotechnic*. The unlikely-looking letter sequence *phth-* begins *phthalein* (a chemical compound), *phthalocyanine* (a pigment used in blue or green dyes), *phthisicky* (suffering from *phthisis*, an archaic term for tuberculosis), and other related words. The equally unlikely *chth-* begins *chthonian* and *chthonic* (both meaning "pertaining to deities below the earth"). And *vr-* begins *vriesia* (a tropical plant), *vrouw* (a term used for a housewife or woman in South Africa), and *vroom*.

Unparalleled Pairs

Double letters in general are unlikely to start words; *oo-* is the most common, sometimes as one syllable (*oomph*, *oops*, *oodles*), sometimes two (*ooblast*, *oocyte*, *oogenesis*). Other words beginning with double letters include *aah*, *aardvark*, *aardwolf*, *eek*, *eel*, *eensy-weensy*, *eerie*, *iiwi* (a Hawaiian bird), *llama*, and *llano*. In proper names, there's *Lloyd*, *Llewellyn*, and author Jasper *Fforde*.

There are more rare beginnings, of course, but for now this is the end.

Words of Wisdom: Beginnings

✳   ✳   ✳   ✳

"Things are always at their best in their beginning."
—Blaise Pascal

"Individuality of expression is the beginning and end of all art."
—Johann Wolfgang von Goethe

*" Great is the art of beginning, but greater the art is of ending;
Many a poem is marred by a superfluous verse. "*
—Henry Wadsworth Longfellow

"A bad beginning makes a bad ending."
—Euripides

*"Begin at the beginning...and go on till you come to the end:
then stop."*
—Lewis Carroll

"It is easier to resist at the beginning than at the end."
—Leonardo da Vinci

*"At birth our death is sealed, and our end is consequent on our
beginning."*
—Marcus Manilius

*"Many a time...from a bad beginning great friendships have
sprung up."*
—Terence

"Look with favor upon a bold beginning."
—Virgil

Isograms

*An **isogram** is a word that contains no letter more than once. Coincidentally, isogram is an isogram, but not the longest one.*

✳ ✳ ✳ ✳

THERE ARE MANY common isograms between 10 and 12 letters long, including *aftershock, bankruptcy, dumbwaiter, judgmental, trampoline, Volkswagen, atmospheric, documentary, lumberjacks, misanthrope, housewarming, lexicography, upholstering,* and plenty of others. But looking at words with 13 or more letters, the pickings get slimmer and include a greater percentage of rare words. Some 13-letter isograms are *flamethrowing, metalworkings, unpredictably,* and *unproblematic.* The most common 14-letter isogram is *ambidextrously,* though there's also *pseudomythical* and *undiscoverably.* At 15 letters there is *dermatoglyphics* (the study of fingerprints), *hydropneumatics,* and *misconjugatedly,* as well as *uncopyrightable,* which can be pluralized to make a 16-letter isogram if taken as a noun that means "things you can't copyright." Finally, the longest one-word isogram, topping out at 17 letters, is *subdermatoglyphic,* which means "pertaining to the layer of skin beneath the fingertips."

If names and phrases are allowed, then we also get the 14-letter *Rhapsody in Blue, blasting powder, quick on the draw,* and *Clyde Tombaugh* (discoverer of Pluto). At 15 letters, there is *tumbledown shack, rhyming couplets, breakdown lights* (aka hazard lights), *Judgment of Paris* (the beauty contest between Hera, Athena, and Aphrodite that sparked the Trojan War, according to Greek mythology), and *Bradley McIntosh* (singer with the band S Club). If we accept any name, without limiting ourselves to the famous, there is the remarkable 18-letter *Deborah Glupczynski,* a doctor in California. If we just throw all the rules to the wind and use any old pair of words together, we can get up to 20 letters with *gunpowdery blacksmith,* a fellow who should probably be careful working around flames.

Catoptrons and Ambigrams

Some of us spend too much time in front of the mirror anyway, so why not incorporate a bit of wordplay? Next time you head to the bathroom to tend to your visage, bring along a notepad and a pen or pencil as well.

✳ ✳ ✳ ✳

Leonardo da Vinci's notebooks were written in what is called "mirror writing"—that is, from right to left and flipped, so that in order to read them one would have to hold them up to a mirror (and know how to read Italian). However, there are some words that, if he'd written them in uppercase letters, would have remained readable without the need for a mirror.

Take the word TOOT, for example; it's a palindrome, but it also looks the same in a mirror. Such words are known as *catoptrons* (named for an old word meaning "mirror").

Get Vertical

If you don't want to limit yourself to palindromes (since there are only so many of those that are also catoptrons—including MOM, WOW, YAY, AHA, and phrases like A TOYOTA), then the thing to do is write the word vertically, like so:

H
I
A
W
A
T
H
A

> *"Let us be grateful to the mirror for revealing to us our appearance only."*
> — SAMUEL BUTLER

If you write vertically, you can find some very long catoptrons, such as MOUTH TO MOUTH, AWAY WITH YOU, HAM WITH MAYO (or WITHOUT MAYO, if you prefer), HOITY-TOITY, MAMMA MIA, VA-VA-VOOM, and more. And it is possible to have lowercase catoptrons. The word *wow* still works, for instance, and *bod* and *bid* also look the same when reflected horizontally even though they aren't palindromes, since the *b* and *d* are mirror reflections of each other.

Another way to read some catoptrons is to stand in front of a mirror with a piece of paper held flat in front you, touching the mirror. Tilting the edge of the paper closest to you upward will cause any words on the reflected page to appear vertically flipped, making catoptrons out of CHECKBOOK, OKEECHOBEE, DIOXIDE, and more.

Head over Heels

Catoptrons are a specific form of *ambigrams,* which are words that can be read from multiple viewpoints—most commonly, rotated 180 degrees (as with the uppercase NOON or the lowercase *pod*), but other orientations are possible. 0.

✳ *Ambigram* has another wordplay meaning unrelated to this one. Turn to page 317 to find out more about the ambigrams of the anagram family.

"Read about Tom Swifties," Tom Said Swiftly

What can we learn about words and language from the speech patterns of characters in a classic series of children's books? Something hilarious, that's for sure.

✳ ✳ ✳ ✳

IN THE EARLY twentieth century, the Stratemeyer Syndicate published many series of children's books featuring such well-known and beloved characters as the Hardy Boys, Nancy Drew, the Bobbsey Twins, and young inventor Tom Swift. The original series of Tom Swift books—which were not, perhaps, written by the most elite ghostwriters in the world—became known for a particular writing tic: Apparently the writers (or editors) felt that using the word *say* by itself too many times would be repetitive, so they used synonyms or added adverbs to offer variation.

Say It with . . . Anything, Really

For example, in the first six pages of the first Tom Swift book (*Tom Swift and His Motor Cycle*, published in 1910), characters *add, remark, comment, exclaim, cry, retort, ask, growl, demand, sneer, advise, threaten, declare, snap,* and *answer,* but never just *say* anything.

Eventually, things are "said," but they are said *earnestly, quickly, stiffly, eagerly, at length, aloud, admiringly, with a sneer, with a smile,* and *with a grim smile.*

This was such a recognizable trait of the Tom Swift series that people began to poke fun at it by creating similarly structured sentences in which the verbs or adverbs used were appropriate to the sentence being spoken (often involving puns and homonyms). Such sentences became known by the name *Tom Swifties.*

A Brief List of Swift Samples

Here are just a few examples:

* "I need a pencil sharpener," Tom said bluntly.

* "I forget what I'm supposed to be shopping for," Tom said listlessly.

* "What are you taking pictures of?" Tom snapped.

* "I was a spy for the FBI," Tom said informally.

* "This is a picture of my new house," Tom said, visibly moved.

* "Can I get you something?" Tom asked fetchingly.

* "My garden needs another layer of mulch," Tom repeated.

* "The girl's been kidnapped," Tom said mistakenly.

* "I dropped the toothpaste," Tom said, crestfallen.

* "That mischievous child didn't tell the truth," Tom implied.

* "I've been selling salmon from a small kiosk," Tom said standoffishly.

Sentences may, of course, be spoken by other people if the joke calls for it.

* "I guess they didn't believe I'm not a crook," Nixon said resignedly.

* "This musical is depressing," said Les miserably.

* "I'm investigating radium," said Marie curiously.

"Obviously there are many more examples, but perhaps we should stop here for now," Tom said haltingly.

At Least They're Not Guarded by Mummies

Only slightly less majestic, mysterious, and awe-inspiring than the famed Egyptian pyramids are **pyramid words.** *Don't believe us? Just try hunting for one that's 15 letters long. If you manage to find one, it may indeed feel as though you've just dug up a pharaoh's treasure....*

✳ ✳ ✳ ✳

PYRAMID WORDS ARE not, contrary to what one might think, the sort of thing that someone like Bernie Madoff would use to convince people to invest in a Ponzi scheme. Rather, a pyramid word is one whose letters, when stacked in increasing order of frequency, create the shape of a pyramid.

Language Lover's Fruit Salad

For instance, the word *banana* has one *b*, two *n*'s, and three *a*'s:

B
NN
AAA

Papaya is another example. (W0hat is it with fruit and pyramids?)

Y
PP
AAA

Every single letter is its own pyramid, unremarkably enough, and many three-letter words form pyramids—*dad, pop, mom,* and *sis* are but a few members of that family—but ten-letter examples are fairly rare. If you want to *go one on one* with someone, you might want to be armed *to the teeth,* and wear a *sleeve-*

less shirt for flexibility. You'll shout, "Here's a little something to *remember me* by" as you knock your opponent out. "*Bye-bye, baby*. Did I just mop the floor with you? *I did indeed.*" To regain your sense of *sereneness*, you might want to visit a *beer brewer* so you can avoid flunking your next *stress test*. (A few more that we couldn't fit into the story are *pepper tree*, the brand name *Roto-Rooter*, and *deadheaded*.)

Rarest of the Rare

Fifteen-letter pyramid words are nearly impossible to find. Part of the problem is that 15-letter words and phrases that only contain five different letters are already somewhat uncommon, and finding one that breaks up into sets of one, two, three, four, and five letters is a tall order indeed. The Jean Cocteau film title *La Belle et la Bête* ("Beauty and the Beast") comes close, with five *e*'s (if you count the *e* with an accent along with the others), four *l*'s, and two each of *a*, *b*, and *t*.

This pyramid phrase is perhaps not in any dictionary, but it is what a demon does: *possesses people*. It breaks down like so:

L
OO
PPP
EEEE
SSSSS

(Interestingly, the pyramid also spells a word from top to bottom: *lopes*.)

A more legitimate 15-letter phrase is *espresso presser*. (That's one *o*, two *p*'s, three *r*'s, four *e*'s, and five *s*'s.) An espresso press is an actual kitchen gadget, so surely someone who uses one is an espresso presser, right?

Centos: The Game of Patchwork Poems

When confronted with a subject or intellectual arena that's new to you, the bold act of diving in and getting your hands dirty can be an effective way to start your education. If that foreign-to-you arena happens to be the world of poetry, perhaps you will find **centos** a good (and suitably messy) starting point for learning about both reading and writing poetry.

✳ ✳ ✳ ✳

A CENTO IS A sort of poetic patchwork (in fact, the word *cento* comes from the Latin word for "patchwork"), constructed of lines from other poems—sometimes all from one poet, sometimes from many. Centos are mostly the province of literature professors and sympathizers of literature professors.

Cento Intro

Centos are often fairly dry, as in these couplets excerpted from a cento published in the late 1800s:

> *Fame runs before us as the morning star,*
> *How little do we know that which we are; ...*
> *Defer not till to-morrow to be wise,*
> *Wealth heaped on wealth, nor truth nor safety buys; ...*

Those four lines are by John Dryden, Lord Byron, William Congreve, and Samuel Johnson, respectively, and one could argue that the poem in its entirety (which also goes on to include lines from Ben Jonson, Robert Burns, Oliver Goldsmith, John Keats, Alexander Pope, and William Shakespeare, among many others) makes some sort of sense—if one were able to stay awake long enough to finish the whole thing.

Penny for Your Cento?

Centos tend to be more entertaining when they juxtapose works unexpectedly or humorously, as in John Ashbery's "The

> *"Poetry is a mirror which makes*
> *beautiful that which is distorted."*
> — PERCY BYSSHE SHELLEY

Dong With the Luminous Nose," a mostly serious cento that takes its title from an Edward Lear poem and draws from a broad range of sources. One pair of lines combines snippets of William Blake and Samuel Taylor Coleridge to amusing effect, as you can read here:

> *Near where the dirty Thames does flow*
> *Through caverns measureless to man, ...*

Admittedly, it's not Monty Python, but it's droll for literary poetry. The cento is in some ways the spiritual ancestor of some Dadaist poetry, which was often constructed from found sources (and which often tended toward the irreverent and humorous).

Here's one last cento, an original one constructed from lines by T. S. Eliot ("The Song of the Jellicles"), Carl Sandburg ("Fog"), Edgar Allan Poe ("The Bells"), and Samuel Taylor Coleridge ("The Rime of the Ancient Mariner"): four literary luminaries combined toward a rather frivolous end.

> *Jellicle Cats come out tonight*
> *On little cat feet.*
> *How they tinkle, tinkle, tinkle:*
> *Water, water, everywhere.*

Words of Wisdom: Poetry

* * * *

"Always be a poet, even in prose."

—CHARLES BAUDELAIRE

"I would define, in brief, the poetry of words as the rhythmical creation of Beauty."

—EDGAR ALLEN POE

"My life has been the poem I would have writ, but I could not both live and utter it."

—HENRY DAVID THOREAU

"One ought, every day at least, to hear a little song, read a good poem, see a fine picture, and, if it were possible, to speak a few reasonable words."

—JOHANN WOLFGANG VON GOETHE

"No poems can please for long or live that are written by water-drinkers."

—HORACE

"A poet can survive anything but a misprint."

—OSCAR WILDE

"Poetry: the best words in the best order."

—SAMUEL TAYLOR COLERIDGE

"A poet without love were a physical and metaphysical impossibility."

—THOMAS CARLYLE

"He who draws noble delights from sentiments of poetry is a true poet, though he has never written a line in all his life."

—GEORGE SAND

Typewriter Words

Office jobs can be dull, so it makes sense that the mind of someone sitting at a typewriter or computer keyboard might wander from time to time and eventually come up with the concept of **typewriter words,** *or words spelled using only specific parts of a keyboard.*

❋ ❋ ❋ ❋

SOME OF THE longest common words that can be spelled using only the top row of a QWERTY keyboard are *perpetuity, proprietor, repertoire, teeter totter,* and, appropriately enough, *typewriter.* If phrases are allowed, there's also *top priority, witty retort,* and *Peter Piper.* With just one vowel, the middle row ends up being less fertile, word-wise; some of the words that can be spelled using only the middle row are *alfalfa, Galahad,* and *Haggadah.* The bottom row, which has no vowels at all, is downright barren. There are a lot of Roman numerals in that row (such as the year *MMX*), but pretty much everything else is an acronym (like *BBC* or *BMX*) or a sound effect (like *zzz,* or the Crash Test Dummies song "Mmm Mmm Mmm Mmm").

Finding the Right Words (and the Left Words)

Other categories of typewriter words are those typed with only the left or right hand (using the standard method of typing). The longest common left-hand-only QWERTY words include *sweaterdresses, aftereffects, desegregated, reverberates,* and *stewardesses;* phrases include *great crested grebe, street addresses, wages after taxes,* and *excess baggage* (which the stewardesses might have to deal with). *Polyphony* is a long right-hand-only word, and right-hand-only phrases include *opinion poll, opium poppy, hoi polloi,* and the flower *Johnny jump-up* (the hyphen seems fair game, since it's also typed with the right hand). Alternating left and right hands gives *sleight of hand* and *antiskepticism* (starting with the left) and *neurotoxicity* (starting with the right).

One, Two, Three ... We Win!

Most games are competitive; there's a winner and a loser, and the spirit of good-natured competition is one of the things that makes the game fun. **One, Two, Three,** *however, is a rarity: an addictive game that's completely cooperative.*

✳   ✳   ✳   ✳

HERE'S HOW IT works: Two players count to three in unison, then they each say a word or phrase at the same time. If they say the same word, they win! Naturally, they almost certainly won't say the same word on the first try, so they count off and do it again. This time, though, they each try to find a word that somehow connects the two previous words, hoping to converge on the same word. If they don't match, they try again to converge from the next two words, and so on.

For instance, say two players start a game by saying "rocks" and "old-fashioned." One player might connect the two words by imagining very old rocks, leading them to say "fossil" in the next round. The other might notice that an old-fashioned is a kind of cocktail (think "on the rocks"), leading them to say "ice." "Fossil" and "ice" aren't a match, so they'd have to try again, perhaps matching on "glacier" in the next round (since a glacier is a large piece of ice that may have fossils in it). Connections can be made however the players like!

The only other rule is that a word can't be repeated during a game. So if one round has the pair of words "fire" and "water," you can't guess "fire hydrant" in the next round, because "fire" has already been used. Just "hydrant," however, would be fine.

A few tips: When in doubt, go for the general instead of the specific; you're more likely to match. But don't be afraid to make a leap of logic. It's possible to get stuck guessing many things conceptually close to each other without matching, and making a lateral jump may be the best way out.

More Word Games

Here are two more great word games, both perfect for groups!

❋ ❋ ❋ ❋

THE CLASSIC **GHOST** can be played by any number of people. One person chooses a letter (let's say *p*). The next person adds a letter after it (say, *h*, bringing us to PH). Play continues in turn, with each person adding a letter while trying to avoid completing a word. PH might become PHA, then PHAN, then PHANT, then PHANTA. At that point someone might challenge, thinking that PHANTOM was the only possible word under construction (it's illegal to make a play without having a real word in mind . . . though you can get away with it if no one challenges you). This one would be a fruitless challenge, though, if the player had PHANTASMAGORICAL in mind . . . though another player would haplessly lose by the time they got to the *m*, since PHANTASM is also a word.

Another fun word game is called **Dictionary Game.** If you've ever played the board game Balderdash, you're familiar with the conceit of this game. One person flips through the dictionary looking for an obscure and unusual word. The player's goal is to select a little-known word that no one will recognize. Each player writes down the word and then thinks of a definition for it—hopefully one that will seem convincing—writes it down, and passes their paper to the leader. Meanwhile, the leader writes down the word and the correct definition. Once everyone has turned in their answer, the leader reads all the definitions out loud (including the real one). Each player guesses which one they think is the real definition. Players get a point for guessing correctly. If they happen to know the correct definition and write it down, they get three points. If no one guesses correctly, the leader gets a point. Play until each person has had a chance to choose a word from the dictionary. After everyone has had a turn, the player with the most points wins.

Chapter 9

As the Word Turns

The Devil May Care

No, the slang exclamation "what the dickens" has nothing to do with the nineteenth-century English writer responsible for such classics as Great Expectations, A Tale of Two Cities, *and* A Christmas Carol—*although that wouldn't be a bad guess. Use of the term* **dickens** *predates Mr. Charles Dickens by a couple of centuries, as it happens, and the word is actually a euphemism for* devil.

✳   ✳   ✳   ✳

S HAKESPEARE, SO OFTEN lauded as a language innovator, is credited with coining the word. It first appears in *The Merry Wives of Windsor* (1602), when Margaret Page is trying to recall Falstaff's name:

> *I cannot tell what the dickens his name is my husband had of him.*

While we know what *dickens* means, no one is exactly sure where the diabolical euphemism comes from. It shares the initial *d* with *devil*, as does the similar euphemism *deuce*, and that undoubtedly plays a role. But beyond that there is no certainty.

What's in a Name?

Some have suggested that *dickens* is an alteration of *devilkin*, but this is mere speculation. More likely it is simply the diminutive of the name *Dick*; the names *Dickin* and *Dickon* were in use long before the euphemism for the devil appeared.

And if substituting a man's name for the devil seems odd—and maybe a trifle unfair to those poor and unlucky souls who bear the moniker—it isn't unique. *Old Nick* is another euphemistic name given to Lucifer, dating to the mid-seventeenth century.

Devilish Developments

In addition to adding color to the English language, Shakespeare's use of the phrase "what the dickens" also marks a shift in attitude about use of the word *devil* in polite speech. *Devil* was quite commonly used in Elizabethan English; Shakespeare, for example, is not shy about using it elsewhere. But starting in the late Elizabethan era, euphemisms like *dickens* started cropping up. The aforementioned *deuce* came somewhat later, making its appearance in 1651, and *Old Nick* is from sometime before 1643. So the Bard's use of "what the dickens" shows that he was on the cutting edge of all the latest slang and linguistic trends.

This shift in what is considered polite speech also demonstrates that what is considered profanity is really a question of fashion. Profanity may not change as fast as hemlines or tie widths, but it does change. And what is considered highly offensive in one era may not be in another. Think of today's vocabulary, in which sexual terms are becoming increasingly acceptable and the ultimate taboos are racial and misogynistic epithets. A century ago, the opposite would have been the case. What the dickens is up with that?

Where Did It Come From?

Daredevil: This one stems from the two English words it contains: *dare* and *devil*. The term describes a person who is so reckless or foolhardy that he or she would be willing to dare the devil.

Lusting After Luxury

We associate the word **luxury** *with wealth, opulence, and indulgence, but when the word first entered English it meant "sexual desire," or plain, unadorned "lust."*

✳   ✳   ✳   ✳

BORROWED INTO ENGLISH from French around 1340, *luxury* was imported by the Normans in 1066. It is ultimately from the Latin *luxuria,* meaning "extravagance, excess," a word the Romans used to emphasize excessive and sinful waste. A milder term that meant "wealth, splendor" was the word *luxus.* By the time the Latin *luxuria* had filtered down into Norman-French, it had taken on the sexual meaning (the Normans even had a verb, *luxurier,* or *luscurier,* which meant "to fornicate"), and it was this sexual meaning that was adopted into English.

This PG-13 version of *luxury* persisted in English for a few hundred years, lasting from Middle English through the beginnings of modern English. In "The Man of Law's Tale" from *The Canterbury Tales* (circa 1386), Chaucer, never shy of bawdy themes, wrote, "O foule lust of luxerie, lo, thyn ende!" Writing in what's known as early modern English, poet and satirist John Marston wrote in his play *Antonio and Mellida* that the romantic comedy's protagonist Mellida is "stained with adulterous luxury." And even as late as 1812—solidly into the period of modern English—the poet George Crabbe wrote of "Grov'ling in the sty...of shameless luxury."

Use of *luxury* in the sense of "wealth, splendor, opulence" came in the early seventeenth century—meaning it existed alongside the "lascivious" sense for a century or so—probably the result of people reinterpreting the word to reflect the Latin meaning. It is this sense that survives today, and the word has lost whatever sexual connotations it once had. But while English speakers may have cleaned up *luxury*'s act, the French have kept it dirty. Their modern word *luxure* still means "lechery" or "lust."

Words of Wisdom: Success

✳   ✳   ✳   ✳

"It is not the going out of port, but the coming in that determines the success of a voyage."

—Henry Ward Beecher

"The play was a great success, but the audience was a total failure."

—Oscar Wilde, commenting on the first performance of his play *Lady Windemere's Fan*

"Let us be thankful for the fools. But for them the rest of us could not succeed."

—Mark Twain

"The success of most things depends upon knowing how long it will take to succeed."

—Charles Montesquieu

"I have learned that success is to be measured not so much by the position that one has reached in life as by the obstacles which he has overcome while trying to succeed."

—Booker T. Washington

"What exactly is success? For me it is to be found not in applause, but in the satisfaction of feeling that one is realizing one's ideal."

—Anna Pavlova

"I cannot ask of heaven success, even for my country, in a cause where she should be in the wrong...My toast would be, may our country be always successful, but whether successful or otherwise, always right."

—John Quincy Adams

R U a Robot?

Chances are, you've at least once gazed sadly at a teetering pile of laundry and longed for a robot of your very own to assign a long list of unpleasant (but programmable) chores. Or maybe your desire for a robotic companion came much earlier, as a child, when you were fascinated by tales of futuristic adventure and machines that were somehow more man than metal. In any case, you may be interested to learn that the history of the word itself has more in common with the former scene than the latter.

✻ ✻ ✻ ✻

THE WORD **ROBOT** was coined in 1920 in the play *R.U.R. (Rossum's Universal Robots),* written by the Czech writer Karel Čapek. It comes from the Czech *robota,* meaning "forced labor" or, figuratively, "drudgery, hard work," referring to the central European system of serfdom that existed before 1848.

Laborious Roots

Čapek's dystopian play, which premiered on Broadway in October 1922, featured a race of enslaved "Robots," humanlike creatures artificially assembled from organic materials. Far from the images of mechanized metal that the word *robot* typically conjures today, these flesh-and-blood beings more closely resembled what we would now call *androids.* But, perhaps because of the relevance of Čapek's theme—the play came about in a time when industrialization and factory labor were combining with rising totalitarianism (the Bolsheviks revolted in Russia in 1917, and Mussolini came to power in Italy in 1922)—the word *robot* caught on, even as the popular conception of one diverged from Čapek's dramatic vision.

As early as 1923, a year after the American debut of *R.U.R.,* *robot* had acquired a figurative sense, that of a person who acts mechanically or with no evidence of emotion. Derivations of the word followed shortly after. Famed science fiction writer Isaac Asimov—who, incidentally, referred to Čapek's play as "a terribly bad one"—coined the adjective *robotic* in 1942, and by 1945 the prefix *robo-* was in use.

A Muddy History

But while Čapek—or, perhaps more accurately, his brother Josef, to whom he gave coinage credit—gave us the word, he did not invent the concept. The idea of humanlike automatons had been around for centuries. The word *android*, denoting an automaton that resembles a human, dates to the eighteenth century. And the Czech origin of *robot* recalls the Jewish tradition of the *golem*, a robotlike servant made from mud. *Golem* is Hebrew for "shapeless mass."

Čapek's Robots were humanlike androids, but the word, especially in its actual application to real-world automatons, is often used for machines that do not resemble humans at all. This shift is not recent, and such usage has been around almost as long as the word has been in use in English.

In 1930, for example, automated traffic signals in London were dubbed *robots*. This particular use of the word, which never caught on in the United States (although the *Oxford English Dictionary* cites an early example from Canada), has fallen out of use in British English but survives in South Africa.

Where Did It Come From?

Android: Popularized in the 1950s by science fiction writers, the word that means "automaton resembling a human being" actually goes back to 1727 (from the Greek *andro-*, "human," and *eides*, "form"). Androids are also known as *replicants* (from *replica*, or "exact copy") in the 1982 film *Blade Runner*, and as *mechas* (mechanical people) in the 2001 film *A.I. Artificial Intelligence*.

An Unimpeachable Etymology

What do presidents Andrew Johnson and Bill Clinton have in common? Born about a century and a half apart, both men share the unenviable distinction of having been impeached while serving as president of the United States.

※ ※ ※ ※

CLINTON'S 1998 IMPEACHMENT, HAPPENING in recent memory and in the age of C-SPAN and 24-hour news channels, ensures that most of us are at least familiar with the term. Although the details of Clinton's impeachment might have encouraged some to associate the process with a juicy story, the word **impeach** has nothing to do with the fruit. It was first spelled *empeche* and comes from a Latin word meaning "entangle, ensnare." It is related to *impede* and first meant, like *impede* does today, "to hinder, prevent." *Impede* comes from a Latin word meaning "tie the feet together," and both *impeach* and *impede* are related to the Latin word for "foot."

Impeach only took on the meaning of "to bring a charge against" in the 1300s, and it was another century before it began to be specifically applied to public officials. Many people today confuse impeachment—the bringing of the charge or accusation against a public servant or politician—with the determination of guilt or being convicted of a crime; impeachment, however, is only the beginning of the process. (Considering that most officials resign once impeached, this confusion is understandable.)

The meaning "to charge, accuse" came about through confusion with the word's association with the Latin word *impetere*, "to attack." The English words *impetus* ("an impulse"), *impetuous* ("impulsive"), and *impetigo* (a type of skin disease) are all related to *impetere*.

Impeach is also related to the obsolete word *depeach*, which means "to finish off quickly, get rid of" or "to make haste."

Word Roots and Branches
Wordamabob

Infixes are elements inserted in the middle of words. English has relatively few infixes (for more on infixes, see page 130), but one of these is -ma-, the insertion of which into a word lends it an air of pseudosophistication, often ironic in that the speaker knows the sophistication to be false. (She knows that you know that she is only pretending to be sophisticated, or sophistimacated.)

❋ ❋ ❋ ❋

THE POPULARITY OF the *-ma-* infix is a rather recent phenomenon, but there are examples of its use that date back a few centuries. The first is *thingamabob*, which first appears in Tobias Smollett's 1751 *The Adventures of Peregrine Pickle*, a picaresque novel poking fun at European society. The *-ma-* in *thingamabob* isn't a true infix, in that it isn't meant to be duplicated in other words as an independent element. Rather it appears as if *thingamabob* is a variation on the older *jiggumbob* (1613), *kickumbob* (1613), and *thingummy* (1737), all meaning "a thing, the name of which cannot be recalled at the moment."

But 1824 saw the introduction of *thingamajig*, and *whatchamacallit* was in use by 1928. The latter appears to be a variation of *what-d'ye-call-it*, which dates to 1639, or *whatcha-may-call-it*, where the *may* has been reduced to *ma*, probably under the influence of *thingamajig* and company. These early uses set the stage for the introduction of the true infix in the 1990s.

The *-ma-* infix flows from the linguistic watershed that is *The Simpsons*, a source of nonce words since 1989. In that show, the infix *-ma-* is a feature of Homer Simpson's speech. The most successful of Homer's *-ma-* coinages is *edumacation*, which has achieved a considerable life outside of the series, undoubtedly due to the comedic irony of mispronouncing *education*. Other notable Homerisms include *macamadamia nut*, *metabamalism*, *pantomamime*, *saxamaphone*, and *sophistimacated*.

A Politician Says "Oink"

If you watch the Sunday morning political talk shows or 24-hour cable news channels, you will inevitably hear talk of **pork,** *or government funds dispensed by politicians to win favor from their constituents. But why* pork? *Where does the tasty term come from?*

✳ ✳ ✳ ✳

THE LITERAL MEANING of the word *pork,* "the flesh of a pig," came into English in the fourteenth century from the Anglo-Norman *porc.* Ultimately it comes from the Latin *porcus,* or "pig." Fairly straightforward so far, right?

Porcine Progress

The political sense of *pork,* however, is American in origin, first appearing in the 1860s. It is a shortening of *pork barrel* and is a reference to such barrels being a communal source for the staple food. It may even be a reference to the pre–Civil War practice of plantation owners distributing salt pork in barrels to their slaves.

David W. Mitchell, an Englishman who traveled the United States and in 1862 wrote about his experiences in the book *Ten Years Residence in the United States,* quotes a Pennsylvania newspaper editor who explained why he declined to run for public office:

> *To put myself in a position in which every wretch entitled to a vote would feel himself privileged to hold me under special obligations, would be giving rather too much pork for a shilling.*

This is the first known use of *pork* in a political context, although Mitchell identifies the phrase "too much pork for a shilling" as "a common expression," and the word *pork* is used with the literal sense of "meat" within it.

Pure Political Pork

The first known unambiguous use of political *pork* is from the September 13, 1873, *Defiance* (Ohio) *Democrat* in an article titled "The Fuss Over the Pork." This use is quite different from the current sense in that it refers to furor over lawmakers raising their own salaries:

> *Recollecting their many previous visits to the public pork-barrel, the much bigger loads lugged away on those occasions... this hue-and-cry over the salary grab puzzles quite as much as it alarms them.*

Within a few years, the familiar sense of *pork* was not only in use, but openly talked about in the halls of Congress. The *Congressional Record* of February 28, 1879, contains the following:

> *St. Louis is going to have some of the "pork" indirectly; but it will not do any good.*

Through these examples, we can see that political pork is just an example of legislators bringing home the bacon to their constituents.

Where Did It Come From?

Hogwash: This term has been around since the fifteenth century. Originally spelled *hoggyswasch*, it first referred to pig swill. Eventually the word morphed into *hogwash*, and its meaning changed, too. It began being used to describe any useless stuff around 1900.

Words of Wisdom:
Freedom & Liberty

✳ ✳ ✳ ✳

"In every human breast, God has implanted a principle, which we call love of freedom; it is impatient of oppression and pants for deliverance."

—Phillis Wheatley

"Carelessness about our security is dangerous; carelessness about our freedom is also dangerous."

—Adlai Stevenson

"Abstract liberty, like other mere abstractions, is not to be found."

—Edmund Burke

"Give me the liberty to know, to utter, and to argue freely according to conscience, above all liberties."

—John Milton

"We lack many things, but we possess the most precious of all—liberty!"

—James Monroe

"Liberty, when it begins to take root, is a plant of rapid growth."
—George Washington, in a letter to James Madison

"Liberty is the most contagious force in the world. It will eventually abide everywhere. No people of any race will remain slaves."

—Earl Warren, Chief Justice of the United States

"Let every nation know, whether it wishes us well or ill, that we shall pay any price, bear any burden, meet any hardship, support any friend, oppose any foe to assure the survival and the success of liberty."

—John F. Kennedy

Infamous Etymology?

*Has the word **notorious** always been so, well, notorious?*

✳ ✳ ✳ ✳

AMERICAN RAPPER Christopher Wallace, more popularly known as The Notorious B.I.G., was killed in a drive-by shooting in 1997. Anyone familiar with Wallace's music— which, typical of the genre during that time, centered on the themes of drugs and violence—would suspect that his moniker capitalizes on the word *notorious* as a denoter of infamy. And they would be right. But, while this word is most commonly used today to describe something that is well known for unenviable reasons, this hasn't always been the case.

Notorious is a Medieval Latin word meaning "famous, well known," and it was adopted into English at the end of the fifteenth century in exactly this value-neutral sense. But very quickly it became associated with fame of an unsavory or infamous nature, and it underwent *pejoration* (the linguistic process by which a word adopts a negative meaning). The Church of England's *Book of Common Prayer* (1549), for example, uses the phrase "notorious synners." It was from oft-heard uses like this that *notorious* acquired its insalubrious reputation.

Despite the fact that the value-neutral *notorious* is still on the books (listed as the primary or secondary definition, depending on which dictionary you consult), usage experts typically advise against its use. Even so, we see professional writers using the word in exactly this sense.

Notoriety, a related word that has maintained an inoffensive reputation, might have something to do with *notorious*'s notorious tenacity in holding on to its neutral connotation—even in the face of grammar police proscription.

Curb Your Enthusiasm

One of the most euphemistic words currently in use today is **enthusiasm.** *Anyone who is batty, kooky, or fanatical about just about anything has been labeled, at some point, an enthusiast. But what does this label really mean?*

✳ ✳ ✳ ✳

NEWS STORIES THESE days mention sports enthusiasts, martial arts enthusiasts, outdoors enthusiasts, and beer enthusiasts. Even people who think the world is ending have been called doomsday enthusiasts. In some of these cases, using *enthusiast* seems to be a polite way of avoiding the word *nut*.

But is *enthusiasm* really such a weak word? As with all words, its meaning has changed over time. It may be diluted these days, but historically it has had an extremely specific and strong meaning. Borrowed wholesale as the Greek *enthusiasmos*, the word first appeared in English texts in 1579 and meant, more or less literally, "possession by a God." The word was soon anglicized but maintained this divine denotation, as the following 1620 use demonstrates: "The Bacchanals runne thorow the streets raging and storming, full of the Enthusiasme of their god." That enthusiasm sounds more like the pains of the little girl in *The Exorcist* than the excitement of a proud Yankees fan.

By the early 1700s, the use of *enthusiasm* was no longer limited to instances of religious ecstasy, but it still carried with it plenty of force, referring to "rapturous intensity of feeling in favour of a person, principle, cause, etc.; passionate eagerness in any pursuit, proceeding from an intense conviction of the worthiness of the object." Although the *Oxford English Dictionary* stipulates this as the "principle current sense," such a definition seems a little excessive when applied to a beer enthusiast or sports car enthusiast, or any of the innumerable other enthusiasts out there today. Or maybe, just maybe, we're simply underestimating these enthusiasts' enthusiasm.

Totally *Awesome*

The word **awesome,** *as it is currently used, seems quite at home next to "Whoa!" and "Dude!" and even "Duuuuuuude." Everything from movies and video games to the weather and what you ate for breakfast can be, and often is, described as "awesome."*

✳   ✳   ✳   ✳

B UT THE ORIGINAL meaning of *awesome* was more literal, as it did mean "full of awe, profoundly reverential." The *Oxford English Dictionary* has this initial meaning dating back to the late sixteenth century, a time when the suffix *-some* was proving productive in the formation of adjectives from nouns.

Variations emerged over the years as the word took a crooked path to its current destination. The seventeenth century saw an increase in *awesome*'s versatility, as it acquired the meaning "inspiring awe; appalling, dreadful, weird." That sense, while not entirely obsolete today, is far less common than the watered-down *awesome* (used to describe something overwhelming or remarkable) that began appearing in the latter decades of the twentieth century. Although the *OED* specifies the "colloquial" status of this sense, *awesome* has been used this way in such respected publications as *The Economist* ("a garrulous old African with an awesome memory") and *The New Yorker* ("an austere ostrich of awesome authority").

It's a small step from this watered-down use to "trivial use," which is the sense we are so familiar with now. Today's *awesome*, an enthusiastic term of commendation, can bear as much or as little weight as needed. It is perhaps most commonly used as a synonym for another popular slang word: *cool.*

Awesome may no longer apply to the most cosmic or cataclysmic events, but as it lost 70 pounds of seriousness, it picked up more than that in versatility and humor. *Awesome* is a fun word to use, and we can never have enough of those.

Words of Wisdom: Ambition

❋ ❋ ❋ ❋

"The ripest peach is highest on the tree."

—JAMES WHITCOMB RILEY

"Avarice, ambition, lust, etc., are nothing but species of madness."

—BENEDICT SPINOZA

"Ambition drove many men to become false; to have one thought locked in the breast, another ready on the tongue."

—SALLUST

"Ambition—it is the last infirmity of noble minds."

—JAMES M. BARRIE

"A pen is certainly an excellent instrument to fix a man's attention and to inflame his ambition."

—JOHN ADAMS

"Ambition is not a vice of little people."

—MICHEL DE MONTAIGNE

"Ambition is so powerful a passion in the human breast, that however high we reach we are never satisfied."

—HENRY WADSWORTH LONGFELLOW

"Ambition is the germ from which all growth of nobleness proceeds."

—OSCAR WILDE

"Ambition may be defined as the willingness to receive any number of hits on the nose."

—WILFRED OWEN

Rise of the Yuppies

Successful, materialistic, and self-indulgent are three of the more polite words used to describe **yuppies,** *the young, urban professionals of the 1980s who measured success by the price tag of their BMWs and the square footage of their condos.*

✳ ✳ ✳ ✳

DEPENDING ON YOUR source, the word *yuppie* was initially coined as a nickname for either "young, urban professional" or "young, upwardly mobile professional." One thing is clear: It refers to the generation of 20-somethings that regarded designer duds, chic coifs, expensive autos, and luxury pads as the gauges for social standing.

This materialist mob gained acclaim in 1984 when *Time* magazine printed an article called "Here Come the Yuppies!" discussing a new book called *The Yuppie Handbook: The State-of-the-Art Manual for Young Professionals*, which documented the dos and don'ts of the Yuppie kingdom. *Newsweek* magazine named 1984 "The Year of the Yuppie." Thus, *Time* and *Newsweek* introduced this lifestyle to middle-class America and lent it cultural credence—but they didn't coin the term.

Joseph Epstein, an American editor and author best known for his book *Snobbery: The American Version*, is often credited with (or accused of, depending on your perspective) originating the term *yuppie* in 1982. But Epstein can't claim the glory (or blame) for coining the term either. The word first appeared—in a convoluted form at least—in a 1980 *Chicago* magazine article about urban renaissance written by Dan Rottenberg. But even that isn't the end of the story.

In 1983, *yuppie* vaulted to popularity when used by *Chicago Tribune* columnist Bob Greene in his article "From Yippie to Yuppie" about Jerry Rubin, a founder of the Youth International Party, and his road from radical activist to regular Joe.

Word Roots and Branches
A Positive Negative

Anti- is a very busy and productive prefix, having been used to form many new words. But it was not always so. The prefix has only been used in English for about 450 years; Shakespeare, for example, didn't use any anti- *words. The prefix comes from the Greek* anti-, *meaning "opposite, against, instead."*

✳   ✳   ✳   ✳

PRIOR TO 1500, there were only two *anti-* words in use in English, and both were borrowed from French and Latin, indicating that the prefix was not a productive source of words within English. These two words were *Antichrist* and *antipodes*, both dating to the fourteenth century. Words using the prefix that were coined in the sixteenth and seventeenth centuries include: *antidote, antipathy, antiphon,* and *antithesis*. In the middle of the seventeenth century, in a fit of negativity, there was a veritable explosion of *anti-* words.

This sudden coining of *anti-* words was part of a fashion for writers of the period to use a vocabulary heavily reliant on Greek and Latin roots. Eager to show off their scholarly chops, these writers used a lot of words that required knowledge of these classical languages to understand. Critics of this fashion derided the new words as *inkhorn terms*—a label that was coined a century earlier in reference to the bottles of ink made from animal horn and used in schools—implying that these writers were showing off their newly acquired erudition, like schoolchildren, rather than displaying an artful use of language.

The popularity of *anti-* came along at the tail end of this particular fashion, but *anti-* has had staying power and, unlike many of the Latinate and Greek roots popular at the height of the inkhorn era, has remained a productive prefix to this day. It has become so common that we don't even think of *anti-* as being foreign or highfalutin anymore.

Don't Take No Fliegerabwehrkanone

Unless you're a flak catcher, that is. Then it's your job. Confused yet? Read on for the flak facts.

✳ ✳ ✳ ✳

IN ITS LITERAL sense, *flak* is antiaircraft fire. The word is a German acronym for *fliegerabwehrkanone,* or "air-defense cannon." It first appeared in English-language publications in 1938, just before the outbreak of World War II. In the ensuing war, *flak* quickly became an integral part of the military vocabulary. Cities were defended with continuous barrages of fire called *flak curtains;* a *flak alley* was a heavily defended airspace; and aircrew wore *flak jackets, flak vests,* and *flak suits.*

Flak also has a metaphorical meaning of "intense negative criticism." This sense arose in the early 1960s, as evidenced by this quotation from an August 1964 issue of *Newsweek:*

> *Congressional flak aimed at the Administration's multibillion-dollar Apollo... program.*

Flak is not to be confused with *flack.* Both words arose about the same time, with *flack* first appearing in print in 1939. But *flack* has nothing to do with the military. A *flack* is a publicist or press agent. The word was coined in *Variety* magazine as a tribute to Gene Flack, a Hollywood press agent of the 1930s.

While they are two distinct words with very different meanings, conflation of *flak* and *flack* may have contributed to the colorful term *flak catcher,* made famous by Tom Wolfe's 1970 book *Radical Chic & Mau-Mauing the Flak Catchers.* A flak catcher is a publicist whose job it is to respond to criticism.

Nowadays, being a flak catcher is a pretty good, if sometimes aggravating, job. That's a big change from what the term would have meant in the skies over Europe in the early 1940s.

A Terrifically Frightening Etymology

Sometimes a commonly used word has a hidden past that surprises its none-the-wiser modern users. Such is the case here: How did one of our brightest and most unabashedly positive words move beyond such a scary start?

✳ ✳ ✳ ✳

IN CONTEMPORARY PARLANCE, the adjective **terrific** is typically used in an emphatic, complimentary manner. But *terrific* meant something quite different historically, and its *morphology* (how a word is built up out of small units) offers some clues as to the road this word has traveled.

The root *terr-*, found in other familiar English words like *terror, terrorism,* and *terrible,* ultimately comes from the Latin verb *terrere,* meaning "to frighten"; the ending *-fic* is an abbreviated form of the Latin adjectival ending *-icus.* So *terrific* began its career as a word describing something frightening or dreadful.

A Scary Semantic Past

Terrific didn't enter English use until the early modern era. The first writer known to use it was John Milton in the 1674 edition of *Paradise Lost.* Milton uses it in the sense of "frightening" as he describes the animals God has created:

> *The Serpent suttl'st Beast of all the field,*
> *Of huge extent somtimes, with brazen Eyes*
> *And hairie Main terrific, though to thee*
> *Not noxious, but obedient at thy call.*

How did this word, originally a descriptor suitable for the scariest of slithering beasts, come to denote something stupendous? Well, *terrific*, like a host of other adjectives—*horrible*, *terrible*, and *awful*, for instance—semantically broadened over time to denote anything excessive or severe. The *Oxford English Dictionary* dates this decidedly less frightening sense to the early nineteenth century, and the adverbial form, *terrifically*, followed about half a century later. In an example from 1859, Charles Darwin—apparently an advocate for semantic evolution as well as genetic—wrote in *The Life and Letters of Charles Darwin* about revising one of his papers: "my corrections are terrifically heavy."

That's Not So Bad

After acquiring this not-so-terrible definition, *terrific* faced a less harrowing leap to get to its current commendatory connotation. It simply needed to go from meaning "great" (as in "a lot") to meaning "great!" (as in "wonderful"). *The Catcher in the Rye* narrator Holden Caulfield, whose colloquial register offers a good barometer of usage contemporary to the book's 1951 publication, deftly demonstrates the latest sense of the word: "This Joe Yale-looking guy had a terrific-looking girl with him. Boy, she was good-looking."

Holden may have been at the front end of semantic innovation, but today this use of *terrific* is so common that the word's original meaning is all but obscure.

Where Did It Come From?

Afraid: This word comes from the less-used verb *affray*, which means "to startle." Someone who is afraid has been startled or frightened.

Flip to the Flop

In the midst of his 2004 presidential campaign, Senator John Kerry famously said of his vote on funding for the war in Iraq, "I actually did vote for the $87 billion, before I voted against it." This may be one of the most naked and succinct examples of **flip-flopping** *in American politics, but it is hardly the first and certainly not the last.*

✳ ✳ ✳ ✳

FLIP-FLOPPERS, OR SIMPLY *floppers*, as they were originally known, have been so-called for more than a century, and they've been around under other names for as long as there have been eager-to-please politicians out currying favor with their constituents.

A Flair for Flopping

The verb *to flop*, a variation on *to flip*, has been in use since the seventeenth century, but it wasn't until the late nineteenth century that the verb and the accompanying noun became part of political jargon. On November 22, 1880, the *New York World* printed this about New York assemblyman Charles R. Skinner:

> *Mr. Skinner's apparent flop on the railroad question is injuring his chances in the Speakership struggle.*

Even then, flopping was considered a somewhat disingenuous thing for a politician to do. At that time, the slang term *flopper* had a more nefarious sense: that of a cheater or swindler. Famed Western writer Bret Harte demonstrates this sense in his 1871 novel *Gabriel Conroy: Bohemian Papers, Stories of and for the Young*, wherein one character insults another by likening him to a not-to-be-trusted "keno flopper."

A Flip-Flop Flap

The addition of *flip* to *flop* in the political sense of the word happened by 1890. A 1901 transcript from the Annual Joint Conference of Coal Miners and Operators includes the following statements:

> We have been accused of being inconsistent, and accused of changing our opinions as compared to what we said in convention three years ago. We may have turned a flip-flop, my friends, but we never turned as quick as the Operators did.

Seaside Flip-Flopping

Since the 1950s it's been possible to be a flip-flopper in another, less incriminating sense. The *Oxford English Dictionary* credits that decade with the first use of *flip-flop* to refer to the simple—and now ubiquitous—flat-soled rubber sandal. So what do you call a politician on vacation? A flip-flopped flip-flopper, of course.

✳ Linguists use the term *reduplication* for the doubling of a syllable—often with a vowel or consonant change—seen in *flip-flop*. Reduplication is a very productive method of word formation; other examples include *helter-skelter, harum-scarum,* and *flimflam.* For more on reduplication, see page 52.

Where Did It Come From?

President: Originally the title of the leader of the United States was supposed to be "His Highness the President of the United States of America and Protector of the Rights of the Same." George Washington, however, disliked the use of "His Highness" and settled upon simply "Mr. President" as an appropriate title for the leader of the new democracy. The word itself is derived from the Latin *praesidere* meaning "to govern."

Bag o' Fleas?

*A **fleabag** is a run-down and shabby establishment, especially a hotel or other lodging place. The word often appears as an adjective, as in "fleabag hotel." It's easy enough to see how fleas are associated with such places, as these insects have become mascots of filth. But how does the bag fit in?*

✳ ✳ ✳ ✳

I T TURNS OUT the original use of *fleabag* was, naturally enough, for a mattress or sleeping bag. The word first appeared in 1837 in *Dublin University Magazine:*

> *"Troth and I think the gentleman would be better if he went off to his flea-bag himself."*

> *In my then mystified intellect this west country synonyme for a bed a little puzzled me.*

The word existed on the fringes of the language until World War I, when soldiers' use of it to refer to sleeping bags cemented it in the popular parlance.

It took a bit longer for *fleabag* to jump from denoting a bed to a hotel. This new sense first appears in *White Light Nights*, a 1924 book by New York journalist Oscar Odd McIntyre, one of the most-read newspaper columnists of his era. His daily column about life in New York City appeared in more than 500 newspapers across North America. At his peak, he made more than $200,000 a year, almost $3 million in today's money. He wrote about fleabags, but he certainly didn't stay in them.

By the 1930s, *fleabag* was used for any type of disreputable or ramshackle establishment, not just hotels and boardinghouses. The 1932 musical *Guys and Dolls*, for instance, mentions a "room on the top of an old fleabag in Eighth Avenue." The word was also applied to disreputable persons, especially prostitutes, and—not surprisingly—dogs and other animals.

Words of Wisdom: Reading

✳   ✳   ✳   ✳

"To rede, and drive the night away."

—GEOFFREY CHAUCER

"Reading furnishes the mind only with material for knowledge; it is thinking that makes what we read ours."

—JOHN LOCKE

"Books must be read as deliberately and reservedly as they are written."

—HENRY DAVID THOREAU

"Reading is to the mind what exercise is to the body."

—JOSEPH ADDISON

"Where the press is free, and every man is able to read, all is safe."

—THOMAS JEFFERSON

"The book which you read from a sense of duty, or because for any reason you must, does not commonly make friends with you."

—WILLIAM DEAN HOWELLS

"The reading of all good books is like a conversation with the most eminent people of past centuries."

—RENÉ DESCARTES

"Let us dare to read, think, speak, and write...Let every sluice of knowledge be opened and set a-flowing."

—JOHN ADAMS

"Wear the old coat and buy the new book."

—AUSTIN PHELPS

Dude, That's Total Buncombe

Buncombe County is located in eastern North Carolina, within the folds of the Appalachian Mountains. Its undeniable beauty aside, Buncombe County isn't remarkable—unless, of course, you count yourself among the ranks of the lexically curious.

✳ ✳ ✳ ✳

THANKS TO EVENTS that took place nearly two centuries ago, this county's name has the unenviable distinction of being synonymous with *nonsense*. The year was 1820. The United States was riven by the issue of slavery. The hot topic of the year was the admission of Missouri into the Union, and in particular whether it would be a slave state or a free one. A decision either way would tip the balance of power in the U.S. Senate, so the issue was critical to both sides. On February 25, as the debate reached a crescendo and representatives started calling for a vote, Felix Walker, representative of Buncombe County, North Carolina, rose to speak. And he spoke. And spoke. And spoke. He droned on and on with florid and interminable verbiage. Others asked him to cease so they could get on with the vote and settle the matter, but Walker just replied, "I am talking for Buncombe," and continued on. Walker was finally shouted down and had to settle for his speech being printed in a newspaper instead of the *Congressional Record*.

Walker's reply struck a chord. *Buncombe*, misspelled *bunkum*, quickly entered Washington parlance, meaning "nonsense, empty oratory" or "speech out of a desire to ingratiate oneself with one's constituents rather than out of conviction." Over the next few decades, *bunkum* passed out of Washington and into the country as a whole. By 1850, the term had drifted across the Atlantic and was being used in Britain. Around the turn of the twentieth century the word was clipped to *bunk*. Evidently the word, like the speech that spawned it, was too long to be tolerated.

Vampires in the Light of Day

Before Buffy the Vampire Slayer *and the* Twilight *series turned the perception of vampires from that of creepy, caped Slavic counts into attractive, glamorous beefcakes, such creatures were a staple of folklore and superstition with one common characteristic: the need for fresh blood.*

✳   ✳   ✳   ✳

THAT NEED HELPED the word *vampire* make its way into the animal world as an adjective describing parasitic or blood-sucking animals: There are vampire bats, vampire bugs, vampire sharks, and vampire squid.

The animal kingdom aside, *vampire* has also become a metaphorical term for any debilitating force that drains the vitality from another entity. *The Wall Street Journal* called Google a "digital vampire" for featuring content from other newspapers on Google News and then profiting from selling advertising to run on those pages. *Rolling Stone* magazine, in an article about Goldman Sachs's supposed predatory policies, referred to the financial behemoth as "a great vampire squid wrapped around the face of humanity." (Ouch!) An online dating advice column commented, "A relationship vampire is a person who goes from relationship to relationship sucking the life and heart out of their victims and all for their self serving drive."

It turns out that metaphorical use of *vampire* has a long history. The *Oxford English Dictionary* includes examples dating back to the eighteenth century of *vampire* as an epithet for an over-bearing or predatory person. By the mid-nineteenth century, one of the slang definitions of *vampire* was "an intolerable bore or tedious person." The word even adopted a specific use in the logistics of live theater: A trapdoor in the stage that was used to suddenly hide a character was called a *vampire*, presumably since the trapdoor looked (and worked) like teeth that opened to swallow an actor. Sounds preferable to a bite, though.

Now Hear This!

This article is brought to you by the ubiquitous Verizon spokesperson: Can you hear him now?

✳ ✳ ✳ ✳

THE COMBINING FORM *audi-* comes from the Latin *audire*, or "to hear," and is used in a number of English words related to sound. Thus something that can be heard is *audible* or has *auditory* qualities. People who listen form an *audience*. Casting directors lis-ten to actors at *auditions*. And an *auditorium* is a room where you go to hear a performance.

The prefix *audio-* is used in all sorts of words relating to sound technol-ogy. An *audiometer* measures sensitivity of the ear to sounds. *Audiotapes* and *audiocassettes* use an obsolescent technology for recording sound. These have been pretty much replaced by *audio-discs* (which have in turn been replaced by MP3 files). We also have *audiogenic* (produced by frequencies correspond-ing to sound waves), *audiology* (a branch of science dealing with hearing), *audiophile* (a person who is enthusiastic about high-fidelity sound reproduction), and *audiovisual* (of or relating to both hearing and sight). *Audiobooks* have been recorded so you can listen to them rather than read them.

Do Auditors Deserve Their Bad Rap?

Even that dreaded IRS *audit* is so called because back in the day relatively few written records were kept, and examination of financial accounts usually consisted of questioning witnesses about their accounts and listening to their responses. This use of *audit* in English dates to 1435. The connection becomes more apparent if we consider the individual who performs an audit—an *auditor*. The word *auditor*, in addition to denoting that much-maligned IRS agent, can simply refer to someone occupying the role of listener. It also refers to someone who learns by oral instruction or attends lectures.

To call an *audible* in football means for the quarterback to verbally change the play at the line of scrimmage, calling for something different than what was planned. The offense better listen up!

They're Listening Now

Oh, and the name of the *Audi* brand of cars is also based on the Latin root. August Horch, the founder of the company, originally manufactured cars under the eponymously named A. Horch & Co. company. Then he lost control of his company due to a dispute with the board of directors. When he started making cars again, he was competing against his old company and could no longer use his own name. Instead, he translated the German *Horch*, which means "hear," into Latin and produced *Audi*.

✳ Also known as "bionic ears," *cochlear implants* are surgically implanted electronic devices that stimulate the cochlear nerves using radio frequency, allowing people who are profoundly deaf to experience sound. Audiologists have studied the electrical methods of stimulating hearing since the late eighteenth century.

Scofflaw: A Truly Winning Word

Word origins can often be tricky to track down, but once in a while, a word's etymology is wholly transparent. **Scofflaw,** *which has its roots in the days of speakeasies, is one such word.*

✳   ✳   ✳   ✳

THE PASSING OF the 18th Amendment made illegal the sale, manufacture, and transportation of alcohol for consumption. It also created a new kind of criminal: the bold boozer who brazenly flouted the new liquor law. Noticing the absence of a word to characterize said lawbreakers, wealthy Quincy, Massachusetts, prohibitionist Delcevare King offered a $200 prize to the person who could come up with the best word to describe those who ignored the 18th Amendment. King received more than 25,000 entries, among them the word *scofflaw*—submitted by two separate contestants, Henry Irving Dale and Kate L. Butler. The word was selected as the winner, and the prize money was split evenly between them.

How Mr. Dale and Ms. Butler conjured up their winning word is clear enough. It's a combination of the verb *to scoff,* meaning "to mock or jeer," and *law.* A *scofflaw,* then, was someone who demonstrated callous contempt for the new liquor law by breaking it. One might have expected the word to fall out of use once the repeal of the 18th Amendment decriminalized the consumption of alcohol (and, in fact, H. L. Mencken wrote in his 1936 edition of *The American Language* that the word "survived until the collapse of Prohibition"), but *scofflaw* has demonstrated a quiet resilience. It is still in use today, just with the generalized meaning of "one who flouts the law."

Not only did *scofflaw* survive the death of Prohibition, but it also enjoyed immortalization on one of TV's most iconic shows. *Seinfeld* fans might remember an episode entitled "The Scofflaw," in which it is revealed that the villainous Newman is a traffic ticket accumulator of monstrous proportions.

Who's Having a Field Day?

It's likely that most children are introduced to the term **field day** *in the context of school. It names that glorious day in late spring when books are closed, desks are vacated, and the student body pours out of the school building for a day of sun and healthy competition. Such a day is nothing short of a rollicking good time (provided you're adept at the three-legged race).*

❋   ❋   ❋   ❋

ALTHOUGH IT'S ONLY a short water balloon toss from this school-age reference to the broader sense of the term—a day occupied with brilliant or exciting events—*field day* has origins away from the playground. As the *Oxford English Dictionary* specifies, back in 1747 it meant "a day on which troops are drawn up for exercise in field evolutions; a military review." Perhaps it's fitting that *field day* has its roots in the military, as there have been many field-derived terms involved in war, including *battlefield* and synonyms such as *field of battle, field of conflict,* and *field of honor.* A soldier *in the field* is engaged with the enemy, and *keeping, holding, maintaining,* or *taking the field* all have specific meanings in war.

It's not quite clear how the term gravitated from a military review to a general term for great success and happiness, but the latter sense is first found in a Thomas Creevey quote from 1827: "Saturday was a considerable field day in Arlington Street, . . . and a very merry jolly dinner and evening we had."

Since then, application of the expression has become as varied as the games that comprise a child's day of diversion. Today's news stories mention field days in relation to pickpockets, point guards, quarterbacks, critics of presidential administrations, conspiracy theorists, Pulitzer Prize–winning authors, and filmmakers. That's a lot of ground for an expression to cover. In fact, *field day* has enjoyed such wild success over the past two centuries, you might say it's had a veritable field day.

Words of Wisdom: Spring

*"A little madness in the Spring
Is Wholesome even for the King."*

—EMILY DICKINSON

*"From you have I been absent in the Spring
When proud-pied April, dressed in all his trim,
Hath put a spirit of youth in everything."*

—WILLIAM SHAKESPEARE

"Youth is like spring, an overpraised season."

—SAMUEL BUTLER

"If we had no winter, the spring would not be so pleasant."

—ANNE BRADSTREET

*"The first day of spring is one thing, and the first spring day is
another. The difference between them is sometimes as great as
a month."*

—HENRY VAN DYKE

"Spring, the sweet spring, is the year's pleasant king."

—THOMAS CAMPION

"Springtime deceives."

—THOMAS HARDY

*"In our springtime every day has its hidden growth in the mind,
as it has in the earth when the little folded blades are getting
ready to pierce the ground."*

—GEORGE ELIOT

*"But [the weather] gets through more business in spring than
in any other season. In the spring I have counted one hundred
and thirty-six different kinds of weather inside of twenty-four
hours."*

—MARK TWAIN

Pop Quiz

Here's your first question: What part did a city full of graffiti play in the history of a popular testing term? Read on for the answer.

✳ ✳ ✳ ✳

THE WORD QUIZ first appeared in the late 1700s as a noun meaning "an odd person," as well as a verb meaning "to make fun of someone." A few decades later, a popular story regarding the origin of *quiz* claimed that the word was coined by an Irish actor and theater manager named Richard Daly, who bet a friend that he could create a nonsense word with no meaning and make it the talk of Dublin within 24 hours. Overnight the letters *q, u, i,* and *z* were graffitied on walls and signs all over the city, and (as the story goes) Daly won his bet and created a word (meaning something like "a peculiar thing" or "a practical joke, a hoax") simultaneously. Unfortunately, there's no hard evidence to support the validity of the Dublin *quiz* story, as good as it is.

The verb *to quiz* later came to mean "to look at something closely" or "to look at something mockingly." Both meanings may be related to *inquisitive*, or the Latin word *quis*, which means "Who?" This sense of asking or investigating may have led to the sense "to ask, question." The use of *quiz* to mean "a set of questions that are asked, especially in school" didn't appear until the late 1800s, almost a hundred years after the word first appeared.

And while quizzes may be the bane of school-age children everywhere, evidence suggests that adults relish the intellectual challenge offered by the concept of a quiz. As proof, consider the popularity of television quiz shows, as well as the recent proliferation of pub quiz games where trivia-loving adults can test their intellects while testing their livers at the same time.

The Elephant in the Room

Perhaps you don't often consider the elephant outside of visits to the circus or zoo (or the massive creature's regular appearances on television nature programs). Well, turns out the world's largest land mammal also carries some significant some linguistic heft.

✳ ✳ ✳ ✳

ALTHOUGH ITS ULTIMATE origin is shrouded in etymological uncertainty, it looks as though the word **elephant** comes from the ancient Greek word *elephas*, meaning "ivory." The Greek word appears with this meaning in the works of both Homer (circa ninth and eighth centuries B.C.) and Hesiod (circa eighth and seventh centuries B.C.).

Writing a few centuries later, Herodotus was the first Greek author to use the word to refer to the large, gray, ivory-tusked and long-trunked animal. And as the creatures became more familiar to the Greeks—Aristotle gave a thorough (if not entirely accurate) description of the giants—their moniker became solidified. By the Roman era, the Latin *elephantus* bore "ivory" as only a secondary meaning.

Language at Large

From its naming of a very large animal with a long trunk, *elephant* has gained broader application as a means of characterizing an animal or plant that is bigger than others of its kind, or one that has a very large nose: hence, *elephant fish*, *elephant grass*, and *elephant shrew*.

Elephant is also an important part of some idiomatic English phrases:

✳ To "see the elephant" (or to "get a look at the elephant") is to see life, or to go out into the world to learn by experience.

✳ A "white elephant" is any unwanted present. In the late nineteenth century, it was the custom of the King of Siam to give an actual white elephant to members of the court who had offended him, so that they would have to pay for its (very expensive) upkeep.

* An "elephant in the room" is a conspicuous situation or controversial issue that no one wants to discuss because doing so would be uncomfortable.

* "Pink elephants" are seen by those who have overindulged in alcoholic beverages.

* To have "a memory like an elephant" is to have the ability to remember things for a very long time. This phrase possibly came about because elephants are known to be both long-lived and intelligent—or perhaps it was due to a historical elephant/camel confusion (unfamiliarity with either animal led to semantic shifts in a number of languages), as the Greeks have a similar proverb: "A camel never forgets."

---

* Have you ever heard an *elephant joke*? It's likely that you have. In fact, you've probably even told one yourself. An elephant joke is an absurd riddle that includes an elephant. For example: **Q:** How do you know if an elephant has been in your refrigerator? **A:** Footprints in the butter. Or how about: **Q:** Why is an elephant big, gray, and wrinkly? **A:** Because if it were small, white, and hard it would be an aspirin. Get the picture? Don't make us break out the one about the elephant packing its trunk before going on vacation. . . .

Words of Wisdom: Words

✳ ✳ ✳ ✳

"Oaths are but words, and words but wind."
—SAMUEL BUTLER

"We don't just borrow words; on occasion, English has pursued other languages down alleyways to beat them unconscious and rifle their pockets for new vocabulary."
—BOOKER T. WASHINGTON

"Kind words do not cost much. Yet they accomplish much."
—BLAISE PASCAL

"If you wish to know the mind of a man, listen to his words."
—JOHANN WOLFGANG VON GOETHE

"When words are scarce they are seldom spent in vain."
—WILLIAM SHAKESPEARE

"Blessed is the man who, having nothing to say, abstains from giving in words evidence of this fact."
—GEORGE ELIOT

"Apt words have power to suage the tumors of a troubled mind."
—JOHN MLTON

"Words are the money of fools."
—THOMAS HOBBES

"I live on good soup, not on fine words."
—MOLIÈRE

"Dictionaries are like watches; the worst is better than none, and the best cannot be expected to go quite true."
—SAMUEL JOHNSON

"As it is the characteristic of great wits to say much in a few words, so small wits seem to have the gift of speaking much and saying nothing."

—François, Duc de La Rochefoucauld

"One of the disadvantages of wine is that it makes a man mistake words for thoughts."

—Samuel Johnson

*"Words are like leaves; and where they most abound,.
Much fruit of sense beneath is rarely found."*

—Alexander Pope

"It took me years to understand that words are often as important as experience, because words make experience last."

—William Morris

"Good words are worth much, and cost little."

—George Herbert

"The finest language is mostly made up of simple unimposing words."

—George Eliot

*"For all sad words of tongue and pen, The saddest are these,
'It might have been.'"*

—John Greenleaf Whittier

"Words, like nature, half reveal and half conceal the soul within."

—Alfred, Lord Tennyson

"A torn jacket is soon mended; but hard words bruise the heart of a child."

—Henry Wadsworth Longfellow

"Words are braver than all fighting."

—The Teaching for Merikare

Chapter 10

To Make a Short Word Long

Kindle: Not Just a Digital Reading Device

Words that define a group of objects (such as people, animals, inanimate things, or concepts), called **collective nouns,** *have been used in English for hundreds of years.*

✳   ✳   ✳   ✳

COLLECTIVE NOUNS WERE popular during the Middle Ages because of the importance of hunting as a primary means of food supply. Many books of courtly behavior produced in the fifteenth century also stressed the importance of knowing these nouns: To know the correct terms was a sign of culture and good breeding. So next time you see a low-flying siege of herons, deceit of lapwings, or convocation of eagles, consult the list below and wow your friends with evidence of your good education.

Animal	Collective Noun	Animal	Collective Noun
badgers	cete	eagles	convocation
bears	sloth	elks	gang
beavers	colony	ferrets	business
boars	singular	foxes	skulk
camels	caravan	geese	gaggle
cats	clowder	goldfinches	charm
cattle	drove	grasshoppers	cloud

Animal	Collective Noun	Animal	Collective Noun
chickens	peep	guillemots	bazaar
coots	covert	hawks	cast
cormorants	flight	hedgehogs	array
crows	murder	herons	siege
deer	herd	kittens	kindle
lapwings	deceit	pheasants	nye
larks	exaltation	polecats	chine
leopards	leap	porpoises	school
lions	pride	ravens	unkindness
locusts	plague	rhinoceroses	crash
magpies	tittering	squirrels	dray
mallards	flush	starlings	murmuration
moles	mumble	thrushes	mutation
monkeys	troop	toads	knot
nightingales	watch	whales	gam/school
owls	parliament	woodcocks	fall
partridges	covey	woodpeckers	descent

✳ **What is a group of dermatologists called? A** *rash,* **of course!**

Having a Bad Day

Sooner or later, it happens to us all: We have a bad day. For better or worse, English is lousy with words describing us when we, or our surroundings, are at our worst.

✳ ✳ ✳ ✳

THE ANCIENT GREEKS attributed our dispositions to four bodily fluids, or *humors*: blood, phlegm, choler (yellow bile), and black bile. Blood (the sanguine humor) gives us vitality, optimism, and a sense of well-being, and phlegm (including saliva, mucus, and other lymphal fluids) induces passivity, lethargy, and sentimentality). But it's the two biles, especially the yellow, that make us cranky.

To be *bilious*, derived from the word *bile*, is to be ill-humored or peevish. Yellow bile is said to produce anger, irritability, and jealousy; and the melancholic humor (black bile) makes us withdrawn, pessimistic, and, well, melancholic. A *choleric* personality is an angry one. To be *splenetic* is to be irritable, and to "vent your spleen" is to release your anger or rage about something (the spleen is the bile-generating organ). *Distemper,* a nerve-related disease afflicting dogs, originally meant "an imbalance of the humors"; when applied to humans, the term indicates testiness or ill humor. *Dyspepsia* (from the Greek *pepsis*, meaning "digest") refers to an upset stomach, but the adjective *dyspeptic* often describes someone with a sour disposition.

Where's the Beef?

Cantankerous people never seem to be at peace with the world unless they're at war with it, and *grouches* and *grumps* will *beef*, bellyache, bemoan, bewail, bitch, carp, fuss, grieve, groan, grouse, growl, grumble, kvetch, nag, snivel, wail, whimper, whine, and yammer about their crummy lives, even—and especially—when their lives aren't so crummy.

To *remonstrate* is to express opposition, usually argumentatively, and if you don't want to do that, you can always *demur*, *inveigh*, or *expostulate*, which are synonyms of *remonstrate*. A *querulous* (*queru*, "complain") individual always sees things at their worst, and a *petulant* (*petu*, "attack") person, much like the *captious* (*cap*, "seize") fellow, is constantly finding fault.

The Latin root *mal* ("bad, evil") is no miserly source for miserable words either: *Maliferous* means "unwholesome," a *malapert* is a disrespectful person, a *malison* is an obscenity, a *malcontent* is a constantly unhappy person, and *malneirophrenia* is a state of depression following a nightmare. The Latin roots of *dismal* literally mean "bad days."

Finally, there are those *quibblers* who only want to *cavil*, *niggle*, *nitpick*, and *pettifog* by finding fault with everything.

Wouldn't it just be easier to have a nice day?

---

* **The word *sanguine* derives from Old French *sanguin* by way of the Latin *sanguis* ("blood"). In this case, *blood* is a happy word, meaning "cheerful confidence and optimism." Based on the ancient Greeks' belief that the body is made up of four humors, or bodily fluids, ruddy faces and cheerful personalities indicated people whose predominant humor was blood. *Sanguinary*, on the other hand, means "bloodthirsty." Although it comes from a similar root, this one is the Latin *sanguineus*, meaning "blood" or "bloody"—but not humorous in the least.**

Here's Looking at You

Humans come in all shapes and sizes, and perceptions of beauty change with culture and the times. In the seventeenth and eighteenth centuries, the Western ideal of female beauty included an hourglass shape and a full figure, which were thought to demonstrate high social status and good health—a stark contrast to today's ultra-skinny standard of perfection.

✳   ✳   ✳   ✳

LOOKS MAY NOT be everything, but it does seem that there's a word for everything when it comes to looks and appearance:

* *abdominous*—big-bellied

* *aspectabund*—having an expressive face

* *bathycolpian*—having large bosoms and deep cleavage

* *bucculent*—wide-mouthed

* *bugle-beard*—a shaggy beard resembling buffalo hair

* *dignotion*—a tattoo, birth-mark, or other distinguishing mark

* *callipygian*—having shapely buttocks

* *embrasure*—the gap between adjacent teeth

* *glabrous*—bald, having no hairs or projections

* *illecebrous*—pretty or attractive

* *imberb*—beardless

* *kalology*—the study of beauty, aesthetics

* *kalopsia*—the overestimation of beauty

* *leggiadrous*—graceful, elegant

* *leiotrichous*—having smooth, straight hair

* *lentiginous*—freckled

* *leptodactylous*—having slender toes

* *leptosome*—a person with a slender, thin, or frail body

* *mouche*—a small patch of beard grown under the lower lip

* *pilgarlic*—a bald person, or someone who is scoffed at

* *platyopic*—having a broad, flat face

* *pyknic*—having a stocky physique

* *rubicund*—having a rosy complexion

* *rugose*—having many wrinkles

* *slangrel*—a long, lean person

* *steatopygic*—having fat buttocks

* *trypall*—a tall, lanky, and slovenly person

* *zaftig*—pleasantly plump

---

* **In 1991, Kate Moss and other super-slim young models (who, in turn, had been preceded by the aptly nicknamed '60s model Twiggy) were dubbed *waifs*, a term that dates all the way back to 1376. In its original meaning, the term denoted unclaimed property, flotsam, or even a stray animal or person. By 1784, it referred to someone, particularly a child, who had no home or community. Since children who have no one to look after them are naturally thin, the word stuck to refer to the physique of such people.**

Words of Wisdom: Beauty

✳   ✳   ✳   ✳

"Love of beauty is taste. The creation of beauty is art."
—RALPH WALDO EMERSON

"Beauty and folly are old companions."
—BENJAMIN FRANKLIN

"Art for art's sake is an empty phrase. Art for the sake of the true, art for the sake of the good and the beautiful, that is the faith I am searching for."
—GEORGE SAND

"Beauty of whatever kind, in its supreme development, invariably excites the sensitive soul to tears."
—EDGAR ALLAN POE

"The soul that sees beauty may sometimes walk alone."
—JOHANN WOLFGANG VON GOETHE

"To look almost pretty is an acquisition of higher delight to a girl who has been looking plain for the first fifteen years of her life than a beauty from her cradle can ever receive."
—JANE AUSTEN

"To love beauty is to see light."
—VICTOR HUGO

"Youth is happy because it has the ability to see beauty. Anyone who keeps the ability to see beauty never grows old."
—FRANZ KAFKA

"Beauty is whatever gives joy."
—EDNA ST. VINCENT MILLAY

Circling *Circum-*

The Latin adverb and preposition circum, *meaning "around, round about," was commonly attached to verbs to add that meaning to the root. There are many* circum- *verbs in Latin, as well as nouns and adjectives formed from those verbs.*

✳   ✳   ✳   ✳

Y OU'LL FIND LOTS of *circum-* words in English as well, but most of these are more-recent coinages and did not exist in classical Latin. Few of the Latin *circum-* words survived into French and hence into English. Two that did are *circoncire,* which we now know as *to circumcise,* and *circonscrire,* or *to circumscribe.* But in the late medieval and Renaissance eras, people coined a whole slew of words using this productive prefix. Some of these *circum-* words are:

✳ *circumagitate*—to move something in a circle

✳ *circumambulate*—to walk in circles

✳ *circumbendibus*—a roundabout process or method; a circumlocution

✳ *circumcircle*—no, it's not a redundancy; it's a circle that passes through the vertices of a polygon

✳ *circumflex*—to bend around

✳ *circumnavigate*—to sail around

✳ *circumstance*—the surrounding condition

✳ *circumvent*—to go around, evade

Perhaps the best *circum-* word is *circumbilivaginate,* "to speak in a roundabout way, to circumlocute." It was coined in sixteenth-century France by writer François Rabelais; it's not much used, but it sure is a fun word to say.

Lexical Gems

You probably know the adage "a revolving lithic conglomerate produces no congeries of a small bryophytic plant." You don't? That's just a fancy translation of "a rolling stone gathers no moss." The English language has a mother lode of words and phrases relating to stones, so we are never more than a stone's throw away from a lexical gem.

✳ ✳ ✳ ✳

GEMOLOGY IS THE study of and professional field relating to precious and semiprecious stones, such as diamonds and emeralds (precious) and opals and garnets (semiprecious).

Lapis It Up

A *lapidary* (from the Latin *lapis*, meaning "stone") is a cutter and polisher of gems—that is, someone engaged in *lapidarian* activities. *Lapis lazuli* is a blue to blue-green semiprecious stone containing the mineral *lazurite*, and *lapis* is a medium to dark blue color. A *lapillus*, however, which also derives from the *lapis* root, is not a precious stone at all but a piece of hardened lava.

English has several *lapid* words no longer associated with gems. *Dilapidated*, with roots that literally mean "stones apart," now means "destroyed, decayed." *Lapidation* is the act of stoning as punishment for a crime. *Inlapidation* occurs when a material *lapidifies*, or gradually turns to stone (see *petrify*, below). *Lapidicolous* (*col*, "dwell") species of beetles live under stones.

Set in *Lith*

The Greek root *lith*, meaning "stone," refers not to gems but simply to stones. The *Paleolithic* (*paleo*, "old, ancient") and

Neolithic (*neo*, "new") periods are the early and later stages of the Stone Age, when humans used stones for tools. *Lithographs* are prints made by etching an image on a flat surface such as stone. A *granolith* is a paving stone made from granite and cement, and a *gastrolith* is a stone used in digestion by an animal, such as a dinosaur. A *lithotomy* (*tom*, "cut") is the surgical removal of kidney stones.

Solid as a *Petr*

The *petr* root from Greek, meaning "rock," gives English *petrify*, meaning "to gradually turn to stone." It can also mean "to paralyze someone with fear" (to turn someone to stone, figuratively). A *petroglyph* (*glyph*, "carve") is a prehistoric carving in rock, and *petroleum* (*ol*, "oil") is extracted from below the earth's surface.

Petrous simply means "rocklike," which gives us another gussied-up adage: "Individuals making their abode in vitreous edifices are advised to refrain from catapulting petrous projectiles," or, "People living in glass houses shouldn't throw stones." Now that's a gem of a phrase!

"Better a diamond with a flaw than a pebble without."

—CONFUCIUS

"There are three things extremely hard: steel, a diamond, and to know one's self."

—BENJAMIN FRANKLIN

"A fine quotation is a diamond in the hand of a man of wit and a pebble in the hand of a fool."

—JOSEPH ROUX

"Wit must be foiled by wit; cut a diamond with a diamond."

—WILLIAM CONGREVE

"Adversity is the diamond dust Heaven polishes its jewels with."

—THOMAS CARLYLE

Now in Print

Extra, extra! Read all about it!

✳ ✳ ✳ ✳

ALL BOOKS (including the one you're holding right now) are made up of different parts, and all those parts have names. This particular book is made up of twenty-two 32-page *signatures* (groups of printed sheets that are folded and stitched together) and is called a *quarto*, because each sheet of paper in a signature was folded four times, then cut. The right-hand pages of the book are called *recto* pages, the left-hand pages are called *verso* pages, and the page numbers themselves are *folios*. The inner margin area of the page, where the book is bound, is called the *gutter*.

Here are some other little-known terms from the world of books:

* *biblioclast*—a destroyer of books

* *biblioklept*—a stealer of books

* *bibliomaniac*—a lover of books; one whose acquisition of them has become an obsession

* *bibliopegist*—a fine bookbinder

* *bouquinist*—a seller of secondhand books of little value

* *chapbook*—a small book or pamphlet, often a collection of poems

* *colophon*—a publisher's emblem, especially one printed on the title page or spine; also, a statement at the end of a book giving details of the typeface, printing history, and so on

> *"There are perhaps no days of our childhood we lived so fully as those we spent with a favorite book."*
> —MARCEL PROUST

* *duodecimo*—a small book in which a sheet of paper has been folded 12 times to make 24 pages, with the sections sewn into the binding rather than glued

* *fascicle*—a section of a book, published separately, as in installments of a novel

* *festschrift*—a collection of articles published in honor of a scholar, from the German words for "celebration" and "writing"

* *frontispiece*—an illustration placed immediately in front of the title page

* *gloze*—a note in the margin, or a comment or explanation within a text

* *holograph*—a document written entirely in the handwriting of the author

* *incunabula*—books printed in the fifteenth century after the invention of movable type in the West

* *marginalia*—notes made in the margins around a text

* *provenance*—the history of ownership of a particular book

* A *genzia* is a repository for books that are damaged or have been discarded, or for books deemed heretical. The term comes from a Hebrew word meaning "set aside" or "hide."

Words of Wisdom: Books

✳ ✳ ✳ ✳

"'Classic.' A book which people praise and don't read."

—MARK TWAIN

"The things I want to know are in books; my best friend is the man who'll get me a book I ain't read."

—ABRAHAM LINCOLN

"You cannot open a book without learning something."

—CONFUCIUS

"If one cannot enjoy reading a book over and over again, there is no use in reading it at all."

—OSCAR WILDE

"Big book, big bore."

—CALLIMACHUS

"Of all the needs a book has, the chief need is that it be readable."

—ANTHONY TROLLOPE

"The World is a book, and those who do not travel read only a page."

—ST. AUGUSTINE

"He who destroys a good book kills reason itself."

—JOHN MILTON

"A book that furnishes no quotations is...no book—it is a plaything."

—THOMAS LOVE PEACOCK

Make Some Noise

The murmur of a babbling brook; the pitter-patter of rain; crickets chirping on a summer night. Sounds can bring peace and contentment. But sound can also be powerful enough to destroy one's sense of calm: a screaming toddler on an airplane; the clatter of breaking glassware; fingernails on a chalkboard.

✳   ✳   ✳   ✳

LISTENING TO THESE sounds can torture the ear, and trying to describe them can challenge the brain. Fortunately, English comes with a collection of unusual words for sounds:

✳ *boation*—a reverberation; a roar; a loud noise

✳ *charivari*—the act or sound of banging objects (such as pots and pans) together to make discordant sounds

✳ *crepitation*—a crackling sound

✳ *foudroyant*—thundering; noisy

✳ *fremescence*—an incipient roaring

✳ *larum*—a loud outburst or noise, as an alarm or warning call

✳ *paradiddle*—a drumroll

✳ *rataplan*—a rapping sound; a drumming noise

✳ *rimbombo*—a loud roar

✳ *scrannel*—having a grating sound

✳ *stramash*—a noisy uproar or argument

✳ *strepitous*—noisy

✳ *taratantara*—the sound of a bugle or trumpet

✳ *tintamarre*—great confused noise

✳ *tonitruous*—reverberating thunderously

Body Works, Body Words

Our bodies are always at work, even when we're sleeping. We breathe in and out, we cough and swallow, our nails lengthen, we sweat and secrete, our hair grows and sheds. And for just about every bit of work our bodies do, English has an interesting word to name or describe it.

✳ ✳ ✳ ✳

LET'S START WITH our windows to the world, our eyes. *Lachrymation* refers to crying or to the excessive secretion of tears. A similar-looking word, *lachrymose*, is an adjective meaning "weeping" or "prone to cause crying"; the word is usually used to describe sad and perhaps melodramatic things. To *nictitate* is to wink, and *ptosis* is the drooping of the eyelids. *Rheum* is the medical term for the natural whitish discharge from the eyes that forms on the eyelids during sleep. (You might call this *sleep*, or the slightly less savory *eye boogers*.) To be *lycophosed* is to have sharp eyesight. *Blepharospasm* names an eye twitch often resulting in excessive blinking. *Saccade* is the term for having rapid or jerky eye movement. A general facial twitch is a *habitual spasmodic muscular contraction*. (With that many syllables, no wonder we usually just call it a "nervous tic.")

The fancy term for earwax is *cerumen*. Impress your friends with this word come cold season: *Rhinorrhea* is the medical term for a runny nose. To *respire* is to breathe in and out (inhale and exhale), and to *suspire* is to sigh. *Pandiculation* is yawning while stetching. Something that is *sudorific* is likely to cause you to perspire.

Medical terms for split fingernails are *onychoschizia* (horizontal splits) and *onychorrhexis* (longitudinal splits). *Bromsteridrosis* is a term for unpleasant body odor, and *kakidrosis* is a term for its excretion. Someone with bad breath is suffering from *ozostomia*, or *halitosis*. To *infrendiate* is to gnash one's teeth. *Eructation* is the act of burping or belching; *flatus* is the gas we expel from our behinds, and *wambling* is the rumbling and grumbling our stomach makes when it's distressed. *Borborygmus* is another name for the rumbling of intestinal gas. *Pyrosis* is the medical term for heartburn (*pyr*, from Greek, means "fire"). *Veisalgia* names what we usually refer to as a hangover. *Cutis anserina* refers to goose bumps, or chill bumps.

Here are some other body words for body works:

* *bruxomania*—the act of grinding one's teeth

* *carphology*—the movement of delirious patients, such as pulling at bedsheets

* *cicatrize*—to heal the skin by forming a scar or scar tissue

* *defluent*—a discharge of mucus from the nose

* *gleet*—inflammation of a bodily oriface

* *deglutition*—the act or process of swallowing

* *horripilation*—bristling of body hair

* *knilb*—the opposite of *blink* (and *blink* spelled backward); to briefly open one's eyes and then close them again

* *singultus*—a hiccup

* *sternutation*—the act of sneezing, or a sneeze

* *tinnitus*—ringing of the ears

Words of Wisdom: Health

✳   ✳   ✳   ✳

"Health and cheerfulness mutually beget each other."
—Joseph Addison

"If I had my way I'd make health catching instead of disease."
—Robert G. Ingersoll

"The only way to keep your health is to eat what you don't want, drink what you don't like, and do what you'd rather not."
—Mark Twain

"The greatest wealth is health."
—Virgil

"It takes more than just a good looking body. You've got to have the heart and soul to go with it."
—Epictetus

"People who don't know how to keep themselves healthy ought to have the decency to get themselves buried, and not waste time about it."
—Henrik Ibsen

"Health and intellect are the two blessings of life."
—Menander

"'Tis healthy to be sick sometimes."
—Henry David Thoreau

"To keep the body in good health is a duty... otherwise we shall not be able to keep our mind strong and clear."
—Buddha

What Do You Mean by That?
Body Parts Edition

✳ ✳ ✳ ✳

Armed to the Teeth

This is said to be pirate terminology that means "to be well equipped with weaponry." In the late 1600s, Jamaica was a British colony surrounded by Spanish and Portuguese property, and the harbor town of Port Royal was a popular center for buccaneers engaged in constant attacks against the Spanish. To boost their efficiency, pirates would carry many weapons at once, including a knife held in their teeth for maximum arms capability.

Cold Shoulder

To give someone the "cold shoulder" means to be aloof or indifferent, intentionally disregarding them. The expression refers to a "cold shoulder of mutton," which is what a host might offer an unwanted guest in lieu of a fine cut of meat and a hot meal.

On the Nose

This term, which means to be "precisely on," comes from the early days of radio broadcasting. Producers would use hand signals to let their announcers (isolated in soundproof booths) know if the program was running on schedule. If it was, they'd touch their finger to their nose.

Pull One's Leg

When you pull a person's leg you are spoofing or teasing him, usually in a good-humored way—but the expression lacked the lighthearted feel when it was first used. Originally, to "pull one's leg" meant to make of fool of him. By tripping a person (pulling his leg) you can make him look very foolish indeed."

Vent Your Spleen

The spleen was once considered to be the seat of melancholy and ill-temper. So, someone who has an explosion of temper is said to be "venting their spleen," or "getting it off their chest."

Not What It Sounds Like

Some English words—beep, hiss, plunk, screech, sizzle—mean what they sound like and sound like what they mean (see page 74 for more on onomatopoeia). But other terms in English show a real disconnect between their sound and their meaning. Here are some terms with meanings that might surprise you.

❋　❋　❋　❋

❋ *doodlesack*—When we think of doodling, we think of scribbling to kill time. In fact, a doodlesack is a sack of sorts that does involve a form of playing: It is a bagpipe.

❋ *dragoman*—It's a bird . . . it's a plane . . . it's Dragoman? No, this is not a new superhero. A *dragoman* is an interpreter or a professional guide for travelers, especially in the Middle East.

❋ *impignorate*—This verb has no connection with *pig*, or with *ignore* or *ignorant*. *Impignorate* is actually an obsolete word meaning "to pawn or sell."

❋ *liripoop*—There's nothing nasty about this word; in fact, it's part of the most formal of occasions. A *liripoop* is a tassel found on the traditional academic robe worn at graduation commencement ceremonies.

❋ *mulligrubs*—Do worms or other creepy-crawly things come to mind when you hear this word? *Mulligrubs* does have some negative connotation, but not in a creaturely sense: It denotes a depressed state of mind.

❋ *nudiustertian*—If you thought this lexical gem might refer to a clothing-optional scene, your imagination is running amok. Sorry, but *nudiustertian* merely means "pertaining to the day before yesterday."

❋ *oxter*—There's no connection here to an ox or bull, though an *oxter* might smell just as bad: It's an outdated term for an armpit.

* *philobat*—A philobat is neither an acrobat nor a type of flying noctural mammal, but someone who enjoys coping with dangerous situations on their own.

* *pilgarlic*—You won't find pilgarlic in the produce section. On second thought, you may find a pilgarlic anywhere in the store, but it won't be for sale. Although the word means "peeled garlic," a pilgarlic is a bald person or someone who is treated with mock condescension.

* *pooter*—Although this word might give little kids the giggles, it has nothing to do with bodily functions. A *pooter* is a suction bottle used for collecting insects and other small invertebrates. The name is likely from American entymologist F. W. Pooter.

* *spondulicks*—This word conjures up a spoonful of delicious ice cream, but it's actually a monetary term. *Spondulicks* is an American slang term for money or cash.

* *Stinking Roger*—Yes, this one stinks, but it's not a fellow named Roger. The term denotes a flower, such as a marigold, that has a strongly distinctive, indelicate fragrance.

* *tittynope*—Nope! Nope! Nope! There's no connection between this lexical oddity and a woman's breast. The word refers to a small leftover, such as a morsel of gristle left on a plate or the dregs at the bottom of a glass of wine.

* *vagitus*—There's no ointment or antibiotic pill to get rid of this, but fortunately it's not contagious: *Vagitus* is the cry of a newborn.

* *yeuk*—Despite its appearance, this strange word doesn't mean "yuck" or anything similar. As a verb it means "to itch," and as a noun it means simply "an itch."

Clearly, the English language retains the ability to surprise us!

Word Roots and Branches
An Enterprising Suffix

The business world has bequeathed many words to the English language, but perhaps one of the most successful and productive has been **entrepreneur**, *a word that really gets down to business.*

✳ ✳ ✳ ✳

FROM THE FRENCH verb *entreprendre,* meaning "to undertake," *entrepreneur* has been used in English since at least 1852 to refer to the founder of a business or enterprise. The word came to the fore during the dot-com boom of the late 1990s, as companies were being created and going public at a furious rate. Being an *entrepreneur,* despite the word's French origin, was, and still is, considered as American a concept as baseball and apple pie.

Given this, it was inevitable that a variety of *-preneur* words would be coined in homage to the all-powerful entrepreneur. Here are just a few, in order of their introduction into the English lexicon:

✳ *intrapreneur* (1978)—an employee who introduces innovation and new business lines within an established company

✳ *infopreneur* (1985)—an entrepreneur in an information-related business

✳ *technopreneur* (1987)—an entrepreneur in a technical business

✳ *homepreneur* (1991)—a home-based business owner

✳ *grantepreneur* (1994)—a businessperson with a focus on obtaining government grant money

✳ *philanthropreneur* (1997)—a philanthropist intent on bringing business principles and tactics to his or her charitable enterprises

> *"I never perfected an invention that I did not think about in terms of the service it might give others. . . . I find out what the world needs, then I proceed to invent."*
> —Thomas Edison

* *ideopreneur* (1998)—an ideologically motivated political power broker

* *alterpreneur* (2005)—a person who founds a business in order to gain more control over and alter his or her life

* *copreneurs* (2006)—a married couple that founds a business

* *momtrepreneur* and *mama-preneur* (2006)—a mother both raising children and running a business from home

* *innerpreneur* (2009)—a person working for personal growth and fulfillment

And while it technically doesn't use the suffix, there is the term *entreprenerd*, a technical person who founds a business, as exemplified by Microsoft's Bill Gates or Google's Larry Page and Sergey Brin.

---

* **Pope Sixtus IV is considered to have been one of the world's early entrepreneurs. Sixtus realized that people would go to great lengths to ensure a better afterlife for their loved ones, and he mined their desperation for profit, collecting money in exchange for what his constituents believed would lessen the time their loved ones would have to spend in purgatory. Sixtus also was the first pope to license brothels. Perhaps religion and entrepreneurship aren't a match made in heaven.**

In with the Old

If you're no longer young—in fact, if you're at or near retirement age—you might be called antiquated, over the hill, past your prime*… or, if you prefer,* experienced, seasoned, *or* practiced. *The ways to describe advanced age are so varied that the challenge to find the right phrase never gets old.*

✳   ✳   ✳   ✳

ENGLISH HAS MANY words that contain the Greek *presby* root, meaning "old man" or "old age." By the age of 50, many people have *presbyopia* (*op,* "see"), a condition requiring reading glasses or bifocals. Some older people might suffer from *presbymnemia* (*mne,* "mind") or *presbyophrenia* (*phren,* also "mind"); the first term denotes age-related forgetfulness, and the second is the term for general mental deterioration due to age. *Presbyacousia* (*acous,* "hear") is age-related loss of hearing, and *presbyasomnia* (*somn,* "sleep") is difficulty sleeping because of old age. No doubt the one *presby* ailment we all want to avoid is *presbymoria* (*mor,* "fool"), which is silliness brought on by advanced years.

Same Old, Same Old

Another family of "old age" words derives from the Greek *ger* ("old"). *Gerascophobia* (*phob,* "fear") is defined exactly as its parts would indicate: "fear of growing old." *Gerocomy,* the medical care of the elderly, has now been replaced by the more familiar *geriatrics.* (Where do you think the over-the-counter multivitamin Geritol got its name?) *Geromarasmus* (from the Greek *marasmus,* meaning "wither, decay") names the emaciation or gradual wasting away of the body due to advanced age. *Eugeria* (*eu-,* "good"), on the other hand, is healthy, happy old age—may we all be so lucky as to enjoy one! *Agerasia* (*a-,* "not") refers to the youthful appearance seen in some older people, which contrasts with *geromorphism* (*morph*, "shape"), the premature appearance of advanced age.

Oldies but Goodies

Here are some other "old age" lexical oddities:

* *alphmegamia*—marriage between a young woman and an older man

* *anility*—behavior like that of an old woman; used especially to denote a man's behavior

* *caducity*—senility, old age

* *matronolaglia*—an attraction to older women, especially those who have children

* *nostology*—the study of senility

* *octogenarian*—a person between 80 and 90 years of age

* *superannuated*—outdated or ineffective due to old age

* *veterascent*—growing old

Anecdotage, coming from a blending of *anecdote* and *dotage*, occurs when an elderly person insists on regaling others with anecdotes about the past.

And finally, there's *antediluvian*, which describes the extremely ancient: Its roots *ante* ("before") and *diluv* ("flood") hark back to the period before the biblical flood of Noah. Now that's old!

---

* **The Presbyterian faith gets its name from the *presby* root, so one might wonder if this Protestant denomination is peopled entirely by senior citizens. Not so. Rather, the term describes a church that is governed by elders, also known as *presbytes*.**

More Questions than Answers

From the temples of ancient Greece to German universities to the blogosphere today, professional and amateur philosophers have often asked the same questions: What does the universe consist of? What is worth knowing? How should we act? Why are we here?

✳   ✳   ✳   ✳

THE MEANING OF life may elude us, but at least we can verify the meanings of these terms about philosophy.

* *axiology*—branch of philosophy studying value judgments

* *dialectic*—a pattern of thinking or argumentation

* *elanguescence*—gradual diminishing of the power of the soul

* *empiricism*—the belief that knowledge can only be gained through experience

* *epiphenomenalism*—the belief that physical reality is primary to thought processes, which are simply a side effect

* *epistemology*—branch of philosophy concerned with knowledge

* *eudaemonism*—an ethical philosophy in which the goal is to achieve a good life

* *noumenon*—a thing that can only be understood through the intellect, rather than by perception

* *phronesis*—practical wisdom or good judgment, as opposed to theoretical understanding

* *solipsism*—belief that only "I" am real, and that everyone and everything else is a product of my consciousness

* *supererogatory*—in ethics, a behavior that is above and beyond what is required by duty

* *voluntarism*—believing in human or divine will

Words of Wisdom: Wisdom

✳ ✳ ✳ ✳

"Knowledge comes, but wisdom lingers."
—Alfred, Lord Tennyson

"So wise so young, they say, do never live long."
—William Shakespeare

"The wise and moral man shines like a fire on a hilltop."
—The Pali Canon

"The art of being wise is the art of knowing what to overlook."
—William James

"Honesty is the first chapter in the book of wisdom."
—Thomas Jefferson

"The only true wisdom is in knowing you know nothing."
—Socrates

"There is a wisdom of the head, and a wisdom of the heart."
—Charles Dickens

"The wise want love; and those who love want wisdom."
—Percy Bysshe Shelley

"Where there is charity and wisdom, there is neither fear nor ignorance."
—St. Francis of Assis

"All human wisdom is summed up in two words; wait *and* hope.*"*
—Alexandre Dumas

The Dark Side

Talk of "the dark side" always conjures up ominous images from the Star Wars movies, and to "go over to the dark side" is to join the enemy. But the dark side is anything but gloom and doom when it comes to unusual words in English.

✳ ✳ ✳ ✳

MANY OF THESE words stem from the same root words: *lygo* (Greek, meaning "shadow, dark, or twilight"), *melan* (Latin, "black, dark"), *scot* (Greek, "darkness" or "blindness"), and *umbr* (Greek, "shade, shadow"). Let's shed some light on "the dark side" of the English lexicon.

✳ *adumbral*—shadowy in appearance

✳ *adumbrate*—to obscure or produce a shadowy image of something

✳ *lygomania*—an obsession with being in dark places

✳ *lygophilia*—love of shade or darkness

✳ *lygophobia*—an excessive fear or panic of the dark

✳ *melanonychia*—black fingernails or toenails, usually caused by bacteria

✳ *melanotrichous*—having black hair

✳ *melanous*—having a swarthy or dark complexion

✳ *obumbrate*—to darken or to becloud so as to partially conceal

✳ *scotobiology*—the study of light pollution at night

✳ *scotograph*—an instrument that allows blind people to write

✳ *scotopia*—night vision

✳ *umbracle*—a shady place

✳ *umbril*—a visor on a helmet to protect the eyes from light

Them's Writin' Words

Spoken language is universal to all human cultures. We seem to be hardwired to speak. Written language, however, develops more slowly and unevenly.

✳ ✳ ✳ ✳

SOME CULTURES NEVER developed writing; others borrowed a writing system from another culture. Along with writing come many terms about written words and the physical process of getting them down on stone, parchment, paper, or screen. Here are a few you may not be familiar with:

✳ *abugida*—a syllabic writing system in which syllables starting with the same sound are based on the same sign

✳ *analphabet*—an illiterate person

✳ *boustrophedon*—a style of writing in which every other line is written right-to-left with mirror-image characters

✳ *flarf*—poetry (often deliberately bad) written by collaging results from Google searches

✳ *graphonomics*—the scientific study of handwriting (not to be confused with *graphology*, a controversial practice of analyzing personality through handwriting)

✳ *griffonage*—sloppy or illegible handwriting

✳ *heterography*—incorrect spelling

✳ *idioticon*—a dictionary of words used only in one region

✳ *lambdacism*—too-frequent or incorrect use of the letter *l* in writing and speaking

✳ *macrography*—abnormally large handwriting

✳ *majuscule*—an uppercase letter

✳ *scoteography*—the art of writing in the dark

Lend Me a Hand

Few words in English are as handy as hand. *It can mean "man" in the navy sense ("All hands on deck!"), or it can refer to the cards dealt to you in bridge or poker ("What a lousy hand!"). The plural* hands *can indicate "power" or "care" ("Joe's fate was in the hands of the jury"). But when we're referring to a hand as a body part, the Greek root* chir *hands English a fistful of interesting vocabulary.*

✳   ✳   ✳   ✳

LONG BEFORE SCHOOLKIDS were texting and tweeting their classmates, they took lessons in *chirography* (*graph*, "write"), or penmanship. While *chirurgeon* (*urg*, "work, worker") has been replaced by *surgeon* in current English usage, people still rely on *chiropractors* (*pract*, "art, technique") to treat back pain. Originally, *chiropodists* (*pod*, "feet") treated disorders of the hands and feet but focused on corns, warts, bunions, and defective nails. Bats are classified as *chiropters* (from the Greek *pter*, meaning "wing") because their handlike forelimbs allow them to fly. To *chirotonize* is to elect someone by a show of hands.

Monkeys and their ape brethren are *chiropodous*, meaning that their feet resemble hands. From Latin we get both *pedimanous* (from *ped*, "foot" + *man*, "hand"), which is synonymous with *chiropodous*, and *quadrumanous* (*quadr*, "four"), which literally means "four-handed." Can apes have a fifth hand? Yes. Their *prehensile* (*prehens*, "grasp") tails help them hang and swing through trees.

Man, Oh *Man*

In addition to *manual*, as in *manual labor* ("work done by the hands"), the *man* root gives English *manicure* (from *cura*, "care"; "treatment or care of the hands and fingernails") and *emancipation*, (from *e*, "out" and *cip*, "take"); literally, "to take out of the hand." *Mano a mano* ("hand to hand") is an expression from Spanish denoting a hostile confrontation between two people, similar to the Greek-derived *chiromachy* (*mach*, "battle"), or fistfighting.

I've Gotta Hand It to You

Chirosophists (*soph*, "wise, clever") are masters of *prestidigitation* (from the Italian *presto*, "nimble" + *digit*, "finger"), which refers to the performing of magical tricks and other "sleight of hand" illusions (*sleight* is an Old Norse word related to the modern-day *sly*). From French we have *legerdemain* (literally "light of hand"), which usually refers to deceit, as in "financial legerdemain." *Chiromancy* (*manc*, "divination"), more commonly known as palmistry, might give you a peek into the future.

The Greek *dactyl*, meaning "finger," is another rich source of 50-cent words in English. *Dactylography*, or fingerprinting, is used in law enforcement. Financial traders use *dactylophasia* (*phas*, "speak") to signal their orders on the trading floor. *Pterodactyls* (*pter*, "wing") were flying dinosaurs, and cartoon characters are usually *tetradactylous* (*tetra*, "four"), meaning that they have only four fingers on each hand.

Let's give English a hand!

Hand-y Idioms

a bird in hand	on the one hand; on the other
blood on my hands	putty in my hands
hand-me-down	reject out of hand
hand-over-fist	throw up one's hands
hands-off approach	upper hand
left hand doesn't know what the right is doing	work hand in glove with
	lend a hand
live hand to mouth	old hand
my hands are tied	

Eu- Know It's Good

Feeling stressed out? That's not necessarily a bad thing.

✳ ✳ ✳ ✳

You MAY NOT think it could exist, but *eustress* (pronounced YOO-stress) is "good stress," a psychological term for the kind of stress that results from good things: the stress of winning the lottery and deciding what to do with all that money, or the stress of having a new baby in the house, or the stress you feel while reading a very suspenseful novel or riding a roller coaster.

Canadian endocrinologist Hans Selye coined the term *eustress* using the word *stress* (obviously) and the Greek prefix *eu-,* which means "well" or "good."

Eustress and its opposite, *distress,* create the same physical effects, but we have different reactions to those physical effects. Eustress feels exciting, manageable, motivating, and as if it takes a short amount of time: Imagine running a race. Distress feels unpleasant, out of control, and anxiety-inducing: Imagine being chased by a bear. The first scenario is exciting and fun, causing eustress, and the second is terrifying, causing distress. Stress that we can't cope with, over time, can lead to problems. Eustress tends to make us more adaptable and stronger.

What's Good for *Eu-* Is Good for Me

Other, more familiar words that start with the same prefix are *eulogy* and *euphemism* (both of which are "good speech"), *eugenics* (from Greek roots meaning "good" and "to produce"), *euphonious* ("well-sounding"), and *euthanasia* ("good death"). Rarer *eu-* words include *eupepsia* ("good digestion"), *euonymous* ("well-named," as in having a fitting or pleasant name), and *eusociality* (an advanced social behavior in animals, such as ants or termites).

The word *eunuch* comes from a different Greek root—which makes sense, as most men wouldn't equate being a eunuch with something "good."

Words of Praise

From the Old English weorth *("worth") +* scipe *("-ship"), or "the state of being worthy,"* worship *has now come to name veneration or adoration, either in a secular or religious sense.* Theriolatry *(worship of animals) refers to religions with animal deities. On the other hand,* plutolatry *(worship of wealth) is metaphorical, even ironic.*

✳ ✳ ✳ ✳

FOR THOSE GIVEN to *epeolatry* (worship of words), here are some more forms of worship you may not be familiar with:

✳ *aischrolatry*—worship of filth

✳ *allotheism*—worship of foreign or unsanctioned gods

✳ *cosmolatry*—worship of the world

✳ *cynolatry*—worship of dogs

✳ *dendrolatry*—worship of trees

✳ *disidemony*—obsolete word for worshipping a god or gods out of fear, not out of love

✳ *gamidolatry*—worship of marriage

✳ *gyneolatry*—worship of or deep respect for women

✳ *heliolatry*—worship of the sun

✳ *mechanolatry*—worship of machines

✳ *onolatry*—worship of donkeys or asses

✳ *pseudolatry*—false worship

✳ *pyrolatry*—worship of fire

✳ *selenolatry*—worship of the moon

✳ *thaumatolatry*—worship of miracles or wonders

To Die For

Wedding vows celebrate the beginning of a life together but often end with the phrase "till death do us part." Benjamin Franklin wrote that "in this world nothing can be said to be certain except death and taxes." And even sporting contests can end in "sudden death." In spite of, or maybe because of, the morbid nature of death, English is alive with words on the topic.

✳　✳　✳　✳

THE LATIN MORT root, found in many English words, means "death." A person who's about to die is *premortient* (*pre*, "before"), and *neomortia* (*neo*, "new") describes the body immediately after death. *Nomomortia* (*nom*, "law") refers to death by natural causes. An accidental death is *tychemortia* (*tych*, "chance"). A sudden or unexpected death is called *oxymortia* (*oxy*, "sharp"), *pnigomortia* (*pnig*, "choke") is death by choking, and *biomortia* (*bio*, "life") is simply the death of any living thing.

Other *mort* words deal with death in a less concrete manner. An *immortelle* (*im*, "not") is a flower that retains its shape and color when dried.

You're Killin' Me

Can death ever be good? The Greek roots *eu* ("good") and *thanas* ("death") suggest this, but *euthanasia* is actually a deliberate ending of life because of an incurable, painful disease. *Aneuthanasia* (*an*, "not, without"), the opposite of euthanasia, means postponing death. *Dysthanasia* (*dys*, "bad, difficulty") and *cacothanasia* (*caco*, "bad") both refer to a painful death. *Lethiferous* (*letum*, "death"; *fer*, "bearing") is causing death, or deadly, and poisons and diseases that bring death quickly are *tachythanatous* (*tachy*, "swift"). *Thanatosis* (*osis*, "condition or process") refers to a state of pretending to be dead (such as might be employed by an animal to ward off a predator). *Hydrothanasia* (*hydr*, "water") is death by drowning.

Finding *Necro*

Rounding out English's deadliest words are those containing the Greek *necro* root, meaning "dead." A *necrology* (*log*, "word") is an obituary, and a *necropolis* (*polis*, "city") was, in ancient civilizations, a cemetery. *Necromancy* (*mancy*, "to prophesy, foretell the future") is the practice of communicating with dead spirits; the word also refers to sorcery and witchcraft. *Necrolatry* (*latry*, "worship") is excessive reverence to the dead, and *necromania* (*mania*, "madness, exaggerated desire") is a morbid attraction to dead bodies, a bizarre condition also shared by *necrophiles* (*phil*, "love"). *Necrophagous* (*phag*, "eat") creatures such as buzzards and vultures feed on the carrion, or dead flesh, of animals. A century ago, a horse trainer treating a bad saddle sore might have put maggots, which are wormlike *necroparasites*, into the infected area to consume the decaying material without eating the healthy tissue.

Death is an emotionally charged topic; thus, it's not surprising that hundreds of euphemisms—and dysphemisms—have been coined. (For more on euphemisms and dysphemisms, see pages 64 and 66, respectively.) Here are a few examples:

Euphemisms	Dysphemisms
bought the farm	become living-challenged
breathed one's last	buy a pine condo
gave up the ghost	go into the fertilizer business
kicked the bucket	
meet one's maker	in the horizontal phone booth
no longer with us	juggling halos
passed away	kicked the oxygen habit
resting in peace	taking a dirt nap
six feet under	worm food

Words of Wisdom: Death

✳ ✳ ✳ ✳

"They that love beyond the world cannot be separated by it. Death is but crossing the world, as friends do the seas; they live in one another still."

—WILLIAM PENN

"Cowards die many times before their deaths; the valiant never taste of death but once."

—WILLIAM SHAKESPEARE

"Death, like birth, is a secret of Nature."

—MARCUS AURELIUS

"Sleep after toil, port after stormy seas,
Ease after war, death after life does greatly please."

—EDMUND SPENSER

"There are but three events which concern man: birth, life, and death. They are unconscious of their birth, they suffer when they die, and they neglect to live."

—JEAN DE LA BRUYÈRE

"One short sleep past, we wake eternally, And Death shall be no more; Death thou shalt die!"

—JOHN DONNE

"As a well-spent day brings happy sleep, so life well used brings happy death."

—LEONARDO DA VINCI

"Thou has all seasons for thine own, O death!"

—FELICIA DOROTHEA HEMANS

"If life had a second edition, how I would correct the proofs."

—JOHN CLARE

Word Roots and Branches
Ab-solutely Fabulous

In Latin, the preposition and prefix ab- means "away, off, from." It has been used to form many new words in English.

✳   ✳   ✳   ✳

CONTRARY TO WHAT Igor from the Mel Brooks film *Young Frankenstein* thought, an *abnormal* brain doesn't come from someone named Abby; rather, it deviates away from the *normal*. To *abduct* someone is to lead them away, from the Latin *ab-* + *ducere* ("to lead"). The verb *to abuse* is from *ab-* + *usus* (Latin for "to use"). To *abhor* something is to recoil in fear and disgust because of it, and the word comes from the Latin *abhorrere*, meaning "to shrink away from something in horror." And the verb *to abort* is from *ab-* + *oriri* (Latin for "to arise, appear"), so to abort something is to cause it to disappear, to be lost.

But not all words that begin with the letters *ab-* are using this prefix. Some may come from roots that begin with those letters, like *abacus*, which is from the Greek *abax*, meaning "board, slab." And other words begin with the prefix *a-* and just happen to have a root that begins with the letter *b*.

The etymology of *abdomen* is uncertain. It may come from the Latin verb *abdere* ("to stow away, to remove"), which in turn is derived from *ab-* + *dere* ("to do, to give"). So the *abdomen* may be the place where you stow away all that fat—but then again, maybe not. It could also come from the Latin *adeps*, meaning "lard, fat," which also gives us the word *adipose*. Some linguists conjecture that the word was originally *adipomen*, but blending together the initial sounds resulted in the word *abdomen*.

✳ Before the abacus, many early number systems consisted of stones placed in lines drawn in the sand. This may explain the root of the word *calculate*, which is derived from *calculus*, the Latin word for "stone" or "pebble."

Chapter 11

Words at Work

Did I Ever Tell You About the Time I Was Bitten by a Snake?

Which is deadlier: a poisonous copperhead or a boring story? I'll tell ya, both can be harmful to your health.

※ ※ ※ ※

AN **ANECDOTE** IS a short retelling meant to be entertaining or educational, and it is usually based in truth. The hilarious story you tell the kids about the time their uncle slipped on a banana peel? That's an anecdote. The boring (and probably untrue) old story about George Washington chopping down the cherry tree and confessing the misdeed to his father? That's an anecdote too.

Anecdote comes from Greek (by way of French) and means, essentially, "unpublished." The adjectival form, *anecdotal*, means "based on the stories that people tell, rather than on scientific truth." It is often heard in the phrase "anecdotal evidence," used to downplay arguments based on observation rather than science. Anecdotal evidence is gleaned from stories. It may or may not be accurate, but it isn't scientific, and it doesn't hold up in court.

So, About That Snake...

But where does that snake from the title of this piece come in? If you are unlucky enough to be bitten by a poisonous snake, you will need an **antidote** to the venom (usually a specific kind of antidote called *antivenom* or *antivenin*). An antidote is a remedy, or something that counteracts the negative effects of something else. *Anti-* means "against" (as in *antidisestablishmentarianism*, of course, but also as in *antivirus* and *antioxidant*), so an antidote works against something bad.

An antidote doesn't have to be something concrete, however. A neighborhood party could be an antidote to loneliness, or a warm cup of hot chocolate might be just the antidote you need against a cold, blustery day. For that matter, an amusing anecdote could be the antidote to a gloomy afternoon!

In any case, *anecdote* and *antidote* are not to be confused. If you offer an antidote when someone wants an anecdote, there could be side effects, but if you offer an anecdote when someone needs an antidote, they might swell up or turn purple with red spots. And you wouldn't want that on your conscience! (Although it may make for an amusing anecdote at a later date.)

---

* **Did George Washington really tell his father, "I cannot tell a lie"? The first U.S. president was renowned for his honor and virtue, but this line was nothing but a fabrication. Biographer Mason Locke Weems published *The Life and Memorable Actions of George Washington* in 1800, a year after Washington's death. An instant hit, it was republished several times, with each edition boasting additions to a section titled "Curious Anecdotes Laudable to Himself and Exemplary to his Countrymen." The fabricated cherry tree story was included in the fifth edition (1806) and in every edition thereafter.**

Bear with Me

Bear with us while we lay bare the differences between **bear** *and* **bare**. *You'll barely blink an eye.*

✳ ✳ ✳ ✳

A BEAR IS A large, mostly omnivorous, dangerous mammal of the genus *Ursus*. A bear figures in one of the most famous and enigmatic stage directions of all time: In Shakespeare's *The Winter's Tale*, Antigonus says, "I am gone for ever," and his speech is followed by the cryptic stage direction "Exit, pursued by a bear." (There is no previous indication of a bear on the stage, and the bear does not return.)

Just Bear with Us, Please

But *bear* is also a verb, and its similarity of pronunciation with *bare* sometimes leads to mistaken substitutions.

To bear means "to carry," both literally and figuratively. (The past tense is *bore*.) In the literal sense: "Fathers bear their children on their shoulders to see the parade pass by." Americans have the right to bear arms. Figurative senses multiply. One is found in President John F. Kennedy's inaugural address, in which he stated that the United States would "pay any price, bear any burden"—assume any responsibility—in the cause of freedom. The word can also mean "to endure some pain or difficulty" ("she could not bear it any longer") or "to give birth" ("she would bear three children").

Bear appears in many stock expressions, including *bear hug* (a powerful hug), *bear market* (a market in which prices are dropping), *bear for punishment* (to be tough and determined; able to

> *"Let us learn to appreciate there will be times when the trees will be bare, and look forward to the time when we may pick the fruit."*
> —ANTON CHEKHOV

withstand rough treatment), *bring to bear* (exert), and *loaded for bear* (ready for action).

The Bare Naked Truth

Bare as an adjective means "not covered" or "naked." A bare patch of ground has no grass or shrubbery growing on it. A baby's bare bottom is in need of a diaper. The word can also describe something reduced to its essentials, such as the bare cell in which some monks live, the "bare bones" of the plot of a movie, or the "bare naked truth." But *bare*—and here is where the trouble often comes in—is also a verb, meaning "to uncover," "to show," or "to strip": "He bared his teeth in a snarl at the insult" or "She bared her soul within the pages of her diary, confident no one would see what she had written."

The stock expression *grin and bear it*, which encourages one to endure without revealing discomfort or distress, has been known to appear as the malapropism *grin and bare it*—quite a mistake indeed. Spelled this way, it describes the sort of action one would see in a strip club.

✷ The *grizzly* (*Ursus arctos horribilis*) is a species of brown bear found in North America, and it is to be avoided. Digging into the root of the word may drive the point home: *Grizzly* is sometimes written for its homophone *grisly*, which means "horrible or disgusting," as in a grisly murder-suicide. *Grizzly* is also sometimes written mistakenly for *grizzled*, an adjective meaning "streaked with gray hair." Note: Grizzled grizzly bears are also to be avoided if you want to escape a grisly fate.

Do You Deserve a Dessert?

What a difference the letter s makes. It can help the reader distinguish between two words with different origins and different meanings, even though they are spelled similarly and are easy to confuse. But there's more, because the English language is addicted to complications: A single word, spelled one way, can have completely discrete meanings.

✳ ✳ ✳ ✳

DESERT, AS A verb, means "to abandon": "Soldiers who desert in the face of the enemy will be subject to court-martial." The word *desert* originally came from the Latin *deserere*, meaning "to leave, forsake." This same root also gave rise to the noun *desert* (below). Stephen Crane's *The Red Badge of Courage* is about a soldier in the Civil War who briefly panics and flees the field of battle. He is a *deserter* who (spoiler alert!) returns and redeems himself.

Desert, as a noun, is the term for a barren stretch of land, often sandy, that lacks water and vegetation. The huge desert in North Africa is the Sahara—and *Sahara* comes from an Arabic word meaning "desert."

Desert is less commonly used, but equally correct, as a noun meaning "what one is entitled to or worthy of." The word comes from the French *deservir*, "to serve well." It is often used in the plural form, *deserts* (pronounced de-ZERTS). Therefore, when you get what is coming to you, for good or for ill, you receive your *just deserts*—that is, what you *deserve*.

But What If I Really Wanted *Just* Dessert?

Dessert, always a noun, names the sweet course at the end of a dinner, or the item featured in that course: "We always have pumpkin pie for dessert at Thanksgiving." The word comes from the French *desservir,* which means "to clear the table."

So, people who skip this article and embarrass themselves by mixing up these words have received their just desserts, right? Not so fast. The error *just desserts* is exceedingly common.

> *"Use every man after his desert, and*
> *who should 'scape whipping?"*
> —WILLIAM SHAKESPEARE

If you keep forgetting which spelling goes with which meaning, here's a handy trick for general use: Let's pretend you're stressed out about something—wouldn't a sweet treat, such as a slice of cherry pie, cheer you right up? Well, if you spell *stressed* backward, you get *desserts.* If you can remember that pairing, you'll know to spell the word for a sugary snack with two *s*'s in the middle; any other situation requires *desert* (with only one *s* in the middle). Simple!

Where Did It Come From?

Saccharine: This word does not refer to an actual sugar substitute, but it can be used literally or metaphorically to mean "overly sweet." (The artificial sweetener doesn't have an *e* at the end, but the word was first used in that form in 1885.) *Saccharine* was first recorded in the 17th century and actually means "of or like sugar." It is derived from the Latin *saccharum* ("sugar"), which came from the Greek *sakkharon,* although it is related to the Sanskrit *sarkara,* which referred to gravel or grit in the fourth century.

Affecting Effective Usage

*Both **affect** and **effect** are associated with bringing things about. There are four possibilities here to be distinguished:* affect *as a verb,* affect *as a noun,* effect *as a noun, and* effect *as a verb. Effective writers use them all in the correct context.*

✳   ✳   ✳   ✳

THE VERB AFFECT means "to influence something; to have an impact on an action or emotional state": "Allegations of misconduct have not affected his determination to run for reelection." It can also mean "to pretend": "She affected unconcern about her tardiness." The noun *affectation* ("artificial behavior intended to impress") is allied to the latter meaning. The root of this sense of the word—the Latin *affectare* ("to aim at")—signified liking and loving, and therefore developed into the English *affection*. You will want to take some care to distinguish between affection and affectation in life as well as on the page.

As a noun, *affect* means "a person's external display of their emotion; demeanor": "The criminal lacked all affect when the verdict was read." That is, he showed no emotion.

When used as a noun, *effect* means "the outcome or result of some action": "Even after the dose was doubled, the medication had no effect on the bacteria, which multiplied wildly." As a verb, *effect* means "to bring about or to cause something to happen; to produce an effect": "The new dean vowed to effect reforms in the university's admission policies." The adjective *effective* ("successful in producing results") is allied to this sense.

Affect as a verb and *effect* as a noun are the senses most commonly encountered in speech and in writing—and as such they are the most commonly confused. The word RAVEN is a handy mnemonic that will help you remember which is which: Remember Affect Verb Effect Noun. As mnemonics go, this one is quite effective.

Words of Wisdom from Winston Churchill

✻ ✻ ✻ ✻

✻ Success is the ability to go from one failure to another with no loss of enthusiasm.

✻ Everyone has his day, and some days last longer than others.

✻ A lie gets halfway around the world before the truth has a chance to get its pants on.

✻ Golf is a game whose aim is to hit a very small ball into an even smaller hole, with weapons singularly ill-designed for the purpose.

✻ We have always found the Irish a bit odd. They refuse to be English.

✻ We are waiting for the long-promised invasion. So are the fishes.

✻ An appeaser is one who feeds a crocodile—hoping that it will eat him last.

✻ A politician needs the ability to foretell what is going to happen tomorrow, next week, next month, and next year. And to have the ability afterwards to explain why it didn't happen.

✻ A prisoner of war is a man who tries to kill you and fails, and then asks you not to kill him.

✻ All the great things are simple, and many can be expressed in a single word: freedom, justice, honor, duty, mercy, hope.

✻ Criticism may not be agreeable, but it is necessary. It fulfils the same function as pain in the human body. It calls attention to an unhealthy state of things.

High Dudgeons and Low Dungeons

The problem with being "in high dudgeon" is that when you're (by definition) in a foul mood or a state of resentment, you're likely to irritate people. You may even annoy them enough that they will wish they could throw you into a dungeon! Luckily, there are few of those around these days. But what is the relationship between these words, and who ever heard of dudgeon, *anyway?*

✳   ✳   ✳   ✳

THE SIMPLE ANSWER is that there is no apparent relationship between **dudgeon** and **dungeon,** despite their similarities in spelling and pronunciation. *Dungeon* comes to us from French, and it originally denoted a tower or keep (the central part of a castle). Over the years, the meaning became more specific, and now *dungeon* is used almost exclusively in reference to a dark prison below a castle—or something dark and confining that conjures up that image. The original "tower" meaning has also stayed in English, but now the French spelling, *donjon,* is generally used in such cases to distinguish it from the later "dark prison" meaning.

Low and Nasty, or High and Nasty?

Dudgeon is an entirely different story. It appeared in English sometime in the sixteenth century, and no one really knows where it came from. In modern English it is only used in the phrase *high dudgeon* (or, rarely, *great dudgeon*). Because it is such a rare word, and most modern speakers don't really know what

> *"What other dungeon is so dark as one's own heart! What jailer so inexorable as one's self!"*
>
> —Nathaniel Hawthorne

it means, it is very easy for a speaker to mistakenly replace it with a much more common word and instead say the phrase as *high dungeon*.

It's also easy, however, to remember the correct word: A dungeon is a low, nasty place, whereas a dudgeon is a high, nasty mood. Your high dudgeon may cause you to be thrown into a low dungeon, and being in a low dungeon may cause you resentment and put you into a high dudgeon, but a dungeon is never high and a dudgeon is never low.

✳ The Tower of London is home to one of the most infamous dungeons in the world, "The Little Ease." The Little Ease was a dungeon so small that the prisoner inside it could do nothing but crouch uncomfortably until released. The Little Ease's most famous resident was Guy Fawkes, who plotted to blow up the British Parliament in 1605. The saga of Mr. Fawkes gave us a word we use every day. Turn to page 125 to find out more.

Where Did It Come From?

Alcatraz: The famous prison in San Francisco Bay actually got its name from the pelicans that live in the area. The word derives from the Spanish *Alcatraces,* which means something akin to "pelican" or "strange bird." Sailors picked up the name, and when they saw the California island filled with these birds, promptly named it Alcatraz.

You Say *Elude*, and I Say *Allude*... Let's Call the Whole Thing Off

*Both **elude** and **allude** are related to the Latin word* ludere, *which means "to play." They're both sneaky little words, but they're sneaky in different ways.*

✳   ✳   ✳   ✳

ALLUDE COMES FROM the Latin word *alludere*, which means "to play with." *To allude* means "to hint at or refer to indirectly." It's a way to be playful with language. In the context of a story, poem, song, or other literary work, a common way to allude is to use a phrase or image from another work without explicit attribution. (See page 68 to read about *allusion* as a literary device.)

I Thought That Sounded Familiar...?

Titles of movies, books, and plays often allude to other movies, books, and plays. Near the end of the classic movie *Casablanca*, the French police captain played by Claude Rains says, "Major Strasser has been shot. Round up the usual suspects." This line inspired the title of the 1995 movie *The Usual Suspects*; it alludes to *Casablanca* by borrowing a signature phrase from the film. The movie *10 Things I Hate About You* is based on Shakespeare's play *The Taming of the Shrew*. The movie title subtly alludes to the play title phonetically, in that it's similar in length and contains sounds that are repeated from the play title, including the *you/shrew* rhyme at the end. We can say that the movie title is *allusive*; it is, or contains, an allusion to the title of the play.

Watch Out!

Elude is derived from the Latin word *eludere*, which means "to stop playing." *To elude* means "to avoid" or "to escape perception or understanding." When *elude* is used in reference to the avoidance of actual physical capture, it implies skill or cunning

> *"It is the Vague and Elusive. Meet it and you will not see its head. Follow it and you will not see its back."*
> —LAO TZU

on the part of the avoider. Escaped convicts sometimes, unfortunately, elude capture; endangered animals sometimes, fortunately, elude hunters. Often the things that elude us are mental, however, so they're probably not purposefully trying to hide from us: "His face looks familiar, but his name eludes me." The related adjective is *elusive*: "The police found the stolen jewels stashed away in an old warehouse, but the mastermind behind the crime remains elusive."

If the distinction between these two words eludes you, just remember that the elusive second *l* avoids capture in the word *elude*.

* In the German version of *Casablanca*, Humphrey Bogart's unforgettable line, "Here's lookin' at you, kid," was translated as "Ich seh' dir in Die Augen, Kleines," meaning "I look in your eyes, honey."

* As the story goes, *Casablanca* director Michael Curtiz's Hungarian accent often caused confusion during filming. When one prop man brought a poodle to the set per Cortiz's instructions (or what he thought were the instructions), Cortiz set him straight, shouting, "A *poodle*! A poodle of water!"

Where Did It Come From?

Extract: To pull forth; from the Latin *extractus*, which comes from *extrahere*, which breaks down as *ex-* ("out of") + *trahere* ("to draw").

Foul or Fair?

A fowl can be foul, but can a foul be fowl? There are several meanings attached to these two homonyms, so it can be tricky to sort out which is which.

❋   ❋   ❋   ❋

THE SIMPLER WORD is *fowl.* Originally it stood for any bird, as in the biblical parable "Behold the fowls of the air: for they sow not, neither do they reap...yet your heavenly Father feedeth them" (Matthew 6:26 KJV). In current English, *fowl* has become more specific and now indicates a bird of the order Galliformes, the order of game birds that includes chickens and turkeys. Some people limit the use of the term to chickens, but in general parlance, *fowl* includes most of the birds that are raised or hunted for food, such as chickens, turkeys, pheasants, and grouse. If you have difficulty remembering the spelling of *fowl,* you could think of the *w* as the first letter of the word *wings,* and that should tell you that *fowl* is for the birds. Or you could notice the word *owl* in *fowl* and remember that owls have wings, too.

Foul, a more complicated word, has several different meanings and can function as adjective, verb, or noun. The most common use is as an adjective meaning "offensive, objectionable, unpleasant," as in a foul (grumpy) mood, a foul (stormy) day, or a foul (unpleasant) smell. The related verb means "to make something objectionable or unpleasant": "The goats fouled the yard with their droppings." The primary noun sense is "a play in certain sports that is not allowed or is outside the boundaries" (with the related verb sense "to make such a play"). In basketball, for example, a foul is an illegal physical contact with an opposing player. In baseball, a foul is a batted ball that goes outside the lines of play.

Obviously, a chicken doesn't belong on a basketball court or a baseball diamond, so a sports foul has to be spelled differently than a chicken fowl. In any case, a fouled fowl would be a hit bird, which would be cruel...and also foul.

Word Roots and Branches
A *Bi-* Word Is Built for Two

A subject so nice, you'll want to read it twice.

✳ ✳ ✳ ✳

THIS PREFIX IS familiar to most people. It is from the Latin *bi-*, meaning "two, twice." A *bicycle* has two wheels, *bifocals* have two lenses for each eye, and to be *bilingual* is to speak two languages. To *bifurcate* is to split into two forks, or branches; to *bisect* something is to divide it in two; and *bilateral* means "two-sided." Some other *bi-* terms include the following:

✳ *Bi-* is all about the numbers, and in mathematics, *binomial* means "having two terms." And the wonderful *biquadrate* is the square of a square.

✳ *Bifoliate* has nothing to do with skin care. It means "consisting of two leaves or pages," like a pamphlet.

✳ To be *bipolar* is to "have two extremes or poles." In the 1970s, this adjective was adopted by the psychological community as a replacement for the more descriptive, but now less acceptable, *manic-depressive*.

✳ *Bigamy* is the state of having two spouses at once.

✳ And to be *bisexual* is to be attracted to both sexes. In the 1990s, *bi-* took on more meaning in terms of sexuality, as in *bi-curious*, describing someone interested in broadening their romantic horizons.

✳ **Perhaps you've heard the medieval tale of two mythological monsters, Bicorne and Chichevache. Bicorne was a human-faced cow who fed on patient and obedient husbands and was fat and content. Chichevache, whose name means "miserly cow" in French, devoured good and faithful wives, but, because such women were deemed scarce in the misogynistic world of medieval literature, was perpetually starving to death.**

Accept Is Like *Except,* Except It's Not

*Although the words **accept** and **except** have nearly identical pronunciations, they have almost opposite meanings. We're sure you'll be accepting of both—although there are sure to be exceptions.*

✳ ✳ ✳ ✳

ACCEPT IS DERIVED from the Latin word *acceptare,* a form of the verb meaning "to receive." To *accept* something is to receive it, or—thinking figuratively—to just say yes to it. You might take it willingly, as when you accept a gift, or you might merely bear it without complaining, as when you accept your lot in life. You can accept a responsibility or accept a new member to your club. You can also accept the truth of a claim or the validity of an idea. The noun related to *accept* is *acceptance.* Everyone seeks it.

Except comes from the Latin word *exceptus,* which means "taken out." It begins with the Latin-derived prefix *ex-* (also found in words like *exterior, exclude,* and *expel*), which

"For the most part, I've led a virtuous life...except for the two years I worked in sales."

means "out" or "outside." When you except something, you push it out of the group, metaphorically speaking.

Except is not typically used as a verb, however. It's much more commonly used as a preposition, occasionally followed by *for.*

> *"Unfortunately, goodness and honor are rather the exception than the rule among exceptional men, not to speak of geniuses."*
> —CESARE LOMBROSO

You might say, "I'll eat any vegetable except cauliflower," or "Nobody except my mother calls me Junior." *Except* can also introduce phrases other than noun phrases, including prepositional phrases: "Put it anywhere except in the refrigerator" or "I'm a vegetarian, except on Thanksgiving."

An Exceptional Exception

The noun related to *except* is *exception*. Sometimes we talk of "making an exception" of someone or something, which means treating that person or thing differently from all the others. In this case, being set apart from the group is more likely to be a positive thing than a negative thing; the phrase is usually used when someone is set to receive special favors or allowances: "Just this one time, I'll make an exception to the 'no dessert until you finish your dinner' rule."

People and things that set themselves apart from the group can be described as *exceptional*. To be exceptional is to have rare and desirable qualities or abilities, so it's almost always a good thing. An exceptional student is someone with grades on the A side of the curve, not the F side.

Here's a way to remember the difference between these words: To accept is to include, and to except is to exclude.

Mind Your *Manners* and *Manors*

Mind your **manners** *when you visit a* **manor,** *or you might be treated in a disdainful* **manner.**

✳   ✳   ✳   ✳

THE SINGULAR NOUN *manner* means "a mode of behaving or doing something." A doctor who has a good bedside manner is attentive and considerate with patients. *Manner* is often used as a fussier way to say *way,* and it tends to occur in combination with "fancy" multisyllabic modifiers: It sounds more natural to say "in an unorthodox manner" or "in an unobtrusive manner" than it does to say "in a cool manner" or "in a fun manner."

Manner, incidentally, is one of the traditional grammatical categories for adverbial expressions, along with Place and Time. In the sentence "I ate with gusto yesterday at the manor," *with gusto* is a Manner adverbial, *yesterday* is a Time adverb, and *at the manor* is a Place adverbial. (The term *adverb* is reserved for single words. An *adverbial* can be a phrase.) *Manner* also used to mean "kind" or "sort," and we still see that meaning in idioms such as "all manner of problems."

Ask Ms. Manners

Plural *manners* are habits of politeness. It's important to mind your manners. People with good manners say "please" and "thank you" and "you're welcome." Those with bad manners might talk too loudly on their cell phones or neglect to leave a tip.

Knowledge of good manners is especially important when one is visiting a *manor.* A manor is a big house on an estate. A word that's similar in sound and meaning is *mansion.* English lords used to live in manors. In medieval England, a manor was also an official territorial unit, and the "lord of the manor" enjoyed certain privileges, such as the right to hold court.

To mind your *manners* and *manors,* you might remember that the word *manor* contains the letters *or,* just like the word *lord.*

Is It *Complementary* to Be *Complimentary*, or the Other Way Around?

If someone tells you what a great job you did, is he or she being **complimentary** *or* **complementary***? Would you choose complimentary or complementary shoes to match your outfit? Pronounced almost identically, these two words are easily and often confused, but there are ways to keep them straight.*

✳   ✳   ✳   ✳

SOMETHING THAT IS *complementary* is something that completes a set, or that goes well with something else. Your shoes and your outfit can be complementary, for example, or the right wine can complement a meal. Complementary medicine is medicine that works alongside standard treatments but doesn't replace them. (Alternative medicine, on the other hand, is a replacement for, rather than an adjunct to, the standard treatment.) More technically, colors and angles can be complementary as well. Complementary colors are those that appear opposite each other on a traditional color wheel and that, when mixed, generally make gray or a neutral color. In geometry, complementary angles total 90 degrees when added together (that is, a 30-degree angle and a 60-degree angle would be complementary). Just remember that something complementary completes a set—all three words are spelled with an internal *e*.

Complimentary has two primary meanings, both closely related. First, a *compliment* is a kind or admiring remark. If a person is complimentary, they are saying something nice or being kind. Second, if an object is complimentary, it is free. Complimentary coffee is coffee that is handed out free of charge, for example. A way to remember the correct spelling in this case is to consider that it is kind to be complimentary—both words are spelled with an internal *i*.

In Spite of Everything

Read this article: You might learn something in spite of yourself!

✳ ✳ ✳ ✳

SPITE IS AN unpleasant word for an unpleasant concept. Deriving from the Old French *despit* ("contempt") and *despiter* ("to show contempt for") and the Latin *despectus* ("looking down on"), it came into English as a noun meaning "an intention to hurt or annoy" and as a verb meaning "to deliberately hurt, annoy, or offend."

Thus, "she sold his books in the divorce out of spite" reflects the unlovely emotions of these painful circumstances. While the proverbial "cut off your nose to spite your face" literally describes harming one part of yourself to injure another, it is (thankfully) a figurative expression for acting out of pique in a self-destructive manner. A

"Have we made a real effort to know the neighbors."

spite fence is a barrier a person erects to annoy a neighbor with whom he is at odds, even though he has no particular need of it and draws no particular benefit from it. The word also gives us the adjective *spiteful*, meaning "malicious" or "vindictive." Spiteful remarks are intended to wound the hearer.

Spitefully Speaking

At some point far back in the language, *spite* also morphed into a preposition, *despite*, meaning "not being affected by":

> *"There is not a more mean, stupid, dastardly, pitiful, selfish, spiteful, envious ungrateful animal than the public."*
> —William Hazlitt

"She held her head up despite the spiteful rumors being spread about her." The phrase *in spite of* is synonymous with *despite*: "In spite of all his efforts, he never succeeded in obtaining a promotion."

Moreover, if you do something "in spite of yourself," you do it even though you do not really want to or did not expect to: "She laughed in spite of herself." No particular malice or ill will may be attached to the expression.

The Latin root *despectus* has another English descendant, *to despise*, which means "to feel contempt for." *Despectus* gave rise to the word *despicable*, or "worthy of contempt." *Despise* has a crowd of closely related words used for identifying hatred and dislike: *abhor, contemn* (not *condemn*), *detest, disdain, loathe,* and *scorn.* Be careful; it can be nasty out there.

✳ The idiom "cut off your nose to spite your face" is thought to date back as far as the ninth century, when devout women would disfigure themselves as a way to protect their chastity. It is said that when Saint Aebbe the Younger, the mother superior of the monastery of Coldingham in Scotland, caught wind of Viking pirates invading, she instructed her nuns to mutilate their faces so as to appear undesirable to the Vikings and protect their virginity. She then cut off her nose and upper lip, with the nuns following suit. On the one hand, the tactic worked: When the Vikings finally arrived, they left the nuns alone. However, it might have worked too well: The invaders were so horrified that they burned down the monastery.

Optimal Options

There is a regular pattern in English in which adjectives are formed from nouns by adding or changing the ending to -al. Someone in hysterics is hysterical, *someone who is talented at music is* musical, *and what happened in the course of history is* historical. *But is the* **optimum** *of something necessarily* **optimal***? That one is a bit trickier.*

✳   ✳   ✳   ✳

Accoring to most dictionaries, *optimal* is an adjective, but *optimum* is both a noun and an adjective. Because *optimum* comes from a Latin noun with the same form and meaning as the English word, some people believe that it should be used only as a noun. But *optimum* has been used adjectivally since the nineteenth century, so there's no real reason to avoid it, even though there is another available adjective (*optimal*). But then the question becomes: What is the difference? Should you use one rather than the other in certain situations, or do they mean the same thing?

Because most dictionaries treat the words as direct synonyms, they can be used interchangeably, with the exception that only *optimal* can take an *-ly*

"We've concluded that our optimal deployment of your services can only be actualized within a downsizing paradigm."

ending to form an adverb: Someone can be *optimally* employed (employed to the best of their advantage), but not *optimumly* employed.

> *"Between the optimist and the pessimist,*
> *the difference is droll.*
> *The optimist sees the doughnut;*
> *the pessimist the hole."*
>
> —Oscar Wilde

But Which One Is Optimal?

There are some people who like to make a distinction between these words, though, and—especially in some scientific fields—there is a subtle difference between their meanings. Among people who differentiate, *optimum* implies the absolute most or best, while *optimal* suggests a relative best; therefore, *optimal* indicates the best that is available, while *optimum* indicates the best that is theoretically possible. The optimum number of people in a room, for example, would be the largest possible number of people that could fit. The optimal number, on the other hand, would be the largest number that could fit comfortably—which is likely to be a significantly smaller number. This distinction is also important in medicine, for example, where the difference between an *optimum* dose and an *optimal* dose could be dangerous!

Unlike many confusing words in English, there is no right or wrong here. If it is helpful to make a subtle distinction in meaning, or if you are working in a field where the distinction is usually made, you should do so—as long as you realize that not everyone will pick up on it.

Is such a situation optimum or optimal? An optimist would certainly say it's both!

✴ Optimus Prime is a character from the *Transformers* movie franchise and line of toys. With a name like Optimus (from the Latin *optim,* meaning "best") and Prime (from the Latin *prima,* or "first"), is it any wonder he's the leader of the good guys?

Words of Wisdom:
Optimism/Pessimism

* * * *

"A pessimist is one who makes difficulties of his opportunities and an optimist is one who makes opportunities of his difficulties."

—HARRY S. TRUMAN

"Optimism...is a mania for maintaining that all is well when things are going badly."

—VOLTAIRE

"Pessimism, when you get used to it, is just as agreeable as optimism. "

—ENOCH ARNOLD BENNETT

"A pessimist is a man who has been compelled to live with an optimist."

—ELBERT HUBBARD

"Optimism—the doctrine or belief that everything is beautiful, including what is ugly."

—AMBROSE BIERCE

"Pessimism leads to weakness; optimism to power."

—WILLIAM JAMES

"I can endure my own despair, but not another's hope."

—WILLIAM WALSH

"Pessimism never won any battle."

—GENERAL DWIGHT D. EISENHOWER

Word Roots and Branches
Doodle-Dos

Most people have, at one time or another, absentmindedly scribbled or scrawled our way through a phone call or a less-than-riveting class lecture; that is to say, we've doodled. We're doodlers. We've engaged in doodling. But has a consideration of the word itself ever accompanied our doodles? Don't bet doodly-doo on it.

❋　❋　❋　❋

THE OXFORD ENGLISH DICTIONARY currently defines *doodle* as "an aimless scrawl made by a person while his mind is more or less otherwise applied." But *doodle* has a résumé of meanings that is as fun as the word sounds. From the seventeenth century to the nineteenth century, *doodle* meant "a silly or foolish fellow; a noodle." The *Historical Dictionary of American Slang* says *doodle* was a term for a Union soldier, perhaps inspired by the song "Yankee Doodle"; it also defines *doodle-doo* and *doodly-doo* as meaning "the least bit."

Here are some additional doodle terms:

❋ It's part of *cock-a-doodle-doo*, the most common onomatopoeic representation of rooster-ese.

❋ A *doodlebug* is a divining rod used by prospectors to indicate the presence of oil, minerals, etc.; also, the larva of an ant lion.

❋ A *fopdoodle* is a fop, with a spritz of idiocy thrown in.

❋ *Monkey doodle* is foolish, meddling, or mischievous activity.

❋ A *snickerdoodle* is a type of soft, sweet cookie, typically sprinkled with cinnamon and sugar.

Ned Flanders, the invariably optimistic neighbor on *The Simpsons*, exploits the combinatory powers of *doodle* to liven up his lexicon. Some of his coinages include: *whoopsie doodle*, *diddly-doodly*, and the greeting *howdy-doodly*.

Take a Deep Breath

In English you have to watch out for that silent e. It can indicate not only a difference in pronunciation, but also a difference in part of speech.

✳ ✳ ✳ ✳

THE WORD **BREATH,** pronounced "breth," is always a noun. It means "the air taken into and expelled from the lungs." *Breathe,* which tacks on an *e* at the end of *breath* and is pronounced with a long *e,* is a verb that describes the action of taking air into the lungs and expelling it.

Breathing being a necessity of life, it is not surprising that the language has developed a rich store of metaphorical associations. Here are a few phrases:

✳ To "wait with bated breath" is to be in suspense.

✳ "Don't hold your breath" warns someone not to expect any quick action.

✳ "Save your breath" advises one not to waste time on a fruitless enterprise. "Don't waste your breath" gives the same advice.

✳ To "take someone's breath away" is to surprise with respect or delight.

✳ "A breath of fresh air" describes a welcome change that takes place for the better.

✳ And "last breath," of course, signifies death. This is sometimes used in exaggeration: "She will fight for her rights to the last breath."

Breathe Easy

✳ To "breathe down someone's neck" is to be oppressively attentive to their actions.

* To "not breathe a word" is to keep a secret.

* To "breathe new life into" is to reinvigorate.

* To "breathe easy" is to relax and be relieved from stress.

* To "breathe one's last" signifies death.

Not only are metaphorical phrases with the word *breath* in them common in spoken English, they also appear often in literarature. In fact, such a phrase occurs as early as 1590, in Shakespeare's *The Comedy of Errors:* "You run this humor out of breath."

Breadth and Butter

Indeed, the breadth of metaphors is large. Wait a minute—*breadth?* Because of the similarity in pronunciation, *breadth* ("the width of an object" or "a wide range or extent") is sometimes confused with *breath.* An expert does not have a wide *breath* of knowledge but a wide *breadth* of knowledge—as you will, after reading this article.

"A man who waits to believe in action before acting is anything you like, but he's not a man of action. You must act as you breathe."

—Georges Clemenceau

"A human being is only breath and shadow."

—Sophocles

"All things share the same breath—the beast, the tree, the man . . . the air shares its spirit with all the life it supports."

—Chief Seattle

Where Did It Come From?

Yawn: An involuntary reaction to tiredness or boredom; opening the mouth wide for an intake or expulsion of breath. This word comes from the Middle English *yenen* or *yanen*, which in turn derives from the Old English *ginian*; akin to the Old High German *ginēn* (to yawn), the Latin *hiare*, and the Greek *chainein*.

Bewitched and Bewildered by *Be-*

As far as English prefixes go, you won't find many much older than be-. *Many English prefixes in use today are from Latin and Greek, and their English uses date to the late Middle Ages or the Renaissance period—but* be- *is older. It dates to Old English, where it was a preposition originally meaning "about, around, near." This preposition still exists today with a somewhat different form; we know it as* by.

✳ ✳ ✳ ✳

BE- IS FOUND in many prepositions and adverbs pertaining
to location. Because it is so deeply
ingrained in the language, we
often don't even realize that
it is present. Something that
is *before* is at the front, while
something *behind* is at the
rear. If something is *below*
or *beneath*, it is at a subordinate spatial position.
Something that is *between* is
near two things, while something that is *beyond* is at a distance, or yonder.

The prefix doesn't always appear as *be-*, either. When it is
accented, we spell it *by-*. Hence we get *bylaws*, *bystanders*, and
byroads. Befuddled? Don't be.

To *Be-* or Not to *Be-*?
Of course *be* by itself is a verb, but it is often combined
with other verbs to form new words. When that happens,
the *be-* prefix comes into its own, boasting a wide variety
of meanings:

* It can signify "about, all-over." So to *bestir* is to rise and move about, to be *bespattered* is to be covered with mud or some other substance, and to be *bespeckled* is to have speckles all over. This use is still active and productive, forming new words.

* *Be-* can act as an intensifier, adding emphasis without changing the fundamental meaning. So to *bemuddle* is more confusing than to *muddle*, and *begrudging* is more reluctant than simple *grudging*. This intensive use also remains productive today.

* The prefix can render a verb figurative or specialize its meaning. So to *befall* has nothing to do with literal falling, but refers to chance and happenstance. To *become* involves a figurative arrival at a new state of being, not a physical one at a new place. And to *behold* something is to see something as if it were in your possession.

* It can change an intransitive verb into a transitive one. So to *belie* is to tell lies about or misrepresent something specific, not simply to speak falsely, and to *bemoan* or *bewail* is to complain about a specific condition, not simply to cry out in pain.

* It can combine with a verb to form a participial adjective meaning "covered, furnished with, overcome by." Hence something can be *bejeweled*, *bewitched*, or *beguiled*. This use of the prefix remains productive.

---

* **The soliloquoy heard 'round the world: Hamlet's "To be or not to be" is one of the most famous literary quotations of all time. Most people can quote the beginning: "To be, or not to be, that is the question: Whether 'tis Nobler in the mind to suffer"... and then everyone other than Shakespearean scholars and theater buffs falters. The prince's speech goes on for 31 more lines—it's 247 words in total.**

His Arrival Is Imminent, Your Eminence

Here's a topic that is eminently confusing to some.

✳ ✳ ✳ ✳

To be **EMINENT** means to be "conspicuous, notable, or important." One way to be conspicuous, or "stick out," is to stick out literally, like a jutting rock. In fact, *eminent* comes from the Latin *eminere*, meaning "to stand out," and in one of its senses it still denotes a physical sticking out. Now it typically applies to people who stand out due to their high level of achievement or status.

Eminence is the noun that refers to the state of being eminent. Some nobles used to be addressed as "Your Eminence," and cardinals in the Roman Catholic Church still are. Used to modify adjectives, *eminently* is an adverb that intensifies meaning in the same way that *very* does, though more emphatically. To say something is "eminently difficult" is to say it's really very difficult, or perhaps that it's conspicuously difficult (since a high degree of some quality is what makes something conspicuous).

Are You Ready?

Imminent means "ready to happen," "about to occur," or "looming." *Imminent* comes from the Latin word *imminere*, meaning "to project or threaten." The kinds of things that are typically described as imminent are danger, deadlines, or that which is bad or scary. In other words, while one probably wouldn't talk about a birthday party as being imminent, an upcoming 40th birthday might well be described as such. Death is often described as imminent: When it is thought to be imminent, a patient may be put into hospice.

The word *imminent* pops up often in legal terminology: In international law, preemptive self-defense is only justified when there's an *imminent threat* that leaves no doubt about the necessary course of action. And *imminent danger* is a legal term used in a variety of contexts to describe an immediate danger. For example, in labor law, a workplace might be said to pose an imminent danger to employees.

A long-lost relative of these words is *immanent*. It means "inherent" and comes from the Latin word *immanere*, meaning "to remain in place" or "dwelling within." This word is rare relative to *eminent* and *imminent*. It is most often used to describe a spiritual presence. Theologians talk about God being immanent in nature, and philosophers talk about things like consciousness being immanent.

Here's a mnemonic to help keep these words straight: In alphabetical order, *eminent* comes first (because it's important, and it sticks out), *immanent* comes in the middle (because it's "inside," or inherent), and *imminent* comes last (because it's waiting to happen).

※ **The legal term *eminent domain* refers to the right of a government to appropriate a citizen's private property for public use, with or without the person's consent, paying "just compensation" to the owner. Common reasons for the government to exert its right to eminent domain are for construction of public utilities, highways, and railroads.**

A Whole Lot Going On

Is there some genetic component in English from its Germanic origins that disposes it to a certain wordsrunningtogetherness?

✳ ✳ ✳ ✳

*T*ODAY USED TO be *to-day*. Jane Austen wrote *everybody* as *every body*. The Who's 1979 film and album *The Kids Are Alright* made English teachers sputter in helpless irritation. While *all right* still prevails in standard written English, *alright* has been steadily gaining on it in informal writing.

The phrase *a lot* means "many" or "much." And as Yogi Berra said, you can observe a lot just by watching—so watch out for the word *alot*, which evokes a lot of scorn. Many would-be grammarians would tell you that *alot* is not a word in English. Unfortunately that response itself is wrong, or at least it's too simplistic to be accurate. What people mean when they say something is "not a word" is that it is not a part of standard written English or formal English or whatever dialect of English the speaker favors. Besides, although *alot* hasn't gained as much ground as *alright*, it is entirely possible that it may one day be standard English.

Don't confuse the noun phrase *a lot* with the identically pronounced verb *allot*, which means "to distribute or apportion": "The moderator will allot equal time for each participant in the debate." Interestingly, the history of the verb *allot* shows that it was formed by joining the Anglo-French prefix *a-* ("to") to the word *lot*, meaning "portion," as in the King James Version of the Bible, which says, "Jacob is the lot of his inheritance" (Deuteronomy 32:9), and in the phrase *to draw lots* ("to make a decision by randomly choosing one out of a set of objects"): "Let's draw lots to see who should ask the boss if we can leave early."

To avoid confusion, it's very important that we don't misuse these words a lot. Alright?

Words of Wisdom: The Power of Words

* * * *

"Broadly speaking, the short words are the best, and the old words best of all."
—WINSTON CHURCHILL

"An honest man's word is as good as his bond."
—MIGUEL DE CERVANTES

*"A word is dead
When it is said,
Some say.
I say it just
Begins to live
That day."*

—EMILY DICKINSON

"Words are, of course, the most powerful drug used by mankind."
—RUDYARD KIPLING

"If you be pungent, be brief; for it is with words as with sunbeams—the more they are condensed the deeper they burn."
—JOHN DRYDEN

"Words—so innocent and powerless as they are, as standing in a dictionary, how potent for good and evil they become in the hands of one who knows how to combine them."
—NATHANIEL HAWTHORNE

"The fewer the words, the better the prayer."
—MARTIN LUTHER

"Value your words. Each one may be the last."
—STANISLAW LEC

Build or Destroy?

Homophones (words that sound the same but are spelled differently and have different meanings) are often confusing, but they are particularly so when the words have opposite meanings. These are called **Janus words**. *(For more on Janus words, see page 126.)*

✳   ✳   ✳   ✳

RAZE AND **RAISE** are just such a pair. The first means "to demolish or destroy completely," while the other means "to build up" or "to create."

Raze came into English from Anglo-Norman (the French language spoken by the Normans who settled in England after the conquest in 1066), and is ultimately Latin in derivation. According to the *Oxford English Dictionary*, it is first found in written English in the late fourteenth century, and it comes from words meaning "to scrape," "to erase," or "to level"—the word *razor* comes from the same root.

To raze, then, is to scrape something down to ground level, implying total destruction. It's fairly common to come across the usage "raze to the ground." But since to raze is to completely destroy or demolish a building, or the fortifications of a village in wartime, or whatever else, the word *raze* suffices on its own.

A *Raise*-in in the Sun

Raise, on the other hand, is a Germanic word, coming into English from a Scandinavian language, and it first appears in written English (again according to the *Oxford English Dictionary*) around 1200. The meaning today remains much the same as it was, with early meanings including "to lift something up or erect something" or "to waken someone from death or sleep." A related Germanic word, in both etymology and meaning, is *rise*.

A Close Shave

Knowing the backstory doesn't always help, but in this case, the etymologies of these words can help you to remember which to use. If you remember that *raze* is related to *razor*, it's easy to make the connection between shaving something down and utterly destroying it. And as *to rise* means "to move higher," so *to raise* means "to move something higher or build something up." The destructive word *raze* is always spelled with a *z*, as in *razor*, and the constructive—or elevating—word *raise* is spelled with an *s*, like *rise*.

You Raise Me Up

You might want to keep in mind that distinction between "moving higher" and "making something move higher." The verb *to rise* is intransitive and does not take an object: Bread rises on its own. The verb *to raise* is transitive and does take an object: A camper raises her own tent. Raising does not have to be literal, physical motion, either: A poker player can raise the ante. A conscientious editor will raise questions about a text. And an exemplary employee will raise the issue of being deserving of a raise (noun, "an increase in wages or salary.")

✳ Occam's Razor is a scientific and philosophic principle attributed to fourteenth-century logician and Franciscan friar William of Ockham. It states: "Entities should not be multiplied unnecessarily," meaning that the simplest of competing theories is preferred to the more complex.

Where Did It Come From?

Ramshackle: From the Icelandic *ramskakkr*, we get this very twisted word that we use to describe something that is falling down or crumbling. *Ramr* means "very," and *skakkr* is Icelandic for "distorted."

What's All the Fuss?

No single writer has contributed as much to the English language as William Shakespeare. In fact, the sixteenth-century playwright is credited with the coinage of more than 1,700 words.

✻　✻　✻　✻

THERE ARE THOUSANDS of words whose first known appearance is in Shakespeare's works, which means that he either coined them himself or was among the first to use them. Some examples: *addiction, bedazzled, clangor, deafening, distasteful, dwindle, eyesore, gossip, impartial, lackluster, mimic, new-fangled, pale-faced, puking, sanctimonious, tardily,* and *well-read.*

The list of common expressions adopted into the language from his plays and poems is equally impressive. It includes: *beggar all description, brave new world, cold comfort, fool's paradise, heart of gold, in my mind's eye, love is blind, milk of human kindness, more in sorrow than in anger, plague on both your houses, sound and fury,* and *too much of a good thing.* These expressions are so familiar that few English speakers will recognize them as having been coined by Shakespeare. And Shakespearean authorship does not protect them from misquotation, as "to gild refined gold, to paint the lily" in Shakespeare's *The Life and Death of King John* has been transformed in common use into "to gild the lily."

✻ Shakespeare's *Much Ado About Nothing* is sometimes misspelled *Much Adieu About Nothing. Ado,* a word seldom in use anymore in modern English, means "difficulty" or "fuss." So, Shakespeare's title indicates great commotion about something of small importance. However, because *ado* has largely dropped out of use except in the title of this play, it is easy for someone who has heard it rather than seen it in writing to mistake *ado* for *adieu. Adieu* is the French word for "good-bye"— literally, "to God," like the Spanish *adios.* Stick to *much ado,* and all's well that ends well.

Words of Wisdom from William Shakespeare

✳ ✳ ✳ ✳

✳ "Be not afraid of greatness: some are born great, some achieve greatness, and some have greatness thrust upon them."

✳ "No legacy is so rich as honesty."

✳ "How far that little candle throws his beams! So shines a good deed in a naughty world."

✳ "Peace puts forth her olive everywhere."

✳ "How sharper than a serpent's tooth is it to have a thankless child!"

✳ "The voice of parents is the voice of gods, for to their children they are heaven's lieutenants."

✳ "Have more than thou showest, Speak less than thou knowest, Lend less than thou owest."

✳ "This above all; to thine own self be true, And it must follow, as night the day, Thou canst not then be false to any man."

✳ "I can easier teach twenty what were good to be done, than be one of the twenty to follow mine own teaching."

✳ "I would I had bestowed that time in the tongues that I have in fencing, dancing, and bear-baiting. O! had I but followed the arts!"

✳ "The better part of valor is discretion."

✳ "All the world's a stage, and all the men and women merely players."

✳ "Conscience does make cowards of us all."

Worms Got Your Tongue?

*Looking for a simple explanation of **bated** vs. **baited**? No need to hold your breath any longer.*

✳ ✳ ✳ ✳

WHETHER YOU'RE WAITING for the sequel to your favorite book to be published, or for your favorite aunt to arrive for a visit, your anxious expectations may result in *bated breath*, or breath that is held or slowed down. The unfamiliar verb *to bate* is a shortening of *abate*, which means "to reduce in amount, degree, or intensity."

In Shakespeare's *The Merchant of Venice*, Shylock says, "Shall I bend low and in a bondman's key, / With bated breath and whisp'ring humbleness, Say this . . . ?" Later authors used "with bated breath" to mean "fearfully," as in: "The pirates no longer ran separate and shouting through the wood, but kept side by side and spoke with bated breath. The terror of the dead buccaneer had fallen on their spirits" (Robert Louis Stevenson, *Treasure Island*).

The most common current meaning of the phrase is "in anticipation," and the most common current confusion is due to the misspelling *with baited breath*. *Bait* and *baited* are more familiar to modern English speakers than the verb *to bate*, so the spoken phrase is likely to bring up images of worms and fishhooks for many. And once you're thinking about fishhooks, it is easy to make the leap from *anticipation* to *temptation*, and then to reinterpret the phrase as meaning "with breath that draws someone or something in." But the image of breath that smells like worms or nightcrawlers is probably not very welcome.

To determine which is the correct word, think of the old story about the cat who eats cheese and sits by the mouse hole waiting for the mouse to appear. The cat's breath is *baited*, but as you wait to learn of the mouse's fate, your own breath is *bated*.

Underhanded Motives

Do you have an ulterior motive for reading this article? Will it alter the course of history?

✳ ✳ ✳ ✳

YOU WON'T FIND the word *alterior* in any standard dictionary, but it is appearing more often in print and on the Internet, especially in the phrase *alterior motives*. It arises from confusion about the adjective **ulterior,** meaning "beyond the meaning or scope," and is likely a combination of *ulterior* and *alternative*.

An *ulterior motive* is one that is kept concealed or hidden; an *alternative motive* is a secondary motive that is not hidden. The initial vowel sounds are very similar in many American dialects, and if you're trying to avoid the negative connotations of *ulterior*, or if you're unsure about the meaning of the prefix *ulter-/ ultra-* (which comes from Latin and means "beyond, farther, exceeding"), then it would be a simple mistake to come up with *alterior motive* instead.

The concept of *alter-* meaning "other" is well established for most native English speakers: Your alter ego is your other self. An alternate choice is another choice. The second common meaning of *alter* is "change," as in "to alter a dress" and "the village has not altered much in three decades." It is easy to combine the two meanings and to think of a motive that has changed or is secondary.

But there's an added layer to *ulterior motive*—that of deceit. *Ulterior* has an implication of something that is not visible, and especially something that is deliberately hidden or concealed. An ulterior motive, then, is one you'd rather other people didn't know about. Such a motive is likely to be underhanded and unfriendly, and is probably unfortunate, so if you remember those words, you should be able to remember that *ulterior motive* starts with a *u*.

Ad(d) This One to Your List

You don't need to pass even the most basic math class to understand the (ad)dition of this prefix.

✳ ✳ ✳ ✳

IN LATIN, THE preposition *ad* means "to," and as a prefix, *ad-* is combined with other roots to indicate direction or motion toward, transformation into, increase, or intensification. A clear example of how this works is the verb *to add*. The English verb is a clipping of the Latin *addere*, which comes from *ad-* + *dare* ("to give"). So *to add* is literally "to give to."

Sometimes the *ad-* prefix can be difficult to spot. In later Latin, the *d* was dropped before most consonants. So, for example, *adscendere* (*ad-* + *scandere*, "to climb") became *ascendere* and, in English, *to ascend*. But Latin kept the *d* before vowels and before *d*, *h*, *j*, *m*, and *v*. Thus, we have *to adhere*, from *ad-* + *haerere* ("to stick").

Adventures in Language *Adaptations*

Many of the *ad-* words in English were borrowed from Old French, brought across the English Channel by the invading Normans in 1066. In Old French, the prefix had been reduced from *ad-* to *a-* in all cases, even before vowels. So the Old French *auenture* is from the Latin *adventura res*, a "thing about to happen," and the Latin *advenire* means "to arrive, come to, develop." If you read Chaucer and other Middle English writers, you will see that they also used *auenture*, with the meaning of "fortune, happenstance, luck."

Starting in the fifteenth century, Latin scholars in England recognized that the French had dropped the *d*, and they started adding it back to conform to the original Latin. So *auenture* became *adventure* once again. Similarly, Middle English borrowed the Old French *aministrer*, but in later centuries it became *administer* (*ad-* + *ministrare*, "to serve").

Not So Fast!

Sometimes those Latin scholars went too far and added the *d* to words that didn't originally come from the *ad-* prefix or even to words that weren't Latin in the first place. So, for example, in a mad bout of hypercorrection, medieval scholars took the word *amiral*, from the Arabic *amir-al-ma* ("commander of the sea"), and made it *admiral*. It just goes to show that grammar and spelling mavens have been busy overcorrecting other people's language for about as long as anyone can remember. You've got to *admire* (*ad-* + *mirari*, "to wonder") their drive, if not the results.

✳ Prefixes are often responsible for semantic ambiguity. For example, *in-* indicates location or intensification, as in *inflate* and *indirect*. However, it also has negative connotations, as in *ingratitude* and *inexact*. So be sure to think carefully with words like *inflame*!

Where Did It Come From?

Admiral: Western seamen in the thirteenth century adopted this title of rank when they came in contact with Arabic ship captains who called themselves *Amir-al-bahl* ("commander of the sea"). Still, the word originated in the desert, as the title of Abu Bakr, who was called *Amir-al-munin* or "commander of the faithful."

The Inside Story of an Everlasting Puzzle

Eternal *vs.* **internal:** *a puzzle that won't take an eternity to solve.*

✳   ✳   ✳   ✳

BOTH ETERNAL AND *internal* are adjectives derived from Latin, and both have the *-al* ending that marks many such adjectives (*moral, feral, viral,* etc.). But these two words have very different meanings.

Something that's *eternal* lasts forever. Or, to use a related noun, it lasts for an *eternity*. Religions often promise eternal life. (But watch your step, because vampires often do as well!) Some things, such as mathematical truths, are eternal because they're abstract, existing outside of time. Sometimes we use the word *eternal* as a bit of an exaggeration for things that just seem unceasing, as when we describe a friend as an "eternal optimist" or a dripping faucet as an "eternal problem."

Something that's *internal* is on the inside; for example, internal organs, which are inside our bodies. The opposite of internal is *external,* meaning "on the outside." This contrast between the Latin-derived prefixes *in-* and *ex-* is found in other pairs of words as well, such as *introvert/extrovert* and *implode/explode* (the *n* changes to *m* in *implode* because of the following *p*).

Because the inside/outside distinction can act metaphorically, the word *internal* has a few more-abstract uses. Police officers who specialize in *internal affairs* investigate crimes committed by members of their own law enforcement agency. A philosopher who talks about *internal states* is referring to states of mind.

Mixing up the words *internal* and *eternal* need not be an eternal problem. Luckily, there's an easy trick you can use to remember the difference between them: *Internal,* which describes whatever is on the inside, starts with the word *in.*

At the Core

Tune in for a hard-core discussion of **core, corps, corp.,** *and* **corpse.**

✳ ✳ ✳ ✳

THE CORE OF something—of an apple, of Earth—is the central part. Moving to more figurative meanings, *core* can refer to the central group in a large body (the core employees in a company, for example) or a central set of qualities (such as the core competencies of those employees). It is a Middle English word that originally referred to the tough center of a piece of fruit. The expression "rotten to the core" denotes someone or something that is completely, fundamentally corrupt and worthless, all the way through.

A *corps* (which is pronounced just like *core*, not like *corpse*) is a division or branch of a military body (such as the U.S. Army's Signal Corps) or a body of people engaged in similar activity (such as the press corps or the corps de ballet). The word is, as the last example suggests, French in origin, deriving in turn from the Latin *corpus*, or "body." If you are dealing with more than one corps, the plural, confusingly, is also spelled *corps*, but it is pronounced "cores."

Corp. is the abbreviation for *corporation*. *Corporation* comes to us from the Latin *corporare*, "to combine in one body," and indeed a corporation is a group of people who have combined to act as a single entity. In U.S. law, a corporation is considered to be a person, with the same rights as an individual human being.

A *corpse*, of course, is the body of a dead person. It also comes into English by way of the Latin *corpus*. *Corpse* is a word reserved for the body of a human being; the body of a deceased animal is not a corpse, but a *carcass*. If a corpse has been donated to a medical school for research, it is called a *cadaver*.

Every Once in a While

*We tend to gloss over short words like **while** while on our way to the main point we are trying to communicate. For example, if we say someone is "fiddling while Rome burns" (meaning he or she is doing nothing or behaving frivolously when urgent action is called for in a serious situation), then all the emphasis falls on the* fiddling *and* Rome burning *and* while *gets forgotten. But let's linger for a few moments and explore the usage of this word.*

❋ ❋ ❋ ❋

THE WORD *WHILE* occurs as both a noun and a conjunction (and as a verb, but more on that later). As a noun, it means "a period of time": "They stayed in the bar for a long while, talking politics." When used as a conjunction it means "during the time; at the time" ("The teacher left the room while the students were finishing the examination"; "Every once in a while, Mary liked to treat herself to an ice cream in the middle of the afternoon") or "whereas; although" ("While he expressed views eloquently, he did not obtain sufficient votes to prevail").

As the English language developed, the noun phrase *a while* evolved into the single-word adverb *awhile*, meaning "for a short time": "They sat awhile on the porch watching the sun go down."

It Would Have Been Easier to Have "Sat a Spell"

While it is easy to confuse *a while* (two words: noun) and *awhile* (one word: adverb), they are distinct constructions with distinct meanings. The mistake that most frequently turns up is the construction *for awhile:* "I need to study this *for awhile* until I understand it" is wrong. The correct phrase is *for a while.* Grammarians take note: An adverb (*awhile*) cannot be the subject of a preposition (*for*). The following shows correct usages: "Rachel is going to leave the house *for a while* until the smell of new paint has faded. She plans to drive *awhile* and find a place to get some lunch."

> *"Be like the bird who, pausing in her flight awhile on boughs too slight, feels them give way beneath her, and yet sings, knowing she hath wings."*
> —Victor Hugo

As Time Goes By

And then there's the verb form, found in the expression *while away*, which means "to pass time in a leisurely way": "He likes to while away the summer afternoons reading murder mysteries in a hammock."

While away is sometimes mistakenly written as *wile away*. *Wile* is an old verb meaning "to entice." It is more familiar in the noun form *wiles*, or "cunning stratagems to manipulate people." If you ever whiled away the time watching Looney Tunes cartoons, you might remember one scheming rascal by the name of Wile E. Coyote. Because Wile E. is forever plotting to trap the Road Runner, his name is about as fitting as you can get—it's a play on the word *wily*, which means "cunning" or "manipulative."

Words of Wisdom: Dreams

✳ ✳ ✳ ✳

"The future belongs to those who believe in the beauty of their dreams."

—ELEANOR ROOSEVELT

"But I, being poor, have only my dreams; I have spread my dreams under your feet; Tread softly because you tread on my dreams."

—WILLIAM BUTLER YEATS

"The woods are made for the hunters of dreams, the brooks for the fishers of song."

—SAM WALTER FOSS

"Those who dream by day are cognizant of many things which escape those who dream only by night."

—EDGAR ALLAN POE

"A dreamer is one who can only find his way by moonlight, and his punishment is that he sees the dawn before the rest of the world."

—OSCAR WILDE

"Those who have compared our life to a dream were right...We sleeping wake, and waking sleep."

—MICHEL DE MONTAIGNE

"To accomplish great things we must not only act, but also dream; not only plan, but also believe."

—ANATOLE FRANCE

"Hope is a waking dream."

—ARISTOTLE

Playing Possum

When is a possum not a **possum***? When it's an* **opossum***!*

✳ ✳ ✳ ✳

EASILY CONFUSED BECAUSE they are rarely seen in the same place, possums and opossums are different types of animals that live on different continents. Possums are native to Australia, New Guinea, Indonesia, and other islands of the South Pacific. Opossums are native to North and South America. The best-known American opossum is the Virginia opossum, *Didelphis virginiana*, common in much of the eastern part of North America. The word *opossum* comes from the name for this animal in the Algonquian language of the native people of Virginia.

Both possums and opossums are marsupials, and most species are nocturnal. But while opossums are all members of the same taxonomic family (Didelphidae) in the order Didelphimorphia, several different families in the order Diprotodontia (the order that also includes koalas, wombats, wallabies, and kangaroos) hold possums as members. A major physical distinction between possums and opossums is that all species of opossum have bare tails, while all species of possum have furred tails. The two groups are similar in appearance, though—enough so that the possums of Australia were originally named for their resemblance to the opossums of the Americas.

One of the reasons these names can be so confusing to residents of the United States is that *opossum* is often shortened in casual speech or writing, so the animal is just called a *'possum*. Especially in the South, where the Virginia opossum is the most common, it's rare to hear someone use all three syllables of the name. To add to the confusion, American English has the idiomatic expression *to play possum*, meaning "to play dead." When faced with possible danger, an opossum will curl up and stiffen its body so that it seems to be dead. Opossums do play possum. Possums, however, do not.

All Right

Some of the simplest words in English are the most complicated. This is because these words often have multiple definitions, covering both literal and figurative usages.

✳ ✳ ✳ ✳

RIGHT IS ONE of those words. It is a word with many senses and uses. As an adjective, it can mean "correct" ("the right answer"); "the best option" ("the right choice"); or "politically conservative" ("the right wing"). It can even be used as an interrogative to invite a response to a statement ("You see what I'm doing here, right?").

As an adverb it is equally useful, meaning "immediately" ("right now"); "correctly" ("She guessed right"); or "satisfactorily" ("Things are finally going right"). It can also be used directionally ("Turn right at the corner").

Rightly Speaking

But *right* really comes into its own as a noun, meaning "the morally correct" ("right and wrong"); "an entitlement" ("the right to trial by jury"); "the conservative element" ("the Right"); "the side opposite the left" ("On my right, you'll see the new office space"); or, in

plural form, "the authority to make use of a creative work" ("He sold the paperback rights to his book").

As a verb, it means "to restore to normal condition" ("They righted the capsized canoe"; "He was determined to right the wrong done to his mother").

As an exclamation, *right* indicates agreement. And it can even serve as a conversational filler, similar to the ever-present *like*.

The idiomatic expressions are also numerous: *not right in the head* ("not altogether sane"); *dead to rights* ("obviously guilty"); *do right by* ("treat fairly"); *right as rain* ("satisfactory, safe"); and *right away* ("immediately").

All these senses come from the Old English *riht*, from Germanic roots. In its original sense it did not refer to a turn or a side but a straight line. In that sense, the word is also related to the Latin *rectus*, meaning "ruled," in straight lines. The Latin also gives us words for "rightness" in figurative senses: *rectify* ("to make right") and *rectitude* ("moral rightness").

Rite Here, Right Now

By contrast, the word **rite** derives from the Latin *ritus*, or "religious usage," and it is a much more limited word. It means "a religious ceremony" ("the rite of baptism") or "the customary practices characteristic of a church" ("the Byzantine rite"). The word can also take on a secular sense, as when one describes graduation from high school as a "rite of passage."

The trend in current spelling to drop the *gh* in words with a *-ght* ending—*lite* for *light*, *nite* for *night*—is whimsical and harmless; no one who drinks lite beer is going to be confused. But that doesn't eliminate all possibilities for confusion . . . right?

---

* The human brain is divided into two hemispheres: the right side and the left. Our personalities are influenced by both sides, but most people have a "dominant" side. People who are right-brained are known for being intuitive, spontaneous, and creative. Left-brainers are typically more cognitive, analytical, and studious, and tend to be science- and math-oriented.

* When Igor Stravinsky's *The Rite of Spring* premiered in Paris on May 29, 1913, the dissonant score and barbaric rhythms first startled the audience, then repelled it. Vaslav Nijinsky's determinedly unconventional ballet choreography further outraged the audience, which rioted in the aisles. The police had to be called.

Chapter 12

Words Will Never Hurt Me

Hopefully You'll Read This Article Hopefully

To some, **hopefully** *is something of a grammatical bugaboo.*
Hopefully this article will clear some things up.

✳ ✳ ✳ ✳

NO ONE OBJECTS when the word is used to mean
"in a hopeful manner": "The odds of winning
were slim, but he hopefully bought a lottery ticket
anyway." What some people object to is the use
of *hopefully* to qualify an entire sentence, meaning "it is to be hoped that": "Hopefully, I will be
accepted into Harvard." Other sentence modifiers, like *fortunately, arguably,* or *strangely,* are
acceptable, but *hopefully* raises the hackles of
some would-be stylists.

The objection to *hopefully* as a sentence modifier is recent, only
dating to the 1960s. Although lexicographers have traced *hope-*
fully's existence as a sentence modifier to 1702, it was rarely
used until the 1930s. By 1960 it was firmly established. Then
the backlash began.

Point . . . and Counterpoint

There are four main objections to *hopefully* as a sentence modifier, all of which can be refuted.

* *Hopefully means "in a hopeful manner," and any other meaning is just wrong.* This argument is simply incorrect. Words do not have intrinsic meanings; they mean whatever people agree they mean. So if enough people use it as a sentence modifier, then it's a legitimate usage.

* *We're losing the old sense.* This seems to be true, as the "in a hopeful manner" sense appears to be fading from use, but this sort of thing happens all the time. And *hopefully*'s popularity as a sentence modifier indicates that this newer usage is even more valuable than the original sense.

* *It ascribes an emotion (hope) to a non-person.* This is not actually correct, as the sentence modifier means "I hope that" or "a generic person hopes that." And besides, we anthropomorphize all the time in our speech and writing. This is nothing new.

* *Sentence modifiers can't be formed into constructions of "in a _____ manner."* Again, this is wrong. While *fortunately* can't mean "in a fortunate manner," words like *happily*, *strangely*, *mercifully*, and *oddly* exist quite happily as both standard adverbs and sentence modifiers.

Arguing against linguistic trends like this is like trying to hold back the tide—it simply cannot be done. *Hopefully* is a case in point. Its use as a sentence modifier has not been slowed in the least. And hopefully the would-be grammarians will give up trying.

"A hopeful disposition is not the sole qualification to be a prophet."

—WINSTON CHURCHILL

"To travel hopefully is a better thing than to arrive."

—ROBERT LOUIS STEVENSON

"While there's life, there's hope."

— MARCUS TULLIUS CICERO

Festivus: For the Rest of Us

Frank Costanza—George's father in Seinfeld—*isn't exactly a grinch, but in one classic episode he is out to change the holiday season as we know it.*

✳   ✳   ✳   ✳

As FRANK EXPLAINS it, the experience of fighting with another father over a toy doll at Christmas years ago led him to seek an alternative to Christmas. "Out of that," he says, "a new holiday was born: a Festivus for the rest of us!" The made-up holiday is commemorated with three primary traditions: airing grievances with family members, performing "feats of strength," and gathering around the Festivus pole (a bare aluminum pole).

Festivus originated with *Seinfeld* writer Daniel O'Keefe, whose family first celebrated their own holiday called "Festivus" in February 1966, to commemorate the anniversary of O'Keefe's parents' first date. The Festivus pole was not part of the original celebration, but it did include a wrestling match between the children and audio recordings in which each family member described how the others had disappointed them over the year.

Seinfeld fans embraced Festivus with glee, and it quickly entered the pop culture lexicon. Festivus celebrations caught on. One entrepreneurial business even began manufacturing Festivus poles. In 2005, Wisconsin's governor displayed a Festivus pole at the governor's residence. Two years later, the mayor of Green Bay rejected a request to display a Festivus pole at city hall, calling the request "silly antics"—which is really what Festivus is all about.

O'Keefe's father (also named Daniel), the founder of Festivus, told *The New York Times* that the name of the holiday "just popped into my head." The English word *festive* comes from the Latin *festum* ("feast"). English also has *festal*, as in "festal atmosphere" or "festal banners," but the adjective now sounds archaic. In case you were wondering, yes, the plural of *Festivus* is *Festivi*.

Atwitter About *Twitter*

Though it's now known mainly as the name of a social network allowing people to write and read short messages (no more than 140 characters) from diverse sources, the word **twitter** *has a long history that's been swept away by the web phenomenon.*

✳ ✳ ✳ ✳

ORIGINALLY, THE WORD applied to birds—specifically, the high-pitched yammering that comprises many birdsongs. *Twitter* is one of many bird-related terms that can be applied to humans in a semi-insulting manner; needless to say, when someone is accused of *chirping* or *squawking*, it isn't a compliment (nor is being called *cuckoo*).

Twitter's meanings are not limited to the aviary, however. It has also meant "ignorant or idle talk," "a suppressed laugh; giggle," "a condition of tremulous excitement; a state of agitation," "to move tremulously; to tremble with excitement," and "to hanker (*after*, or *to do* something)." *Twitter* also inspired variations such as *twitteration, twitterpated*, and *atwitter*, the last of which is still commonly used.

A rare meaning of *twitter* is "one who twits," or a storyteller. That meaning is much in line with today's Twitter users, who are called *Twitterers* or—more commonly—*tweeters*. *Twitterer* does have some older recorded uses, first in keeping with *twitter's* bird-related sense: "When the forest howls to its fury, driving the twitterers from the spray" (Robert Mudie, *The Feathered Tribes of the British Islands, Vol. 1*, 1834).

Twitterpated is a 1940s-era word meaning "lovestruck" or otherwise dazed and confused. Perhaps it stems from the older words *addlepated* and *muddlepated*, or simply that *pate* is a mostly archaic word meaning "top of the head" (and, by association, one's intellect). In modern parlance, *twitterpated* might well describe those obsessive Twitterers who tweet morning, noon, and night.

Poly- Want a Prefix?

The prefix poly- *is one of the most productive in English. It comes from the Greek, meaning "many, much." The* Oxford English Dictionary *lists around a thousand words beginning with* poly-, *most of them scientific or technical terms. (Note that the prefix is not the same as the ending* -poly *found in words like* monopoly. *That ultimately comes from the Greek* poles-, *meaning "seller, dealer." So a* monopoly *is literally "one seller.")*

T HE GRANDDADDY OF *poly-* words is *polytrichon.* It's one of those rare words borrowed from Latin directly into Old English, making its first English appearance more than a thousand years ago. While English took the word from Latin, it is ultimately Greek in origin, where it means "very hairy" or "very bushy." In Latin and in English the word is used as a name for the hop plant *Humulus lupulus,* used in brewing beer.

Other *poly-* words include:

* *polyandry*—having multiple husbands or male sexual partners at the same time; and its counterpart, *polygyny*

* *polyanthus*—a type of plant that has many flowers

* *polyarchy*—a government with many leaders

* *polychromatic*—having many colors

* *polydactyl*—having more than the usual number of fingers or toes

* *polygamy*—having multiple husbands or wives

* *polyglot*—characterized by multiple languages

* *polyhistor*—a great scholar

* *polymorphous*—having mutiple forms or styles

* *polynomial*—a mathematical expression consisting of multiple variables

* *polyopia*—double (or greater) vision

* *polypharmacy*—prescribing multiple drugs for various ailments suffered by a patient, often elderly; usually used negatively

* *polysemy*—of a word, having multiple meanings

* *polytechnic*—relating to multiple technical or vocational disciplines

* *polytheism*—belief in or worship of many gods

* *polyurethane*—a polymer whose units are joined by a urethane ester

---

* The phrase "Polly wants a cracker?" was Nabisco's original slogan for saltine crackers when they were first produced in 1876.

* A polyglot Bible is any version of the Bible that consists of translations in various languages arranged in parallel columns. Polyglot Bibles allow scholars to compare ancient and modern versions of the text, as well as to compare the translation from one language to another. Several of the most famous polyglot Bibles are the Complutensian (published in Spain in 1522); the Biblia Regia, or Antwerp polyglot, (printed in Antwerp in 1572); and the London Polyglot, also called the Londoninesis or Waltonian (published in England in 1657). The Waltonian comprises six volumes that contain a total of nine languages: Hebrew, Samaritan, Aramaic, Greek, Latin, Ethiopic, Syriac, Arabic, and Persian.

Is Our Children Learning?

The night before the 2000 presidential election, in a final stump speech in Arkansas, Texas governor George W. Bush reflected on his rise to the brink of the presidency, in particular his defeat of John McCain in the South Carolina primary race. "They misunderestimated me," he said. It was both a slip of the tongue and a brilliant coining of a new portmanteau: a word that wraps up underestimate *and* misunderstand *in one neat package. If only he'd done it on purpose.*

✳ ✳ ✳ ✳

THE WORLD ENJOYED two presidential terms full of malapropisms, spoonerisms, eggcorns, and other amusing slip-ups.* Over the course of nine years, *Slate*'s Jacob Weisberg collected more than 500 so-called **Bushisms.** He placed *misunderestimated* in his top 25, along with "Well, I think if you say you're going to do something and don't do it, that's trustworthiness" (#18) and "You teach a child to read, and he or her will be able to pass a literacy test" (#6).

Some of the Bushisms stem from simple grammatical confusion. In the oft-quoted "Rarely is the question asked, is our children learning?" the humor comes from contrast between the content of the statement and its form. President Bush's simple error in subject-verb agreement made some wonder if he was perhaps "left behind" in grammar class. Other statements would be impossible to understand even if the grammar was spot on. Take this 2009 declaration: "One of the very difficult parts of the decision I made on the financial crisis was to use hardworking people's money to help prevent there to be a crisis."

Folk "Hero"

Many Bushisms stem from Dubya's well-known folksy manner and off-the-cuff speaking style. In fact, in the 2000 election, his casual charisma helped him defeat Al Gore, who seemed stiff and wooden by comparison. But Bush's folksiness was poorly timed when, in 2008, he complimented Pope Benedict XVI with "Awesome speech!" On the other hand, Bush's 2002 characterization of the economy as "kind of ooching along" was accurate, if a bit vague.

Bush has shown that he can even misquote his own malapropisms. Reflecting on his lexical legacy in March 2001 at the White House Correspondents' Association Dinner, he boasted, "You have to admit that in my sentences I go where no man has gone before. I've coined new words, like 'misunderstanding.'"

For more on portmanteau words, see page 586; malapropisms, page 16; spoonerisms, page 10; and eggcorns, page 60.

✳ As *awesome* the adjective has inched its way into slang vocabulary, so too have other spin-off parts of speech stemming from the word. The most popular is likely the noun *awesomeness,* defined as "something that inspires or defines awe" and often used as an exclamation all on its own.

Where Did It Come From?

Boomer: The phrase *baby boom* was coined in 1941, four years before the start of the most iconic spike in American births to date; the derivative term *baby boomer,* which connotes someone born during that time (1946–1964, although the exact years are somewhat debated), was first recorded in 1974. The lexical clipping *boomer* appeared in *The New York Times* in 2007. Those born between 1958 and 1964 are known by some as *shadow boomers.* And the children of the boomers (born 1982–1994) have been dubbed *echo boomers.*

Words of Wisdom: Children

✳ ✳ ✳ ✳

"We find delight in the beauty and happiness of children that makes the heart too big for the body."
—RALPH WALDO EMERSON

"Make me a child again just for tonight!"
—ELIZABETH AKERS ALLEN

"The most interesting information comes from children, for they tell all they know and then stop."
—MARK TWAIN

"There can be no keener revelation of a society's soul than the way in which it treats its children."
—NELSON MANDELA

"Children and fools cannot lie."
—JOHN HEYWOOD

"The great man is he who does not lose his child's-heart."
—MENCIUS

"One must ask children and birds how cherries and strawberries taste."
—JOHANN WOLFGANG VON GOETHE

"As much as I converse with sages and heroes, they have very little of my love and admiration. I long for rural and domestic scene, for the warbling of birds and the prattling of my children."
—JOHN ADAMS

"The childhood shows the man, as morning shows the day."
—JOHN MILTON

Word Roots and Branches
Ex-citing

*The prefix ex- is actually two different prefixes, both with the
same essential meaning but with origins in different languages.*

✳ ✳ ✳ ✳

THE PREFIX EX- comes to us from the Latin preposition *ex-*
and the Greek *ex*, both of which mean "out of." To figure
out which of the two is being used in a particular English word,
you must look at that word's history. But such analysis becomes
complicated by the fact that *ex-* changes form depending on the
word to which it is attached. If the word begins with a vowel,
the form of the Greek prefix remains *ex-*, but before consonants
it becomes *ec-*. The Latin *ex-* keeps its form before vowels and
the consonants *c, h, p, q, s*, and *t*. Before the letter *f*, the Latin
becomes *ef-*; before other consonants it becomes *e-*.

The Greek prefix gives us a number of words in which its "out of"
sense is more or less transparent. It isn't hard to see this prefix
at work in *exodus* ("departure, especially that of the Jews from
Egypt") or *exorcize* ("to cast out, especially a demon or evil spirit"),
but other words, like *exegesis* ("explanation, analysis"), *eccentric* (in
geometry, "pertaining to two circles that do not share the same
focus"; also, regarding human behavior, "odd, not typical"), and
ecstasy ("a state of rapture, trance, joy, exaltation"), require a little
out-of-the-box thinking to make the etymological connection.

The Latin gives us such words as *ebullient* ("agitated, overflow-
ing, enthusiastic"), *effervesce* ("to bubble"), *extend* ("to stretch,
reach"), *exasperate* ("to intensify, aggravate, embitter"), and
excommunicate ("to exclude from a group, especially the sacra-
ments of a church").

In English, the Latin prefix has acquired another meaning,
that of "former" or "formerly." It is often used with a hyphen to
make words like *ex-husband* or *ex-wife*.

Civil War-isms

People who spend an excessive amount of time together—training, marching, attacking—are bound to develop their own nicknames and slang. The common words and phrases listed below weren't typically used in letters home but were used regularly among the soldiers themselves.

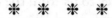

* *Arkansas toothpick*—a knife

* *blizzard*—a volley of musket fire

* *bowlegs*—a cavalry soldier

* *Bragg's bodyguard*—lice

* *bull pit*—a confinement area for those under arrest

* *bumblebee*—the sound of flying minie balls

* *bummers*—soldiers sent out to forage for food or other supplies from the land

* *butternut*—the yellow-brown uniforms of Confederates; or, a rebel soldier

* *chicken guts*—the gold braid on an officer's uniform

* *copperhead*—a Northerner with Southern sympathies

* *deadbeat*—a person exempt from fighting

* *dog robber*—the soldier designated as cook

* *doughboy*—an infantry soldier

* *embalmed beef*—official-issue canned beef

* *forty dead men*—a full cartridge box, which usually consisted of forty cartridges

* *French leave*—absent without leave

* *fresh fish*—raw recruits

* *graybacks*—lice, or a derogatory term for a Confederate soldier or Confederate dollar

* *greenbacks*—money

* *hayfoot/strawfoot*—commands used to teach raw recruits the difference between left and right

* *hospital rat*—someone who fakes illness

* *lucifers*—matches

* *pig sticker*—bayonet

* *play old soldier*—to fake illness

* *Quaker gun*—a tree trunk made to look like a cannon

* *quick step, flux*—diarrhea

* *salt horse*—salted or pickled meat

* *seeing the elephant*—to experience combat

* *Sherman's neckties*—bent railroad rails after being heated in fire then wrapped around trees to make them useless

* *Sherman's sentinels*—chimneys left standing in the army's wake after the house was burned down

* *Sunday soldiers, parlor soldiers*—insults for soldiers who were of little merit

* *sutlers*—vendors who followed the armies and sold goods to them that were not provided by the government

* *tumbled over*—to be killed in action

* *web feet*—a cavalry term for the infantry

Take Me Out to the Ball Game: Baseball Lingo

To live in the world of baseball, one must speak the language. Below is just a sampling of common slang terms and their origins.

✳ ✳ ✳ ✳

✳ *airmail*—a throw, often from the outfield, that overshoots its intended target. Origin: Descriptive.

✳ *bag*—base. Origin: From nineteenth-century equipment guides describing a base as a sack of sand or sawdust.

✳ *balloon*—a pitch that's easy to hit. Origin: Descriptive of a sphere that's larger than a baseball.

✳ *barnstorming*—a tour, often of exhibition games. Origin: A vaudeville term that implied the performers were so eager to strut their stuff they'd even play in a barn during a storm.

✳ *battery*—the pitcher and catcher, together. Origin: Telegraphy, referring to the transmitter (pitcher) and the receiver (catcher).

✳ *bees in the hands*—the "stinging" sensation that occurs after swinging the bat, particularly when not wearing protective gloves and/or in cold weather. Origin: Descriptive of stings.

✳ *blue*—an umpire. Origin: Historically, the color of an umpire's uniform.

✳ *bush*—unprofessional. Origin: Refers to "bush league."

✳ *can of corn*—an easy basket catch. Origin: Refers to a grocer retrieving canned goods from high shelves by pushing them with a stick and allowing them to drop into his smock.

✳ *chin music*—inside brushback pitch close to the jaw. Also "a close shave." Origin: Descriptive. "Music" is the whooshing of the ball.

✳ *cleanup hitter*—the fourth batter in the lineup. Origin: He clears, or cleans, the bases occupied by the first three hitters.

✳ *deuce*—curveball. Origin: Usually signaled for with two fingers.

✳ *fungo*—fielding practice retrieving hit balls, and the special bat used to hit those practice balls. Origin: Numerous theories, ranging from a combination of the words "fun" and "go," to the cricket expression "fun goes," to the German word "fungen," or catch.

✳ *get the thumb*—to be ejected from the game. Origin: Descriptive of an umpire's hand signal.

✳ *gopher ball*—a pitch hit well, often for a long home run. Origin: A pun on "go for," as in a hit that will "go for extra bases," or a pitch a batter will "go for."

✳ *in his wheelhouse*—a pitch precisely where the batter likes to hit it. Origin: Nautical term referring to the room where the boat is controlled.

✳ *paint the black*—a pitch on the inside or outside corners of the strike zone. Origin: Descriptive of the black outline of home plate.

✳ *pull the string*—to fool a batter with an off-speed pitch. Origin: Descriptive of a ball arriving later than the hitter anticipated, as if pulled back by a string.

✳ *rubber arm*—a pitcher who is, or can be, used frequently. Origin: Descriptive of the flexibility and durability of rubber.

✳ *The Show*—the major leagues, often from the perspective of a minor-leaguer. Origin: Descriptive of larger crowds, parks, and more media and amenities relative to the minors.

✳ *southpaw*—a left-handed pitcher. Origin: In most ballparks, home plate faces east so as to keep the sun from a batter's eyes, meaning south would be on the pitcher's left side.

Words of Wisdom: Fun and Games

✳   ✳   ✳   ✳

"If all the year were playing holidays,
To sport would be as tedious as to work."

—WILLIAM SHAKESPEARE

"If a man insisted always on being serious, and never allowed
himself a bit of fun and relaxation, he would go mad or
become unstable without knowing it."

—HERODOTUS

"Come, Watson, come! The game is afoot."

—ARTHUR CONAN DOYLE

"I've taken my fun where I've found it."

—RUDYARD KIPLING

"Though boys throw stones at frogs in sport, the frogs do not
die in sport, but in earnest."

—BION

"The Puritan hated bear-baiting, not because it gave pain to
the bear, but because it gave pleasure to the spectators."

—THOMAS BABINGTON, LORD MACAULEY

"The chase, the sport of kings;
Image of war, without its guilt."

—WILLIAM SOMVERVILLE

"Good ballplayers make good citizens."

—PRESIDENT CHESTER A. ARTHUR

Q and Not U

If you thought this article was going to be about the now-defunct dance-punk rock band Q and Not U, you're wrong (but you have an impressive knowledge of indie rock). It is, in fact, simply about words in which the letter q is not followed by a u, as it usually is in English.

✳ ✳ ✳ ✳

I F YOU'RE A Scrabble player, you probably already know a lot of words fitting that description; once you've drawn the *q* tile, you don't want to just store it away until you find a *u*. So instead, you might find it useful to play *qi* (an alternate spelling of the Chinese *chi*, meaning "energy"), *qat* (a Middle Eastern shrub used to make a narcotic), *Qoph* (the nineteenth letter in several Semitic languages), *faqir* (a Hindu or Muslim ascetic), or *qintar* (an Albanian currency), among other options. And of course there are *Iraq* and *Qatar*, though, being proper names, they are not Scrabble-legal. You could also play *suq* (an Arabian market), but there are almost certainly better words you could spell with that *u* in there.

One thing you may have noticed about those words is that they are all loanwords from foreign languages—specifically, foreign languages that did not descend from Latin (which spelled its *kw-* sounds as *qu-*, or, more accurately, *qv-*, via a linguistic evolution that passed from the Phoenicians to the Greeks to the Etruscans). Transliteration from these languages varies, and thus alternate spellings abound in which the guttural *k-* sound represented by the *q* might be rendered as *k*, *kh*, or *ch*.

Of course, there are a few other *q*-without-*u* words that don't fall under that umbrella, like *QWERTY*, the first six letters on the top row of a standard keyboard or typewriter, and *Qix* (pronounced *kicks*), a video arcade game of the 1980s. *NASDAQ* and *tranq* (short for *tranquilizer*) both end in *q*, pronounced *k*, and there's also the actor *Eriq La Salle*; if you ever meet him, ask him if he misses *u*.

Google, Kozmo, and Kerbango

In the early 1970s, the Internet Assigned Numbers Authority (IANA) was created to manage the assignment of unique numbers to each computer connected to the Internet. It quickly became clear that it was impractical to use only numbers in these "labels"—what are now known as IP addresses. In the early '80s, the Domain Name System was created, allowing computers to be referenced by name instead of by number.

✳ ✳ ✳ ✳

WHEN THE INTERNET was commercialized in the mid-1990s, domain names began flying off the shelves. The new dot-com businesses needed unique, memorable names that could be made into brands. Without the high-quality search engines of today, it was important for domain name to be memorable—and easy enough for users to type accurately—or traffic to the site would suffer. The amount of characters allowable in a domain name was limited, making things even harder. As the pool of available domain names dwindled, entrepreneurs got more desperate, turning to creative spellings, foreign words, and nonce words.

Dot What?

In some cases, company names or domains were created by combining existing words or word parts. Some names were created with prefixes, such as *e-* (as in *electronic*): eBay, Epinions, eToys, and Evite, for example. Others added suffixes, such as *-ster* (probably borrowed from words like *gangster* and *mobster*): Napster and Friendster, for example. And still others were coined as portmanteau words by combining parts of two words, as in Wikipedia (*wiki* + *encyclopedia*) and Netfolio

(*Internet* + *portfolio*), an online investing service. (See page 586 for more on portmanteau words.)

In other cases, entrepreneurs strung together consonants and vowels to make names that were meaningless, sometimes barely pronounceable, and even unrelated to the goods or services provided by the site. Companies from Akamba.com (which produced and sold web server accelerator cards) to Zooba.com (an online bookstore) appeared, developed products or services, and gradually failed, changed their names, or merged with companies with more memorable names. The list of vanished domains reads like a register of comic book sound effects: Kozmo (home delivery), Flooz (virtual money), Kerbango (Internet radio), Oingo (search engine), Yazam (venture capital), and so on. The registered domain names multiplied like flies until the dot-com crash of 2000 stopped the madness.

Having a high-quality, meaningful domain name is no guarantee of business success: Just ask the founders of Pets.com, which went belly-up in 2000. And with the right business model and marketing, even a made-up word can be made into a great brand. After all, look at Google—a purposeful misspelling of *googol* (a very large number: 1 followed by 100 zeros). Google is now not only one of the most powerful brands in the world, but has even earned an entry in the *Oxford English Dictionary*, with *to google* being a verb meaning "to use an Internet search engine."

＊ **Domain registration was managed by the government for the first three decades of its existence, and there was no cost to register a domain name. But beginning in 1995, after the privatization of the industry, private registry operators (called network information centers, or NICs) were given the authority to begin charging for domain name registration. Today, domain registration is big business.**

Worldly Wisdom:
European Proverbs

✳ ✳ ✳ ✳

✳ Children have a hair of their father. (Belgium)

✳ A good horse has many faults; a bad one barely any. (Croatia)

✳ The road to a friend's house is never long. (Denmark)

✳ Who takes the child by the hand takes the mother by the heart. (Denmark)

✳ Begin to weave and God will give the thread. (Germany)

✳ God gives the shoulder according to the burden. (Germany)

✳ Even a clock that does not work is right twice a day. (Poland)

✳ What kind of parents, such children. (Poland)

✳ All goats jump onto leaning trees. (Poland)

✳ There is no shame in not knowing...
      ...the shame lies in not finding out. (Russia)

✳ Any fish is good if it is on the hook. (Russia)

✳ As you cooked the porridge, so must you eat it. (Russia)

✳ A drop hollows out a stone. (Russia)

✳ Better to blush once than pale a hundred times. (Serbia)

✳ He that sleeps soundly feels not the toothache. (Switzerland)

✳ If you close one eye you will not hear everything. (Switzerland)

✳ Only when you have eaten a lemon do you appreciate what sugar is. (Ukraine)

Welcome to Wordistan

Afghanistan, Pakistan, and the other -stans—including Tajik-istan, Turkmenistan, and Uzbekistan—often make today's news.

✳ ✳ ✳ ✳

THE NAMES OF some countries end in *-istan*, which means "place" or "home" in various Indo-European languages of Central Asia and the Indian subcontinent. *Afghanistan*, then, is "home of the Afghans."

An exception to the pattern is *Pakistan*. There is no people named "the Paks" who call the region their home. Rather, the word was coined in 1933 by South Asian Muslim nationalist Choudhary Rahmat Ali as an acronym denoting the regions of British India that were predominantly Muslim. These regions were: *P*unjab, the *A*fghan border region, *K*ashmir, *S*indh, and Baluch*istan*. The acronym also has a double meaning in Urdu (the national language of Pakistan), where *pak* means "pure, perfect, complete."

Since 1932, the word *stan* has also been used on its own as a noun referring to any or all Central Asian countries, particularly those that end in *-istan*. Sometimes the noun appears with an apostrophe, *'stan*, denoting the missing initial element.

In recent decades, since at least the 1960s, the *-istan* suffix has been used in a tongue-in-cheek manner to create names for supposed or fictional backwaters, like *nerdistan*, *absurdistan*, *Blogistan* (more provincial than the blogosphere), *somewhereistan*, and *nastystan*. Not all of the fictional formations are jocular, however. The coinage *Islamistan*, for instance, denotes the people of Islam without reference to ethnicity or nationality. There is also *Hindustan*, which has been in English use since the early seventeenth century. To many living in the region, the name *Hindustan* refers only to the Hindi-speaking parts of India, but in the West it is often used to refer to the subcontinent in general.

Faster than a Science Fiction Plot Device

Why does lightning-quick travel in science fiction happen at **warp speed**? *What exactly is undergoing the "warping"?*

✳   ✳   ✳   ✳

THE ANSWER IS, basically, the fabric of space and time. If a spaceship were able to use antimatter to generate a special magnetic field around itself, it could slip through the seams of the space-time continuum and travel light-years in an instant.

So far the concept of warp speed is just science fiction (the most famous example appears in *Star Trek*). Warp speed takes antimatter, and that's not exactly something you can pick up at the gas station just yet. But it's probably not mere fantasy. William Shatner claims that when scientist and *Star Trek* fan Stephen Hawking toured the set of *Star Trek: The Next Generation*, he paused at the warp engines of the starship *Enterprise* and said, "I'm working on that." Researchers today are working on a design for an engine partly propelled by tiny amounts of antimatter.

By the time NASA actually launches something at warp speed, the phrase may have lost its scientific meaning through widespread general use of the words to simply mean "fast." A headline about the release of the Apple iPad referred to "Warp Speed Publishing." An article about the Arizona State football team's fast-paced offense said the team would play at warp speed. An article about Toyota's faulty accelerator pedals said that victims were thrust into warp speed.

This follows a common pattern of specific terms entering general use by extension or association of meaning. But it raises the question of the limits of our exaggeration. What hyperbole can we turn to next when *warp speed* loses its power, when we need something faster than the starship *Enterprise* just to brag about running backs?

One-Hit Wonders

*A **nonce word**—a word contrived for a unique occasion—is the last resort of a desperate Scrabble player. In an early episode of* The Simpsons, *Bart plays* kwyjibo, *defining it as "a big, dumb, balding North American ape. With no chin." Homer's reaction leads Bart to yell, "Uh oh. Kwyjibo on the loose!"*

✳   ✳   ✳   ✳

BUT NONCE WORDS aren't acceptable in Scrabble, since by definition they have no history and no future—and leave no trace in a dictionary. They are one-hit wonders, created for one purpose and then left to their own devices.

Nonce words can be self-explanatory. Even without Lewis Carroll's explanation of *slithy* as a combination of *slimy* and *lithe*, the meaning is clear because of sound symbolism. The sounds remind us of *slippery*, *slithery*, and *sly*. Other nonce words might need an entire song's worth of explanation, such as *supercalifragilisticexpialidocious* in *Mary Poppins*.

If a nonce word turns out to be reusable, it graduates to the level of *neologism*—a new or recent word that has entered wider use but may or may not be found in a dictionary. Recent neologisms include *generonym* (used to refer to a common brand name that is universally used to refer to a generic product, such as *Kleenex*, *Coke*, and *TiVo*); *slackademic* (a student who prefers to have fun and lighten their workload rather than buckle down to their studies); and *blamestorm* (a meeting, especially in a corporate setting, whose purpose is to try to figure out who and what to blame for a failure or mistake).

Writers, comedians, and average Joes who have coined various nonce words over the years probably had no idea they would someday be elevated to the level of a real word. So hold onto those Scrabble tiles: In a few years, you might just be able to play *kwyjibo*.

A Modern Dilemma

Creating names for artistic and literary periods is fairly easy when we have the benefit of hindsight. We often name periods after important people (Victorian era, Homeric Age), major events (Revolutionary period, Reconstruction era), or main features of the period (the Romantic period, Age of Enlightenment, the Renaissance). Coming up with a name for the current era, however, may prove to be more difficult.

✳ ✳ ✳ ✳

WHEN NAMING THE current, present-tense era, it's tempting to choose a moniker that refers only to the time period. Consider, for example, the peculiar case of the *modern* period (from the Middle French *moderne*, "of the present time," from the Latin *modo*, "just now"). The literal meaning of *modern* is "current, present, or up-to-date." At the time when the modern periods in dance, literature, art, philosophy, and architecture were blossoming, the name *modern* was apt. After all, the modernists were concerned with shedding classical and traditional forms and styles for entirely new ones. "Modern art" is abstract rather than striving for more realistic representation. "Modern dance"

James Joyce

is a form defined in contrast to the highly stylized traditional forms, such as ballet. In literature, writers of the "modernist" period, such as Ezra Pound, James Joyce, and Virginia Woolf, tampered with the structure of literature itself.

But like an avocado-and-marigold kitchen of the '70s, once stylish but now dated, many "modern" styles are now looking, well, old-fashioned. In fact, the blush is off the word itself, and describing a style as *modern* sounds frumpy and not at all up-to-date.

Cutting-Edge Terminology

Terms that are used to describe the newest movements of today, especially in the arts, are *contemporary* and *avant-garde*. In the sciences, technology is more likely to be described as *cutting-edge* or *state-of-the-art* than *modern* or the even-more-outdated *futuristic*.

In literature and art, twentieth-century works that came after the modernist period might be referred to as *postmodern*. The word was seen as early as the 1870s but didn't become conventional until the latter half of the twentieth century. Now a period in its own right, *postmodernism* is defined, in part, by a rejection of objective truth and the reintroduction of traditional elements, often in unexpected ways. But now that postmodernism is its own literary period, what comes next? Yes, it's not unusual to hear the term *post-postmodernism*.

Perhaps it's time for a new naming convention—this time, one that will stand the test of time.

What Do You Mean by That? The Food Edition

If yo've ever wondered about the source of some food phrases, we've got answers.

✳   ✳   ✳   ✳

Cool as a Cucumber

Even on a warm day, a field cucumber stays about 20 degrees cooler than the outside air. Though scientists didn't prove this until 1970, the saying has been around since the early eighteenth century.

Egg on Your Face

During slapstick comedies in the Victorian theater, actors made the fall guy look foolish by breaking eggs on his forehead.

Spill the Beans

In ancient Greece, the system for voting new members into a private club involved secretly placing colored beans into opaque jars. Prospective members never knew who voted for or against them—unless the beans were spilled.

Bring Home the Bacon

This expression is used to denote the person in a marriage who earns the larger monetary share of household income, but it once meant exactly what it says. In the twelfth century, at the church of Dunmow in Essex County, England, a certain amount of cured and salted bacon was awarded to the couple that could prove that they had lived in greater bliss than any of their competitors. The earliest record of this contest was 1445, but evidence exists that the custom had already been in effect for at least two centuries. In the sixteenth century, proof of devotion was determined through questions asked by a jury of unmarried men and women. The curious pork prize continued, albeit in irregular intervals, until the late nineteenth century.

Words of Wisdom: Food

✳ ✳ ✳ ✳

*"Man and the animals are merely a passage and channel
for food."*

—Leonardo da Vinci

*"One finds many companions for food and drink, but in a
serious business a man's companions are very few."*

—Theognis

*"If you are ever at a loss to support a flagging conversation,
introduce the subject of eating."*

—Leigh Hunt

*"'Tis an old maxim in the schools,
That flattery's the food of fools;
Yet now and then your men of wit
Will condescend to take a bit."*

—Jonathan Swift

"One should eat to live, not live to eat."

—Molière

*"Our minds are like our stomachs; they are whetted by
the change of their food, and variety supplies both with
fresh appetite."*

—Quintilian

*"So long as you have food in your mouth, you have solved all
questions for the time being."*

—Franz Kafka

"The best of all physicians is apple pie and cheese."

—Eugene Field

Slang: Letting It All Hang Out

*Everyone is a **slang** expert. That's because slang is inherently from and of the people; it's the language that thrives outside the halls of power and starched collars of formal society.*

✳   ✳   ✳   ✳

"**S**LANG IS A colourful, alternative vocabulary," says the *Oxford Dictionary of Modern Slang.* "It bristles with humour, vituperation, prejudice, informality: the slang of English is English with its sleeves rolled up, its shirt-tails dangling, and its shoes covered in mud."

It can be hard to put your finger on exactly what qualifies a word as "slang," but typically words and expressions that are classified as such are informal, are known throughout a certain subculture or region, and are synonymous with another, more conventional term or phrase.

The origins of slang words are almost always murky. By the time a catchy word or phrase gets popular enough to be worth noticing—like *cool* for "interesting and exciting," *stiff* for "corpse," or any of the hundreds of slang synonyms for "drunk," such as *sloshed* or *wasted*—it's too late to know who or what started it. Over time, a slang word may work its way into the popular vernacular and become widely used, thus passing into mainstream speech.

Slang Myths: Busted

So anyone can be a slang expert. But that doesn't mean that folk wisdom about slang always holds up. In fact, there are numerous myths about the sources and spread of slang. Linguist Arnold Zwicky says there are three myths about language use in particular, including slang, that capture the public's imagination. These are:

1. The Recency Illusion: "the belief that things you have noticed only recently are in fact recent"

2. The Frequency Illusion: "once you notice a phenomenon, you believe that it happens a whole lot"

3. The Adolescent Illusion: "the consequence of selective attention paid to the language of adolescents . . . by adults"

The root myth that might sum up the other myths is that slang is a danger to a language. According to some, slang is often lazy, vulgar, or cynical, and it threatens to lower the quality of a society's language—if not social health in general! This accusation has been made for centuries, and it's almost always wrong. Slang is language at its liveliest and most earnest—and, arguably, its most healthy.

"Such is slang, or indirection," wrote poet Walt Whitman, "an attempt of common humanity to escape from bald literalism, and express itself illimitably."

Is to fear slang, then, to fear poetry?

✳ **Many slang words have a surprisingly long history. The slang meaning of the word *cool*, for example, goes back to the early twentieth century.**

Where Did It Come From?

Dude: Originally from a German word meaning "fool," this term eventually came to mean a city slicker vacationing in the Wild West. It has since evolved into a general term for a guy, or in some cases, it's an affectionate word for a member of someone's own group. Basically, "dude" has come full circle from outsider to insider.

Gridiron Grammar

From the battlefield to the sewing circle: the origins of some common football terms.

✳ ✳ ✳ ✳

CONSIDERING THAT THE quarterback is often referred to as the *general* and his players are known as *troops*, it's not surprising that many football terms, such as *bomb*, *trenches*, and *gunners*, have been borrowed from the military. The *blitz*, like its wartime connotation, is a bombardment, but not from the air. It is an all-out frontal attack, bolstered by 300-pound behemoths intent on launching the quarterback face-first into the turf. The football *bomb* is an aerial assault, but instead of an explosive-laden shell, this weapon is a perfectly delivered spiral pass. The *trenches*, much like their World War I counterparts, are found along the line of scrimmage, an all-man's land where hand-to-hand combat determines who wins the day. Like their combative comrades, gridiron *gunners* are responsible for thwarting the enemy's attack. On the battle lines that are drawn between the boundaries, these gunners set their sights on the kickoff and punt-return specialists.

"Sew" Tough

Now, it's doubtful that too many pigskin pundits would equate the quaint image of a sewing circle with the hard-nosed ferocity of the football field, but why else would words such as *patterns*, *buttonhooks*, and *seams* be instrumental entries in the gridiron lexicon? Tailors depend on *patterns* to guide them, much like the offense on the football field depends on well-executed play patterns to move the ball foward. The *buttonhook* is an important tool for a tailor and a nifty maneuver for a receiver, who races down field and then hooks back toward the line of scrimmage. Tailors and seamstresses know that working along the seams takes a delicate touch. In football, the *seam* is a narrow gap in the defense that must be worked to "sew up" a reception.

Words of Wisdom: Competition

✳   ✳   ✳   ✳

"The way of the sage is to act but not to compete."

—LAO TZU

"Our doubts are traitors, and make us lose the good we oft might win, by fearing to attempt."

—WILLIAM SHAKESPEARE

"The praise of living authors proceeds not from the reverence of the dead, but from the competition and mutual envy of the living."

—THOMAS HOBBES

"That is the happiest conversation where there is no competition, no vanity, but a calm quiet interchange of sentiments."

—SAMUEL JOHNSON

"Tradition approves all forms of competition."

—ARTHUR CLOUGH

"Those who know how to win are much more numerous than those who know how to make proper use of their victories."

—POLYBIUS

"Let this be your motto—Rely on yourself!
For, whether the prize be a ribbon or throne,
The victor is he who can go it alone."

—JOHN GODFREY SAXE

"Strive, and hold cheap the strain."

—ROBERT BROWNING

Weasel Words

Advertisers, politicians, and corporations are infamous for using doublespeak, jargon, and euphemisms to either hide or neutralize what they're trying to sell or say. **Weasel words** *drain the meaning from a thought or action, just as a weasel sucks the contents from an egg.*

✳   ✳   ✳   ✳

Here are a few common weaselly words and phrases, along with what they really mean:

* *bad patient outcome*—doctor prescribed wrong medication; sponge left in patient during surgery; wrong limb amputated; death

* *core strength*—the one product customers are still buying

* *destination icon*—tourist trap

* *dysfunctional family*—more like the Sopranos, not so much the Cleavers

* *empowerment*—the illusion of having a say in what gets done and who does it

* *exit strategy*—a plan for leaving an awkward situation with as much subtlety as possible

* *fixer-upper*—does it need "some" work, or is it a piece of crap? You decide.

* *head count reduction*—"You're fired"

* *human resources*—the first and highest hurdle to getting hired

* *immersive experience*—say good-bye to your lunch plans; you're here for the long haul

* *lifestyle destination*—if you have to ask, you can't afford it

* *loss prevention associate*—security guard; Rent-a-Cop

* *mainstreaming*—dumped into the regular classroom without support

* *network-centric*—paper is obsolete, work is all online, and everything is 24/7

* *new and improved*—same stuff, but less of it, in flashier packaging

* *non-ongoing position*—why not just say "temporary"?

* *outside the box*—tell me something I don't know

* *partner* (as a verb)—you'll do the work; he'll get the credit

* *positive birth experience*—obstetrician didn't skimp on the drugs

* *preowned vehicle*—probably not by a little old lady who only drove to church on Sundays

* *productivity gains*—half the staff has been sacked; everyone else does double the work

* *quality face time*—the boss pretends to listen to you for ten minutes (see also *touch base*)

* *retail landscape*—used to be downtown, then the mall, now it's Amazon.com

* *self-regulation*—just get your work done, okay? I'm too busy to supervise.

* *touch base*—you pretend to listen to your boss for ten minutes

Origins of Standard Symbols

Removing a colon is pretty serious business—whether you're a surgeon or a copy editor. You use punctuation marks and other symbols on your computer keyboard every day, and here is an explanation of their origins.

* * * *

¶—The pilcrow is a typographical character used to indicate a new paragraph. The name may have come from *pylcraft*, a derivation of the word *paragraph*, and the symbol that resembles a backward P may have originated as a C for *chapter*, or to represent a new train of thought.

!—Usually used after an interjection or other word to indicate strong feeling, the exclamation mark is a pictographic device believed to have originated in the Roman empire. Its resemblance to a pen over a dot was thought to represent a mark a writer might make when surprised or overjoyed at completing a long writing project.

@—If "you've got mail," then you have seen @, or the "at" sign, which is in the middle of every e-mail address. Before this use, the symbol was most commonly used as an abbreviation in accounting ("3 apples @ $2 each = $6"). Its symbol may be derived from the Norman French symbol à, meaning "at" in the sense of "each." Another theory is that it originated from the Latin word *ad*, which means "at, toward, or by."

*—The asterisk gets its name from *astrum*, the Latin word for "star," which the asterisk is also called. It is not an "asterix"—that's the name of the star of a French cartoon. The asterisk was created in feudal times when the printers of family trees needed a symbol to indicate date of birth, which may explain why it's shaped like the branches of a tree.

;—The semicolon was invented by an Italian printer for two main purposes: to bind two sentences that run on in meaning and to act as a "super comma" in a sentence that already contains many commas. Excessive use of the semicolon is considered showy by many writers, especially when employed to create long, multisegmented sentences.

?—What is the origin of the question mark? The symbol is generally thought to originate from the Latin *quaestio*, meaning "question," which was abbreviated to Qo, with the uppercase Q written above the lowercase o. The question mark replaces the  period at the end of an interrogative sentence. There's a superstition in Hollywood that movies or television shows with question marks in the title do poorly at the box office. That may explain its absence in the title of the game show *Who Wants to Be a Millionaire*, a program that would not exist without questions!

&—The ampersand, used to replace the word *and*, has been found on ancient Roman sources dating to the first century A.D. It was formed by joining the letters in *et*, which is Latin for "and." Through the nineteenth century, the ampersand was actually considered the 27th letter of the English alphabet.

%—The percent sign is the symbol used to indicate a percentage, meaning that the number preceding it is divided by 100. The symbol appeared around 1425 as a representation of the abbreviation of *P cento*, meaning "for a hundred" in Italian.

=—The equal sign is a mathematical symbol used to indicate equality and was invented in 1557 by Welsh mathematician Robert Recorde. In his book *The Whetstone of Witte*, Recorde explains that he invented it "to avoid the tedious repetition of these words: 'is equal to.'" Recorde's invention is commemorated with a plaque in St. Mary's Church in his hometown of Tenby, Wales.

Solid: A Favor from a Faithful Friend

To the unfamiliar, the beseeching phrase "do me a solid" might seem a mysterious request—a solid what?

✳ ✳ ✳ ✳

A PLEA TO "DO ME A SOLID" is one to reserve for those you trust and cherish the most, a phrase to make use of when you're asking them to do you a huge favor. Sometimes a *really* huge favor: "Mark, just do me a solid and stay with your wife," pleads the pregnant protagonist in the movie *Juno*.

The phrase was introduced by the television show *Seinfeld* in a 1991 episode. "Hey, would you do me a solid?" asks Kramer. "Well, what kind of solid?" Jerry asks. Kramer needs him to sit in a car while it's double-parked. Jerry refuses, so Kramer asks George the same question. George also declines, but says, "I'd like to; I've never done a solid before."

Before *Seinfeld*, use of the word *solid* as a noun was mostly reserved for science classrooms, where students learned about the three states of matter: solids, liquids, and gases. "Do me a solid" utilizes the word's sense of reliability, implying that the person accepting the request will prove they can be counted on in a pinch. Doing the solid will prove how solid the relationship is.

The blog Clarion Content picks up on a refreshing nuance of "do me a solid." While the phrase "do me a favor" is loaded with a sense of obligation—"do this for me and I'll do a favor for you" or "I'll owe you one"—"do me a solid" comes with no strings attached. The "solidity" is a characteristic of the friend, but also of the friendship. If the friendship truly is solid, good deeds will be traded back and forth naturally. The act itself doesn't create any obligation, but true friends are expected to naturally care for one another, help one another, and be able to ask for help from one another, without feeling that they have to pay a price.

That's what solid friends are for.

Talking About the Weather

The phrase "talking about the weather" may be just another way to say "meaningless chitchat," but the weather is anything but unimportant.

❋ ❋ ❋ ❋

SINCE THE ADVENT of dependable furnaces, widespread air-conditioning, and reliable meteorologists, weather idioms seem to have fallen out of favor. Here are a few now-obsolete weather idioms:

❋ *Keep one's weather eye open*—to be keenly aware, especially for possible trouble. At least as old as 1929, the saying appeared in a 1981 newspaper article that said, "The Russians...are keeping a weathereye on other navies."

❋ *Make fair weather*—a maker of fair weather is offering an olive branch and being diplomatic (or at least giving the appearance of doing so).

❋ *Stretch wing to weather*—the *Oxford English Dictionary* has one 1825 citation for this rather poetic synonym for flight, mentioning "the fairest falcon that ever stretched wing to weather."

❋ *Weather a point*—weathering a point involves gaining an advantage or accomplishing a purpose against opposition.

❋ *Weather breeder*—literally or figuratively, a weather breeder is a warm, gorgeous day, and one indicating that bad storms are coming.

❋ *Weatherheaded*—an insult meaning something close to *air-headed* and *light-headed*, with the connotation of fickleness.

❋ *Weather-wiser*—this noun, used in the seventeenth and eighteenth centuries, referred to any weather forecasting device. A synonym is *weatherometer*.

Out to Save Us from Ourselves

Almost everyone has their pet peeves when it comes to English usage. Like matching everyone *and their* in the previous *sentence (which has been done, it turns out, since Shakespeare's time). Or using* hopefully *to mean "I hope." Or splitting infinitives—or was that hairs?*

✳   ✳   ✳   ✳

ANYONE CAN BE annoyed, but a self-righteous few elevate their annoyances to a quest to save the English language itself. Slipping standards, lack of sentence diagramming in schools, text messaging—it all adds up to doom in the eyes of these crusaders. In order to decry every misplaced participle, misused adverb, and misunderstood idiom, many of them turn to our era's preferred megaphone: the blog.

Linguist Ben Zimmer called this phenomenon *peeveblogging*. Apparently inspired by that term, *Boston Globe* language columnist Jan Freeman coined the term *peeve-ology* for the study of peeves, eventually settling on *peevologist* for those who analyze the peeves of others (as opposed to those who are themselves peevish).

Join the Peeve-fest: It Starts At or About Now

Peevologists lament that logic and mere historical fact are rarely enough to deter these linguistic malcontents. At a peeve-fest on the website of *The Daily Telegraph*, which invited readers to name "the most annoying phrase in the English language," one commenter derided the phrase "at about 10:30 P.M.," saying that one should just use *at* or *about* but not both. University of Pennsylvania linguist Mark Liberman pointed out that "at about" is "not intrinsically inconsistent" and can be traced back to such prestigious writers as Jane Austen, who wrote in *Northanger Abbey* in the early 1800s: "At about half past twelve, a remarkably loud rap drew her in haste to the window."

He Blinded Me with Science

The peevish mindset is opposite from the scientific, linguistic view that accepts, analyzes, and documents language change. The peevish are preoccupied with upholding what Zimmer has called a kind of "verbal hygiene." They may take a perverse pleasure in their self-righteous rightness. But in fact, these "mistakes" often indicate language change. Language is naturally dynamic; if it were not, we'd still be speaking the English of Shakespeare or Chaucer. Just as the ocean waves and tidal forces change the shape of coastlines, speakers sculpt language itself into new forms.

Geoffrey Chaucer

Look at the word *grow*, for example. Until recently, its primary use was as an intransitive verb (a verb that has no direct object). For example, "Jimmy grew two inches over the summer." It appears as a transitive verb in the sense of "grow a beard," but trends in business language have turned *grow* into a transitive verb. It's common to hear MBAs talk about "growing an investment" or "growing the client base." Upon first hearing this usage, peevologists shuddered in horror and labeled it jargon, but sure enough, the use of *grow* as this type of transitive word has continued to, well, grow, and has entered the English lexicon, if not the dictionary—yet.

Top Most Irritating Peeves

Well, folks, that subhead right there would earn a spot on many peevologists' list. It's superfluous to use *top* if *most* is used, and vice versa. But you'll often see "Top 10 Most" lists, and even though using both terms is redundant, it's not incorrect.

＊ *Dictioneer* is a slighting term for someone who criticizes others' diction or writing style.

Words of Wisdom: Anger

✳ ✳ ✳ ✳

"Man should forget his anger before he lies down to sleep."
—THOMAS DE QUINCEY

"Holding on to anger is like grasping a hot coal with the intent of throwing it at someone else; you are the one who gets burned."
—BUDDHA

"Speak when you are angry and you will make the best speech you will ever regret."
—AMBROSE BIERCE

"A man that studieth revenge keeps his own wounds green."
—FRANCIS BACON

"Anger and jealousy can no more bear to lose sight of their objects than love."
—GEORGE ELIOT

"Anger is a short madness."
—HORACE

"Heaven has no rage like love to hatred turned, nor hell a fury like a woman scorned."
—WILLIAM CONGREVE

"How much more grievous are the consequences of anger than the causes of it."
—MARCUS AURELIUS

"When angry count to ten before you speak. If very angry, count to one hundred."
—THOMAS JEFFERSON

"When angry, count to four; when very angry, swear."
—MARK TWAIN

Unfriend Is an Unfriendly Word

The New Oxford American Dictionary's 2009 Word of the Year—
unfriend*—gained fame thanks to Facebook, where people can be "unfriended" just as easily as they can be "friended."*

✳   ✳   ✳   ✳

NOT EVERYONE IS a fan of the term. Linguist Michael Quinion claims that the main objection is that the proper word form should be *defriend*, which parallels *befriend*. He suggests that the word is instead modeled on *unsubscribe*, and also that *friend* is relatively uncommon as a verb. But, as the *Oxford English Dictionary* shows, *friend* has been a verb for a long time—since 1225 at least. *Unfriend* was even spotted as a verb hundreds of years before Facebook—in this case, back in 1659: "I hope, Sir, that we are not mutually Unfriended by this Difference which hath happened betwixt us" (Thomas Fuller).

If the etymology of the word isn't the problem, then what is? It's more that the word simply sounds cruel. It rings of third-grade playground battles and broken relationships ("I'm not your friend anymore!"). But *unfriend* is just a technical term for breaking an association between yourself and another party in a particular company's database.

Do You Want Fries with That?

Of course, in practice, changes to friend rosters on Facebook can and do affect real relationships. In 2009, Burger King unveiled the "Whopper Sacrifice" app, in which, by simply unfriending ten people, users could earn a free Whopper. But those who thought they'd get a free lunch had another think coming. Facebook normally doesn't tell the unfriended they've been dumped, but Burger King deliberately twisted the knife by sending each victim a notification that they'd been unfriended for one-tenth of a deluxe hamburger. You know what they say: A friend in need (of a tasty burger) is an unfriend indeed!

Pardon My French

When Bart gets a stomachache in the 1995 Simpsons *episode "'Round Springfield," he goes to the school nurse's office—and finds Lunchlady Doris instead of a nurse. "Budget cuts," Doris explains. "They've even got Groundskeeper Willie teaching French."*

✳ ✳ ✳ ✳

CUE GROUNDSKEEPER WILLIE in the classroom, and cue a political catchphrase. "Bonjourrr," Willie says to the French students, rolling his r's in his Scottish brogue, "you cheese-eating surrender monkeys!" *Cheese-eating,* of course, comes from the popularity of cheese in France. However, if Willie had used *baguette-eating* or *champagne-swilling,* the impact wouldn't have been the same. The word *cheese* is inherently funny (think of a "cheesy grin"). And there's something twisted about poking fun at French cheese, which is some of the finest in the world.

The phrase came at a singular point in history when it was popular for Americans to loathe the French. Soon enough, hawkish writer (and *Simpsons* fan) Jonah Goldberg was using the phrase "cheese-eating surrender monkeys" in the *National Review Online,* blasting the French for their supposed military wimpiness. The term gained even more traction in 2003, when France declined to ally with the United States for an invasion of Iraq. The British newspaper *The Guardian* summed up the conflict by stating that Americans perceived France's unwillingness to join the war effort in Iraq as a "genetic weakness." A fresh wave of anti-French outrage crested in Washington, where Congress officially renamed "French fries" as "freedom fries" in its cafeteria.

The *New York Post* used an abbreviated version of the *Simpsons* phrase in 2006, in a headline (sans dietary element) about the

Iraq Study Group's recommendation to withdraw combat troops from Iraq. "Surrender Monkeys," read the headline, next to pictures of two monkeys with the faces of the report's authors.

But It Isn't Nice, No Matter What You're Eating

From there, the term spread to the lexicon of political invective, and it became a variable formula (like a *snowclone*—see page 77). In recent years, various writers have replaced *cheese* with *borscht, cheeseburger, cod, couscous, curry, donut, falafel, gazpacho, goat, granola, hummus, kielbasa, McDonald's, sauerkraut, tofu, tortilla, Velveeta, waffle,* and even *whale,* all to suit their purpose *du jour.*

By focusing on an aspect of culture (food preferences), "X-eating surrender monkeys" has become a politically and socially acceptable way to insult another culture while also poking fun at the pacifistic nature of its leaders. Perhaps Groundskeeper Willie should have followed up with: "Pass the ammo. And the haggis."

"Accurst be he that first invented war."

—CHRISTOPHER MARLOWE

"There are many causes I would die for. There is not a single cause I would kill for."

—MAHATMA GANDHI

✳ French translators struggled to find the right words to properly convey the sentiment behind "cheese-eating surrender monkey." They settled on *primates capitulards et toujours en quête de fromages.*

Adios, Muchachos

So long, farewell, auf Wiedersehen, good night. These are just a few of the many things you can say when you take your leave around the world.

❋   ❋   ❋   ❋

1. Afrikaans	Totsiens
2. Chinese (Cantonese)	Joi gin
3. Chinese (Mandarin)	Zai jian
4. Danish	Farvel
5. Dutch	Vaarwel
6. English	Goodbye
7. French	Au revoir
8. German	Auf Wiedersehen
9. Greek	Adio
10. Hawaiian	Aloha
11. Hungarian	Viszontlátásra
12. Irish Gaelic	Slán
13. Italian	Arrivederci/ciao
14. Japanese	Sayonara
15. Polish	Do widzenia
16. Portuguese	Adeus
17. Russian	Do svidaniya
18. Scottish Gaelic	Beannachd leibh
19. Spanish	Adiós
20. Swedish	Adjö

Words of Wisdom: Travel

✳   ✳   ✳   ✳

"I never travel without my diary. One should always have something sensational to read on the train."

—Oscar Wilde

"Travel, in the younger sort, is a part of education; in the elder, a part of experience. He that traveleth into a country before he hath some entrance into the language, goeth to school, and not to travel."

—Francis Bacon

"For my part, I travel not to go anywhere, but to go. I travel for travel's sake. The great affair is to move."

—Robert Louis Stevenson

"The man who goes alone can start today; but he who travels with another must wait till that other is ready."

—Henry David Thoreau

"I love to travel, but hate to arrive."

—Hernando Cortez

"A good traveler has no fixed plans, and is not intent on arriving."

—Lao Tzu

"I have found out that there ain't no surer way to find out whether you like people or hate them than to travel with them."

—Mark Twain

"Like all great travelers, I have seen more than I remember, and remember more than I have seen."

—Benjamin Disraeli

Chapter 13

Word History

Lunar Love

How much control do you believe the heavenly bodies—that is, the sun, moon, stars, etc.—exert over our lives? What about our love lives? The notion perhaps sounds crazy to our modern ears, but belief in a connection between moon and man is evidenced in our linguistic history.

※　※　※　※

IS SOMEONE IN LOVE in a rational state of mind? The history of the word *moonstruck* would tell us no, and we have all seen examples of people who seemed to get a little loopy in the presence of a significant other. The word *moonstruck* first appears in John Milton's 1674 version of *Paradise Lost* in a long list of ailments visited upon humanity because of Adam and Eve's indiscretion with the apple:

> *Deamoniac Phrenzie, moaping Melancholie,*
> *And Moon-struck madness, pining Atrophie,*
> *Marasmus and wide-wasting Pestilence,*
> *Dropsies, and Asthma's, and Joint-racking Rheums.*

Crazy in Love

Milton's use of *moon-struck* to describe madness, while new, isn't just crazy talk. The moon has long been connected with madness, and evidence for this association shows up in the English lexicon. The Latin word for moon, *luna*, gives us *lunatic*—a word originally applied to someone afflicted with what were believed to be moon-triggered bouts of insanity—and its derivative, *lunacy*.

In the mid-nineteenth century, Charles Dickens was the first to use *moonstruck* in association with love, describing the title character of *David Copperfield* as "the moon-struck slave of Dora." In *Tristram and Iseult* (1852), Matthew Arnold described Tristram as a "moonstruck knight." These uses, aided perhaps by the accompanying imagery of a moonlit lovers' tryst, erased the sense of plain madness, as *moonstruck* came to mean "in love." By the Victorian era, to be moonstruck was to be madly in love.

Reach for the Stars

The moon isn't the only celestial body employed in amorous description. The term *star-crossed*, whose coinage is credited to Shakespeare (in the prologue of *Romeo and Juliet* the bard refers to the doomed young lovers as "star-cross'd"), describes a pair whose love is thwarted by outside forces. Like *moonstruck*, *star-crossed* arose from the belief that our fates are determined by astrological events.

There are some other senses of *moonstruck*, based on various superstitions about the effects of moonlight. Some believed that sleeping in moonlight could cause blindness, and those afflicted with this supposed moon-blindness were, at least up until the mid-1800s, sometimes called *moonstruck*. Nineteenth-century sailors believed that the tropical moon would spoil fish, and such fish were said to be *moonstruck*. Of course, it was the tropical heat, and not the moonlight, that caused the fish to spoil, but superstition seldom has anything to do with common sense, does it?

Where Did It Come From?

Lovebird: This figurative description of a human lover dates back to 1911, but it's taken from the 1595 definition for a "small species of West African parrot, noted for the remarkable attention mating pairs pay to one another." Aww.

Words of Wisdom: Love

✳   ✳   ✳   ✳

"Two persons love in one another the future good, which they aid one another to unfold."

—MARGARET FULLER

"To love deeply in one direction makes us more loving in all others."

—ANNE-SOPHIE SWETCHINE

"Love comforteth like sunshine after rain."

—WILLIAM SHAKESPEARE

"What is life without the radiance of love?"

—J.C.F. VON SCHILLER

"What is love without passion?—A garden without flowers, a hat without feathers, tobogganing without snow."

—JENNIE JEROME CHURCHILL

"Love is a great beautifier."

—LOUISA MAY ALCOTT

"You know . . . nothing about the sort of love of which I am capable. Every atom of your flesh is as dear to me as my own; in pain and sickness it would still be dear."

—CHARLOTTE BRONTË

"All, everything that I understand, I understand only because I love."

—LEO TOLSTOY

"Absence sharpens love, presence strengthens it."

—THOMAS FULLER

"True love is a durable fire."

—SIR WALTER RALEGH

"Love makes up for the lack of long memories by a sort of magic. All other affections need a past: love creates a past which envelops us, as if by enchantment."

—Benjamin Constant

"Love is the vital essence that pervades and permeates, from the center to the circumference, the graduating circles of all thought and action. Love is the talisman of human weal and woe—the open sesame to every soul."

—Elizabeth Cady Stanton

"What know we of the Blest above But that they sing, and that they love?"

—William Wordsworth

"There is no remedy for love but to love more."

—Henry David Thoreau

"There is only one happiness in life, to love and be loved."

—George Sand

"If you would be loved, love and be lovable."

—Benjamin Franklin

"All love is sweet, given or returned."

—Percy Bysshe Shelley

"The supreme happiness of life is the conviction of being loved for yourself or, more correctly, being loved in spite of yourself."

—Victor Hugo

"He prayeth best who loveth best all things both great and small; for the dear God who loveth us, He made and loveth all."

—Samuel Taylor Coleridge

"I hold it true, whate'er befall; I feel it, when I sorrow most; 'Tis better to have loved and lost, Than never to have loved at all."

—Alfred, Lord Tennyson

A Lousy Article

Here's an opening sentence you might recognize: "If you really want to hear about it, the first thing you'll probably want to know is where I was born, and what my lousy childhood was like…"

✳ ✳ ✳ ✳

THUS STARTS J. D. Salinger's 1951 classic *The Catcher in the Rye*. No one familiar with the book and its economically privileged but disenchanted narrator, Holden Caulfield, would understand "lousy childhood" to mean that Caulfield's upbringing was defined by the presence of pesky parasitic insects. But, then again, it's likely that not many of us have considered the entomological origins of *lousy*.

Dirty Language

The word comes from *louse*, and the original meaning was "infested with lice," as demonstrated in William Langland's fourteenth-century poem *Piers Plowman*:

> *With an hode on his hed a lousi hatte aboue.* (With a hood on his head, a lousy hat above.)

But the figurative meaning of "bad, worthless, contemptible" wasn't far behind—most of the time, something infested with lice isn't in very good shape or particularly desirable. Geoffrey Chaucer, a contemporary of Langland's, used this figurative meaning in his *The Friar's Tale*:

> *A lowsy jogelour kan deceyve thee.*(A lousy juggler can deceive you.)

So the figurative meaning has been around almost as long as the literal one.

A Swarm of New Usage

There is another, more recent sense of *lousy* that plays off the metaphor of infestation rather than the unhygienic insect itself. That is the use of the word to mean "teeming or swarming with, full of." This sense arose in the United States in the middle of the nineteenth century. The *Democratic State Journal* of Sacramento, California, would write of a gold rush claim in October 1856: "The bed of the river is perfectly 'lousy' with gold."

(The placing of the word in quotes is a giveaway that it is being used in a new sense that the writer or editor does not expect the reader to be familiar with.)

We don't often see the original, literal meaning of *lousy* anymore. That's probably because in our modern, ultra-hygienic society of disinfectants, soaps, and regular bathing, lice—except for the occasional outbreak among schoolchildren—aren't that big of a problem. But because the spelling of the word has remained the same, and because the metaphorical meanings haven't strayed too far from the literal, the etymology of the word is still easily recognizable.

Where Did It Come From?

Pack rat: Interestingly, some believe that this term (meaning a person who can't or won't discard anything—a condition that can sometimes be a variant of an anxiety disorder), came from the North American bushy-tailed woodrat, a rodent that has a habit of dragging objects back to its home and packing them in. But that meaning only came into usage around 1885, whereas the use of pack rat for human hoarders dates to 1850. So, either the rat's name is really older than the dictionary states, or the reference to humans was the term's original usage.

Any Volunteers?

Those who volunteer to distribute food at a local soup kitchen or who travel across the country to help rebuild homes after a natural disaster may not think of themselves as soldiers, but at one time that's precisely what a volunteer was.

✳   ✳   ✳   ✳

THE WORD **VOLUNTEER** dates to the beginning of the seventeenth century and originally referred to soldiers who had enlisted of their own free will. The word's first known appearance is in poet Michael Drayton's *The Miseries of Queene Margarite* (circa 1600):

> *And with five thousand valient Volunteers, Of native French, put under her Command, With Armes well fitted she towards Scotland steeres.*

In the Army Now

English borrowed the word from the French *voluntaire*, which in turn came from the Latin *voluntarius*, which means "of one's own free will."

The military did not have exclusive command of *volunteer* for very long, however. By 1638 the word was being used broadly to refer to anyone who offered his or her service without being under obligation to do so.

Evidence for *volunteer* as a verb doesn't show up until the mid-eighteenth century, when Samuel Johnson chose to include it in *A Dictionary of the English Language*—regarded as the forerunner of modern dictionaries— with the definition of "to go for a soldier." Johnson's goal was to make a record of the English lexicon as it existed among speakers of the language; that he chose to include *volunteer* as a verb suggests that folks had been using it

> *"It is easier to find men who will volunteer to die, than to find those who are willing to endure pain with patience."*
> — Julius Caesar

as such for some time before his dictionary first went to press in 1755.

Beyond the Battlefield

The adjective *voluntary*, on the other hand, is older than both the noun and verb *volunteer*. It dates to the late fourteenth century, and it never had an exclusive military connotation. It originally meant "spontaneous, without external prompting," developing the sense of choice around the middle of the fifteenth century.

In botany and gardening, *volunteer* has a very different connotation. A *volunteer plant* is one that grows spontaneously, without being deliberately planted. So a botanical volunteer is a weed and, far from being welcomed, is often set for eradication.

✻ Tennessee is known as the "Volunteer State." This nickname harks back to the original military meaning of the word and dates to the Mexican-American War of 1846 to 1848, during which a call went out for 2,800 volunteers from the state to join the army. Some 30,000 answered the call.

Where Did It Come From?

Rookie: A large, annoying black bird found in rural medieval England was known as a *rook*. When young farmers went to the local fairs and were taken by the swindlers there, they compared the thieves to the rooks; ultimately, those conned in the swindle became known as *rookies*. The word came to be used in modern language to describe anyone young, naive, or new at something.

Words of Wisdom: Courage

✳ ✳ ✳ ✳

"Courage is almost a contradiction in terms. It means a strong desire to live taking the form of a readiness to die."
—G. K. CHESTERTON

"Courage is what it takes to stand up and speak; courage is also what it takes to sit down and listen."
—WINSTON CHURCHILL

"It is curious that physical courage should be so common in the world and moral courage so rare."
—MARK TWAIN

"Oh courage...oh yes! If only one had that...Then life might be livable, in spite of everything."
—HENRIK IBSEN

"Courage is like love; it must have hope for nourishment."
—NAPOLEON BONAPARTE

"For it giveth unto all lovers courage, that lusty month of May."
—SIR THOMAS MALORY

"One man with courage makes a majority."
—ANDREW JACKSON

"I refer those actions which work out the good of the agent to courage, and those which work out the good of others to nobility."
—BENEDICT SPINOZA

"Without justice, courage is weak."
—BENJAMIN FRANKLN

Mighty Hunter to Mighty Idiot

In contemporary slang, the term **nimrod** *is no compliment. It's a word in the same vein as* doofus *and* idiot, *with a hint of jerkdom thrown in for good measure.*

✳   ✳   ✳   ✳

Y ET NIMROD HAS a considerably prouder history as an *eponym*, or a common noun derived from the name of a person or place. (For more on eponyms, see page 136.) It comes from the biblical figure Nimrod, great-grandson of Noah, who is described in Genesis 10:9 as "a mighty hunter before the LORD" (KJV). According to the textual evidence dug up by the *Oxford English Dictionary*, this oblique reference to Nimrod lay dormant for centuries before being lexically resurrected in the sixteenth century. After a brief incarnation as another word for *tyrant*, *nimrod* returned to its biblical roots. By the mid-1600s, "skilled hunter" or, more simply, "a person who likes to hunt," had emerged as the primary meaning for *nimrod*.

But how did the word make the semantic jump from mighty hunter to mighty idiot? A widely circulated explanation attributes the shift to none other than cartoon character Bugs Bunny, who in a 1940s cartoon refers to his hapless nemesis, hunter Elmer Fudd, as a "poor little Nimrod." As the explanation goes, cartoon audiences unfamiliar with the biblical reference took this use of *nimrod* not as a nod to Fudd's hunting hobby but as a characterization of his slow-wittedness.

While it's perfectly plausible for a popular cartoon to influence the semantic development of a word in the way that this Looney Tunes tale suggests, there is one problem here. The *OED* dates the earliest use of the dumbed-down *nimrod* to 1933 (in the play *The Great Magoo*)—about a decade before Bugs and Fudd ever crossed paths. Is this evidence completely damning to the theory of cartoon coinage? Perhaps, but don't let that stop you from hunting down another explanation!

Resting on Etymological Laurels

The word **triumph** *comes from Latin, but its meaning in that language is not the one we commonly use today. To the Romans, a* triumph *was a parade celebrating a great military victory.*

✳ ✳ ✳ ✳

IN THE DAYS of the Roman republic, generals were forbidden to enter the environs of Rome with their armies. The only time armies were allowed to enter was after a major victory in battle, when the senate granted the victorious general permission to hold a *triumph.* The general would ride a chariot through the streets of Rome to the steps of the senate, a slave standing beside him holding a crown of laurels over his head. The general's army would follow, leading the commander of the defeated enemy, captured slaves, and great wagons of spoils from the victory. The day was a holiday, and the entire city would turn out to cheer, to feast, and to celebrate. (See page 551 to read about *ovation,* a word with related roots.)

Roman poets also used the word *triumphus* to refer to a victory itself—as opposed to the lavish post-battle ceremony—as did later prose writers in imperial Rome. But this sense was relatively rare in Latin, and the word usually referred simply to the processional and accompanying celebrations.

Both of these senses were borrowed into English. There is one Old English work that uses the word: King Alfred's translation of the works of Orosius, a late Roman historian. But the word really makes its English appearance in the fourteenth century, during the Renaissance, when classical culture was being studied and revived. Today, the sense of the victory processional is still used in reference to Roman history, but the transferred sense of *triumph* meaning "victory, conquest" is the more usual English use. Another subtly different sense, referring to the elation or joy that accompanies a victory, comes a little later, with the *Oxford English Dictionary* dating it to 1582.

Meat Market

A vegetarian *is someone who doesn't eat meat, or at least that's what the word means today. Had there been vegetarians a millennium ago, however, they would have eaten plenty of meat. That's because* **meat** *did not always mean "the flesh of animals": In Old English, the word* mete *meant simply "food."*

✳ ✳ ✳ ✳

IT WASN'T UNTIL the Middle English period, specifically the early fourteenth century, that *meat* narrowed in meaning to apply only to animal flesh. In modern times, the word is used variously to include or exclude different types of animal flesh. The International Vegetarian Union, for example, adopts a narrow definition of the word, specifying that its members do not eat meat, poultry, or fish. The Roman Catholic Church, which has long proscribed the eating of meat on certain days, includes beef, pork, and poultry under its definition of *meat*; fish and reptiles are fair game.

Many people use the term *meat* to refer only to beef, excluding poultry and products that come from pigs. The *Dictionary of American Regional English* records a sign seen as late as 1972 in a Honolulu shop window: "No meat today, only pork." However, the National Pork Board begs to differ. You may be familiar with their slogan: "The Other White Meat."

Some specific non-animal foods are also referred to as *meat*. The meat of a nut is the part inside the shell that you eat. Likewise, the word can denote the fleshy, edible part of a fruit.

The role of meat as an important dietary staple has given rise to a number of metaphorical phrases and sayings. *Meat and potatoes*, used to label a staple commodity or an unsophisticated offering, dates to at least 1846. And the use of *meat* to denote the main part or gist of a story or a matter of importance came along a couple of decades later.

Please, May I Have Another Meaning?

If you've ever struggled to develop your proper social graces—
perhaps you are continually showing up late to dinner parties, or
saying the wrong thing when the right thing is sorely necessary—
it will be a comfort to know that even the word **polite** *itself hasn't*
always had it all figured out, either.

✻ ✻ ✻ ✻

IT IS VERY common for a word with a specific, literal meaning to develop figurative or metaphorical meanings that are
related to the literal one. This process is one type of what linguists refer to as *semantic broadening*, and the word *polite* offers
a good illustration of it.

A Smooth Transition

We can see a parallel change in *polite* across multiple languages.
A semantic change occurs in the original Latin, and then the
same pattern repeats itself centuries later in a number of languages that borrowed or inherited the word with its original
meaning.

The English word *polite* comes from the Latin verb *polio*,
meaning "to smooth, to polish." Its past participle, *politus*, and
adverbial form, *polite*, came in that language to mean "cultured,
refined"—a metaphorical polish.

The adjective *polite* first appears in English in the late fourteenth century, apparently adopted directly from the Latin
rather than via French (as is normally the case). The original
meaning in English was a literal one of "smooth, polished." As
it happened in Latin, by 1500 *polite* was being used to mean
"refined, cultured, elegant," a sense that survives today chiefly
in the term *polite society*. Finally, the sense of "courteous, well-
mannered" developed in the mid-eighteenth century.

It's a Small World

We see the same development of meanings in French, where the word *poli* appears around the year 1160 with the meaning of "smooth, shiny." By the late twelfth century, the word was being applied to words and diction with a meaning of "careful, well-chosen." It acquired the meaning of "cultured" in the late sixteenth century, then "well-mannered" in the late seventeenth. A similar pattern occurred at about the same time in Spanish and Italian.

Interestingly, in Occitan (a Romance language spoken in southern France and parts of Spain and Italy), the pattern is reversed. In Old Occitan the word *polit* was first used in the mid-twelfth century, metaphorically, to describe "well-chosen" words; the literal meaning of "smooth, polished" did not develop until the fourteenth century.

Is this a case of inevitable semantic development? Is a word in any language meaning "smooth" going to develop a metaphorical sense meaning "cultured, well-mannered"? Or were these languages influenced by the senses of the word already at work in the older Latin? At the risk of seeming impolite, we'll go ahead and leave these questions open-ended.

Where Did It Come From?

Gossip: Once an approved manner of discussing someone's business, this word came from the religious rite of baptism. Those adults who stand up for a baby during the ceremony are known as godparents. The godparents of one child were considered "related" to the godparents of another child in that family and became known to each other as *godsibb*. These insiders were given the right to discuss family business among themselves. A little too much discussion might have made way for a broader definition of *godsibb*, or *gossip*, to mean people who tell tales, spreading both truth and rumor.

A Trinity of Prefixes

Language often blesses its users with an abundance of options. Even small concepts or limited topics can produce a staggering volume of accompanying vocabulary. You can then imagine what a wealth of words are available to one who wants to discuss the divine, a subject as massive as they come.

✳ ✳ ✳ ✳

THE ENGLISH LANGUAGE has a trinity of prefixes that are used to express thoughts about gods and goddesses: *dei-*, *div-*, and *theo-*.

A Godly Beginning

Dei- comes from the Latin word *deus* ("god") and has given us a number of words relating to the divine. The most notable of these, of course, is *deity*. This came into English in the late fourteenth century from the French *déité*, which in turn is from the Latin *deitas*, a late Latin variation on *deus* coined by St. Augustine in the fifth century. Other *dei-* words include:

✳ *deicide*—the (presumably theoretical) killing of a god; Nietzsche would be proud

✳ *deific*—no, it's not a blend of *deity* and *terrific*; it's an adjective pertaining to making something divine, as in "deific transformation"; also *deifical*

✳ *deification*—the act of making something divine

✳ *deiform*—having the form of a god, godlike

✳ *deism*—a doctrine that accepts a divine creator but rejects a personal God that plays an active role in the universe; also *deist*, one who subscribes to this doctrine

This Prefix Is Simply Divine

Div- and *divine* come from the Latin word *divus*, another word for "god." *Diva* is the feminine form (a goddess) and, through Italian, is the source for the word denoting a self-important female performer. And the practice of *divination*, the foretelling of events and the discovery of the hidden, comes from the same Latin root. *Div-* words include:

* *divinely*—in a godlike manner

* *divinity*—the quality of being a god; also *divineness*

* *divino-political*—a seventeenth-century adjective relating to theocracy

And *Theo-* Makes Three

The third prefix, *theo-*, is not Latin; it is from the Greek *theo-*, also meaning "god." *Theo-* is much more productive in English than the two Latin roots. It gives us, among others:

* *theocracy*—rule by priests or religious leaders

* *theodicy*—the justification of God's actions, an explanation of "why bad things happen to good people"

* *theodidact*—one who is taught by God

* *theology*—the study of gods and religion

Where Did It Come From?

Xmas: Those who believe that this word is a cheap and potentially blasphemous abbreviation for *Christmas* forget that since at least A.D. 1100 the symbol *X*, derived from the Greek word for "Christ," has been used in reference to Jesus Christ. In fact, the word *Xmas* has been around since at least the mid-1500s.

Words of Wisdom: Faith

✳ ✳ ✳ ✳

"Faith is love taking the form of aspiration."
—WILLIAM ELLERY CHANNING

"The principal part of faith is patience."
—GEORGE MacDONALD

"Faith makes the discords of the present the harmonies of the future."
—ROBERT COLLYER

"Understanding is the reward of faith. So do not seek to understand in order to believe, but believe so that you may understand."
—ST. AUGUSTINE

"Faith is an excitement and an enthusiasm: it is a condition of intellectual magnificence to which we must cling as to a treasure, and not squander."
—GEORGE SAND

"The improver of natural knowledge absolutely refuses to acknowledge authority, as such. For him, skepticism is the highest of duties, blind faith the one unpardonable sin."
—THOMAS HUXLEY

"Faith is a living, daring confidence in God's grace. It is so sure and certain that a man could stake his life on it a thousand times."
—MARTIN LUTHER

"Love is faith, and faith, like a gathered flower, will live rootlessly on."
—THOMAS HARDY

It's Alive!

*Did you know the word **quick** did not always mean "fast"?*

✳ ✳ ✳ ✳

THE WORD QUICK comes from the Old English *cwic*, meaning "alive." This original sense of the word is still occasionally used, but outside of the stock phrases "the quick and the dead" (i.e., the living and the dead) and "cut to the quick" (i.e., seriously wounded; a reference to living flesh and to cutting a nail down to the living tissue), it is pretty rare nowadays. Furthermore, the rarity of the original meaning is demonstrated by how often these stock phrases are reinterpreted to use the "fast" meaning. "The quick and the dead" is often reinterpreted to mean "be fast or you will die." And "cut to the quick" is often erroneously used to mean "get to the heart of the matter, stop beating around the bush."

The original sense appears in the phrase "quick with child," meaning "pregnant." (This is an inversion of the original "with quick child.") The word *quickening*, once common but now quite rare, refers to the first movements of a fetus in the womb.

The original meaning also survives in *quicksilver* (another name for mercury), a word that goes back to the Old English *cwicseolfor* and is a reference to the fact that drops of liquid mercury move as if they were alive.

Around the year 1300, *quick* acquired the sense of "moving, shifting" and also "fast, swift." The first gives us *quicksand*, or moving sand, and the latter is the dominant sense of the word today. The sense of *quick* meaning "mentally agile" or "smart" appears around 1450, although there is a single use of *cwices modes*, or "quick mind," in surviving Old English texts.

So, while language has evolved gradually over the centuries, at the same time it can be called *quick*—because it is metaphorically alive, constantly moving and changing.

Good, Gooder, Goodest

Everyone knows that gooder *and* goodest *are bad English, and unless you're using urban slang, there's nothing worse than* baddest. *But why do we say* good-better-best *and* bad-worse-worst *instead of* good-gooder-goodest *and* bad-badder-baddest?

✳   ✳   ✳   ✳

ALL LANGUAGES HAVE "holes" in their lexicons; that is, entries that should be present in their vocabularies but, strangely, are missing. Think about the plural of *deer*: No competent speaker of English would say, "I saw three deers in the nature preserve." Such gaps or irregular patterns in a language's word stock are instances of **suppletion;** the missing *gooder* and *goodest* (and *badder* and *baddest*) are examples of this.

In a Past Life, I Was a Noun

Linguists believe that *good* and *bad*, historically, are not true adjectives, a category that typically allows for the *-er* and *-est* comparative and superlative forms. Rather, these words were originally nouns that over time morphed into adjectives because of their ability to modify nouns

("the good shepherd"; "the bad dog"). In fact, no comparative or superlative forms for *good* or *bad* probably ever existed in English.

English bases the comparative and superlative forms of *good* on an Old English word, *bot* (which meant "aid" or "remedy"), so *better* and *best* became linked to *good*. *Bot* still exists in the phrase "to boot" (meaning "as well" or "also"), and it is possible that *booty*, an archaic term referring to loot or stolen goods taken by pirates on the high seas, also comes from the Old English *bot* form.

Instead of *badder* and *baddest,* the comparative and superlative forms of *bad* are based on the Old English *wyrsa* (meaning "to confuse, mix up"), giving us *worse* and *worst.*

Wending, Wending, Went!

The English verb *to go* reveals another example of suppletion. The past tense form *went* actually comes from the archaic English verb *wend,* which also means "to go." It is likely that English once had a past tense form of *go,* which it lost sometime during the language's early formation.

Returning to *baddest* for a moment: In urban slang, this term does not denote anything negative at all. In fact, a good synonym for *baddest* is *best!*

✳ Interestingly, Romance languages also exhibit suppletion in their words for *good* and *bad.* The Spanish *bueno,* French *bon,* and Italian *buono* have *mejor, meilleur,* and *migliore,* respectively, as their comparative forms. Similarly, the comparatives of the Spanish *malo* and French *mauvais* are *peor* and *pire.*

✳ Speaking of good and bad, here's a word with meanings that have encompassed both: *Egregious* is a word that experienced a fall from grace with a major semantic shift. It comes from the Latin *ex* ("out") + *greg* or *grex* ("flock"), literally meaning "towering above the flock." Historically, *egregious* was used to describe something "remarkable in a good sense, of distinguished, eminent personal qualities." Over time, the term took on a negative slant and is now used to describe something that is "extraordinary in a bad way."

Where Did It Come From?

Hoosegow: Now a slang term meaning "jail," the word gets its original meaning from the Spanish *juzgado,* meaning "court of justice." Mexican usage shortened it to *juzgao,* using the word in reference to a jail. It later became popular in the American Old West, spelled just the way it sounded to the American ear.

That's Nice, Dear

Many words have seen their meanings change over the centuries, but seldom has a word changed so significantly, so many times, or had so many different meanings as **nice.** *Today, the word means "pleasant, good-natured, attractive" and has a positive connotation. (Although describing a potential romantic interest as "nice" can certainly be damning with faint praise.) But it was not always the case.*

✳   ✳   ✳   ✳

THE EVERYDAY WORD *nice* has exhibited a surprisingly wide range of meanings over the years, including—but not limited to, believe it or not—"silly," "wanton and lascivious," "discriminating, delicate, and tactful," "shy," "strange," "cowardly," and "refined, cultured."

You Don't Know Nice

Nice was originally an Old French word meaning "silly, simple, and unsophisticated." Ultimately, it comes from the Latin *nescius,* meaning "ignorant." It took a few centuries for *nice* to filter down from the French-speaking English nobles to the Anglo-Saxon populace, but by 1300 English speakers were using the word to mean "foolish" or "ignorant."

In the latter part of the fourteenth century, *nice* had a semantic explosion, coming to mean a great variety of things—some of them contradictory. It could, as before, be used to mean "silly or ignorant," but it could also mean "clever and cunning," "wild and primitive," "sluggish and slothful," "cowardly and timid," "fastidious and scrupulous of manner," "dainty and delicate," and "extravagant, wanton, and sinful." Often the same writer would use the word in contradictory senses.

Many of these senses are now obsolete, but some continue to survive—*nice* can still mean "fastidious, precise," for example. The most common sense in use today, that of "pleasant, agreeable, attractive," is of relatively recent vintage and didn't appear until the mid- to late eighteenth century.

Linguistic Development Sure Can Be Exhausting

A significant factor in the word's flexibility in meaning is the inventiveness of language users. One surefire way to liven up your lexicon is to use an old word in an unexpected way. And when lots of folks start following suit, we end up with a new meaning for a word. Consider the word *bad*, for instance. Thanks to linguistic innovators in the twentieth century— perhaps most notably pop star Michael Jackson—the word acquired the meaning "extremely good." The older and quite contradictory meaning of "not good" persisted, and now the two senses coexist.

Centuries of semantic heavy lifting have left *nice* a little tired, and today it's a word that carries with it very little weight. In fact, the word is so void of semantic heft that you might say it functions as a disparaging term—in certain contexts, at least. (Think again of one using the word to describe a potential romantic suitor.)

✳ *Nice* could also be considered a *capitonym*. Capitonyms are another category of *homonyms*. As the name implies, capitonyms are words that have the same spelling, but they have different meanings and potentially different pronunciations when capitalized. For example, the words *polish* ("to make shiny") and *Polish* ("from Poland") are capitonyms. The words *nice* (as defined, quite extensively, in this article) and *Nice* (the coastal city in France) would be another example. (For more on homonyms, turn to page 271.)

A Timely Word

*The history of the word **tidy** is anything but tidy.*

✳ ✳ ✳ ✳

THE ORIGINAL MEANING of *tidy* was "timely, opportune," used particularly in regard to crops, referring to fruit in its proper season. It comes from the Old English *tid*, a versatile little word that meant "time," "a measure of time" (anything from one hour to many years), or "season," and from which we get the words *tide* and *tidings*. In the mid-fourteenth century, during the period known as Middle English, *tidy* appeared as an adjective meaning "timely."

The Middle English *tidy* also meant "in good condition, healthy, plump." This usage, which survives today only as a dialectal variation, is undoubtedly an extension of the sense of *tidy* meaning "in season." Originally reserved for crops and livestock, this *tidy* eventually gained currency as a descriptor for people, particularly comely young females.

From the sense of *tidy* meaning "in good condition, healthy" came the meaning "admirable, possessing desirable qualities"; this *tidy*, like its forebearer, described both things and people. This sense can still be found today, although it has been downgraded a bit to "satisfactory, pretty good." It is also found in the sense meaning "considerable, big," as in "a tidy sum of money."

Today's principle meaning, that of "orderly, clean," dates to at least the beginning of the eighteenth century, when the word was included in a 1706 dictionary with the definition "handy, neat, clean, as [a] tidy servant." A century later, thanks to a linguistic process called *functional shift*—by which a word changes part of speech without any changes to its form—English speakers gained the option of using *tidy* as a verb. As a verb *tidy* often pairs with *up* (a development likely due to *tidy*'s semantic closeness to *clean*, a word that can also pair with *up*).

Words of Wisdom: Gardening

✳ ✳ ✳ ✳

"A good garden may have some weeds."

—THOMAS FULLER

"To know of someone here and there whom we accord with, who is living on with us, even in silence—this makes our earthly ball a peopled garden."

—JOHANN WOLFGANG VON GOETHE

"A Garden is a lovesome thing."

—THOMAS EDWARD BROWN

"Gardens are not made by singing, 'Oh, how beautiful,' and sitting in the shade."

—RUDYARD KIPLING

"If you have a garden and a library, you have everything you need."

—MARCUS TULLIUS CICERO

"The toad, without which no garden would be complete."

—CHARLES DUDLEY WARNER

"May I a small house and a large garden have."

—ABRAHAM COWLEY

"Exclusiveness in a garden is a mistake as great as it is in society."

—ALFRED AUSTIN

"Give me odorous at sunrise a garden of beautiful flowers where I can walk undisturbed."

—WALT WHITMAN

Reworking Words with *Re-*

Sometimes even the smallest and simplest of prefixes can have complicated histories behind them. Get ready to take another look at a prefix you likely use every day.

✳ ✳ ✳ ✳

THE PREFIX RE- is one of the most used in English, added to an uncounted number of words. It has its origins in Latin, but its use in English is somewhat different than its ancient forebearer.

Revealing the Past

In Latin, the prefix had four basic meanings, which can each be illustrated by English verbs borrowed from Latin, courtesy of Norman French:

1. "back to a previous position," as in *recede* (*re-* + *cedere*, "to go"), *reduce* (*re-* + *ducere*, "to lead"), and *refer* (*re-* + *ferre*, "to carry")

2. "again," as in *re-create* (*re-* + *creare*, "to produce"), *reform* (*re-* + *formare*, "to shape"), and *renovate* (*re-* + *novare*, "to make new")

3. "remaining in position," as in *retain* (*re-* + *tenir*, "to hold"), *refrain* (*re-* + *frenum*, "bridle, harness"), and *relinquish* (*re-* + *linquere*, "to leave, abandon")

4. The prefix was also used to indicate a reversal of meaning, similar to our use of the prefix *un-*; some examples are *resign* (*re-* + *signare*, "to mark, sign"), *reveal* (*re-* + *velum*, "veil"), and *reprobate* (*re-* + *probare*, "to approve")

Rehashing *Re-*

In early Latin, *re-* would be used before consonants and *red-* would be used before vowels. Some English words that start with *red-* offer examples of this prefix, such as *redeem* (*re-* + *emere*, "to buy").

> *"Suppose you were an idiot. And suppose you were a member of Congress. But I repeat myself."*
> —MARK TWAIN

Classical Latin was spoken over a period of about a thousand years, and over that time meanings shifted and connotations built up to the extent that it is not always possible to decipher precisely what a word originally meant. A good example is *religion*. It's not exactly clear how this word came to be. It probably derived from *re-* + *legere*, "to read," which is also the source for our adjective *legible*. From "read again" the word probably developed into "repeatedly observing divine rites and practices," hence our modern sense of *religion*.

In English, however, the use of *re-* to form new words (as opposed to ones borrowed from French and Latin) is much more limited. When forming new words, the prefix is almost always used in the sense of "again." Some examples include: *reapportion, reempower, reinitialize, relubricate, rephotograph, resubmerge,* and *retarget*.

Where Did It Come From?

Cult: This well-known term denotes a small group of devotees, or an offshoot from a mainstream religion. You may be surprised to learn that this word comes from the French *culte,* which is in turn derived from the Latin *cultus,* meaning "care, adoration."

The Longest (History of) *Yard*

How can such a simple four-letter word (but not that kind of four-letter word) have such a complex history? Well, because it is actually two words.

✳   ✳   ✳   ✳

THE WORD **YARD** names both a unit of measurement and the land around your house, but there is a different origin for each meaning. Although both come from Old English, they derive from different roots.

As in Yardstick

Yard as a unit of measure comes from the Old English *gyrd*, which originally meant "stick, twig." It came to mean a "staff or pole" used for various purposes (for example, a *seglgyrde*, or *sail-yard*, was a spar from which a ship's sail was spread, as in our modern *nautical yard*). The Anglo-Saxons also used *gyrd* to refer to a unit of measure, but one considerably longer than our modern 36 inches. An Anglo-Saxon *gyrd* was roughly 16.5 feet, equivalent to our modern *rod*. (The exact standard for all these measures varies both regionally and over time.) For distances approximating today's yard, Anglo-Saxons used the *eln*, later modernized to *ell* and standardized to 45 inches.

In the fourteenth century, 13.5 feet were lopped off the length of a yard, and King Edward III standardized the unit of measure at a length of three feet. Three accounts for this shortening exist. The primary reason appears to be the introduction of the Roman 12-inch foot, which was brought to England by the Normans in the 1066 conquest.

Another explanation is that the shorter length was derived from the girth of a man's waist or, more specifically, from the length of the sash or girdle worn around the waist. The other oft-cited postulate suggests that King Henry I, who reigned in the early 1100s, declared a yard to be the distance between the tip of his nose and the end of his thumb. Whatever its origin, the unit of measure was standardized at a length of three feet by both King Edward I (1305) and King Edward III (1353), giving us the yard we know today.

As in Cookout Space

The grassy area around your house, on the other hand, comes from the Old English *geard*, meaning "an enclosure, a dwelling place"—specifically the grounds around a building that were not used for cultivation, but for other work or for living. There is a wonderful elegiac moment in the Old English epic poem *Beowulf* (thought to have been written in the year 1000) in which the word is used in the description of mourning for a young nobleman who has died:

> *The riders sleep,*
> *heroes in their graves; there is no music of the harp,*
> *no cheer in the yard; as there was of old.*

So we may measure our yards in yards, but despite looking and sounding the same, these are very different words.

✳ For several centuries after the Norman Conquest, England had two vernacular languages, divided by class. The nobles spoke Anglo-Norman, and the commoners Old English. Eventually the two languages blended to form what we call Middle English, and over time both Anglo-Norman and Old English disappeared into the new amalgam language.

Where Did It Come From?

Acre: At one point in its history, this word referred to a measurement of the amount of land a yoke of oxen could plow from sunrise to sunset.

Words of Wisdom: Distances

✳ ✳ ✳ ✳

"'Tis distance lends enchantment to the view,
And robes the mountain in its azure hue."

—Thomas Campbell

"Our sympathy is cold to the relation of distant misery."

—Edward Gibbon

"Bad news travels fast and far."

—Plutarch

"How far that little candle throws his beams!
So shines a good deed in a naughty world."

—William Shakespeare

"Slight not what's near through aiming at what's far."

—Euripides

"Once the realization is accepted that even between the closest human beings infinite distances continue to exist, a wonderful living side by side can grow up, if they succeed in loving the distance between them which makes it possible for each to see the other whole against the sky."

—Rainier Maria Rilke

"Better is a neighbor that is near than a brother far off."

—Proverbs 27:10, KJV

"I do not want the constellations any nearer,
I know they are very well where they are,
I know they suffice for those who belong to them."

—Walt Whitman

The Taming of the Shrewd

*Today, being labeled **shrewd** may or may not be a compliment. The adjective can be used to indicate that a person is clever and astute, or alternatively, that a person is crafty and conniving, cold and calculating. Some 700 years ago, however, the word bore no such ambiguity, being reserved for the wicked and depraved.*

❋　❋　❋　❋

TODAY'S SHREWD HAS its roots in Middle English, where it first appears around the year 1300 in the work of a Gilbertine monk, Robert Manning of Brunne, titled *Handlyng Synne*: "Ryche men haue shrewed sonys." This adjectival form is derived from the Middle English noun *shrewe*, a word denoting a wicked or villainous person. This word is, in turn, generally understood as a figurative application of an earlier *shrewe*— ultimately from the Old English *screawa*—that denoted a small, sharp-nosed mammal. In the Middle Ages, shrews were thought to be venomous and their bite highly injurious—hence the word's association with evil things.

After its appearance in Middle English, *shrewd* spent the next couple of hundred years undergoing *amelioration*, the linguistic process by which a word loses its negative meaning over time. Many of its incarnations have relied on figurative senses of the word *sharp* ("the shrewdest pain," "a shrewd right winde"). These senses suggest, perhaps, a metaphorical play on the critter's pointy-nosed appearance rather than (like the original sense) on its supposed malignance.

The modern sense of *shrewd*—that is, "clever," or intellectually sharp—did not appear until the first part of the sixteenth century. Even then it retained something of an unsavory connotation; the inaugural usage ("serpently shrewd") pairs it with the snake, another much-maligned animal. The intervening centuries have mitigated this negative connotation, however, and now it's possible to be *shrewd* without being shrewlike.

Words of Wisdom: Happiness

✳ ✳ ✳ ✳

"Thousands of candles can be lighted from a single candle, and the life of the candle will not be shortened. Happiness never decreases by being shared."

—BUDDHA

"Happiness is when what you think, what you say, and what you do are in harmony."

—MAHATMA GANDHI

"Our greatest happiness does not depend on the condition of life in which chance has placed us, but is always the result of a good conscience, good health, occupation, and freedom in all just pursuits."

—THOMAS JEFFERSON

"We know nothing of tomorrow; our business is to be good and happy today."

—SYDNEY SMITH

"Since you get more joy out of giving joy to others, you should put a good deal of thought into the happiness that you are able to give."

—ELEANOR ROOSEVELT

"It is not how much we have, but how much we enjoy, that makes happiness."

—CHARLES SPURGEON

"Happiness: an agreeable sensation arising from contemplating the misery of another."

—AMBROSE BIERCE

A Triumphant Ovation

*You're familiar with the kind of **ovation** that follows a breath-taking performance, but did you know there's another kind?*

* * * *

THE WORD *OVATION* has a résumé quite apart from the concert hall and sports arena. The word originated in classical Latin, and in the world of ancient Rome it had a rather specific, war-oriented application. Upon his victorious return from battle, a Roman commander would receive a *triumph*, a lavish ceremony with a procession of his army and spoils and the conferring of a laurel crown. (See page 530 for more on *triumph*.) One who did not achieve a complete victory would receive an *ovation*, a sort of ancient Roman runner-up prize. This silver-medal ceremony was less of a to-do, and the commander had to settle for a myrtle crown rather than one of laurel.

Used in its literal sense to describe aspects of ancient Roman civilization, the word *ovation* first showed up in English texts in the 1500s. Over the next few centuries, the word underwent semantic broadening. This process was spurred by its figurative application, as demonstrated in the seventeenth-century religious text *Christian Morals*, by Sir Thomas Browne: "Rest not in an Ovation but a Triumph over thy Passions." By the early 1800s, application of the word had been stretched further, giving us the meaning we know today—that of enthusiastic public acclaim, especially in the form of sustained applause.

This is a word that has spawned many variations, such as *standing ovation*, *ovationary*, and *ovational*. Another word stemming from *ovation* is *ovate*, defined as "giving an ovation" or "to applaud a person enthusiastically." Also, *ovator* is a rare word—the *Oxford English Dictionary* specifies it as a colloquialism, a sort of lexical red flag—for one who takes part in an ovation. We may rarely get to be the recipient of a standing ovation, but we can at least, at times, settle for the status of ovator.

Zombies: Feeding on Flesh (or Bailout Money)

You may have seen an alarming number of them walking the streets on Halloween in recent years: zombies. Popular culture has been infatuated with the undead of late, but do you know where and when the term **zombie** *first came to, um, unlife?*

✳ ✳ ✳ ✳

WHAT IS IT about zombies that we find so scary? Author Max Brooks has a theory: "Other monsters may threaten individual humans, but the living dead threaten the entire human race. Zombies are slate wipers." Brooks dutifully—and, of course, satirically—came to civilization's aid with his 2003 book *The Zombie Survival Guide: Complete Protection from the Living Dead.*

Zombie stories have deep roots in African and Haitian voodoo; the *Oxford English Dictionary* says the word *zombie* is of obscure western and central African origin and compares it to the African words *nzambi* ("god") and *zumbi* ("fetish"). In 1940, *Time* magazine said that W. B. Seabrook's book *The Magic Island*, a fictional account of voodoo cults in Haiti, "introduced 'zombi' into U.S. speech."

Onslaught of the Undead

Although Haitian voodoo mythology gave birth to the concept of zombies, zombies were permanently put on the map of horror lore by the 1968 film *Night of the Living Dead*, with its iconic staggering, disheveled corpses roaming in search of flesh to feast upon. (Without that movie, we may never have had

Michael Jackson's video for "Thriller," one of the most influential music videos of all time.)

Zombies made a comeback in the twenty-first century thanks to a new wave of horror films, TV shows, and books—including a 2004 remake of *Dawn of the Dead*, and AMC's television series *The Walking Dead*, based on the comic books of the same name. Writer Seth Grahame-Smith's unexpected pairing of zombies with Jane Austen resulted in 2009's *Pride and Prejudice and Zombies*.

Don't Panic, But
Zombies Are Everywhere

Zombie has also found its way into general usage, usually in the sense of "a catatonic or mentally dim or distant person," as evidenced in this quote from the Woody Allen film *Whatever Works*: "I can't teach an empty-headed zombie chess." Someone suffering from a migraine might be described as a zombie, for instance, as might someone suffering from a debilitating lack of sleep. Another type of zombie is a person who accepts the status quo without thought or questioning, who doesn't show their own strong or passionate beliefs, and who quietly shuffles along with the masses.

The sense of "dead but feeding off the living," meanwhile, was preserved in financial lingo after the Wall Street meltdown of 2008 with the term *zombie bank*—a bank that is dead, or worthless, but feeds on government bailout money.

✳ Legend has it that the only way to kill a zombie is to destroy its brain—before it succeeds in eating yours, that is.

✳ For more linguistic monster mayhem, turn to page 381 to read up on the many uses of *vampire*—if you dare.

Words of Wisdom
from Jane Austen

* * * *

* "A lady's imagination is very rapid; it jumps from admiration to love, from love to matrimony in a moment."

* "For what do we live, but to make sport for our neighbors and laugh at them in our turn?"

* "Friendship is certainly the finest balm for the pangs of disappointed love."

* "How quick come the reasons for approving what we like!"

* "I cannot speak well enough to be unintelligible."

* "Let other pens dwell on guilt and misery."

* "Life seems but a quick succession of busy nothings."

* "Nobody minds having what is too good for them."

* "Nothing is more deceitful than the appearance of humility. It is often only carelessness of opinion, and sometimes is an indirect boast."

* "The person, be it gentleman or lady, who has not pleasure in a good novel, must be intolerably stupid."

* "There are people, who the more you do for them, the less they will do for themselves."

* "Vanity and pride are different things, though the words are often used synonymously. A person may be proud without being vain. Pride relates more to our opinion of ourselves; vanity, to what we would have others think of us."

* "We have all a better guide in ourselves, if we would attend to it, than any other person can be."

Tawdry or Saintly?

*Something that is **tawdry** is cheap and gaudy. The word dates to the seventeenth century, when it was also a noun meaning "cheap, showy finery." Only the adjective is used much today.*

✳ ✳ ✳ ✳

TAWDRY COMES TO us from *tawdry lace*, an alteration of *St. Audrey's lace*, a silk neckerchief popular with women in the sixteenth and seventeenth centuries. The term *tawdry lace* predates *tawdry*, first appearing in the mid-sixteenth century.

The name comes from the story of Ethelreda, also known as Audrey, a seventh-century Anglo-Saxon princess, the daughter of Anna, king of East Anglia. As legend has it, Audrey took a vow of perpetual virginity and got through two marriages without having sexual relations. Her first husband died before he could get her into the marital bed. The second marriage was eventually annulled, much to the relief of the very frustrated young groom, who had gone so far as attempting to bribe the local bishop to release her from her vow and who, when she fled his advances, chased after her across England. After the annulment, Audrey went on to found an abbey in the town of Ely in East Anglia. Audrey died of a large tumor on her neck, which she attributed to divine punishment for having worn many expensive jeweled necklaces in her younger years.

After Audrey's canonization, it became fashionable for medieval English women to wear lacy silk scarves around their necks in tribute to her. Cheap and gaudy versions—of the sort you'd find at any tourist trap today—were sold to the country women at the annual St. Audrey fair at Ely, and after a time such inferior finery gained inextricable association with the chaste saint. This association led to the term *St. Audrey's lace*, eventually contracted to *tawdry lace*. By the late seventeenth century the word *tawdry* had gained stand-alone status, leaving its connection to the virgin Ethelreda quite obscure.

Why You Need Smart Friends

Moron. Simpleton. Muttonhead. Nincompoop. Oaf. Ignoramus. Numbskull. Bonehead. Dullard. Half-wit. Idiot. Goose. Dunderhead. Dolt. Nitwit. English certainly offers a plethora of dumb-denoting insult options. With so many words at hand, how is one to choose? For the history of one such term in this crowded category, read on below. (And for more original insult ideas, see page 164.)

page 164.)

✳   ✳   ✳   ✳

ONE LEXICAL CHOICE for characterizing the demonstrably dense, *dunce,* has an interesting history: It actually comes from the name of a *smart* person. The word began as an eponym of the thirteenth-century theologian and thinker Jon Duns Scotus. Duns was never considered a dunce himself, but he attracted many followers, and they developed a not-so-bright reputation.

Duns and the Dunsmen

Up until the sixteenth century, Duns was considered a formidable intellectual figure. His texts on theology, philosophy, and logic were staples in respected English universities. His followers were among the who's who of scholasticism. As time went on, however, Duns's ideas became outdated, and adherents of other schools of thought pounced on them as objects of ridicule.

Duns's loyalists—the Dunsmen, or Dunses—were not easily moved. They remained steadfast in their increasingly unpopular beliefs, making them easy academic targets. Eventually, *Dunse* adopted the connotation of—as the *Oxford English Dictionary* so delicately puts it today—a "blockhead incapable of learning or scholarship."

Dunce Is as Dunse Did

Within only a few decades, the word was being applied more broadly. You no longer had to be a stubborn follower of Duns to be a *Dunse*; you simply had to be "a dull-witted, stupid person." With this more liberal application came a change in the spelling and the loss of the initial capital letter, alterations that have obscured the word's etymological connection to the thirteenth-century thinker.

We can also thank Duns and the dunces for inspiring the *dunce cap*, a schoolchild's variety of public humiliation that made its first appearance in Charles Dickens's 1840 novel *The Old Curiosity Shop*.

✳ The change from *Duns* or *Dunse* to the spelling we know today is a function of the variation characteristic of early English texts. Without the regularizing influence of dictionaries—the earliest of which postdates *dunce* and its variants by a couple of centuries—it was common for words to co-occur with many different spellings. Even when the word was still being used to characterize the actual followers of Duns, the modern variation popped up. By the early 1600s, however, the switch from *Duns(e)* to *dunce* appears to have been ubiquitous.

Where Did It Come From?

Ignoramus: Commonly applied to fools, the term derives from the plural Latin for "we don't know." Until the seventeenth century, it was used in British courts when juries could not decide a case due to lack of evidence. The 1615 George Ruggle play *Ignoramus*, about a clueless attorney, gave the term its current meaning.

Chapter 14

Spread the Word

Put Away That Red Pen

Has anyone ever insisted that you can't end a sentence with a preposition? Or maybe they insisted nauseous *only describes something that causes nausea. Or perhaps you were scolded for using* can *instead of* may, *even though the words have interchangeable meanings. If so, you were a victim of* **paradiorthosis,** *or "a false correction."*

※ ※ ※ ※

THE PRACTICE OF paradiorthosis is unfortunately more common than the word, which has all but disappeared from usage. Today it is more commonly known as *incorrection.* William Safire used the term on December 10, 2006, in his *New York Times Magazine* "On Language" column, defining it as "a correction that is itself incorrect."

More recently, University of Pennsylvania linguist Mark Liberman discussed the phenomenon, speculating on the reasons behind incorrection. He theorized that incorrections are essentially contagious. Once we've been incorrected by a person of suitable authority—say, an English teacher or Great-Aunt Nellie—we may be so convinced of their correctness that we confidently go about spreading the incorrection, unaware of the error.

Liberman also mentions that most people—even English teachers, language columnists, and other would-be language advisers—are "untrained and deeply confused about the analysis of language." In other words, they don't know linguistics. Was there a required linguistics course at your school? Unlikely.

That's What You Think

So the combination of loud, incorrect voices from childhood and loud, misinformed voices throughout life fuels a perfect storm for paradiorthosis.

One author plagued by incorrection was J.R.R. Tolkien. In a 1953 letter to his son Christopher, he complained of the "impertinent" editors trying to change his deliberately eccentric spelling and grammar in *The Fellowship of the Ring*, such as "altering throughout *dwarves* to *dwarfs*, *elvish* to *elfish*, *further* to *farther*, and worst of all *elven* to *elfin*."

Paging Mr. Murphy

Speaking of editors, copy editors have been known to suffer from *Muphry's Law*. (And no, that's not a typo, for those of you who were ready to incorrect the term.) In the *Society of Editors Newsletter* (1992), John Bangsund coined this term to describe another hazard of attempting to fix others' "mistakes." He wrote: "Any correction of the speech or writing of others will contain at least one grammatical, spelling, or typographical error." Although this prediction hasn't been scientifically proven, it makes a good point: Be very careful when altering someone else's work.

"Substitute 'damn' every time you're inclined to write 'very'; your editor will delete it and the writing will be just as it should be."

—MARK TWAIN

"In composing, as a general rule, run your pen through every other word you have written; you have no idea what vigor it will give your style."

—SYDNEY SMITH

For Richer or for Poorer

The world is sometimes divided into the "haves" and the "have nots," and the English language has many words and phrases to cover both ends of the continuum.

✳ ✳ ✳ ✳

THE WORD **RICH** derives from the Middle English *riche*, which was borrowed from Old French. Old English had the related word *rice* (pronounced REE-chay), which as an adjective meant "wealthy, powerful" and as a noun meant "kingdom" (and is related to the German word *Reich*, as in the Third Reich). The French phrase *nouveau riche* ("new rich"), which denotes those who have recently acquired wealth and tend to display it ostentatiously, is now part of our language. In colloquial language, we use such phrases as *loaded*, *rolling in money* (or *dough*), and *flush* to describe someone with cash to spare.

In Poor Taste

Poor, from the Middle English *poure*, entered the language through the Old French *povre*, which derived from the Latin *pauper*, itself now an English word. The related roots *pau* and *pov*, meaning "few, little," have enriched the English lexicon with such words as *paucity* (scarcity), *pauciloquence* (the use of few words, extreme brevity in speech), and the more familiar *poverty* and *impoverished*.

English has a wealth of informal words and phrases denoting poverty, among them *broke, hard up, strapped, down-and-out, short of cash, pinched, unable to make ends meet,* and *in the poorhouse.* In some churches you'll find a *poor box* in which parishioners can make contributions to help the less fortunate. The *poor farm* and *poorhouse* were nineteenth-century institutions that fed and housed the indigent at public expense.

"For Munificence or for Impecuniousness" Just Didn't Have the Same Ring

Benefactors, people who are extremely generous, are said to be *munificent* or *unstinting.* The man who hoards his wealth without spending it is a *skinflint,* a *miser,* or a *Scrooge,* this last term coming from the name of the avaricious character in Charles Dickens's *A Christmas Carol.* A person who spends money like there's no tomorrow is a *profligate,* a *spendthrift,* or a *wastrel.* Another word for someone who foolishly spends his fortune is *prodigal;* we're all familiar with the biblical parable of the prodigal son, who left his family's home, lived lavishly, and returned home *impecunious,* another word for *penniless.* And we call someone who is frugal to the point of stinginess *parsimonious.*

"Life is a dream for the wise, a game for the fool, a comedy for the rich, a tragedy for the poor."

—Sholom Aleichem

"Content makes poor men rich; discontent makes rich men poor."

—Benjamin Franklin

✳ The etymology of *poor boy,* a submarine sandwich associated with Louisiana and locally called a *po'boy,* is much disputed. One theory is that it derived its name from the French *pourboire* ("for drinking"), terminology denoting money left as a tip for service. Other explanations have linked the word to "a poor boy's lunch," referring to its low price, or to strikers (or "poor boys") in a 1929 streetcar strike who were fed sandwiches during the work stoppage.

Words of Wisdom: Money

✳ ✳ ✳ ✳

"Never spend your money before you have it."
—THOMAS JEFFERSON

"To have done anything just for money is to have been truly idle."
—HENRY DAVID THOREAU

"Though mothers and fathers give us life, it is money alone which preserves it."
—IHARA SAIKAKU

"Writing is the only profession where no one considers you ridiculous if you earn no money."
—JULES RENARD

"Money begets money."
—JOHN RAY

"The civility which money will purchase, is rarely extended to those who have none."
—CHARLES DICKENS

"This will never be a civilized country until we spend more money for books than we do for chewing gum."
—ELBERT HUBBARD

"Business, you know, may bring you money, but friendship hardly ever does."
—JANE AUSTEN

"Money is like manure, of very little use except it be spread."
—FRANCIS BACON

"I can make more generals, but horses cost money."
—ABRAHAM LINCOLN

Achieving Buzzword Synergy

Words come into and go out of fashion. Sometimes a particular word—a **buzzword**— *will catch a wave of popularity and become overused to the point where it becomes essentially meaningless.*

✳   ✳   ✳   ✳

BUZZWORDS ARE OFTEN found in business writing, as firms compete to show they are hip to new and improved language. A good example of a buzzword is *synergy.* The word hit its peak of popularity in the early 1990s. It is still common but is no longer as overused as it once was.

Synergy is the cumulative effect of coordinated action by a number of independent factors—the whole becomes greater than the sum of its parts. It's a modern word coined from Latin roots. The *Oxford English Dictionary* has one citation of *synergy's* use from 1660, but this appears to be an outlier. It was coined again in the mid-nineteenth century in medical jargon, where it described the effects of multiple organs working together.

Synergy began appearing in business writing in the late 1950s. It continued to be used unremarkably for several decades, until suddenly, in the 1990s, synergy became a business imperative. Every company had to be exploiting the "synergistic effects" of something or other. The word appeared on just about every executive résumé. Companies even changed their names to incorporate the word.

Of course, in reality nothing had changed. Businesses had been "exploiting synergistic effects" for as long as there had been business. The word synergy became so overused that it became something of a joke. Since then, synergy has settled back into the frequency of use it had prior to the furor of the 1990s. It can again be used without triggering rolling eyes and skepticism— maybe—but one should be careful not to overuse it.

Funny Things Are Everywhere

In 1960, Theodor Geisel, better known as Dr. Seuss, was challenged by his publisher to write a book using only 50 unique words. He came back to win the bet with Green Eggs and Ham, *which uses exactly 49 one-syllable words and a single multisyllabic word (*anywhere*).*

✳ ✳ ✳ ✳

D R. SEUSS GEARED many of his books (including *Green Eggs and Ham*) toward beginning readers, using rhythm, compelling storylines, and, of course, fantastical illustrations to create interest, while keeping vocabulary straightforward and simple.

But other Dr. Seuss books use an altogether different strategy. Dr. Seuss is the uncontested master of the nonsense word. Making up silly words is an obvious way to fill a challenging line with words of the right meter and rhyme: *Lake Winnebango, Katroo, sneetch,* etc. The entire book *There's a Wocket in My Pocket* is formed around rhyming nonsense words—even up to the ridiculous "a nooth grush on your toothbrush."

Taking Words Apart;
Putting Them Back Together

In other places, Seuss combines two or more words or sounds into a portmanteau that creates a strong image. (See page 586 for more on portmanteaux.) The Lorax gave us *snergelly* (describing a phone line that is crooked, dirty, and causes a nasal transmission), *schloppity schlop* (liquid pollution), and *lerkim* (a hidden lair). Even the word *truffula* uses sound symbolism: It evokes *truffle* (something rare and expensive but completely natural), *fluff,* and *trifle* (something light and delicate).

These Seussisms could be called *ideophones,* or words that make a vivid sensory impression. (For more on ideophones, turn to page 50.)

What a *Nerd*

Some Dr. Seuss words have made it into everyday usage. Possibly the most recognized is *nerd*, which was coined in *If I Ran the Zoo* (1950): "And then, just to show them, I'll sail to Ka-Troo / And bring back an It-Kutch, a Preep, and a Proo / a Nerkle a Nerd and a Seersucker, too!" Seuss's *nerd* was just a quirky zoo animal, but by the mid-1950s, *nerd* became a synonym for *square*, meaning "an unfashionably academic person." Another word that caught on is *oobleck* (*Bartholomew and the Oobleck*, 1949). It's the perfect name for the bizarre mixture of cornstarch and water that's a solid under pressure but then turns into an oozing, gooey liquid. The *thneed* ("a Fine-Something-That-All-People-Need," from *The Lorax*) has become the ultimate symbol of wasteful consumption of useless consumer products.

And we love to hate a *grinch*, which today is used to refer to any unnecessarily negative person, not just a Christmas hater. Although Dr. Seuss popularized the word *grinch*, he did not coin it. *Grinched* appears in the *Oxford English Dictionary* as early as 1635, with the meaning of "tightly closed, clenched" (in reference to teeth), and in 1892, as "to make a harsh, grating noise."

Dr. Seuss words can hardly help but make us smile. And that's—to quote *Oh, the Places You'll Go!*—"ninety-eight and three-quarters percent guaranteed."

✳ **Roald Dahl, author of *Charlie and the Chocolate Factory* and many other children's books, delighted in using wordplay in his writing. His work brims with made-up words that evoke wonderful imagery, such as a repulsive vegetable called a *snozzcumber* and dangerous beasts like *hornswogglers*, *snozzwangers*, and *whangdoodles*.**

The Same Old Shtick

Since about the tenth century, Yiddish has been the primary language of Ashkenazi Jews. It's a mixture of German, Hebrew, and Aramaic, with a smattering of Slavic words thrown in. Today, about three million people speak it, but millions more use Yiddish words and phrases every day without realizing it. Plop your tuchus (tush) in a comfy chair and check out these favorites.

✳ ✳ ✳ ✳

BECAUSE YIDDISH IS written in the Hebrew alphabet, English spellings may vary, giving a proofreader a whole lot of *tsuris* (trouble).

Oy Vey!

* *bris*—circumcision ceremony
* *bubkes*—nothing; an inadequate reward or compensation
* *chutzpah*—arrogance, conceit, nerve
* *dreidel*—traditional wooden top
* *kibitz*—offer unwanted advice; chat, converse
* *klezmer*—a musical genre
* *klutz*—a clumsy person
* *kvetch*—complain
* *maven*—expert, "know-it-all"
* *mensch*—a person of integrity or character
* *meshuga*—crazy
* *meshuggener*—a crazy person
* *mitzvah*—a good deed
* *nebbish*—a weak or unimportant person

* *nosh*—eat (verb); a small snack (noun)

* *putz*—stupid or worthless person

* *schlep*—to drag or haul something that's especially burdensome, or to make a tedious journey (verb); a boring person (noun)

* *schlock*—cheap, shoddy, inferior

* *schmear*—spread

* *schmendrick*—a sucker, someone who is easily fooled or taken advantage of

* *schmooze*—chat, gossip, or make small talk in an attempt to win favor

* *schmuck*—a despicable or foolish person

* *schnook*—a gullible person

* *shtick*—a comic routine or affected manner put on as a performance

* *spiel*—a sales pitch or persuasive speech

* *tuchus*—rear end

* *yarmulke*—skullcap used to cover one's head during prayer

* *yenta*—a talkative or gossipy woman; a blabbermouth

* *zaftig*—curvy, overweight

---

* **It's said that a *schlemiel* (chronically clumsy person), like a *klutz*, is the person who spills his soup, but the *schlimazel* (chronically unlucky person) is the person on whom the soup lands.**

Worldly Wisdom: Yiddish Proverbs

✳ ✳ ✳ ✳

✳ God gives burdens, also shoulders.

✳ A wise man hears one word and understands two.

✳ A man should live if only to satisfy his curiosity.

✳ If you ever need a helping hand, you'll find one at the end of your arm.

✳ What soap is to the body, laughter is to the soul.

✳ God could not be everywhere, and therefore he created mothers.

✳ Surrounding yourself with dwarfs does not make you a giant.

✳ Time and words can't be recalled, even if it was only yesterday.

✳ Those who tease you, love you.

✳ What you don't see with your eyes, don't invent with your mouth.

✳ Prayers go up and blessings come down.

Yada Yada About *Yada Yada*

We spend so much of our lives talking, and it's hard to argue with the notion that most of it is just a bunch of **blah-blah**.

✳ ✳ ✳ ✳

THE TERM BLAH-BLAH is at least as old as 1918, and it was used in the following example from 1921: "Then a special announcer began a long debate with himself which was mostly blah blah." But *blah-blah* has been old news since *Seinfeld* came on the scene and, in the 1997 episode "The Yada Yada," introduced the term to viewers:

> Marcy: *You know, a friend of mine thought she got Legionnaires' disease in the hot tub.*
>
> George: *Really? What happened?*
>
> Marcy: *Oh, yada yada yada, just some bad egg salad. I'll be right back. (She leaves.)*
>
> Jerry: *Nice girl.*
>
> George: *Lovely.*
>
> Jerry: *I noticed she's big on the phrase* yada yada.
>
> George: *Is yada yada bad?*
>
> Jerry: *No, yada yada is good. She's very succinct.*

The show sent *yada yada* hurtling across the pop culture firmament, but the term had already been around for a while. The *Oxford English Dictionary* suggests it may be related to *yatter* ("to talk incessantly; chatter"). That seems plausible, since variations include *yatta yatta*, *yattata-yattata*, and *yaddega-yaddega*.

Any way you slice it, reduplicative terms like *yada yada*, *blahblah*, *tittle-tattle*, and *mumbo jumbo* lend themselves very well to describing nonsense, maybe because they sound as meaningless as their meaning. (For more on reduplication, see page 52.)

A Wise Strategery: Don't Disregard *Saturday Night Live*

One central rule of presidential politics is to take Saturday Night Live *seriously. The show's caricatures of big-name pols can help shape the national imagination about who a leader is: Gerald Ford was clumsy; Bill Clinton libidinous; George W. Bush bumbling; vice-presidential candidate Sarah Palin clueless.*

✳ ✳ ✳ ✳

WHILE EACH OF these stereotypes may have been influenced by general public perceptions, when enacted on *SNL*'s stage, the portrayals were hammered home to voters. To their credit, Al Gore's advisers in the 2000 presidential campaign realized this and showed him *SNL*'s take on his first presidential debate. The debate sketch portrayed Gore as patronizing and professorial, and the real Gore noticeably loosened up in the second debate.

The longest lexical legacy of that particular *SNL* skit, though, came at the very end, from Will Ferrell's George W. Bush. Asked to make the case for his candidacy in a single word, Ferrell squinted at the camera and proclaimed—with great self-satisfaction—"strategery" (pronounced struh-TEE-juh-ree).

It wasn't the first or funniest faux Bushism to gain cultural currency, but *strategery* had staying power. The word caught on not only with *SNL* fans, but also with Bush fans, Bush bashers, and even Bush staffers. Three months after Bush's first inauguration, *The Washington Post* reported that Bush adviser Karl Rove was convening a meeting of senior staffers and calling it the "Strategery Group." Rove told the *Post*, "We tried to come up with a nice sounding name. We meet in the Cordell Hull Room, but nobody's buying off on the 'Hull Group.' I think we're going to be stuck with Strategery."

A *Strategery* Meeting of the Minds

One of the lighter findings from Bush aide Scooter Libby's federal trial was an official schedule for June 10, 2003, that showed Libby had a "Strategery Meeting" on the docket. Conservative pundit Bill Sammon's 2006 book about the Bush presidency was called *Strategery*. And today there's an iPhone app for a game called Strategery, the objective of which is to rule the world.

Strategery takes the adjective *strategic*, which comes from the noun *strategy*, and applies *-ery* at the end to make it a noun all over again. It's a method for malapropism that fit a candidate known for mangling multisyllabic words. And as Bush and his Strategery Group proved, there's no better way to take a joke than to get in on it yourself.

Since Chevy Chase debuted his Gerald Ford impersonation in 1976, *SNL* actors have gleefully sunk their teeth into political impersonations. Here are some of the most memorable:

Saturday Night Live Actor	Impersonation
Fred Armisen	Barack Obama
Dan Aykroyd	Jimmy Carter
Dana Carvey	George H. W. Bush; Ross Perot
Chevy Chase	Gerald Ford
Chris Farley	Newt Gingrich
Will Ferrell	George W. Bush
Tiny Fey	Sarah Palin
Darrell Hammond	Bill Clinton; Al Gore
Phil Hartman	Ronald Reagan
Norm MacDonald	Bob Dole
Amy Poehler	Hillary Clinton

Mind Meld: Ancient Vulcan Technique, Modern English Term

The advance of science and technology is a fertile ground for growing neologisms (new words). As new technologies and concepts are invented, we need words to describe them. Science fiction can also be a productive source of new words.

✳ ✳ ✳ ✳

WHEN PEOPLE CONSIDER the intersection between sci-fi and popular culture, conversation turns to *Star Trek.* The original TV series ran from 1966 to 1969 and bequeathed us a number of spin-off series and movies, but it also left us with an enriched vocabulary. Alongside *phasers* and *warp drive* (see page 496 for more on warp speed), *Star Trek* gave us **mind meld.**

In the TV series, *mind melding* described the Vulcan ability to create a telepathic link with another being. The term first appears in the episode "Elaan of Troyius" (1968): "Mr. Spock, . . . he refuses to talk. I'll need you for the Vulcan mind meld."

However, the mind meld isn't just a one-way extraction of thoughts. It's a genuine connection between individuals. While mining thoughts from others, the Vulcans also expose their own inner thoughts and emotions. Both parties in the exchange typically come out with a deeper understanding of the other.

Mind meld now sometimes refers to a deep understanding or nonverbal communication between people. In business, *mind meld* can also refer to any intensive transfer of information or knowledge between people, especially if they have different perspectives. For example, a briefing between the engineering and design teams might be called a mind meld.

Out of the Blue

The primary colors red, yellow, and blue are sources for many terms and idioms in English. But neither red nor yellow gives us the multitude of phrases and coinages that blue provides.

✳ ✳ ✳ ✳

MANY BLUE PHRASES pertain to the positive side of things. A *blue ribbon* goes to the winner. *Blue bloods* were originally members of the aristocracy, and today this term still designates people of noble or privileged pedigree. It is generally assumed that the term comes from the Spanish *sangre azul* (literally "blue blood"), which denoted the visible blue veins of the fair-complexioned royalty. A *blue book* lists the names of the elite and the socially prominent. *Blue-chip* stocks and investments are of the highest quality and lowest risk, and the origin of the term comes from gambling, where blue poker chips had the highest value. In earlier times, a restaurant or diner might feature a *blue plate special*, a meal offered at a special price.

Not All That's Blue Is Good

No one likes *feeling blue*. *The blues*, a musical genre that grew out of the African American religious musical tradition, often deals with melancholy and sadness. *Singing the blues* means crying over a lost love or another of life's rough spots. A *blue movie* or *blue humor* has overtly indecent sexual content. *Blue laws* were instituted during colonial times to promote public morality, and you still see their aftermath in localities that ban alcohol sales on Sunday.

Once in a blue moon means "very rarely" and comes from the old term *blue moon*, a second full moon occurring in the same month as a first. Being *between the devil and the deep blue sea* forces you to choose between two equally bad options. A *bolt from the blue* is a complete surprise; that is, it's something right *out of the blue*.

As you can see, it's easy to *talk a blue streak* about blue!

How Sweet It Is

The English language dishes out a supersize serving of vocabulary words to help you express your sweet nothings and somethings.

✳ ✳ ✳ ✳

LET'S BEGIN WITH sweet sounds. The Latin *dulc* and Italian *dolc*, meaning "sweet," give English *dulcet*, an adjective meaning "pleasing to the ear," and *dolce* (pronounced DOL-chay), a musical term that tells a musician to play in a sweet, gentle manner. The *dulcimer* is a stringed instrument placed across the thighs when sitting and plucked or strummed. Other musical instruments with sweet-sounding etymologies are the *euphonium* (the root parts mean "good sound"), a brass instrument similar to the tuba, and the *celesta* ("heavenly"), a keyboard instrument that produces bell-like sounds.

If a human voice is sweet, we call it *mellifluous* (*mel*, "honey"), literally meaning "honey flowing." This *mel* root also appears in *melittology*, the study of bees.

Ambrosia, the food of the gods in ancient Greece, today refers to a dessert made of sugar, oranges, and coconut. *Nectar*, the drink of the gods, now names a delicious, invigorating drink, as well as the sweet fluid that bees gather from flowers to make honey. This word also gives us the name of the peachlike fruit *nectarine*. Strangely, however, *nectar* includes the *nec* root, meaning "death," along with *tar*, "avoiding"; it was believed that the gods avoided death by drinking nectar.

> *"Sweet is the memory of past troubles."*
> — MARCUS TULLIUS CICERO

Visions of Sugar

English also has a pantry full of *sugar*-y words and phrases. In New England people gather for a *sugaring off*, where they boil maple sap to make maple syrup and maple sugar. The *sugarplum* you hear about in Clement C. Moore's poem "A Visit from St. Nicholas" isn't a plum at all; it's a small, round piece of candy. A *sugar apple*, more popularly known as a *sweetsop*, is the fruit of a tropical evergreen tree. Finally, a *sugar daddy* is an older (usually wealthy) man who gives gifts or financial support to a much younger woman in return for companionship and more.

Can something be too sweet? Indeed, it can. *Treacle* is the British English word for molasses, but it and its adjectival form, *treacly*, refer to that which is sickeningly sweet or sentimental. To *cloy* is to be too rich, too filling, too sweet—and therefore overwhelming; *cloying*, when referring to one's behavior, means "overly sappy" or "mushy." *Saccharin*, a noun, is a calorie-free artificial sweetener that you'd put in coffee, but *saccharine*, the adjective, means "artificially ingratiating to the point of insincerity."

The English language is sweet!

✳ A Sugar Daddy candy is a caramel-flavored sucker manufactured by Tootsie Roll Industries. Sugar Babies are a bite-size version of the same candy, and for a time candy aficionados could also find Sugar Mamas—chocolate-covered Sugar Daddies. Sugar Mamas were discontinued in the 1980s.

Where Did It Come From?

Choconiverous: This nonce word was coined as a humorous way to describe a person who likes to bite off the head of a chocolate Easter Bunny before any other part.

By the Letters

What do laser, radar *and* scuba *have in common? They're all examples of* **acronyms,** *a rich source of new words coming into the English language.*

✳ ✳ ✳ ✳

CRONYMS (FROM THE Greek *acro,* meaning "topmost," and *onym,* "name") combine the initial letters of a series of words to form a new word: *Laser* is Light Amplification by Stimulated Emission of Radiation; *radar* is RAdio Detecting And Ranging; *scuba* is Self-Contained Underwater Breathing Apparatus. Similar to acronyms are *initialisms,* which are pronounced not as words but as a series of letters (e.g., FBI, IRS, and ASAP).

There are quite a few initialisms associated with Christianity. From the first three letters of the name "Jesus" in Greek, *IHS* is commonly used to represent Jesus. INRI is the Latin initialism for *Iesus Nazarenus Rex Iudaeorum,* or "Jesus of Nazareth, King of the Jews." The fish as a Christian symbol even comes from an acronym: ICHTHYS, an acronym for the Greek "Jesus Christ, God's Son, Savior," is the Greek word for "fish." Modern-day religious acronyms, some of them playfully facetious, include ASAP (Always Say A Prayer), BIBLE (Basic Instructions Before Leaving Earth), EGO (Edging God Out), and TGIF (Thank God I'm Forgiven).

World War II produced an alphabet soup of acronyms. Female combatants became WACs (Women's Army Corps) and WAVES (Women Accepted for Volunteer Emergency Service), a branch of the navy. *Gestapo* (GEheime STAatsPOlizei, or "Secret State Police") entered English through German, along with *flak* (FLiegerAbwehrKanone, or "aircraft defense gun"), this latter term now a thoroughly English word meaning "excessive criticism or opposition." (See page 373 for more on *flak*.)

Now That's a Mouthful!

One of the longest acronyms in English is a coinage from the U.S. Navy: ADCOMSUBORDCOMPHIBSPAC, which stands for "ADministrative COMmand, AmPHIBious ForceS, PACific Fleet SUBORDinate COMmand." (It's pronounced just as it looks: "ad com sub ord com phibs pac.") The U.S. commander in chief is POTUS (President Of The United States), and the judiciary is headed by SCOTUS (Supreme Court Of The United States).

Computer technology has given us thousands of acronyms and initialisms, including ASCII (American Standard Code for Information Interchange) and the programming language BASIC (Beginner's All-purpose Symbolic Instruction Code).

Initialisms and acronyms abound in everyday life. You need a PIN (Personal Identification Number) to access an ATM (Automatic Teller Machine), and a VIN (Vehicle Identification Number) to register your car, which you hope has ABS (an Anti-lock Braking System) for safety.

✳ What does the initialism DVD stand for? Are you stumped? There's a good reason for that: Originally the initials stood for "digital video disc," but when that term became outdated it was reinvented as "digital versatile disc."

✳ A *pseudo-acronym* (or *anti-acronym*) is created when the letters of an acronym no longer stand for what they originally meant. KFC, for example, used to stand for "Kentucky Fried Chicken," but the company has now officially changed its name to "KFC," short for nothing at all.

Monologophobians, Unite

The story of Dr. Peter Mark Roget illustrates what can be accomplished through a life of curiosity and discovery—and if it doesn't illustrate it, then it may well demonstrate, exemplify, *or even* illuminate *it. The man was an accomplished scientist, physician, and inventor before he became one of the world's leading lexicographers.*

✳ ✳ ✳ ✳

USING THE SAME word more than once can be an effective technique, or it can plunge the thought into an unwanted abyss. The world may never know if Dr. Peter Mark Roget suffered from *monologophobia*, the obsessive fear of using the same word twice, but he did spend his life compiling a classed catalog of words to facilitate the expression of his ideas. His thesaurus, he claimed, would "help to supply my own deficiencies." Roget's definition of deficiencies might conflict with most, since he was an accomplished scientist, physician, and inventor before he became one of the world's most famous lexicographers.

What Was I Going to Say?

The thesaurus, now 160 years in print, has sold more than 30 million copies worldwide and has become an institution of the English language. Despite critics' complaints that this reference book plunges people into "a state of linguistic and intellectual mediocrity" in which language is "decayed, disarranged, and unlovely," Roget set out to create a tool that would offer words to express every aspect of a particular idea, rather than merely list alternative choices. He believed that people often just forget the precise word they're looking for and that his book would help them remember.

Roget was 70 years old when he began compiling the thesaurus (he borrowed the Greek word for "treasure house") that would later bear his name, and he was 73 by the time it was published. Roget's system, compiled from lists he had been saving most of his life, instituted a brand-new principle that arranged words and phrases according to their meanings rather than their spellings.

Facts, Data, Scoop, Straight Stuff, and Information

Here are some facts about the thesaurus:

* In 1852, Roget's first thesaurus contained 15,000 words. The sixth edition, published 149 years later in 2001, includes 330,000 words and phrases.

* Anyone can use the name Roget on their thesaurus, but only the publisher HarperCollins has trademark-protected *Roget's International Thesaurus*.

* New editions of the thesaurus are greeted by the press and public as a mirror of the times in which we live. Such terms as *acid rain, creative accounting, insider trading,* and *bag lady* were added in the 1980s. The '90s ushered in new terms such as *eating disorder, Tamagotchi, double whammy, zero tolerance, air kissing, focus group, spin doctor, road rage,* and *bad hair day.*

* The twenty-first century is bringing into play such phrases as *Ashtanga yoga* and *WAP phones.*

It's Wordalicious!

Ready to feast on a savory selection of scrumptious vocabulary? Using a well-known and simple suffix, one can easily prepare a veritable buffet of new words and terms to describe some of the finer things in life. If you're hungry for new language, read on!

❊   ❊   ❊   ❊

THE SUFFIX -LICIOUS is not a traditional one by any means. It's primarily found in nonce and humorous slang coinages. It comes from the word *delicious*—from the Latin *deliciae* ("delight") + *-ous*—and is added to nouns and adjectives to mean "excellence in or fullness of quality of trait X."

Great Taste in Language

Although modern use of this suffix's source word is most often tied to the titillation of our taste buds, the original sense of *delicious* was not specific to food. It meant "highly pleasing or delightful; affording great pleasure or enjoyment." So even though the *-licious* suffix has considerably broadened beyond things that taste great, the word it comes from started off a bit broad itself.

The tasty suffix is invariably used positively, and it even has the power to turn a disparaging term into a complimentary one. Some of the most delicious (if not entirely ubiquitous) *-licious* words are:

❊ *brownie-licious*—of good-tasting brownies

❊ *e-licious*—of something good found online

❊ *Mac-a-licious*—like a product from Apple Inc.

❊ *nerd-a-licious*—especially nerdy, but in an appealing way

* *penguin-a-licious*—really cool (get it?)

* *read-a-licious*—good to read

* *swishalicious*—of a basketball shot that is nothing but net

* *turkey-licious*—of good-tasting turkey

Another Batch of Fresh Coinages

Although *-licious* is atypical as an affix, it isn't exactly unique. The suffix *-rific*, derived from the common adjective *terrific* (in the sense of "superlatively good"), is the result of the same kind of process. What's more, many words that can bear one of these two suffixes can also bear the other for a subtly different effect.

In a few cases, a *-licious* word has broken out to become a more commonly used slang term. Perhaps the most notable of these deliciously catchy coinages is the term *bootylicious* ("beyond sexy"). The word, boasting an entry in the online edition of the *Oxford English Dictionary*, has been around since at least the early 1990s, when it was used in the rap community to mean "lackluster, laughable." The term owes today's decidedly more positive definition to the Destiny's Child 2001 anthem (off their album *Survivor*) for curvaceous women titled—you guessed it—"Bootylicious."

Where Did It Come From?

Gourmet: This term originally referred to a horse groom, then to minor household servants who tasted the wine for quality. In time, this position at a wine shop was used to refer to a connoisseur of fine wines. This led to the modern meaning of one who prefers, can distinguish, or can create fine food and drink.

Weapons of Mass Destruction

We heard the term **weapons of mass destruction** *during the 1991 Gulf War, and again during the second (2003) war with Iraq. Both times Saddam Hussein was believed to have developed these nuclear, biological, and chemical weapons, an assessment that was only correct the first time. But the term is much older than this.*

✳ ✳ ✳ ✳

I T DATES TO at least 1937, when *The Times* of London printed an article that used the term:

> *"Who can think without horror of what another widespread war would mean, waged as it would be with all the new weapons of mass destruction?"*

The article was referencing the destructive power of modern conventional weapons, however, and not the nuclear, biological, and chemical weapons with which the term *weapons of mass destruction* is now usually associated.

The phrase became associated with nuclear weapons after the 1945 bombings of Hiroshima and Nagasaki, Japan, and by the 1960s biological and chemical weapons were also being included in the term's definition. The phrase was adopted by the international arms control community as an emotionally loaded term to refer to those weapons they meant to reduce or eliminate.

Conventional Tension

The counterpoint to a weapon of mass destruction is a *conventional weapon*. *Conventional*, when applied to non-nuclear warfare, is a *retronym*, a term coined when a previous word has been rendered inadequate by technological advances. The use of *conventional weapon* and *conventional war* dates to the early 1950s and the start of the Cold War.

The consequences of nuclear, chemical, and biological warfare are so appalling that "conventional warfare" sounds practically peaceful by comparison. But we must not forget that *weapons of mass destruction* is a political catchphrase. Most of the wars in human history have been fought with "conventional" weapons, and they have still caused mass destruction. The 1994 genocide in Rwanda, for example, was largely carried out with nothing more than clubs and machetes, and yet approximately 800,000 Rwandans were killed in just a few months. In times of war, human ingenuity is the most destructive force of all.

✳ The United States, the United Kingdom, and Canada collaborated on a top-secret research and development project—known as the Manhattan Project—that ultimately produced the first atomic bomb. Albert Einstein was among those who supported the program, and he signed a letter to President Roosevelt to that effect, but he later had great regrets about it.

Where Did It Come From?

Agent Orange: The experimental herbicide used to disastrous effect by the United States during the Vietnam War derived its name from the orange stripe on the side of its containers. The coloring distinguished it from the equally toxic but lesser-known Agents White, Purple, and Blue.

Words of Wisdom: Justice

✳ ✳ ✳ ✳

"Thwackum was for doing justice, and leaving mercy to heaven."

—HENRY FIELDING

"Justice without strength is helpless, strength without justice is tyrannical."

—BLAISE PASCAL

"It is justice, not charity, that is wanting in the world."

—MARY WOLLSTONECRAFT

"Why should there not be a patient confidence in the ultimate justice of the people? Is there any better or equal hope in the world?"

—ABRAHAM LINCOLN

"I believe that religious duties consist in doing justice, loving mercy, and endeavoring to make our fellow creatures happy."

—THOMAS PAINE

"Extreme justice is often injustice."

—RACINE

"In the course of justice, none of us should see salvation: we do pray for mercy."

—WILLIAM SHAKESPEARE

"The love of justice in most men is simply the fear of suffering injustice."

—FRANÇOIS, DUC DE LA ROCHEFOUCAULD

"Revenge is a kind of wild justice, which the more man's nature runs to, the more ought law to weed it out."

—FRANCIS BACON

Yoink!

*When it comes to a **yoink**, you always want to be the yoink-er, never the yoink-ee. That's never stated explicitly in* The Simpsons—*where the word, an exclamation made when stealing something out from under someone's nose, originated— but after numerous "yoinks" on the show, it goes without saying.*

✳ ✳ ✳ ✳

FAMED PERIODICAL *The New Yorker* credits *Simpsons* writers with coining *yoink*, first used in a 1993 episode in which Marge shows Homer the money he's saved by not drinking for a month. "Yoink!" says Homer, snatching the cash and heading for the bar. The Simpsons Archive (www.snpp.com) keeps a "'Yoink!' List" of such uses on the show, listed by episode and situation ("Mr. Burns, pulling the plug on Homer"; "Bart, taking Kent Brockman's danish").

Yoink lacks the morphological complexity of, say, *embiggen* (another *Simpsons* coinage, the opposite of *belittle*). Instead, like *meh*, an apathetic utterance, *yoink* works because it's part word, part sound effect. Clearly, people tend to think loss should have a sound effect: Remember Ross Perot's description of American jobs going to Mexico as a "giant sucking sound"? In fact, Wikisimpsons, an online encyclopedia of *Simpsons* knowledge, speculates that *yoink* is meant to imitate a specific cartoon sound effect that accompanies taking or stealing: sort of a mixture of a "zip" and a "whoosh," made with a violin. (You can hear it in the intro to *The Jetsons*, when Jane Jetson underhandedly snatches her husband's wallet.)

In its life beyond *The Simpsons*, *yoink* has become a verb meaning "to steal" or "to snatch." But some have tried to give it kinder connotations. An app with the name Yoink lets you move fies around more easily!

Portmanteau Words

Also known as blended words, **portmanteau words** *are created by splicing two other words together, merging both their sounds and their meanings.*

✳   ✳   ✳   ✳

THE TERM *PORTMANTEAU* appears in Lewis Carroll's *Through the Looking-Glass,* when Humpty Dumpty uses it to explain nonsense verse, such as *slithy* (*slimy + lithe*) and *mimsy* (*flimsy + miserable*), in the poem "Jabberwocky." An actual *portmanteau* (from the French *porter,* meaning "to carry," and *manteau,* meaning "cloak") is a leather traveling case that opens into two hinged compartments.

Portmanteaux are different from contractions, which are also formed by blending two words together, in that contractions are made from combining two words that follow each other in sequence (*don't = do + not*), while portmanteaux can combine any two words to create a singular concept.

Some blends are so common that we take them for granted and have all but forgotten that they are blends. These include *brunch* (*breakfast + lunch*), *electrocute* (*electro- + execute*), *motel* (*motor + hotel*), *newscast* (*news + broadcast*), *slumlord* (*slum + landlord*), *smog* (*smoke + fog*), and *televangelist* (*television + evangelist*).

These Animals Are Wild

The animal kingdom enjoys a lion's share of portmanteaux. The difference here is that these hybrids are literal—the blended words are coined to describe the blending of species. A *zedonk* is a hybrid of a zebra crossed with a donkey. A *liger* is a hybrid cross between a male lion and a female tigress. A *beefalo* is a cow crossed with a buffalo. And the trend toward breeding so-called "designer dogs" has introduced dozens of hybrid breeds and portmanteau names, including *chiweenie* (chihuahua + dachshund), *cockapoo* (cocker spaniel + poodle), *labradoodle* (Labrador + poodle), *schnoodle* (miniature schnauzer + poodle), and *St. Weiler* (St. Bernard + Rottweiler).

Blended Families

Portmanteaux are very common in computer technology: *alphanumeric* (*alphabetic* + *numeric*), *animatronics* (*animation* + *electronics*), *bit* (*binary* + *digit*), *blogcast* (*blog* [which itself is a blend of *web* + *log*] + *broadcast*), *Internet* (*international* + *network*), *pixel* (*picture* + *element*), *podcast* (*iPod* + *broadcast*), and *webinar* (*Word Wide Web* + *seminar*).

Brand names and new products are often coined by blending two words: *Breathalyzer* (*breath* + *analyzer*), *Frappuccino* (*frappé* + *cappuccino*), *Groupon* (*group* + *coupon*), *Plytanium* (*plywood* + *titanium*), and *Verizon* (the Latin *veritas* ["truth"] + *horizon*), to name just a few.

Name meshing is a popular form of blending. Celebrity couples are ripe for name blending, such as *Brangelina* (Brad Pitt + Angelina Jolie). Of course, these terms can fizzle as quickly as a failed relationship: *TomKat* (Tom Cruise + Katie Holmes), anyone? The resulting moniker is also called a *uniname*, and hey, if the celebs can do it, why can't you?

✳ **Author Lewis Carroll created a wide variety of puzzles and riddles for children. *Lewis Carroll's Games and Puzzles* can still be purchased today. Carroll is also credited with creating an early version of the game Scrabble.**

Indulging in a Reverie

For many English speakers, French is the language of refinement and elegance. Those who might shy away from "egg pie" will devour a quiche. *Fattened goose liver? No, thank you, but please pass the* foie gras. *In ballet, French prettily turns squats into* pliés *and spins into* pirouettes.

＊　＊　＊　＊

WORDS BORROWED FROM French are often associated with good food, entertaining, etiquette, aristocracy, and the arts. These loanwords may retain French spellings not found in native English words (such as letters with accent marks) and French pronunciations (such as nasalized vowels, silent consonants, and that challenging r found in *croissant* and *genre*). Over time, borrowed words tend to become anglicized in spelling and pronunciation, as in *encore*, *critique*, and *debutante*. Eventually, we might not realize they were borrowed at all.

Perhaps you have always thought of yourself as a *gourmet*, a *connoisseur* of fine food. Well, then, let's journey to a *restaurant* or *bistro* to explore *nouvelle cuisine*. The *maître d'* reminds us that we can order *à la carte* or select from the *buffet*. Perhaps you would like an *aperitif* before your *hors d'oeuvre*? For your *entrée*, you might try *bouillabaisse*, a *casserole*, or *filet mignon*. And for dessert, why not try a *crepe* with *café au lait* or *cognac*?

During the meal, you may enjoy the *milieu* as you watch the other guests. You have a strange feeling of *déjà vu*: Have you been here before, or are you indulging in a *reverie*? That *chic* couple over there—is their *rendezvous* the cover for a *liaison*? The *petite brunette* woman, is she his *confidante* or perhaps his *protégée*? Your eye lands on her ring, a diamond *baguette*. It's nothing *risqué*, then; she is his *fiancée*. You may wish the evening would never end, but of course it does. But you may keep the empty *champagne* bottle as a *souvenir*.

Worldly Wisdom: European Proverbs

✳ ✳ ✳ ✳

✳ The heart that loves is always young. (Greek)

✳ A thousand men can't undress a naked man. (Greek)

✳ A different man, a different taste. (Greek)

✳ A miser is ever in want. (Greek)

✳ By learning you will teach; by teaching you will learn. (Latin)

✳ He who dares wins. (Latin)

✳ To be successful is to be in solitude. (Latin)

✳ If you scatter thorns, don't go barefoot. (Italian)

✳ After the game, the king and the pawn go into the same box. (Italian)

✳ We learn by teaching. (Italian)

✳ If the beard were all, the goat might preach. (Italian)

✳ If the young only knew; if the old only could. (French)

✳ A bad craftsman blames his tools. (French)

✳ A good reputation is better than riches. (French)

✳ The absent are always wrong. (French)

✳ An ounce of mother is worth a pound of clergy. (Spanish)

✳ No revenge is more honorable than the one not taken. (Spanish)

✳ It is good fishing in troubled waters. (Spanish)

✳ There are no worse blinds than those who do not want to see. (Portuguese)

✳ What is cheap is costly. (Portuguese)

From *Aa* (Lava) to *Zyzzyva* (a Weevil)

A common misconception is that a good vocabulary makes a good Scrabble player. Sure, if that vocabulary includes words like adze (a tool that cuts tile), ourie (an adjective meaning "shabby"), or ratites (large, flightless birds).

✳   ✳   ✳   ✳

THE GAME OF Scrabble is a fascinating mixture of luck, strategy, and word knowledge. The ability to spell helps, as does having an extensive vocabulary. But that's not enough. To really excel at the game, top Scrabble players study and memorize specialized word lists. For the most part, players don't worry too much about what the words mean. They're just valid combinations of letters. Here are some of the most important lists.

Two-letter words: The fourth edition of *The Official Scrabble Players Dictionary* contains 103 acceptable two-letter words to use in Scrabble, and top players have memorized them all (even if they haven't memorized their definitions). They include the names of musical notes (*la, ti, fa*), interjections (*hm, oy, mm, uh, um*), shortened forms (*ed* for *education, za* for *pizza*), and spelled-out letter names (*ay, ef, el, ar, ex*).

Two-to-make-three: A study list for learning three-letter words made from two-letter words might look like this: *g / nu / bnst.* That tells us that given the word *nu* (a Greek letter), a three-letter word can be made either by putting *g* in front of it (*gnu*) or by adding *b, n, s,* or *t* after it (*nub, nun, nus, nut*).

Vowel and consonant dumps: While it's disheartening to look at your tiles and see a sea of low-scoring vowels, a number of words with a high vowel-to-consonant ratio will help you get rid of them. Such words include *aioli, eerie, ilia, miaou, luau,* and *oidia.* Also useful to know are the words with no vowels, including: *brr, cwm* (a valley), *crwth* (an ancient harplike instrument), *nth, shh,* and *tsk.*

Bingo-prone stems: Putting down all seven letters at once (a "bingo") earns a 50-point bonus. To achieve this, top players study the combinations of letters that will make valid words, starting with the most frequent letter combinations. These six-letter combinations are called "stems," and experts have learned how to use them. For example, given the six letters in *tisane* (an infusion used as a beverage or for medicinal effects), any seventh letter except *j, q,* and *y* will provide at least one seven-letter word. Given a *t,* the stem makes *instate* or *satinet;* even a *z* will produce *zeatins* (a substance that comes from Indian corn) or *zaniest.*

❋ A National Scrabble Championship is held annually in the United States, with a grand prize of $10,000.

❋ Words with Friends is a modern-day version of Scrabble. People play it through Facebook or as an app on their smart-phone. Just as in Scrabble, the more obscure words you know, the better chance you have of winning.

❋ If you think *zyzzyva* (a weevil) is a funny word, how about *zenzizenzizenzic*—a number raised to the nth power. (That's one you won't be playing in Scrabble!)

Least-Favorite Words

Certain words have an unexplainable adverse effect on some people, making them shudder or setting their teeth on edge for reasons they can't explain. It might be something about the spelling or pronunciation—or is there something more?

✳   ✳   ✳   ✳

SOME WORDS GET a bad rap because they are overused and nonspecific. Parents get tired of hearing *like, whatever,* and *random* from their teens. Meaningless corporate-speak words like *incentivize, leverage,* and *synergy* can grate, especially when we strongly suspect that the person using them is hiding their incompetence behind vague buzzwords.

Some words are off-putting because of the images they evoke—words like *pimple, armpit, nostril,* and *vomit.* You can put them in a nicer font or whisper them softly, but they'll always be the pariahs of the lexicon. We can create euphemisms (like *upchuck* or *zit*), but over time, those words too become contaminated with unpleasantness.

Thick and Oafish; Short and Ugly

But then, some words are just inherently unlovable. They have thick, oafish consonants combined with short, ugly vowels—words like *chunk, smock,* and *gruel.*

People also dislike, and will go out of their way to avoid, words they aren't sure how to pronounce. The worst are words that have not—or have only partway—migrated from their original foreign pronunciations to fully English ones. We keep our eyes downcast as we mumble our way through *chipotle, croissant,* and *mauve.* Winemakers, take note: The names of most wines fall into this category, possibly leading linguistically humble Americans to opt for "house white" over "sauvignon blanc." Perhaps your marketing team could leverage that know-how into a win-win scenario.

The Word that Keeps on Giving

*Like the phenomenon it names, **regifting** just keeps giving and giving....*

✳　✳　✳　✳

THE PRACTICE OF *regifting* is a perfect solution to an annoying problem: A thoughtless (or clueless) friend or relative gives you something useless—say, a ceramic panda. And soon after, lo and behold, it comes time for you to give someone else a little something, and you can't figure out what to get. While you're racking your brain, you happen to see the ceramic panda sitting on a shelf in the closet. Oddly enough, it's still in the original wrapping. That's how regifting happens.

Though the act of regifting is probably centuries old, it didn't have a proper name until the TV show *Seinfeld* came along. In the 1995 episode "The Label Maker," Elaine realizes something is wrong when Jerry receives a Label Baby Jr. (a label maker) as a gift from dentist Tim Whatley. Elaine rants, "I think this is the same one I gave him. He recycled this gift. He's a regifter!"

The term is used many times in the episode, and even inspired another variation: *degift* (taking back a gift you give to someone).

George: *Well, didn't he regift the label maker?*

Jerry: *Possibly.*

George: *Well, if he can regift, why can't you degift?*

The term *regift* caught on quickly, perhaps more than any other *Seinfeld* coinage. The practice has been catching on quickly as well. According to the website Regiftable.com, the majority of people (60 percent) believe regifting has become an acceptable practice. Maybe they're just looking for excuses, but they say it's a good way to help maintain the budget at holiday time, and it's also a useful method of recycling.

Words of Wisdom: Truth

✳   ✳   ✳   ✳

"Hard are the ways of truth, and rough to walk."

—JOHN MILTON

"Often truth spoken with a smile will penetrate the mind and reach the heart; the lesson strikes home without wounding because of the wit in the saying."

—HORACE

"In the mountains of truth, you never climb in vain. Either you already reach a higher point today, or you exercise your strength in order to be able to climb higher tomorrow."

—FRIEDRICH NIETZSCHE

"There is no truth existing which I fear, or would wish unknown to the whole world."

—THOMAS JEFFERSON

"When in doubt tell the truth."

—MARK TWAIN

"If you would be a real seeker after truth, it is necessary that at least once in your life you doubt, as far as possible, all things."

—RENÉ DESCARTES

"Truth is the cry of all, but the game of the few."

—GEORGE BERKELEY

"All truth passes through three stages. First, it is ridiculed. Second, it is violently opposed. Third, it is accepted as being self-evident."

—ARTHUR SCHOPENHAUER

"Three things cannot long be hidden: The sun, the moon, and the truth."

—CONFUCIUS

The Truth About Truthiness

There were already plenty of words—such as balderdash, bunk, crapola, hooey, *and* hokum—*that mean "nonsense" or "baloney." It's not like the world was crying out for a new addition to this family. Or, based on the way the public eagerly embraced the coinage of the word* **truthiness,** *maybe it was.*

✳ ✳ ✳ ✳

COMEDY CENTRAL'S *The Colbert Report* was sharp from day one: Its most famous new word—*truthiness*—was coined on the debut show. It was part of a segment called "The Word," in which Stephen Colbert ranted (in a satirical fashion, of course) about the "elitist" sources—such as dictionaries and encyclopedias—that insist on promoting their own truth as *the* truth. ("Who's Britannica to tell me the Panama Canal was finished in 1914? If I wanna say it happened in 1941, that's my right," he protested, tongue in cheek.) As a closing, Colbert said, "The truthiness is, anyone can read the news to you. I promise to *feel* the news at you."

Just months after that episode, the American Dialect Society voted *truthiness* Word of the Year for 2005, which propelled the word into the headlines. Combined with Colbert's increasing popularity and the word's relevance to scandals involving government, religion, and business, the term hit the popular culture lexicon and hasn't left since. It was named Word of the Year again in 2006, this time by *Merriam-Webster's Collegiate Dictionary* and Dictionary.com.

Believe it or not, the term had popped up in the past, specifically in 1824, in a bit of text recorded under the *Oxford English Dictionary's* definition of *truthy*: "Everyone who knows her is aware of her truthiness." This example seems to present a more sincere form of truthiness, with none of the Colbert snark. *The Century Dictionary* cites a usage from 1832: "Truthiness is a habit, like every other virtue." Ain't that the truth?

What Do You Mean by That?

Let's take a look at some common phrases and see if we can't track their origins down.

✳   ✳   ✳   ✳

Clean as a Whistle

Since when has the whistle been synonymous with cleanliness? Back in the prehistoric day when reeds were used to make whistling sounds, they had to be free of all debris to attain the desired tone.

Down in the Dumps

The word "dump" calls to mind nasty stuff, but this phrase has nothing to do with garbage or bodily functions. The origin of this expression is from the German word dumpf, which means "oppressive" or "heavy." To be "down in the dumps" means to feel weighted down by worry.

Gone to Pot

This phrase, meaning not much good for anything, originated in the Elizabethan era with the forerunner of beef stew, when any tidbit of meat too small for a regular portion was thrown into a big pot always boiling over the fire.

In Cahoots

When two or more people are up to no good, they're said to be "in cahoots." The phrase may well come from France, where a small cabin was called a *cahute*. If these cabins were occupied by bandits and robbers planning a heist, the name of the cottages may have become a sort of shorthand to signify what went on inside them.

It's Greek to Me

This phrase, used by someone to indicate that he or she doesn't understand a word of what's being said, is really a quotation from the first act of William Shakespeare's *Julius Caesar*. The character Casca, one of the plotters who participates in Caesar's assassination, describes overhearing Cicero, who was speaking in Greek to deter eavesdroppers. The ploy obviously worked.

Mad as a Hatter

The Mad Hatter was popularized in Lewis Carroll's *Alice's Adventures in Wonderland*, but Carroll did not coin the phrase. Making hats had already been linked with madness. During the early days of processing felt to use in hatmaking, the toxic substance mercury was used, which resulted in many industry workers developing mental or neurological disturbances. From this unfortunate situation, the phrase "mad as a hatter" came to indicate anyone who had gone insane.

The Luck of the Irish

The roots of this phrase vary according to the person you ask. Some say the "luck" of the people of Ireland is anything but: They've dealt with Viking wars, English takeovers, potato famines, terrorism, etc. Others believe that the Irish people's ability to persevere through such hardship is actually a testament to their incredibly good luck.

Nest Egg

A "nest egg" refers to the practice of placing an egg, either real or made of china, into a hen's nest in order to encourage her to lay an egg of her own. By that token, putting some money in a bank account should encourage you to add more money to the account. A noble idea, but I'll bet that hen didn't know about the 50 percent off shoe sale at Nordstrom's!

Up for Grabs

This phrase, which means that something is available to anyone who wants it, is a fairly recent expression, dating back to the Great Depression, when restaurants saved every scrap of excess food. The leftovers were put into bags and set at the end of the counter, where any person in need could take one without suffering the indignity of having to beg.

Crazy for -*Mania*

Mania is a form of madness. As a suffix, -mania is extremely productive in English, forming words that denote a particular type of mental illness or an excessive desire for something. The word comes from postclassical Latin and ultimately from Greek.

✷ ✷ ✷ ✷

Some -manias are genuine illnesses, like *erotomania* ("extreme sexual desire"—1874) and *megalomania* ("delusions of power"—1885). But others are faddish and popular coinages. The most famous of these is perhaps *Beatlemania*, that extreme fondness for the Fab Four that swept the world starting in 1963. The -*mania* suffix is particularly interesting in that the dates of coinage of the various words reveal trends across the centuries. Some of the other maniacal words, both serious and tongue-in-cheek, are:

✷ *bibliomania*—excessive enthusiasm for books (1734)

✷ *politico-mania*—excessive enthusiasm for politics (1785)

✷ *Anglomania*—excessive enthusiasm for all things British (1799)

✷ *monomania*—compulsion or obsession relating to a single area (1815)

✷ *egomania*—morbid love of self (1825)

✷ *kleptomania*—compulsion to steal (1830)

✷ *dipsomania*—alcoholism (c. 1843)

✷ *arithmomania*—compulsion to count and perform calculations (1890)

✷ *micromania*—delusion that one's body or a body part is abnormally small (1892)

✷ *oniomania*—compulsion to purchase things (1895)

Cloaked in Secrecy

In 1966, the first season of Star Trek *introduced a frightening futuristic plot device. A Romulan starship, anathema to Captain Kirk and his crew, was on the move and employing a previously unknown technology: a* **cloaking device,** *which rendered it invisible. This bit of technological whimsy has been a staple of science fiction and video games ever since.*

* * * *

THE TERM CLOAKING DEVICE relies on the figurative use of the verb *to cloak* (the verb itself deriving from the noun denoting a loose-fitting garment), an application that dates to the 1500s. But while *cloak* has enjoyed semantic flexibility for centuries, we owe this manifestation to *Star Trek.*

Cloaking device is of relatively recent coinage, but the notion of manufacturing invisibility didn't originate in the mind of *Star Trek* creator Gene Roddenberry. In fact, the idea dates back thousands of years: There is a prototype for the technology in the ancient Greek myth of Perseus. In addition to his iconic winged sandals, this son of Zeus used a helmet of invisibility.

Returning to this millennium, we find another fictitious cloaking device—this time, in a clever marrying of the term's literal and figurative meanings, taking the form of an actual cloak. Those familiar with J. K. Rowling's *Harry Potter* series might recall Harry's invaluable invisibility cloak, a magical garment Harry wears for missions that are variously mischievous and noble.

It isn't just Trekkies and wizard wannabes who can vouch for the usefulness of a cloaking device; nor is this far-fetched technology only the stuff of fantasy. Scientists today are exploring the real-life possibility of manufactured invisibility—and with encouraging results. So, while there's still a formidable gap between reality and fiction, it may not be light-years before *cloaking device* is as much a part of our daily vocabulary as *Internet* and *cell phone.*

I Spy Something Secret

Spies have their own secret language to keep from being discovered. By spying on these spies, we've managed to uncover the meaning of some of their covert terminology.

✳   ✳   ✳   ✳

Black Bag Job: A black bag job, or black bag operation, is a covert entry into a building to plant surveillance equipment or find and copy documents, computer data, or cryptographic keys. The name is derived from the black bags spies used to carry the equipment for such operations. In 1972, the Supreme Court declared black bag jobs unconstitutional.

Brush Contact: A brush contact is a brief and public meeting in which two spies discreetly exchange documents, funds, or information without speaking to each other, except perhaps to utter "Excuse me" or other pleasantries. To the average person, the interaction would seem like an accidental encounter between two strangers.

Canary Trap: Do you suspect a leak in your organization? Even if the leakers aren't small yellow birds, you might be able to catch them by setting a canary trap—giving different versions of sensitive information to each suspected leaker and seeing which version gets leaked. Although this method has been around for years, the term was popularized by Tom Clancy in the novel *Patriot Games*.

Dangle: In spy terminology, a dangle is an agent who pretends to be interested in defecting to or joining another intelligence agency or group. The dangle convinces the new agency that they have changed loyalties by offering to act as a double agent. The dangle then feeds information to their original agency while giving disinformation to the other.

Honeypot: A honeypot is a trap that uses sex to lure an enemy agent into disclosing classified information or, in some cases, to capture or kill them. In the classic Hitchcock film *North by Northwest*, Eva Marie Saint's character was both a honeypot and a double agent. In real life, in 1961, U.S. diplomat Irvin Scarbeck was blackmailed into providing secrets after he was lured by a female Polish agent and photographed in a compromising position.

L-Pill: An L-pill is a lethal pill carried by spies to prevent them from revealing secrets if captured and tortured. During World War II, some L-pills contained a lethal dose of cyanide encased in a glass capsule that could be concealed in a fake tooth and released by the agent's tongue. If he bit into the capsule and broke the glass, he would die almost immediately. But if the pill came loose and was swallowed accidentally while the agent was sleeping or chewing gum, it would pass through his system without causing any harm, as long as it didn't break and release the poison.

Starburst Maneuver: How does a spy lose someone who is tailing him? One way is by employing a starburst maneuver—a tactic in which several identical looking vehicles suddenly go in different directions, forcing the surveillance team to quickly decide which one to follow. A classic example of this strategy was utilized in the 2003 film *The Italian Job*. Similar-looking agents can also be used instead of vehicles. Kids, don't try this with your parents.

Sheep Dipping: In farming, sheep dipping is a chemical bath given to sheep to rid them of bugs or disease or to clean their wool before shearing. In CIA terminology, sheep dipping means disguising the identity of an agent by placing him within a legitimate organization. This establishes clean credentials that can later be used to penetrate adversary groups or organizations. Similar to the real sheep, the agent is cleaned up so that nobody knows where he's been, kind of like money laundering.

Chapter 15

Where There's a Word, There's a Way

You Talk Too Much

We all know people who are never at a loss for words, don't we? We call them voluble, *which comes from the Latin root* vol, *meaning "roll, flow." The English language has no shortage of fancy words to describe people who are never at a loss for words.*

✳ ✳ ✳ ✳

WE'VE ALL MET (and usually try to avoid) *bloviators*, those people who ramble on pompously at great length. In fact, we often call their verbal gassiness *perorations*, which are high-flown, flowery speeches. *Logorrhea* (from the Greek *log*, meaning "word," and *rrhea*, meaning "run, flow") produces an excessive stream of words (think of it as verbal diarrhea). *Polylogizers* (*poly*, "many" + *log*, "word"), or excessive talkers, are prone to this.

A person who is full of idle, inane chatter is *inaniloquent*, and *bablatrice* and *chaterestre* are both words used to describe talkative women. A *battologist* repeats the same thing unnecessarily. The English language also has a host of odd words to describe incessant, inconsequential talk, including *blather, blatherskite, gabble, galimatias, jabber, jabberwocky, palaver, prate, prattle,* and *twaddle*—all of which are likely to be spouted by a *phylarologist*, or someone who talks nonsense.

Speak Up, I Can't Hear You

If we're stuck listening to a bunch of jabberwocky, we might at least hope it's *eutrapely,* or "pleasant conversation"; unfortunately, we're often forced to listen to a lot of *kvetching,* which is Yiddish for "nagging complaints." A *smellfungus* is someone who always complains, and to *peenge* is to complain in a whiny voice. To *confabulate* (*con,* "with" + *fabul,* "talk") means to chat casually—though do we need such a stuffy word to say this? If you want people to hear you, you speak in a *stentorian* voice (Stentor was a loud-speaking character in Homer's *The Iliad*) and try not to be *blesiloquent* (speaking with a lisp or stammer).

To *brabble* is to talk noisily, which, if you pride yourself on your skill in *deipnosophy* (the art of skillful dinner conversation), you will wisely choose to avoid so as not to offend your dinner companions. *Lexiphanicism* is the practice of using pretentious words, and a *blaguer* is the person using these words. To be *spadish,* on the other hand, is to be direct and blunt in speech.

Please Don't Drumble

What about those people who *entermate* (meddle) and those who *prevaricate,* or don't tell the truth (not to be confused with *heterophemists,* who simply say something other than what they mean)? A *leighster* is a female liar. (It doesn't seem fair that English lacks a term to denote males who tell tales.) And speaking of tales, a *snurge* is a tattletale. To *drumble,* which is a combination of *drone* and *mumble,* means "to talk in a slow, sluggish manner." *Blandiose* people think they sound grandiose, but we know they're bland.

And finally, what about people whose hands do a lot of their speaking? We call this practice *hypermimia,* or waving and gesticulating with the hands while talking.

Personality Plus

We are defined not just by our appearances—hair color, height, facial features, and the like—but also by our personalities, including our moods, our dispositions, and our behaviors. And for just about every personality trait we possess, the English language provides an interesting word.

❋   ❋   ❋   ❋

HERE'S A LISTING of odd words that describe many things we are, and many more things we hope we aren't.

❋ *agathist*—an optimist

❋ *amadelphous*—outgoing, sociable, gregarious

❋ *boeotian*—culturally backward and stupid

❋ *caitiff*—a base, wicked, or cowardly person

❋ *cockalorum*—a boastful or self-important man

❋ *dyspeptic*—having a morose or unhappy disposition

❋ *eleemosynary*—charitable, generous, philanthropic

❋ *eupeptic*—cheerful

❋ *flaskisable*—flaky

❋ *gobemouche*—a very gullible person; someone who believes everything that's said

❋ *grobian*—a sloppy or crude person

❋ *hautain*—proud, arrogant

❋ *huderon*—lazy

❋ *inadvertist*—someone who is oblivious

❋ *kalokagothia*—goodness of character; nobility

❋ *lickerish*—greedy, desirous, lecherous

* *lickspittle*—a fawning, servile flatterer; a toady

* *mammothrept*—a spoiled, brattish child

* *meacock*—a coward; or an effeminate person

* *morate*—well-mannered, moral

* *mountebank*—a fraud or imposter, a charlatan, a quack

* *myrmidon*—one who is unquestioningly obedient

* *mythomaniac*—a habitual, compulsive liar

* *nacket*—a rude and impertinent boy

* *nithing*—a contempible, reprehensible person

* *orgulous*—proud, haughty

* *oultrepreu*—remarkably brave

* *peramene*—very pleasant

* *philobat*—a thrill seeker; someone who enjoys dangerous activities

* *pococurantish*—careless; indifferent

* *pudibund*—prudish

* *quidnunc*—a busybody, meddler, or gossiper

* *rantipole*—a wild, unruly young person

* *subdolous*—sly, crafty, cunning

* *thrasonical*—bragging or boastful

* *varlet*—a rascal

* *volpone*—cunning; a schemer

* *zoilist*—a severe critic; someone who constantly finds fault in others

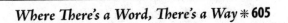

Words of Wisdom: Character

✳   ✳   ✳   ✳

"Character, that sublime health which values one moment as another, and makes us great in all conditions."
—RALPH WALDO EMERSON

"Education has for its object the reformation of character."
—HERBERT SPENCER

"The real character of a man is found out by his amusements."
—JOSHUA REYNOLDS

"The beginning is the most important part of any work, especially in the case of a young and tender thing; for that is the time at which character is being formed and the desired impression is more readily taken."
—PLATO

"A talent is formed in stillness, a character in the world's torrent."
—JOHANN WOLFGANG VON GOETHE

"To enjoy the things we ought and to hate the things we ought has the greatest bearing on excellence of character."
—ARISTOTLE

"Character is much easier kept than recovered."
—THOMAS PAINE

"The measure of a man's real character is what he would do if he knew he would never be found out."
—THOMAS BABINGTON, LORD MACAULAY

"Instill the love of you into all the world, for a good character is what is remembered."
—THE TEACHING OF MERIKARE

From Alpenglow to Dimpsey

Carpe diem, carpe noctem . . . seize the day—and the night!

* * * *

THE ENGLISH LEXICON seizes the concept of time with a multitude of interesting and unusual vocabulary terms for all hours of day and night. Here are a few:

* *alpenglow*—the pink light that covers snowy mountains, especially at dawn and dusk

* *antelucan*—before dawn (from Latin meaning "before light")

* *aubade*—a song about daybreak or dawn or that is sung at dawn, especially one that is intended to warn lovers that the day is approaching

* *cathemeral*—active during both day and night

* *crepuscular*—of or like twilight; dim

* *dimpsey*—dusk

* *gloaming*—twilight, as at early morning or (especially) early evening; dusk

* *hebdomad*—a period of seven days; a week

* *matutinal*—of, relating to, or occurring in the morning

* *mesonoxian*—having to do with midnight

* *nycthemeron*—a period of 24 hours (one day and one night)

* *quotidian*—something that returns or is expected every day, especially in medicine

* *rosicler*—the rosy light of dawn

* *vespertine*—of, relating to, or occurring in the evening

* *yestreen*—yesterday evening

Colorful Language

Traditional Irish and Welsh have no word for the color blue—the word referring to that color, glas, also refers to certain shades of green and gray. The Navajo language also does not distinguish between blue and green, but it has two words for the color black. The ancient Greeks take the prize when it comes to odd color perception: Authors such as Homer and Euripides consistently described the sky as bronze; the sea and sheep as wine-colored; and blood, tears, and honey as green.

✳ ✳ ✳ ✳

ONE MIGHT WONDER if the ancient Greeks were color-blind. If they were, they may have had little use for these colorful and unusual words:

* *aeneous*—shining bronze

* *argent*—silver or white

* *atrous*—jet black

* *aurulent*—gold

* *badius*—chestnut

* *bloncket*—gray, or light gray-blue

* *bombycinous*—pale yellow

* *butyraceous*—resembling butter

* *canescent*—gray or dull white

* *castory*—dull brown

* *celeste*—sky blue

* *feuillemorte*—yellowish-brown

* *fulginous*—soot black

* *fulvous*—tawny

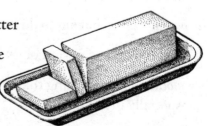

> *"We are like chameleons, we take our hue and the color of our moral character, from those who are around us."*
> —JOHN LOCKE

* *gamboge*—reddish-yellow
* *greige*—gray-beige
* *griseous*—grayish-blue
* *infuscate*—muddy brown
* *jacinthe*—orange
* *leucochroic*—white, pale
* *luteolous*—yellowish
* *mazarine*—rich blue or reddish-blue
* *melanic*—black
* *pavonated*—peacock blue
* *rubiginous*—having the color of rust
* *sarcoline*—having the color of flesh
* *sinopia*—red-brown
* *smalt*—deep blue
* *stramineous*—having the color of straw
* *sulphureous*—bright yellow
* *vinaceous*—having the color of red wine
* *wallflower*—yellowish-red
* *watchet*—light blue
* *whey*—off-white
* *xanthic*—yellow

Shop Till You Drop

As shopaholics will tell you, if you choose to wander through the mall or knackatory (a place to buy knickknacks), there will be no shortage of goodies to tempt your pocketbook.

❊   ❊   ❊   ❊

BUT BUYERS BEWARE—ESPECIALLY those who suffer from *oniochalasia* (buying things as a form of mental relaxation) or *emacity* (an uncontrollable urge to buy things). Some *finnimbruns* (knickknacks, trinkets) are more valuable than others, and you'll want to steer clear of *brimborion* items (those of no value) and anything that looks *brummagem* (cheap and gaudy).

However, shoppers who have engaged in *pismirism*, or the hoarding of money, may have the urge to pull out their credit cards and *spheterize* (take for their own) all the *curwhibbles* (thingamajigs) they can afford. Hopefully none of the shopkeepers will attempt to *gazump* the sale (raise the price of something after agreeing on a lower price). They may be rightfully angry, however, if a customer attempts to pay for goods with *exonumia* (items that resemble money but do not circulate—as in coupons, tokens, etc.).

Speaking of shopkeepers, there are a number of interesting words pertaining to the business of selling. If you're looking to pick up a *colliby* (a small, useful present) or perhaps some *dabbities* (little ornaments or decorative items for the mantel), perhaps you'd like to visit some of these vendors:

❊ *aginator*—a seller of small things

❊ *colporteur*—someone who peddles books

❊ *costermonger*—a seller of fruits and vegetables

❊ *draper*—someone who deals in cloths and dry goods

❊ *duffer*—a peddler

> *"Every man is a consumer, and ought to be a producer. He is by constitution expensive, and needs to be rich."*
> —RALPH WALDO EMERSON

* *haberdasher*—someone who sells men's clothing

* *higgler*—an itinerant peddler

* *huckster*—someone who sells small wares (*outdated*); today, an aggressive promoter of promotional ideas and wares

* *jagger*—a fishmonger

* *kurveyor*—a traveling merchant who sells dry goods from a cart

* *milliner*—a vendor of hats and lace

* *pharmacopolist*—a person who sells medicine

* *seplasiary*—a perfumer

* *tragematopolist*—a seller of confections and sweets

* *xylopogist*—one who sells wood products

No matter where you shop, beware of *scowbankers* (unscrupulous and dishonest merchants) who may try to *honeyfuggle* (swindle, cheat) you by trying to sell you items of *viliority* (items that are cheap, or of lesser value).

Where Did It Come From?

Sawbuck: Slang for an American ten-dollar bill. This term originally referred to cross supports used to hold wood for sawing, also called a "sawhorse." The use of the term to reference a $10 bill most likely derives from the Roman numeral X, which appears on the currency.

Words of Wisdom from Voltaire

✳ ✳ ✳ ✳

✳ "Judge people by their questions rather than by their answers."

✳ "Every man is guilty of all the good he did not do."

✳ "A witty saying proves nothing."

✳ "Appreciation is a wonderful thing: It makes what is excellent in others belong to us as well."

✳ "Behind every successful man stands a surprised mother-in-law."

✳ "Common sense is not so common."

✳ "Faith consists in believing when it is beyond the power of reason to believe."

✳ "I do not agree with what you have to say, but I'll defend to the death your right to say it."

✳ "Never argue at the dinner table, for the one who is not hungry always gets the best of the argument."

✳ "No snowflake in an avalanche ever feels responsible."

✳ "The multitude of books is making us ignorant."

✳ The secret of being a bore is to tell everything.

✳ "To succeed in the world it is not enough to be stupid, you must also be well-mannered."

Word Roots and Branches
The Many Uses of *Multi-*

There is a multiplicity of multi- *words. This is quite appropriate, as the prefix comes from the Latin* multus, *meaning "many, great."*

✳ ✳ ✳ ✳

THE EARLIEST MULTI- words in English are either lifted directly from Latin (e.g., *multiplex*, "having many aspects," and *multiformity*, "having diverse shapes") or borrowed from Anglo-Norman and Old French during the Middle English period (e.g., *multiply*, "to increase," and *multitude*, "a great number"). Starting in the early seventeenth century, people began creating *multi-* words within English, but this remained fairly rare until the nineteenth century, when multitudes of *multi-* words began to be created. And in the twentieth century, *multi-* really took off. Other *multi-* words include:

✳ *multibillionaire*—a person worth many billions of dollars

✳ *multicausal*—having many causes

✳ *multidirectional*—emitting in or coming from many directions

✳ *multidrug-resistant*—a bacteria resistant to a number of antimicrobial compounds

✳ *multiethnic*—composed of many ethnicities

✳ *multifunctional*—having many uses

✳ *multigrain*—composed of many types of cereal

✳ *multihued*—having many colors

✳ *multilateral*—having many sides

✳ *multinational*—involving many countries

✳ *multiparous*—producing many offspring at one time

✳ *multitask*—to conduct many activities at once

Building Vocabulary

Whether it's an A-frame or a ziggurat (a stepped pyramid of Mesopotamia) or anything in between, all buildings are designed with their own specific architectural features, each with a specific architectural term to name it.

❋ ❋ ❋ ❋

START YOUR CRASH course in architectural terminology by perusing the list below:

* *acanthus*—a stylized leaf design, patterned after acanthus plants, used especially on the capitals of Corinthian columns

* *ambulatory*—a covered passageway, either outdoors or indoors; especially, the passageway around the apse and choir of a church

* *balistraria*—a narrow opening, shaped like a cross, through which arrows can be shot

* *breastsummer*—a large beam supporting the whole weight of a wall; a long lintel or girder

* *caryatid*—a supporting column sculpted in the form of a human figure

* *clerestory*—the upper part of a wall, particularly in a church, containing windows (pronounced "clear-story")

* *corbel*—a bracket of wood or stone projecting from a wall to support a cornice or arch

* *coulisse*—a place behind the scenes, such as a lobby or corridor; the backstage

* *cubiculum*—a mortuary chapel attached to a church

* *decastyle*—a portico with ten columns

* *encarpa*—architectural designs featuring fruit

* *entasis*—a slight outward curvature in a column that corrects an optical illusion and gives the appearance of being straight

* *escutcheon*—a decorative metal plate set around a keyhole, doorknob, or handle of a drawer

* *fastigated*—pointed, rising to a point; narrowing to the top, as with a sloping roof

* *gambrel*—a two-sided roof with a double slope on each side, the lower side having the steeper pitch (also called a barn roof)

* *hypaethral*—wholly or partly open to the sky

* *inglenook*—a nook or corner beside an open fireplace

* *rustication*—masonry cut in large blocks, often with a rough exterior to emphasize texture in a wall

* *sitooterie*—a summerhouse or gazebo; an out-of-the-way place to sit with a partner during a dance

Where Did It Come From?

Threshold: Long before it was used to refer to the entry-way of a house, this word was used by farmers to refer to the process of separating the grain from the chaff by stepping upon it.

Cap-a-Pie

No, it's not a dessert. Pronounced cahp-ah-PEE, cap-a-pie comes from Middle French and means "from head to foot." The English language is up to its ears in interesting words to describe our top- and bottommost body parts: Let's start at the top!

✳ ✳ ✳ ✳

THE GREEK CEPHAL, referring always to the head of a living thing, gives us a heady assortment of technical vocabulary: *hydrocephaly*, a dangerous buildup of fluid near the brain in infants, also known as "water on the brain"; *cymbocephalous*, having a boat-shaped skull; and *cynocephalous*, having a face or head shaped like a dog's. *Leptocephaly* is the condition of having an abnormally long and slender face.

Face Facts

Alae are the bulbs on each side of the nose, and *leptorrhinic* denotes someone with an unusually long, skinny nose. The *vomer* is the bone that separates the *nares* (singular *naris*), or nostrils. *Murfles* (freckles) look cute scattered across the *proboscis* (nose). Above the nose is the *glabellum*, the smooth place between the eyebrows. The *philtrum* is the groove in the center of the upper lip, and *labrose* people have very full lips. *Mompyms* are teeth. *Mentum* is just a fancy word for "chin," but *pogonion* is the part of your chin that sticks out the farthest, and *choller* is a double chin. People with very large ears are *macrotous*. The hollow of the ear is called an *alveary*, and have you ever noticed that little flap on the inner side of the ear? That's a *tragus*, and the rim opposite it is called the *helix*. *Dundrearies* are sideburns on an epic scale. The *trichion* is the place where the hairline meets the center of the forehead (if the trichion is V-shaped, we call it a *widow's peak*).

Put One -*Pod* in Front of the Other

Many obscure words pertaining to the foot refer to animals rather than humans, and they contain either the Greek -*pod* or

-*pus* suffix, both meaning "foot." A *bradypod* (*brady*, "slow") is a sloth (i.e., the animal). Curiously, the scaly armadillo is classified as a *dasypod* (*dasy*, "hairy"). More logically, the sea-animal grouping *Decapoda* (*deca*, "ten") includes the shrimp, the lobster, and the crab—all of which are ten-footed crustaceans. *Myriapoda* (*myria-* meaning "ten thousand") includes centipedes and millipedes, wormlike creatures with many legs along their sides—but not 100 or 1,000, as the *cent* and *milli* roots would suggest. A kangaroo, with its giant feet, is of the *Macropus* genus (*macro*, "large"), and the duck-billed *platypus* (*plat*, "flat"), an egg-laying mammal native to Australia, has wide webbed feet. Creatures that "walk" on their undersides rather than on feet, such as the lowly snail and slug, are *gastropods* (*gastr-*, "belly").

Finally, in the true etymological spirit of *cap-a-pie*, we have the octopus, the squid, and the cuttlefish—the *cephalopods*. That's head to toe in one term!

✳ **Pelmatogram is a fancy way to say "footprint."**

Where Did It Come From?

Philtrum: Derives from the ancient Greek term *philtron*, which means "love potion." Although the philtrum may seem pointless to modern humans, the ancient Greeks believed this groove in the center part of the upper lip to be one of the most erogenous parts of the human body.

Walk This Way

Ambul- is a combining form (a root that cannot occur on its own but rather must attach to an affix) that refers to motion, especially walking. It comes from the Latin ambulare, *meaning "to walk, to travel."*

✳   ✳   ✳   ✳

S O THE ADJECTIVE *ambulatory* means "pertaining to walking," or, more figuratively, "shifting, mutable," and the verb *to ambulate* is just a fancy way of saying "to walk." Even fancier, perhaps, is the derivative *perambulate*. Although the word boasts a range of definitions that are derived from its original meaning ("to survey while passing through"), the most unapologetic bombasts may show off by using it as a substitute for "to walk" or "to wander."

Call 911!

The world of medicine, never shy about adopting and adapting Latinate roots, has made good use of *ambul-*, as a number of the words formed from this root have a medical sense. Patients who are not confined to a bed—those able to walk about—are *ambulatory* or *ambulant*. Sometimes it's not the patients that are moving, but the hospital. The French *hôpital ambulant*, or "walking hospital," was the precursor for what we know today as an *ambulance*. And *ambulancier* is a rare word for an ambulance driver, or in modern parlance, a paramedic. But you can bet the best EMTs aren't going to amble anywhere—they're going to get to the scene of the accident as quickly as they can.

There is an old sense of *ambulant*, no longer in use, that describes a disease that moves from one part of the body to another. And there is the seemingly oxymoronic *ambulatorium*, literally "walking place," used to refer to a dispensary or outpatient clinic, especially one in Russia (the word is from the Russian *amulatoriya*).

I Was About to Say That!

From the world of mysticism and magic, we get *ambulomancy*, or foretelling the future by walking around. It may sound silly, but it makes as much sense as any other type of *-mancy* (see page 634), and at least you get some exercise while doing it.

✳ **Ambulances haven't always been the flashing, noisy vehicles that they are today. The earliest ambulance, invented by the Anglo-Saxons around A.D. 900, was simply a cart with a hammock. This simple machine was used to forcibly move incurable patients—most likely people suffering from leprosy or severe psychological disorders. It wasn't until the 1400s that ambulances were used more like they are today, as emergency transport vehicles.**

Where Did It Come From?

Taxi: Manhattan resident Harry N. Allen coined this term in the early twentieth century by combining *taximeter*, the name for the device that calculates passenger fees in gas-powered cabs, with the French *cabriolet* (a horse-drawn carriage with two wheels and a single horse). Allen imported these taxicabs from France and started The New York Taxicab Co. to compete with the increasingly high fares being charged by the city's horse-drawn variety.

A to Z in the Animal Kingdom

Some words for animals are misleading. A mongoose isn't a goose (it's a furry, squirrellike mammal), a titmouse isn't a rodent (it's a bird), and a wolverine isn't a wolf (it's a weasellike creature—or, if you're a college sports fan, a University of Michigan athlete).

✳ ✳ ✳ ✳

Some names of animal species are simply odd collections of consonants and vowels. Here is an A to Z listing of animals that you may never have heard of, even if you consider yourself a devoted *philotherian* (animal lover):

* ✳ *aasvogel*—a South African vulture

* ✳ *bulbul*—a gregarious songbird

* ✳ *colocolo*—a wild South American cat

* ✳ *douroucouli*—a small South American nocturnal monkey

* ✳ *earwig*—a small, pestering insect

* ✳ *froghopper*—a leaping and spitting insect

bulbul

* ✳ *gowk*—a cuckoo bird

* ✳ *hellbender*—a North American salamander

* ✳ *iiwi*—a brightly colored Hawaiian bird

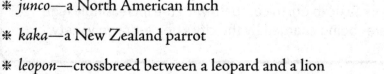

hellbender

* ✳ *junco*—a North American finch

* ✳ *kaka*—a New Zealand parrot

* ✳ *leopon*—crossbreed between a leopard and a lion

* ✳ *muntjac*—a small deer, also known as a barking deer

> *"In the long history of humankind (and animal kind, too) those who learned to collaborate and improvise most effectively have prevailed."*
> —CHARLES DARWIN

* *nightjar*—a nocturnal migratory bird

* *ouzel*—a blackbird

* *phoenicopter*—a flamingo

* *quokka*—a short-tailed wallaby

* *raad*—an electric catfish

raad

* *sunbittern*—a brightly colored South American bird

* *titi*—a South American arboreal monkey

* *urubu*—a black, tropical vulture

* *vireo*—an olive-gray, insectivorous American bird

* *wobbegong*—a carpet shark

* *xenurine*—a species of armadillo

* *yowie*—a little ewe

* *zyzzyva*—a South American weevil

xenurine

---

* ***Agrizoophobia*** is "fear of wild animals"—whether they are found in a zoo or not, one would presume! *Zoophobia* is the fear of all animals.

Where Did It Come From?

Ermine: Although the term now refers to a particularly smooth and beautiful fur often used for luxury coats and coverings, it's derived from the Latin word for weasel, *Armenius mus*, which was originally believed to be a rat from Armenia.

Words of Wisdom: Animals

✳   ✳   ✳   ✳

"Animals are such agreeable friends—they ask no questions, they pass no criticisms."

—George Eliot

"A dog is the only thing on earth that loves you more than he loves himself."

—Josh Billings

"I wish the bald eagle had not been chosen as the representative of our country; he is a bird of bad moral character; like those among men who live by sharping and robbing, he is generally poor, and often very lousy. The turkey is a much more respectable bird, and withal a true original native of America."

—Benjamin Franklin

"Until one has loved an animal, a part of one's soul remains unawakened."

—Anatole France

"Man is neither angel nor beast; and the misfortune is that he who would act the angel acts the beast."

—Blaise Pascal

"He who is cruel to animals becomes hard also in his dealings with men. We can judge the heart of a man by his treatment of animals."

—Immanuel Kant

"I like pigs. Dogs look up to us. Cats look down on us. Pigs treat us as equals."

—Winston Churchill

"Love the animals: God has given them the rudiments of thoughts and joy untroubled."

—Fyodor Dostoyevsky

Double-Barreled Words

Not all words with two sets of double letters are funny: Committee, coffee, success, and cheerfully don't particularly make us smile, but many words with two sets of double letters are odd enough to deserve a second look.

✳ ✳ ✳ ✳

IF YOU'RE FEELING *footloose*, see if these words can put some *pizzazz*—and maybe some *silliness*—into your writing.

✳ *boondoggle*—a useless undertaking; a wild goose chase

✳ *gobbledygook*—unclear language, nonsense

✳ *flibbertigibbet*—nonsense, balderdash

✳ *fuddy-duddy*—an old-fashioned, "square" person

✳ *hootenanny*—an informal performance by folksingers, or any rambunctious gathering

✳ *lillypilly*—an Australian evergreen tree

✳ *massiness*—the quality of being large

✳ *mollycoddle*—to indulge or be over-protective of someone

✳ *muumuu*—a loose-fitting dress

✳ *pettifogger*—someone who is deliberately obscure in speech

✳ *puttyroot*—a species of orchid

✳ *razzmatazz*—a showy exhibition or performance

✳ *riffraff*—unruly or uncouth people

✳ *skullduggery*—deception or trickery

✳ **Subbookkeeper is the only word in English that has four sets of double letters in a row. Cooee (a signal call of Australian Aborigines) is the shortest word with two sets of double letters.**

Victuals and Libations

If it's true that you are what you eat, then you might want to stay away from slimehead, toad in the hole, *or* bang belly . . . *except that the first is a fish we also call orange roughy, the second is sausage baked in batter, and the last one is a dessert. Looking at these and other examples, it's easy to see that the English language serves up a feast of interesting words for what—and how—we eat and drink.*

❋ ❋ ❋ ❋

YERD-HUNGER IS AN overwhelming desire for food, just as *dipsomania* is a craving for alcohol. A *libation* is a beverage—generally an alcoholic one, which would be tempting for someone who is *bibulous*, or fond of drinking. The foam on beer is called *barm*. Total abstention from alcohol is called *nephalism*. On the other hand, if you've had too much to drink you may be *temulent*, or intoxicated, or just a little *crapulous* (tipsy). When you've overimbibed, you might be *adrip, anchored at Sot's Bay, bosko absoluto, capernoited, impixlocated, incog, lappy, pruned, swozzled, whooshed,* or *zissified.*

Dig In

To *gourmandize* is to overeat: You might do this if you are suffering from *edacity*, or great hunger. To *englut* or to *ingurgitate* is to gulp excessively. When you hear your stomach growling, that's *borborygmus.* Following a Thanksgiving feast or
other *bouffage* (a filling meal) you might feel *farctate*, which is the state of having overeaten. *Lurcation, gulosity,* and *edacity* all

refer to gluttony. The opposite of a glutton is a *jejunator*, which is a person who is fasting. To break your fast, you *genticulate*, or eat breakfast. Still hungry? A *bever* is a snack between meals. To *degust* is to savor good food, and *abligurition* is the practice of spending lavishly for food. *Magirology* is the art or science of cooking. *Commensality* (*mensa* is the Latin word for "table") is the act of eating with other people. Something edible is called *comestible*, and a *knabble* is a bite or nibble of food. People who *fletcherize* chew their food at least 30 times before swallowing. To *masticate* is to chew.

Masticate on This

The mouth-filling word *brychomnivorous* describes someone who eats in a furious manner. Perhaps those people are worried about protecting themselves from *cleptobiosis*, or having their food plundered by others. *Polyphages* are those who eat many kinds of food, while *opsomaniacs* love a certain kind of food, to the point of near madness. *Equivores*, *erucivores*, *nucivores*, and *ranivores* have diets of horsemeat, caterpillars, nuts, and frogs, respectively. An onion eater is a *cipovore*, and an *alliaphage* dines on garlic. Newborn babies are *lactiphagous*, meaning that their diets consist solely of milk. Animals that feed on grasses are *ambivores* or *graminivores*. Finally, the proper—and only correct—pronunciation of *victuals*, which means "food" or "food provisions," is "vittles" (VIT-uhls). The *c* and *u* are not pronounced.

Bon appétit, and cheers!

＊ Legend has it that ancient Romans entered a room called a *vomitorium* to purge themselves after a feast. That's a myth. While Romans weren't averse to the occasional binge-and-purge, they didn't use the vomitorium for that purpose. A vomitorium was the passageway between the entrance to an amphitheater and the seats, so-called because the audience was "discharged" quickly through the passageway at the end of an event.

Chances Are

Do you consider yourself a lucky person? Perhaps you once won a lottery pool at work, or took home a few bucks after a card game with some old pals. Maybe you've even claimed a prize of some kind. Or maybe, like most of us, you've never been fortunate enough to win big. In any case, read on to discover the origins behind some of our luckiest—and unluckiest—language.

✳ ✳ ✳ ✳

BASEBALL LEGEND AND 1930s All-Star pitcher Lefty Gomez once said, "I'd rather be lucky than good." We all know there's good luck and bad luck, and some luck—like dumb luck or the luck of the draw—is just a matter of chance. Luckily the English language has its own treasure trove of "chance" words.

More than Just a John Cusack Movie

The word *serendipity*, used when one comes into fortunate circumstances by accident, is derived from the old Persian fairy tale "The Three Princes of Serendip," in which three royal figures keep making lucky discoveries during their travels. Today, serendipity comes in many forms, such as meeting an old friend by chance or finding the perfect parking spot on a crowded downtown street.

The discovery of vulcanization (a manufacturing process that makes rubber suitable for commercial use) is a famous example of serendipity: Tire magnate Charles Goodyear made this breakthrough when he accidentally left rubber and sulfur on a hot surface.

What Luck!

The *fortu* root—from Latin, meaning "chance, fate, or luck"—gives English the words *fortune* and *fortunate*, as well as *fortuity* and *fortuitous*; good writers, however, should be careful not to

> *"Shallow men believe in luck. Strong men believe in cause and effect."*
> —Ralph Waldo Emerson

interchange them. *Fortune* and *fortunate* always refer to something desirable; *fortuity* and *fortuitous* denote something that happens by chance or accident, whether favorable or not. A *fortuitous* encounter with someone to whom you owe a lot of money is probably not a *fortunate* encounter.

The Greek root *aleat,* meaning "chance or luck," is the source of several less-common words. An *aleatocracy* (*-cracy,* "rule") is a government in which the leaders are decided by chance, such as by drawing names from a hat. The adjective *aleatoric* refers to something that is done randomly, or by chance. Some art critics might characterize the paintings of Jackson Pollock as aleatoric because he splashed paint across his canvases.

Finally, the *tych* root—from Greek, meaning "accident or fate"—provides some unusual terms in English. *Dystychiphobia* (*dys-,* "bad"; *phob,* "fear") is a morbid fear of accidents, and *tychastics* is the study of accidents, especially industrial accidents. *Tychemortia* (*mort,* "death") means exactly what its parts would indicate: accidental death.

Chances are you won't always know the right word to describe your lucky situations. Let us hope that a dose of serendipity in those moments can help you find it.

✳ **Pseudoserendipity** (*pseudo-,* "false") refers to a fortunate discovery of something that you are seeking to find.

So Smart

You'll need plenty of book smarts to wrap your head around these outrageous and unusual words.

✳ ✳ ✳ ✳

WARNING: IF YOU suffer from *sophophobia* (the fear of learning), you're not going to like this list. But if you're a *polymath* (a person with encyclopedic knowledge), you may be familiar with these words already!

* *chrestomathic*—devoted to knowledge; also, teaching what is useful

* *daedalian*—extraordinarily inventive

* *invigilate*—to supervise an examination

* *isagoge*—introduction to a scholarly subject

* *logastellus*—a person whose love of words is greater than their knowledge of words

* *omnilegent*—having read extensively and exhaustively

* *opsimath*—a late learner; a person who begins to learn or study late in life

* *palladian*—relating to wisdom

* *peirastic*—experimental

* *perlustrate*—to examine thoroughly

* *phrontistery*—school; a place for thought or study

* *pysmatic*—questioning constantly

* *quodlibet*—scholastic debate over a subtle point

* *sciolist*—a pseudointellectual

Words of Wisdom: Knowledge

✳ ✳ ✳ ✳

"Knowledge which is acquired under compulsion obtains no hold on the mind."

—PLATO

"The time for acquiring knowledge is so short . . . that it is folly to expect it should be sufficient to make a child learned. The question ought not to be to teach it the sciences, but to give it a taste for them, and methods to acquire them when the taste shall be better developed."

—JEAN-JACQUES ROUSSEAU

"Some books are to be tasted, others to be swallowed, and some few to be chewed and digested."

—FRANCIS BACON

"Science is organized knowledge."

—HERBERT SPENCER

"Knowledge is proud that he has learned so much; Wisdom is humble that he knows no more."

—WILLIAM COWPER

"Knowledge is in every country the surest basis of public happiness."

—GEORGE WASHINGTON

"When you know a thing, to hold that you know it; and when you do not know a thing, to allow that you do not know it— this is knowledge."

—CONFUCIUS

"All our knowledge has its origins in our perceptions."

—LEONARDO DA VINCI

"Knowledge is the antidote to fear."

—RALPH WALDO EMERSON

Seeing Red

In 1969, anthropologist Brent Berlin and linguist Paul Kay published a study of color words in the languages of the world. They found that some languages had basic color words only for black and white. But of the languages that added only a third basic color word, it was always for the color red.

✳ ✳ ✳ ✳

T HE MOST LITERARY of *red* words must be *scarlet*. If Margaret Mitchell had consulted the following list before she penned *Gone with the Wind*, we might have read about "Cinnabar O'Hara." Nathaniel Hawthorne might have written *The Flammeous Letter*, and Sir Arthur Conan Doyle might have titled his first Sherlock Holmes story *A Study in Cramoisy*. Here's a list of more red words than you'll probably ever need:

✳ *cinnabar*—deep red; scarlet

✳ *coccineous*—bright red

✳ *coquelicot*—brilliant red; poppy red

✳ *cramoisy*—crimson

✳ *erythraean*—reddish

✳ *flammeous*—having the color of flame

✳ *haematic*—blood-colored

✳ *incarnadine*—carnation-colored; blood red

✳ *kermes*—brilliant red

✳ *lateritious*—brick red

✳ *madder*—red-orange

✳ *miniaceous*—reddish lead

✳ *minium*—vermilion

* *modena*—crimson

* *nacarat*—bright orange-red

* *phoeniceous*—bright scarlet

* *piceous*—reddish-black

* *ponceau*—poppy red

* *puccoon*—blood-root; dark red

* *puniceous*—bright or purplish-red

* *pyrrhous*—reddish; ruddy

* *rubious*—ruby red; rust-colored

* *rufous*—reddish; brownish-red

* *sanguineous*—blood-red

* *stammel*—bright red

* *testaceous*—brick red

* *vermeil*—bright red or vermilion

* *vinous*—deep red; burgundy

---

* **Beginning with the 2000 United States presidential election, the color red has been used to represent the Republican Party, and so-called "red states" are states that tend to favor the Republicans. "Blue states" are those that have a majority of Democrats.**

* *Erubescent* **is a rare word that means "blushing" or "reddening."**

Words of Wisdom: Style

✳ ✳ ✳ ✳

"The poor King Reignier, whose large style agrees not with the leanness of his purse."

—WILLIAM SHAKESPEARE

"Style is the dress of thought; a modest dress, neat but not gaudy, will true critics please."

—SAMUEL WESLEY

"The style is the man himself."

—GEORGE LOUIS LECLERC DE BUFFON

"In matters of style, swim with the current; in matters of principle, stand like a rock."

—THOMAS JEFFERSON

"One man's style must not be the rule of another's."

—JANE AUSTEN

"The proper words in the proper places are the true definition of style."

—JONATHAN SWIFT

"Only great minds can afford a simple style."

—STENDAHL

"I want to be seen here in my simple, natural, ordinary fashion, without straining or artifice."

—MICHEL DE MONTAIGNE

"He has found his style, when he cannot do otherwise."

—PAUL KLEE

Word Roots and Branches
The *-Ism* System

Let us begin with the words of Ferris Bueller, from the 1986 movie Ferris Bueller's Day Off: "'Isms' in my opinion are not good. A person should not believe in an 'ism,' he should believe in himself."

* * * *

ERRIS BUELLER, PLAYED by actor Matthew Broderick, objects to one of the definitions of the suffix *-ism*, that of denoting a system or theory of religious, political, or social practice. From this sense we get words like *communism, empiricism, fascism, socialism, Catholicism, heathenism, polytheism,* and *Protestantism.* The suffix can also be applied to types and classes of behavior, such as *barbarism, despotism, evangelism, fanaticism, hedonism, heroism,* and *jingoism.* Presumably Ferris wasn't objecting to these *-isms*; after all, he is well known for his *absenteeism.*

The *-ism* suffix comes from the French *-isme*, and ultimately the Latin *-ismus* and the Greek *-ismos*, where it forms nouns out of verbs. It does this in English as well, especially with verbs that end in *-ize*: *baptize/baptism, exorcize/exorcism, mechanize/mechanism, ostracize/ostracism,* and *plagiarize/plagiarism.*

In a similar fashion, *-ism* can attach itself to an adjective to form a noun denoting something that is characteristic of a language—like *Americanism, Briticism, colloquialism,* and *witticism.* This same process forms the names of intellectual and artistic schools of thought, as in *classicism, modernism,* and *poststructuralism.* Sometimes the suffix is used to denote something that is characteristic of or in the style of a person, either real or fictional—especially writers. Hence we have *Brontëism, malapropism, Menckenism, spoonerism,* and *Tolstoyism.*

Many *-isms* have been coined in a lighthearted manner, meant to be taken only semiseriously. Thus we get nonce coinages such as *devil-may-careism...or,* perhaps, *Buellerism).*

Future Words

The suffix -mancy is added to roots to form nouns that mean "divination or prophecy by X." So -mancy words are all about predicting the future. The suffix comes into English from the Old French -mancie, which in turn is from the Latin -mantia, and ultimately from the Greek -manteia.

❋   ❋   ❋   ❋

THE -MANCY WORDS in English—and there are over 200 of them—span the alphabet, from *abacomancy* (using funerary ashes to foretell the future) to *zygomancy* (divination by weights). Animals are a rich source of divining words: *aeluromancy* (prophecy by observing a cat jumping), *arachnomancy* (interpreting the future through the behavior of spiders), *apantomancy* (prophecy through a chance meeting with a rabbit, an eagle, etc.), *hippomancy* (prophecy using horses), and *hyomancy* (divination using wild pigs).

We associate some *-mancy* words with fortune-tellers: *astragalomancy* involves the throwing of dice or bones to divine the future, and *cartomancy* uses playing cards or tarot cards. *Chiromancy* is another term for palm reading. With *christallomancy*, a psychic gazes into a crystal ball. *Demonomancy*, which calls upon demons for prophecies, is also known as "black magic." Other *-mancy* words include:

* *aeromancy*—using birds, clouds, or weather phenomena

* *alectoromancy*—using a rooster and grains of corn

* *aleuromancy*—using flour

* *anthomancy*—using flowers

* *anthropomancy*—using human entrails

* *astromancy*—by the stars; astrology

* *austromancy*—using the wind

* *bibliomancy*—using books or Bible verses
* *brontomancy*—using thunder
* *catoptromancy*—using a mirror
* *ceneromancy*—using ashes
* *cephalomancy*—by boiling an animal's head (usually a donkey)
* *ceromancy*—by dropping melted wax into water
* *enoptromancy*—using mirrors
* *gastromancy*—using a crystal ball
* *graptomancy*—using handwriting
* *gyromancy*—by walking in a circle until you fall down
* *hematomancy*—using blood
* *ichnomancy*—using footprints
* *macromancy*—using the largest object in the area
* *mecanomancy*—using sleep
* *oenomancy*—using wine
* *oneiromancy*—using dreams
* *onomancy*—using names or the letters in a name
* *ophiomancy*—using snakes
* *ossomancy*—using bones
* *pyromancy*—using fire
* *rhabdomancy*—using a divining rod
* *scatomancy*—using feces
* *tyromancy*—using cheese
* *uromancy*—using urine

Pain and Suffering

The English language isn't hurting for words pertaining to pain and suffering. It offers many interesting words that describe our afflictions, agonies, distresses, torments, and woes.

✳   ✳   ✳   ✳

ENGLISH SUFFERS FROM no shortage of interesting "pain" words containing the Greek *algia/algo* root. *Abdominalgia* and *cephalalgia* are fancy words for a bellyache and headache, respectively. If you're suffering from *odontalgia*, you have a toothache, but if your teeth hurt on an airplane because of lowered air pressure, then you've got *aerodontalgia*. *Ombrosalgia* is the pain some people experience during rainy weather. With *pantalgia* you're suffering from pain all over. *Algophobia* is a morbid fear or dread of any sort of pain, and *algophilia* refers to taking pleasure in the pain of others. A German word that has entered the English lexicon also carries this meaning of pleasure taken in the suffering of other people: *schadenfreude* (SHAH-den-froy-dah).

Not the "Suffer in Silence" Type

We articulate emotional pain and suffering using the Latin *dol/dolor* root. Besides the familiar *condolence*, there is the musical term *doloroso*, which indicates a passage that should be played mournfully, and *dolor capitas*, or extreme mental suffering. *Dolorology* is a medical specialty concerned with the study and treatment of pain. A *dolorifuge* is something that reduces or eliminates grief and sorrow. The route that Jesus took through Jerusalem on the way to his crucifixion is called the *Via Dolorosa* (*via* is Latin for "road").

Another productive word part for denoting pain is the Greek suffix *-odyn*. An *anodyne* is a medicine or remedy that relieves pain, and its related form *anodynia* refers to the absence of pain in a previously inflamed area of the body. If you're afraid of pain, you have *odynophobia*.

It's Your Body

Most parts of the human body have a name—even those parts you might usually think of only in informal terms. Learn these names, and you'll know yourself as well as the back of your hand—which is called the opisthenar, *by the way.*

✳ ✳ ✳ ✳

✳ *acronyx*—an ingrown nail

✳ *antecubitis*—the front of the elbow

✳ *calcaneus*—the heel

✳ *coccyx*—the tailbone, the final section of the vertebral column

✳ *eponychium*—the cuticle of a finger or toe

✳ *hallux*—the big toe

✳ *humerus*—the long bone from the elbow to the shoulder

✳ *hyponychium*—the "quick" of a fingernail or toenail

✳ *lunula*—the half-moon or crescent-shaped pale area at the base of a fingernail or toenail

✳ *minimus*—the little finger or toe

✳ *nates*—buttocks

✳ *olecranon*—the bony tip of the elbow

✳ *oxter*—armpit; also *axilla*

✳ *phalanges*—the bones that form the fingers and toes

✳ *popliteal*—pertaining to the hollow behind the knee

✳ *tarsus*—ankle

✳ *whirlbone*—kneecap; also *hurlbone*

Feeling Groovy

Happy. Sad. Bored. Scared. Angry. When it comes to feelings and emotions, that's just the tip of the iceberg. The list of emotions people feel on a daily basis is longer than you might imagine. Just take a look at this list—its breadth and scope will likely leave you a bit verklempt *(overcome with emotion).*

✳   ✳   ✳   ✳

✳ *abulia*—loss or lack of will or motivation; also *aboulia*

✳ *alexithymia*—difficulty in experiencing, expressing, and describing emotional responses

✳ *anhedonia*—inability to experience happiness

✳ *anomie*—alienation and purposelessness resulting from a lack of standards and values

✳ *atrabilarian*—affected with melancholy, which the ancients attributed to black bile; also *atrabilious*

✳ *callosity*—lack of feeling or capacity for emotion; callousness

✳ *cathexis*—concentration of mental and emotional energy on a particular person, idea, or object, often to an unhealthy degree

✳ *dysphoric*—depressed, anxious, irritable, restless

✳ *erotomania*—a delusion in which a person believes wrongly that another person, often a stranger or famous person, is in love with him or her

✳ *eupeptic*—cheerful

> *"Any emotion, if it is sincere, is involuntary."*
> —MARK TWAIN

* *euthymia*—the normal, nondepressed, positive state

* *flebile*—filled with grief or sadness; mournful

* *furibund*—frenzied, raging

* *hebetude*—lethargy, dullness

* *hypomanic*—literally "below manic"; persistently elated or irritated, energetic and hyperactive, but not out of control

* *flebile*—mournful; filled with grief or sadness

* *ignavy*—sluggish; slothful

* *labile*—subject to constantly shifting emotions, possibly indicating instability

* *momurdotes*—an archaic word for the sulks

* *pruriginous*—irritable or uneasy

* *rhathymia*—cheerful and optimistic

* *thymogenic*—brought about by emotion

* *tracasserie*—a state of annoyance

* *wabbit*—exhausted

* *wraw*—angry, vexed, wrathful

---

* **Pathogamy is the study of emotions or of the physical expressions caused by emotions.**

Chapter 16

A Passing Phrase

The Comedown

Your new house is beautiful! It's really too bad that it's right next to the freeway.

✳   ✳   ✳   ✳

I N **ANESIS,** A concluding sentence, clause, or phrase is used to diminish, or undercut, the importance of what has come previously. The word is from the Greek for "loosening" or "abating." Anesis is the opposite of *epitasis.* Typically with anesis, a lofty or dignified statement introduces the text, and the conclusion blasts that idea to shreds.

Here's an example of anesis from the Bible, found in 2 Kings: "Now Naaman, captain of the host of the king of Syria, was a great man with his master, and honourable, because by him the Lord had given deliverance unto Syria: he was also a mighty man in valour, but he was a leper" (5:1 KJV). The contrast between Naaman's capability and his physical health sets up a tension to be resolved in the course of the narrative.

I Love You...Like a Brother

Another example of anesis involves the softening-up before one partner attempts to dump another: "You're really smart and very attractive, and we've had a lot of great times together. But I think we should just be friends." The listener might wish that the preliminary compliments had been cut short!

Well, That Was Disappointing

Anesis is allied to *anticlimax*, in which a buildup is suddenly reversed, the rug pulled out from under a reader's expectations, as in this Woody Allen quote: "Not only is there no God, but try getting a plumber on weekends."

An extreme form of anticlimax is *bathos*, a word coined by poet Alexander Pope to indicate an attempt at high-flown sentiment that collapses through the incompetence of its execution—the poetic equivalent of a pratfall.

The opposite of anesis is *epitasis*—"stretching"—in which a concluding sentence or clause restates and reinforces (amplifies) what has come before. Imagine a parent confronting a refractory child at the dinner table: "I worked hard to earn the money to buy this food, and I took a lot of trouble to prepare it as a healthful meal. So now I want you to eat it. All of it." "All of it" is an epitasis.

✳ Baseball historian John Thorn pointed out a purposeful (and clever) use of anesis in the real world: the decision of Major League Baseball's Anaheim Angels to change their name to the Los Angeles Angels of Anaheim. By moving "Anaheim" to the end of the name, the team was able to capitalize on the use of "Los Angeles" to establish its presence in L.A.'s larger media market.

A Beastly Moral Tale

From Aesop to George Orwell, writers have used stories about animals to teach morality lessons. Most people would call these stories fables, after the collection we call Aesop's Fables, *but both those and Orwell's novel* Animal Farm *are more properly called* **apologues.**

❇ ❇ ❇ ❇

AN APOLOGUE GENERALLY features animals or inanimate objects behaving in ways that should serve as a lesson to readers. "The Tortoise and the Hare" is a classic example of one of Aesop's apologues: A tortoise, tired of being mocked by a hare, challenges him to a race. The overly confident hare stops to take a nap and wakes to find that the tortoise is about to cross the finish line, and the hare has lost. The moral that most people remember from this story is "Slow and steady wins the race." Today, we might also hear it expressed as "You snooze, you lose." This moral has shown astonishing longevity, considering the story was probably first told more than 2,500 years ago!

Animal Farm, published in 1945, is a lengthier (and grimmer) apologue. Generally considered a treatise against Stalin-era communism, the book shows what happens when a farmyard of animals starts a revolution against their leaders (the pigs), who are corrupt and indifferent to the needs of the other animals. The line most often remembered from the book is, "All animals are created equal, but some are more equal than others." Orwell's moral may not be as easily reduced to a pithy statement as Aesop's morals are, but it is clear that he was trying to teach a lesson about how people and government should—and shouldn't—interact.

All Apologues Are Fables, But Not All Fables Are Apologues

What distinguishes apologue from fable, parable, or allegory is a fuzzy line at best. In very broad terms, a *fable* is the umbrella category under which the others fall: a tale told to teach a lesson. An apologue is such a tale using nonhuman characters, while a *parable* is such a tale involving human characters. *Allegory* is slightly more complex, being a rhetorical device that uses extended metaphor or symbolism within a story, but a story using the device of allegory can also be either a parable or, as with *Animal Farm,* an apologue.

"Appearances often are deceiving."

—AESOP

"Do not count your chickens before they are hatched."

—AESOP

"A crust eaten in peace is better than a banquet partaken in anxiety."

—AESOP

"People often grudge others what they cannot enjoy themselves."

—AESOP

"Any excuse will serve a tyrant."

—AESOP

"It is thrifty to prepare today for wants of tomorrow."

—AESOP

Where Did It Come From?

Fib: This word originated during the fifteenth century, and it was associated with the word *fable,* which could mean both an interesting story and a lie. A couple hundred years later, a small lie became commonly known as a "fibble-fable." The word eventually was shortened to fib—and that's no lie.

Words of Wisdom: Forgiveness

✳ ✳ ✳ ✳

"Children begin by loving their parents; as they grow older they judge them; sometimes they forgive them."

—Oscar Wilde

"They who forgive most shall be most forgiven."

—William Blake

"To err is human, to forgive divine."

—Alexander Pope

"He that cannot forgive others, breaks the bridge over which he himself must pass if he would ever reach heaven, for everyone has need to be forgiven."

—George Herbert

"The heart of a mother is a deep abyss at the bottom of which you will always find forgiveness."

—Honoré de Balzac

"Good, to forgive;
Best, to forget!"

—Robert Browning

"Only the brave know how to forgive."

—Laurence Sterne

"Forgive your enemies, but never forget their names."

—John F. Kennedy

"The public seldom forgive twice."

—Johann Kaspar Lavater

"We pardon to the extent that we love."

—François, Duc de La Rochefoucauld

Payback Time

The most common meaning of to recompense *is "to make amends for some loss, or to compensate for it." But in addition to this financial or economic meaning,* **recompenser** *also has a literary meaning: making up for something in the first half of a statement with something in the second.*

✳ ✳ ✳ ✳

THE WORD COMES from the Old French *recompenser,* which means "to do a favor to requite a loss." But, as is so often the case, there is also a Greek term for the same figure of speech: *antanagoge,* meaning "leading" or "bringing up."

For example, consider the familiar saying "When life hands you lemons, make lemonade." The first half is negative, but the second half is positive. The goal of recompenser is to rhetorically balance a negative statement with a positive one.

Finding something positive in a negative situation can be a way to soften unpleasant truths: "I was laid off today, so now I'll be able to spend more time with my family." Sometimes it can be a way of preempting blame for a mistake: "Yes, I got lost, but at least we got to explore a new neighborhood."

This sort of balancing act will be familiar to anyone who has read or written student or employee evaluations: "Dudley is regularly inattentive, but his written exercises show real promise"; "Bob is late for meetings, but he always comes prepared."

The term *recompenser* can also apply to a strategy in argument wherein one party, unable to defend against an accusation, turns around and accuses the accuser of wrongdoing. This strategy is also known as the *tu quoque* reply, from the Latin for "you also" or "you're another." *Recrimination* is a common word for the same thing, and if such tactics are left to simmer long enough, they can morph into mudslinging, feuds, and revenge. Payback can be satisfying, but it can also turn ugly very quickly.

On the One Hand, On the Other

Antithesis: *It can't be wrong if it sounds so right.*

✳ ✳ ✳ ✳

ONE OF THE most common patterns in writing is *antithesis*, in which antonyms (opposites) or contrasting words are paired. This device comes from a Greek word meaning "set against" or "oppose." It suggests pitting one opposite against another—a balancing act—and rather than merely juxtaposing contradictory words, it usually makes use of parallel sentence structure. (See page 660 for more on parallelism.)

One of the most famous examples is Neil Armstrong's statement as he set foot on the moon in 1969, "That's one small step for a man, one giant leap for mankind," opposing in parallel both *small step* and *giant leap,* and *a man* and *mankind.* (Interestingly, the quote has often been misstated as it's been handed down over the years. It is often quoted as, "That's one small step for man, one giant leap for mankind"—probably because that sounds more parallel in structure.)

Charles Dickens uses antithesis to great effect in the opening lines of *A Tale of Two Cities*: "It was the best of times, it was the worst of times, it was the age of wisdom, it was the age of foolishness, it was the epoch of belief, it was the epoch of incredulity, it was the season of Light, it was the season of Darkness, it was the spring of hope, it was the winter of despair..." *Best/ worst, wisdom/foolishness, belief/incredulity, light/darkness,* and *spring of hope/winter of despair*: Each parallel pair of antonyms makes the use of antithesis more effective. (This passage is also an example of *anaphora*—see page 676.)

Are True Politics the Antithesis of True Patriotism?

As the Republican candidate for the presidency in 1964, Barry Goldwater notably proclaimed: "Extremism in the defense of liberty is no vice... moderation in the pursuit of justice is no virtue." *Extremism* and *moderation* are balanced against each other, along with *vice* and *virtue*. *Liberty* and *justice*, however, are parallel, but certainly not opposed. It is not unusual to employ direct parallelism and antithesis in the same sentence. Patrick Henry's "Give me liberty, or give me death," for example, has the parallel uses of *give* as well as the antitheses *liberty* and *death*.

Antithesis is familiar in stock expressions as well, found in "rags to riches" and "easy come, easy go." It is also common in advertising: "Everybody doesn't like something, but nobody doesn't like Sara Lee." The balance of opposites helps make the phrase or sentence stick in the memory.

The term itself can also be used to indicate a comparison of opposites: Novelist William Styron wrote, "The madness of depression is the antithesis of violence."

The Yin to Their Yang

Fictional characters in books and movies can also be understood as antitheses to each other: Snow White and the Evil Queen; J. K. Rowling's Albus Dumbledore and Lord Voldemort. This works for the writer because the extreme opposites—good versus evil in these cases—set up a conflict that the writing can exploit in the action of the narrative.

Where Did It Come From?

Villain: If you used this word in feudal England you would have been referring to a poor but honest person who worked as a serf on a noble's estate. The name comes from the Latin *villanus* ("farm servant") and evolved to mean a person capable of base acts. Its first recorded use to refer to a dastardly character is in an 1822 play by Charles Lamb.

I'm Not Meek, I'm Mild-Mannered!

If you don't find this article fascinating, you're crazy. Or maybe you just have discerning taste.

✳   ✳   ✳   ✳

IT'S ENTIRELY HUMAN to consider your own faults to be virtues in disguise while judging other people's faults to be, well, faults. This has been going on for a long time—even the ancient Greeks had a word for it: *paradiastole* (par-uh-dy-uh-STOL-ay, from the Greek *para*, "next to" + *diastole*, "difference"), meaning "using a positive term to disguise a negative trait."

Anal Retentive vs. Detail-Oriented

There are many classic examples or paradiastole: She's scrawny, but I'm slim. Those kids are weird; my kid is quirky. He's loud; she's assertive. Some people battling for an independent homeland are terrorists; others are freedom fighters. Like euphemism, paradiastole rephrases a negative concept. But while euphemism exchanges a negative term for a neutral one, paradiastole suggests a positive way of seeing. (See page 64 for more on euphemism.)

There are a few types of writing where extremes of paradiastole are common. One is the family holiday letter, composed as a reflection of the year to share with family and friends. A family member is unemployed? The letter may describe her as "between jobs." Not much of interest to report at the close of a long, boring year? How about calling it "a peaceful, quiet year in which we've been able to take a break from life's whirlwind of activity"?

Don't Speak Ill of the Dead . . . Even If They Deserve It

Another form of writing in which paradiastole is practically required is in obituaries. To avoid speaking ill of the dead, an obit writer might reinvent a stingy, curmudgeonly, antisocial old lady as "a no-nonsense, independent woman who wasn't afraid to speak her mind." In the same way, a notorious rake might be described as having had "an eye for the ladies."

In these cases, vices are recast as virtues. But paradiastole can also be used not to deceive, but simply to present the world in a more positive way, to *reframe* it. *Reframing* is a simpler name for paradiastole. Self-help and self-esteem books often recommend that people reframe their images of themselves. For example, instead of labeling yourself "a chronic procrastinator," consider yourself to be "working on self-scheduling." Try reframing "the worst year of my life" into "a challenging time."

The ancient Greeks may not have had the modern mania for self-help, but they had the same inclination to make negatives into positives, and they gave us a useful word for it.

Where Did It Come From?

Supercilious: This word applies to people who think they are better than their peers, showing haughty disdain. Interestingly, the word's origin perfectly describes the actions of these very people, with chins raised and eyebrows lifted. The Latin word *supercilium* can be broken down into two words that mean "eyebrow" and "pride."

Only a Dramatization

Read on for more information on two common word endings that you may or may not have known were related. If you don't currently realize their connection, we're sure you'll have a realization by the time you're done reading this article.

✳ ✳ ✳ ✳

THE SUFFIX -IZE is added to nouns or adjectives to create verbs, usually meaning "to make something X." The suffix comes from the late Latin *-izare*, and ultimately from the Greek *-izein*. In English, the suffix *-ization* then replaces the *-ize* in the verb to create a noun denoting the action of the verb.

So, for example:

* A *monopoly* (noun, 1534) is the exclusive ability to sell a commodity.

* To *monopolize* (verb, 1601) is to corner the market.

* And *monopolization* (noun, 1727) is the action or process of cornering the market.

There are hundreds of such English words from Greek and Latin, or modern creations using the Greek and Latin roots. A small sampling includes: *baptize, canonize, cauterize, familiarize, fertilize, harmonize, nationalize, systematize, tantalize,* and *vocalize.* The suffix can also mean "to follow a particular practice or process," as in *agonize, brutalize, dogmatize, philosophize,* and *theorize.* There is a corresponding *-ization* noun for most of these *-ize* verbs. (There even is a *baptization,* but it is obsolete, having been victimized by the much more common *baptism.*)

With -*Ize* Open to the World

But *-ize* and *-ization* can be added to nonclassical roots as well, and to people's names or the names of nations and ethnic groups, meaning "to act or speak (like that person or group)." Many of these are nonce (one-time) coinages or intended to be somewhat humorous. On the serious side, we've got words like *bowdlerize* ("to censor," after Thomas Bowdler, who in 1818 published an expurgated, "family-friendly" collection of Shakespeare consisting of 24 of the Bard's plays), *Americanize*, *Anglicize*, and *galvanize* ("to stimulate," after Luigi Galvani, who discovered in 1771 that he could get dead muscle tissue to twitch by applying an electrical current to it).

The suffix is also used in chemistry to denote "adding to, impregnating with," as in *alkalize, oxidize,* and *ionize.*

We also see the suffix creatively exploited to characterize contemporary life in words like *McDonaldization* (turning an industry into one characterized by low-skilled workers, low pay, and high employee turnover), *organ-donor-ization* (the process by which a failing company purchases a successful competitor and then replaces its own executives with the acquired ones, as in "Disney underwent *organ-donor-ization* when it bought Pixar"), and *purpleization* (increasing the Democratic vote in traditionally Republican districts, or vice versa).

Where Did It Come From?

Plagiarize: To plagiarize is to use the writings or ideas of someone else as your own. *Plagiarize* comes from the Latin *plagiarius,* meaning "kidnapper." Yep, just like your English teachers always told you, it's serious business!

Lend Me Your Ears

The literary term **metonymy** *comes from an ancient Greek word meaning "change of name," and that comes pretty close to explaining the function of metonymy today.*

✳ ✳ ✳ ✳

GENERALLY CONSIDERED A type of metaphor (although some scholars say that it is distinct from metaphor), metonymy is a rhetorical device that replaces one thing with something closely associated with it—like using "Washington" to refer to the U.S. government, or "the Crown" to refer to the British government. The city of Washington is not a part of the federal government, but as the United States' capital city and the location where most federal business takes place, it is so intrinsically associated with the government that it functions well as a vibrant, evocative stand-in. Likewise, the British government does not have a literal crown, but the monarch does. That crown has come to symbolize the power of the government as a whole.

A Two-Way Street

When a news headline reads "White House Reports Million Jobs Lost," obviously the building is not doing the reporting. Rather, someone who works in the building has reported the job losses. But people also use "the White House" to mean the entirety of the executive branch of the U.S. government (not just those who work in the building itself). When headlines blare "Congress Battles White House Over Reform," for example, it's not just the workers from one building who are fighting, but the entire executive branch.

In this way we can see how metonymy works in two directions: A larger thing can represent a smaller thing (the White House standing in for a single employee), or a smaller thing can represent a larger thing (the White House standing in for the executive branch).

But I've Grown So Attached to Them

Misunderstood metonymy can lead to some strange images. Consider, for instance, Mark Antony's words from Shakespeare's *Julius Caesar:* "Friends, Romans, countrymen, lend me your ears." Does anyone from Mark Antony's audience actually remove their ears and pass them up to the speaker? It's unlikely. The ears in this case are metaphorical—actually metonymical. Antony is asking not for literal ears from his audience, but for their focus and attention.

Metonymy is more common in general speech than people usually realize, but it's useful to know how to use it deliberately, as well as how to recognize it when you hear it used by others. After all, it would make for a rather awkward—and perhaps painful—social situation if you ever felt you had to actually pass someone your ears.

---

* A device related to metonymy is *synecdoche,* in which a part of something stands in for the whole of it (or the other way around). You can read more about synecdoche on page 671.

* Encompassing approximately 55,000 square feet, the White House has 132 rooms, including 35 bathrooms and 16 family and guest rooms. It is the world's only private residence of a head of state that is open to the public.

* The Cullinan Diamond is the largest diamond ever found. Unearthed in South Africa in 1905, this 3,100-carat monster was cut into several stones that are still part of the British crown jewels.

The Best Entry in the Whole Book!

Any time we exaggerate to make something seem worse—or better ("I feel like a million bucks")—than it really is, we're using **hyperbole,** *a conscious overstatement of facts for dramatic or comedic effect.*

✳ ✳ ✳ ✳

FOLKSINGER CHRISTINE LAVIN wrote a song called "Katy Says Today Is the Best Day of My Whole Entire Life." She explains in the next line: "Katy is three years old." Children's author Judith Viorst wrote a book called *Alexander and the Terrible, Horrible, No Good, Very Bad Day.* Like many children, the fictional Katy and Alexander are given to hyperbole, or exaggeration. *Hyperbole,* like most rhetorical terms, comes to us from ancient Greek, and back then it meant pretty much what it means in English today: "excess" or "exaggeration."

Hyperbole is often used in everyday speech, such as when we refer to someone as "older than dirt" or say, "this box weighs a ton." Any parent of a teenager will be familiar with the "I'm the only kid in the entire school, maybe the entire world, without a [insert trendy object here]!" speech, or perhaps the "Everyone else's parents let them [insert forbidden activity here]!" lament. Hyperbole isn't meant to be taken literally (except maybe when uttered by 3-year-olds). Even a teen knows there are others in the world in a similar (or worse) state of deprivation.

Hyperbole—both the word and the rhetorical device—has been used for a very long time. Shakespeare used it in *Macbeth* in Lady Macbeth's famous line, "all the perfumes of Arabia will not sweeten this little hand," and so have many other authors, down to the present day. In fact, even the Greek philosopher Aristotle stated that hyperbole has a "juvenile character" and is most often used by people when they are angry (or vehement). In other words, children in ancient Greece must also have had terrible, horrible, no-good, very bad days.

Words of Wisdom: Memory

✳ ✳ ✳ ✳

"It's a poor sort of memory that only works backwards."
—Lewis Carroll

"Memorable sentences are memorable on account of some single irradiating word."
—Alexander Smith

"Many a man fails as an original thinker simply because his memory is too good."
—Friedrich Nietzsche

"There is no hopelessness so sad as that of early youth, when the soul is made up on wants, and has no long memories, no super-added life in the life of others."
—George Eliot

"Memory in youth is active and easily impressible; in old age it is comparatively callous to new impressions, but still retains vividly those of earlier years."
—Charlotte Brontë

"Fond Memory brings the light of other days around me."
—Thomas Moore

"How vast a memory has Love!"
—Alexander Pope

"A liar should have a good memory."
—Quintilian

"A great memory does not make a philosopher, any more than a dictionary can be called a grammar."
—John Henry Cardinal Newman

By the Way...

As any traveler knows, sometimes prompt and speedy arrival at a firm destination is critical above all else. But at other times, the stops and side excursions made along the way hold just as much importance, and often bring unexpected rewards and pleasures. A similar truth can be seen in writing and literature.

✻ ✻ ✻ ✻

An EXCURSUS (FROM the Latin *excurrere*, meaning "to run out of") is an anecdote or episode inserted into a work. It is usually a digression, but it could also be backstory or even a thematically linked element with an importance to the main work to be revealed at a later time.

Some works are particularly notable for digressiveness. Robert Burton's *The Anatomy of Melancholy* is one of those "great baggy monsters" of the seventeenth century in which the writer pours everything he or she knows into the text, with endless notes, digressing incessantly into side topics in an almost stream-of-consciousness style.

(Samuel Johnson was fond of Burton's *Anatomy*, by the way. James Boswell records Johnson as having said that it was "the only book that ever took him out of bed two hours sooner than he wished to rise." But I digress....)

As I Was Saying...

Influenced heavily by Burton, Laurence Sterne's *The Life and Opinions of Tristram Shandy, Gentleman* also makes deliberate use of digression. While the book is meant to be about the title character's "life and opinions," the digressions are such that Tristram has not yet been born by the third volume of the nine-volume book! In Jonathan Swift's *A Tale of a Tub*, the digressions form a large portion of the book and incorporate most of the political satire. In fact, the author devotes an entire chapter, Section VII, to a digression in praise of digressions, for comic effect.

> *"Digressions, incontestably, are the sunshine—they are the life, the soul of reading; take them out of this book for instance—you might as well take the book along with them."*
> —LAURENCE STERNE

(Swift was so adept at wielding irony that some critics struggle with *A Tale of a Tub* to determine what he meant ironically and what he meant satirically. The bitter ironies are more obvious in "A Modest Proposal," in which he advocates that the English eat the children of the Irish, since their policies are already effectively consuming the population. But again, I digress.)

Now, Where Was I?

Early examples of excursus are the satyr plays of Greek drama, in which actors portraying satyrs performed in comic burlesque after a sequence of tragedies. Their pranks and off-color jokes, which had nothing to do with the plays themselves, were intended to lighten the somber mood of the audience. Similar use of digression is found in Shakespeare's tragedies, where the "fool" characters merely provide comic relief.

There are works in which the reader can find as much satisfaction in the assorted digressions as in the main text. One modern example of this is William Goldman's *The Princess Bride*, which is filled with footnotes of his supposed abridgment of the book from a (wholly fictional) original. Another example is Douglas Adams's *The Hitchhiker's Guide to the Galaxy*, which is packed full of meta-commentary on and outtakes from *The Guide* itself.

Metaphorically Speaking

When it comes to comparing two things that are separate and distinct, the English language has many useful devices from which to choose. One of the most important of these devices is detailed here.

✳ ✳ ✳ ✳

AN *ANALOGY* IS an identification of resemblances in two things that are otherwise unalike. A ***metaphor*** is a form of analogy. While analogies generally use logic to demonstrate how things are alike by pointing out shared characteristics, metaphors specifically offer a visual image that reinforces meaning. (For more on analogies, see page 684.)

In the narrowest definition, a metaphor is an implied comparison. This is how a metaphor differs from a *simile*, in which a comparison is made explicitly. Thus, William Blake's "When the stars threw down their spears, / And watered heaven with their tears" uses metaphor, and Lord Byron's "She walks in beauty, like the night" uses a simile. As a general rule, similes employ the words *like* or *as*, and metaphors do not. (For more on similes, see page 94.)

William Blake

Metaphors Are Everywhere

Metaphor is one of the great tools of poetry, but it is commonly embedded in prose writing and everyday speech as well. Fresh metaphors breathe life into staid writing. Sometimes metaphors spring to mind; other times a writer must dig deep to bring one to life.

> *"The folly of mistaking a paradox for a discovery, a metaphor for a proof, a torrent of verbiage for a spring of capital truths, and oneself for an oracle, is inborn in us."*
> —PAUL VALÉRY

English is full of *dead* or *buried* metaphors—metaphors that may once have been fresh, thoughtful, and arresting but have become so commonplace through repetition that no one thinks of them as metaphorical anymore. ("Buried metaphor" is itself a metaphor—see?)

We speak, for example, of "the mouth of a river," the place where it flows into a lake or sea, originally because of its resemblance to an open mouth. But now we use this terminology without recognizing that we are speaking metaphorically, that these words were once intended to conjure an image.

Metaphorical Mishaps

It is usually best for writers to hit a metaphor quickly and move on. Drawing metaphors out into extended metaphors can begin to look silly.

Another hazard to be mindful of is the mixed metaphor, in which a speaker or writer cobbles together two metaphors, leaping from one association to another without regard to consistency, resulting in a confusing mash-up of images. An unfortunate mixed metaphor can take the wind out of the sails of a sentence, making a train wreck out of it. (You see what we did there?)

Every Tick Should Have a Tock

Language, like music, has patterns and balance. And, like music, language has rules about what kinds of patterns are acceptable. An abrupt change in pattern can leave a reader feeling disoriented, distracted, and puzzled. One source of balance in writing is **parallelism.**

✳ ✳ ✳ ✳

FAILING TO MAINTAIN parallel structure is often a grammatical error. Words or phrases joined with a conjunction must be the same part of speech and/or share the same form.

Mind the Pattern

Thus, a sentence like "They enjoy swimming in the river and to run in the forest" is flat-out incorrect. *Swimming* is a gerund, while *to run* is an infinitive. Grammatically, this is like putting a square peg in a round hole. (The sentence should read as follows: "They enjoy swimming in the river and running in the forest." Much better, right?)

Some changes in patterns aren't grammatical errors. An author could write, "I have two hands, two feet, two ears, and a pair of eyes." But the sudden break in an established pattern leaves the reader with unfulfilled expectations, as if a melody didn't come back to the expected resolution with its home note. The author has thrown away a chance to use rhythm and expectation to create a satisfying conclusion.

Unparalleled Parallelism Usage

When used deliberately as a literary device, however, parallelism creates a pleasant combination of repetition of form and novelty of content. Here are some famous examples of effective parallelism:

* Sergio Leone used parallelism in the title of his 1966 film *The Good, the Bad and the Ugly*.

* The Declaration of Independence makes use of parallelism, saying of the king of Great Britain: "He has plundered our seas, ravaged our coasts, burned our towns, and destroyed the lives of our people."

* In traditional wedding vows, couples committing their lives to each other pledge to endure "for better or for worse, for richer, for poorer, in sickness and in health."

* In his historic Gettysburg Address, Abraham Lincoln entreated Americans to resolve "that government of the people, by the people, for the people, shall not perish from the earth."

* In Shakespeare's *Macbeth*, the witches use parallelism (along with rhyme) to emphasize the ingredients in their ghoulish brew: "Eye of newt and toe of frog. Wool of bat and tongue of dog."

Hopefully you enjoyed reading this article and to learn more about parallelism. (And hopefully that sentence just made you do a double take.)

Where Did It Come From?

Honeymoon: This word was first used to describe the love of a newly married couple—sweet as honey, but apt to wane like the moon sometime in the future. Sad but true.

Words of Wisdom from Abraham Lincoln

✳ ✳ ✳ ✳

✳ "Am I not destroying my enemies when I make friends of them?"

✳ "America will never be destroyed from the outside. If we falter and lose our freedoms, it will be because we destroyed ourselves."

✳ "A house divided against itself cannot stand."

✳ "Avoid popularity if you would have peace."

✳ "Books serve to show a man that those original thoughts of his aren't very new at all."

✳ "Fourscore and seven years ago our fathers brought forth on this continent, a new nation, conceived in Liberty, and dedicated to the proposition that all men are created equal."

✳ "How many legs does a dog have if you call the tail a leg? Four. Calling a tail a leg doesn't make it a leg."

✳ "I don't like that man. I must get to know him better."

✳ "You have to do your own growing no matter how tall your grandfather was."

✳ "Give me six hours to chop down a tree and I will spend the first four sharpening the axe."

✳ "Common looking people are the best in the world; that is the reason the Lord makes so many of them."

✳ "My concern is not whether God is on our side; my greatest concern is to be on God's side, for God is always right."

✳ "Whatever you are, be a good one."

Word Roots and Branches
It's a *Mega*-Prefix

It weighs in at only four letters, but mega- *is a really big prefix.*

✳ ✳ ✳ ✳

THE PREFIX MEGA- comes from the Greek *-megas*, meaning "great." It's used in many English words, both technical and colloquial, to mean "big," as in *megafauna* ("big animals"; used by paleontologists to describe dinosaurs and giant mammals of ages past) and *megamillionaire*, which, according to the *Oxford English Dictionary*, was coined as early as 1970. In technical contexts, where the prefix is used to describe a unit of measure, it generally means "a million." So a *megawatt* is one million watts of power, and a *megabyte* is a million bytes of information (actually 1,048,576 bytes, to be precise). Other *mega-* words include:

✳ *megabank*—a giant financial institution, one that is "too big to fail"

✳ *megabid*—a giant financial offer

✳ *megachurch*—a really big church, usually an evangelical one

✳ *megadeath*—a million deaths, usually used in describing the effects of a nuclear war

✳ *megadontia*—really big teeth (think saber-toothed tiger)

✳ *megahit*—a great popular success, usually a film, TV show, song, book, etc.

✳ *megalomania*—delusions of grandeur

✳ *megamall*—a huge shopping center

✳ *megaphone*—a device to amplify the sound of one's voice

✳ *megaton*—a unit of explosive power equal to one million tons of TNT, used mainly in reference to nuclear weapons

✳ *megatrend*—a major social shift

If I Am Late, Cheese Is Made from Curds

*This is an article about **non sequiturs**. Did you know that bacon comes from a pig?*

✳ ✳ ✳ ✳

IN LOGIC, A *non sequitur* (Latin for "it does not follow") is defined as a fallacy. It is a conclusion that is not supported by its premise. The conclusion may be correct or it may be incorrect, but in either case, the conclusion does not properly follow from the premise given. For example, "Jenny lives in a large house; therefore, she must have a big family." It may be true that Jenny has a big family, of course, but it could be that Jenny just likes to have a lot of space.

In literature, the use of non sequitur offers many comic possibilities. In Lewis Carroll's *Alice's Adventures in Wonderland*, for example, when Alice says that she doesn't want to be among mad people, the Cheshire Cat replies, "We're all mad here. I'm mad. You're mad." Alice asks in response, "How do you know I'm mad?" And in a grand non sequitur, the Cat says, "You must be . . . or you wouldn't have come here." Jonathan Swift's satiric essay "A Modest Proposal" is based entirely on this non sequitur: The Irish are poor and starving, so the English should eat their children.

Because I Said So!

Real life is full of non sequiturs as well. An example familiar to many adolescents: "You will do as I say, because I'm the parent."

(In this case, the non sequitur may be a matter of opinion.) For the parent, the logic is perfectly clear: I'm your parent; therefore, I'm in charge. You listen to me. For the adolescent, on the other hand, this may be the non sequitur of all non sequiturs—who says that being the parent means you're automatically in charge?

Inadvertent non sequitur is common in journalism, particularly when writers try to wedge background information into sentences where it does not logically fit: "Sweeney grew up in Cleveland and married three elderly widows, each of whom he killed so he could collect the insurance money." If Sweeney had come from Akron, would those old ladies still be alive?

Does A+B=C?

The reason it's so easy to slip into a non sequitur is that syntax implies relationship. When you put two or more ideas in a sentence, you are telling the reader that there is a relationship, a connection. If there is no real connection, you either mislead the reader or produce nonsense.

In other words, it's important to make sense unless your intention is to be silly, so keep soup stains off your lapels.

Where Did It Come From?

Teenager: This word dates back only to 1941, although the word *teenage* was first used in 1921. *Teen* was used as a noun to describe a not-quite-adult person in 1818. *Teenaged*, though, comes from 1952. The latest spin-off is *tween* (although usually used solely to describe girls between childhood and adolescence, a formidable marketing target). More interesting, perhaps, is the now-archaic Middle English meaning of the word *tene*: "misery; grief."

All Generalizations Are False, Including This One

Sing along if you know it: "A paradox? A paradox! A most ingenious paradox," goes the song from Gilbert and Sullivan's The Pirates of Penzance.

❋ ❋ ❋ ❋

YOUNG FREDERIC OF *The Pirates of Penzance* has been apprenticed to pirates until he reaches age 21. However, owing to his bad luck of having been born on a leap day, he has had only five birthdays (though he has lived 21 chronological years) and thus cannot be said to have met the terms of his indenture. A most ingenious ***paradox*** indeed! In this case, the entire situation is paradoxical, although the result, which at first appears absurd, is proven to be true upon closer observation.

Statements of paradox are often used as a literary device: sentences that seem not to make sense, leading the reader to deeper consideration of the ideas contained therein. Consider the familiar "The more things change, the more they stay the same." Saying "Amid many changes, certain things remain constant" would not have the same impact. Both statements are true, but the first strengthens the underlying truth by compelling the reader to ponder the paradox.

Nothing Is Impossible

"Nothing is impossible" is a classic example of an unsolvable paradox. If it is impossible for something to be impossible, the statement contradicts itself. And what will happen if Pinocchio were to say, "My nose will grow now"? The puppet's nose grows when he lies ... but if he is telling the truth his nose will not grow ... however, if his nose does not grow, then he has lied! This is called vicious circularity, or infinite regress. The very essense of paradox is this: "This sentence is false." This is contradictory because the sentence can't be true and false at the same time.

> *"In theory, theory and practice are the same. In practice, they are not."*
> —ALBERT EINSTEIN

The First Will Be Last, and the Last Will Be First

Religious and philosophical writing often makes use of paradox to shake the reader loose from conventional patterns of thinking. In Christianity, the Prayer of St. Francis states, "For it is in giving that we receive, it is in pardoning that we are pardoned, and it is in dying that we are born to eternal life." Think that one through!

In other cases, paradoxes can be used to make ideas *less* clear, not more. In George Orwell's *Nineteen Eighty-Four*, the government of Big Brother proclaims a series of paradoxes to unsettle the thinking of the populace and make them more malleable: "War Is Peace, Freedom Is Slavery, Ignorance Is Strength." The slogans lead to dissonance in the citizens, who become unable to think logically about abstract ideals such as peace and freedom.

Who Could Resist a Paradox?

Possibly most important, paradoxes make us laugh. The playful use of words to compose impossible situations gives our brains something to chew on, often creating a brand of incongruence that is the perfect breeding ground for humor. Paradox is one of the essential elements of comedy and has been used by everyone from Oscar Wilde ("I can resist everything except temptation") to Groucho Marx ("I intend to live forever or die trying"). Another head-scratcher stems from the combination of two adages: If a cat always lands on its feet, and buttered bread always lands butter side down, what would happen if you tied buttered bread on top of a cat?

Apt Alliteration's Artful Aid

Have you ever pondered how you can possibly turn prose and poetry into more memorable and monumentous pieces of literature? Attempt **alliteration,** *the repeating of the same initial sound or sounds at the beginning of two or more words in close proximity.*

✳ ✳ ✳ ✳

ALLITERATION ADDS MUSICAL cadence to a work, helps emphasize a point, and sets a mood or tone. It can also can make the work easier to memorize and recite. Poets use alliteration to great effect: The line "Apt alliteration's artful aid" appears in Charles Churchill's eighteenth-century poem "The Prophecy of Famine." Wilfred Owen's World War I poem "Anthem for Doomed Youth" describes "the stuttering rifles' rapid rattle," and Edgar Allen Poe smoothly sketches a scene, "While I nodded, nearly napping, suddenly there came a tapping" ("The Raven"). The technique is often used to memorable effect in speeches, such as in the phrase "nattering nabobs of negativism," which William Safire wrote for Spiro Agnew.

Alliteration's distinctive tone is also utilized in the titles of many books, plays, and films: *Of Mice and Men, The Pilgrim's Progress, Love's Labour's Lost, The School for Scandal,* and *The Great Gatsby.* We encounter alliteration in newspaper headlines: "Troubled Tyson in $30 Million Tussle" and "Binge Kills Boozy Boss" (*News of the World*). And alliteration is the key feature of tongue twisters: "Peter Piper picked a peck of pickled peppers" and "She sells seashells by the seashore," for example, which we find next to impossible to get our tongues around.

Healthy as a Horse, Proud as a Peacock

Alliteration also features in our ordinary language: It's a player in such similes as "cool as a cucumber," "fit as a fiddle," and "green as grass," and in such everyday stock phrases as "belle of the ball," "part and parcel," "it takes two to tango," "no rhyme or reason," and "go to rack and ruin."

Businesspeople often use alliteration to make a service or product memorable, as well as to communicate their points more effectively in a presentation. Alliteration can help a speaker remember what to say, and it also works as a mnemonic device to help people remember what they have heard—for example: "Don't drink and drive." It's also a great tool in ad campaigns, where witty advertisers dream up memorable catchphrases ("Don't dream it. Drive it.") as well as in political slogans ("Black is beautiful"; "Reformer with Results"; "Tippecanoe and Tyler, Too").

Catchy but Cliché

So why is alliteration effective? In short, alliterative language sticks firmly in your head and can help evoke a picture. It can change language from being as "dry as dust" into something that is "larger than life." But beware! Although it works as a lovely literary device in poetry, and as a handy memory aid in slogans and catchphrases, it can become intrusive and distracting if overused in prose. Or, to put it differently, relentless repetition rubs readers the wrong way.

✳ It is the sound of the letter rather than the letter itself that makes a phrase alliterative. So, "giant" and "green" do not alliterate, but "jolly" and "giant" do.

Worldly Wisdom: Native American Proverbs

❋ ❋ ❋ ❋

❋ It is better to have less thunder in the mouth and more lightning in the hand. (Apache)

❋ If we wonder often, the gift of knowledge will come. (Arapaho)

❋ Don't let yesterday use up too much of today. (Cherokee)

❋ If a man is as wise as a serpent, he can afford to be as harmless as a dove. (Cheyenne)

❋ All who have died are equal. (Comanche)

❋ Listen or your tongue will keep you deaf. (Cree)

❋ We will be known forever for the tracks we leave. (Dakota)

❋ All dreams spin out from the same web. (Hopi)

❋ Don't be afraid to cry. It will free your mind of sorrowful thoughts. (Hopi)

❋ The greatest strength is gentleness. (Iroquois)

❋ A good chief gives; he does not take. (Mohawk)

❋ You can't wake a person who is pretending to be asleep. (Navajo)

❋ Every animal knows more than you do. (Nez Perce)

❋ Make my enemy brave and strong, so that if defeated, I will not be ashamed. (Plains)

❋ Cherish youth, but trust old age. (Pueblo)

❋ With all things and in all things, we are relatives. (Sioux)

All Hands on Deck (and Bring Your Bodies with You)

What do head of cattle, deckhands, and a new set of wheels have in common? They are all examples of **synecdoche,** *a rhetorical device in which a part or quality of something stands in for the whole (or the other way around).*

✳ ✳ ✳ ✳

SYNECDOCHE (PRONOUNCED SIN-EK-DUH-KEE) is a useful rhetorical shorthand. When you "break bread," for example, you are likely to be eating more than just bread, but the bread stands in as a symbol for the rest of the meal. One part stands in for the whole.

But synecdoche can also work the other way, with a larger category standing as a symbol for one member. When a chicken farmer says, "I've got to go feed my birds," she's more likely to mean her chickens than all the crows, sparrows, and blue jays that happen to be flying around the farm. A similar synecdoche is the use of *America* to mean the *United States:* The term *America* more properly labels the two continents of which the United States is only a part, but the word is commonly used to refer to just the United States—somewhat to the annoyance of the other residents of North and South America.

Sometimes a synecdoche involves something other than an obvious part or whole, such as the material something is made out of. A swordfighter drawing steel is really drawing something made of steel, and a football player tossing the pigskin around is tossing something made of (or at one time in history made of) pigskin. These are both examples of synecdoche.

Metonomy (in which one attribute stands for a whole thing) is related to synecdoche. See page 652 for more on metonomy.

Gathering Mo- and Other -*Mentums*

As a suffix, -mentum isn't all that productive. There are just a couple dozen words ending in -mentum, and all of them are direct borrowings from Latin. But the suffix has gathered some, well, momentum in recent U.S. political campaigns, generating a few trendy words.

✳ ✳ ✳ ✳

Isaac Newton

THE SUFFIX COMES from the word *momentum*, which in modern parlance is usually defined as the inertia an object possesses— its mass times its velocity. Physicist Isaac Newton's first law of motion tells us that objects at rest stay at rest and objects in motion stay in motion unless an external force is applied to them. An object with a lot of momentum is quite difficult to stop.

Momentum of the Past

Momentum, originally meaning "a brief period of time," comes from Latin. In Anglo-Saxon England, a *momentum* was a fortieth of an hour—a minute and a half, to be exact. In the Newtonian physics of the late seventeenth and early eighteenth centuries, the force of an object's motion over an infinitesimally small period of time began to be called the object's *momentum*.

The suffix's political life began in the 2004 presidential race when campaigners for Joe Lieberman, senator from Connecticut and 2000 Democratic vice-presidential nominee, coined the term *Joementum* to describe the supposedly unstoppable momentum that he had in the race for the Democratic presidential nomination. But as it turned out, Lieberman the candidate either lacked some weightiness or failed to move fast enough, because his Joementum wasn't enough to get him across the finish line.

Low- to No-mentum

For years, a new crop of candidates attempted to coin fresh *-mentum* terms based on their names. Most were clumsy, lacking the phonetic link *Joementum* had with *momentum*, and died quick deaths along with the aspirations of the associated candidates. Neither former Massachusetts governor Mitt Romney's *Mittmentum*, former Arkansas governor Mike Huckabee's *Huckmentum*, or Republican nominee John McCain's *McCainmentum* ever built up enough momentum to lead their candidate to triumphant victory in the 2008 presidential election.

---

* Despite a striking similarity to his last name, one word that wasn't used in Barack Obama's 2008 presidential campaign was *obambulate*—meaning "to walk about or wander here and there." Although the stem could easily be mistaken to be *obam-*, it is actually *ob-*, the Latin preposition meaning "in the direction of" or "toward."

* If Bo, the Obama family's Portuguese water dog, were able to run for any kind of public office, perhaps the nation might find itself witness to an inaugural rush of *Bomentum*? Or maybe that word just names the tug of the leash that the First Family feels as they lead their canine pal on a stroll over the White House grounds.

A Banana by Any Other Name

This article isn't the Holy Grail on **periphrasis**—*a form of paraphrase in which a writer varies the text by substituting a descriptive term or phrase for a proper name—but it is a pretty definitive explanation.*

✳ ✳ ✳ ✳

PERIPHRASIS COMES FROM the Greek *periphrazein*, from a root meaning "to point out." A sportswriter who refers to Babe Ruth by his nickname, "The Sultan of Swat," is using periphrasis, as is a journalist who uses the phrase "the white-robed pontiff" for the pope.

Michael Jackson is widely known as "The King of Pop," which is itself a reference to Elvis Presley's periphrastic name, "The King of Rock 'n' Roll." Another artist with a periphrastic name is "the artist formerly known as Prince," who changed his name in 1993 to an unpronounceable symbol. (He changed it back to Prince in 2000.) William Shakespeare is known as "The Bard," or "The Bard of Avon."

No Kidding, Sherlock

Another form of periphrasis uses a proper name to stand for a quality that person is associated with. A figure may become so identified in the public mind with some quality—intelligence, for example—that a sentence like "You're no Einstein" is immediately comprehensible. ("You're no Einstein" is also an example of *meiosis*—see page 678.) Calling a promising tennis player "a real Navratilova" means the writer ranks that player in a class with female superstars. Someone who is considered a traitor or backstabber might be called Judas (after the apostle who betrayed Jesus) or "a Benedict Arnold" (after the American general who plotted the surrender of an American fort to the British and eventually switched sides to join the British army).

Periphrasis is also called *circumlocution,* from *circum* ("around") + *locutio* ("speech"), or *antonomasia,* from *anti* ("instead of") + *onomazein* ("to name"). People use circumlocution as a way to avoid the monotony of repeating words too frequently. It can be used for humorous or euphemistic effect. The classic example, repeated endlessly in journalism classes, is that of the writer who apparently became bored with the word *banana* in an article about, yes, bananas, and decided to mix things up by calling it an "elongated yellow fruit." Now, that "elongated yellow fruit" has itself become a periphrastic term for hack writing.

✳ *Periphrastic* **is also a big word for a simple grammar concept: It denotes a form created with a phrase instead of word endings. In English, the future tense is periphrastic because it uses an auxiliary verb to form a phrase (e.g., "will help"), in contrast to the simple past, which is not periphrastic ("helped").**

✳ **General Benedict Arnold, whose name has become synonymous with treason in the United States, was a friend of George Washington and a hero of the Revolutionary War. When he was passed over for promotion and received a court martial for violating military regulations, he went over to the side of the British, committing treason against the colonies.**

Once More, with Feeling

Sometimes writers will repeat the same word or group of words at the beginning of successive sentences or clauses. In conversation this might be annoying, but in literature it is known as **anaphora,** *from the Greek meaning "to carry back," and it is a technique often used to great effect.*

✳   ✳   ✳   ✳

REMEMBER THE OPENING of Charles Dickens's *A Tale of Two Cities?* It is perhaps the most classic example of anaphora:

> *It was the best of times, it was the worst of times, it was the age of wisdom, it was the age of foolishness, it was the epoch of belief, it was the epoch of incredulity, it was the season of Light, it was the season of Darkness, it was the spring of hope, it was the winter of despair…*

Another example is found in John of Gaunt's speech in Shakespeare's *King Richard II:*

> *This royal throne of kings, this sceptred isle,*
> *This earth of Majesty, this seat of Mars,*
> *This other Eden, demi-paradise;*
> *This fortress built by Nature for herself*
> *Against infection and the hand of war;*
> *This happy breed of men, this little world,*
> *This precious stone set in the silver sea,*
> *Which serves it in the office of a wall,*
> *Or as a moat defensive to a house,*
> *Against the envy of less happier lands;*
> *This blessed plot, this earth, this realm, this England.*

Anaphora is most appropriately used when the writer wants to stress a central point or stir the reader with emotion through the heavily rhythmic pattern of repetition. The repeated words capture the reader's attention and give rise to a feeling of familiarity.

Repeat, Repeat, Repeat

Anaphora is one of a set of patterns of repetition. The others are *epistrophe*, *epanalepsis*, and *anadiplosis*.

In **epistrophe,** words are repeated at the end of phrases or clauses rather than at the beginning:

✳ "There's not a liberal America and a conservative America. There's the United States of America. (Barack Obama)

✳ "I scream, you scream, we all scream for ice cream!"

In **epanalepsis,** a word from the beginning of a clause is repeated at the end:

✳ "Mankind must put an end to war—or war will put an end to mankind." (John F. Kennedy)

✳ "The king is dead; long live the king."

✳ "Next time there won't be a next time."

In **anadiplosis,** words at the end of one clause or sentence are repeated at the beginning of the next, reinforcing the importance of the word or idea:

✳ "Once you change your philosophy, you change your thought pattern. Once you change your thought pattern, you change your attitude. Once you change your attitude, it changes your behavior pattern and then you go on into some action." (Malcolm X)

✳ "Not only so, but we glory in tribulations also: knowing that tribulation worketh patience; and patience, experience; and experience, hope." (Romans 5:3–4, KJV)

Less Is More

*Those who paid attention in biology class probably remember that **meiosis** is the process by which the genome of a diploid cell in animals and plants divides, splitting the number of chromosomes in half, as part of the sexual reproductive process. But this isn't biology class.*

✳   ✳   ✳   ✳

T HE WORD MEIOSIS, deriving from the Greek *meioun* ("to make smaller"), has a place in rhetoric class as well. There the word means "to understate, to make to seem less important." Meiosis is the opposite of exaggeration, or *hyperbole* (see page 654 for more on hyperbole).

Meiosis is often used for humorous effect, employed to exploit the potentially comic gap between the reality of a situation and how it is described. When King Arthur lops off the left arm of the Black Knight in *Monty Python and the Holy Grail*, the knight says, "'Tis but a scratch." When Arthur cuts off his other arm, the knight says, "Just a flesh wound." In his mad determination to keep fighting, the knight employs meiosis.

In the Nixon administration's first public statement about the Watergate scandal in 1972, Ron Ziegler, Nixon's press secretary, called the break-in "a third-rate burglary attempt," trying to dismiss its significance. It was soon clear that meiosis doesn't always work, however—by 1974, the consequences of this "third-rate burglary" drove President Nixon from office.

If the reader is meant to be in on the joke, however, it must be obvious that a comparison is being made, that the larger meaning is there in the background. When Bruce Banner says, "Don't make me angry. You wouldn't like me when I'm angry," our knowledge of his alternate persona—The Incredible Hulk—drives the humor.

Words of Wisdom from Harry S. Truman

✳ ✳ ✳ ✳

✳ "There is nothing new in the world except the history you do not know."

✳ "The only things worth learning are the things you learn after you know it all."

✳ "A President cannot always be popular."

✳ "America was not built on fear. America was built on courage, on imagination and an unbeatable determination to do the job at hand."

✳ "If you can't convince them, confuse them."

✳ "In reading the lives of great men, I found that the first victory they won was over themselves . . . self-discipline with all of them came first."

✳ "It is amazing what you can accomplish if you do not care who gets the credit."

✳ "Men make history and not the other way around. In periods where there is no leadership, society stands still. Progress occurs when courageous, skillful leaders seize the opportunity to change things for the better."

✳ "You can always amend a big plan, but you can never expand a little one. I don't believe in little plans. I believe in plans big enough to meet a situation which we can't possibly foresee now."

✳ "A statesman is a politician who's been dead for 10 or 15 years."

✳ "You want a friend in Washington? Get a dog."

To Question or Not to Question?

Is it best to explain rhetorical terms in contrast to each other? Is it acceptable to use rhetoric to explain itself? Is there any way to write this so that it makes sense?

✳   ✳   ✳   ✳

PERHAPS NOT, but questioning oneself or the reader is a rhetorical device with a long and honorable history. Like many rhetorical terms, *aporia,* meaning "real or feigned self-doubt and questioning," comes to us from the ancient Greeks. In Greek, it meant "to be at a loss," coming ultimately from a word meaning "impassable." In philosophy, *aporia* is an insoluble problem; in rhetoric, it is a problem that may or may not have a solution, but the writer is working it out by arguing both sides, pretending to doubt something before coming to a conclusion (or not). Aporia, also known as *dubitatio,* often involves the use of rhetorical questions. (For more on rhetorical questions, see page 82.)

Aporia is a statement of doubt—either real or imagined— and writers often use it sarcastically, "playing dumb" so they can then drive home their point. By first expressing doubt, writers encourage others to consider how something may be doubted—thus causing confusion, sowing seeds of uncertainty, and challenging others to seek certainty.

When You Really Don't Want an Answer

Hamlet's "To be or not to be, that is the question" is possibly the most recognizable rhetorical question in English literature, but the whole speech from which it's taken is a masterful use of aporia. As the Danish prince works through his decision process out loud, he repeatedly asks himself questions: "Whether 'tis nobler in the mind to suffer... or to take arms against a sea of troubles" (*Is it better to suffer or fight?*); "For who would bear the whips and scorns of time,... when he himself might his quietus make with a bare bodkin?" (*Why*

suffer when you could end your suffering by killing yourself?). These questions pull the reader into the conflict and make the decision seem immediate.

How Am I Supposed to Live Without You?

Aporia does not need to be couched in fancy language, nor does it need to reflect fundamental questions like those of Prince Hamlet. Popular music is full of examples. The theme from the 1970 movie *Love Story* gives us an example: "Where do I begin / To tell the story of how great a love can be?" The singer wonders what would be the best way to tell his story. Cat Stevens wants to know, "Where do the children play?" The rest of the song's lyrics give examples of technological advances and overdevelopment, driving home the idea of a loss of innocence.

Rarely Is the Question Asked

President George W. Bush's much-ridiculed comment, "Rarely is the question asked, is our children learning?" could also be an example of aporia: He sets up his subject as a question to be answered, and though he does not go on to argue both sides, it could be argued that there is no definitive answer to his question. It certainly could be considered insoluble—especially as phrased!

Where Did It Come From?

Reflect: To think quietly and calmly, or in the case of a highly polished surface, to give back an image or likeness; from the Latin *reflectere* (to bend back): *re-flectere* (to bend)

Studying Suffixology

Perhaps you'll want to look into these areas of study before declaring your college major.

✳ ✳ ✳ ✳

THE SUFFIX -OLOGY is extremely productive in English, usually meaning "the study of" or "manner of speaking." It comes, via Latin and French, from the Greek *logia*, a declension of the word *logos*, meaning "word, speech, reason." In Greek, *-o-* is used to connect nouns with suffixes, and Greek words formed with the *-logia* suffix almost invariably end in *-ologia*. This has carried over into English, where most *-logy* words also have the *-o-*, although there are a few exceptions—such as *eulogy*, meaning "words of praise, especially of a dead person" (*eu-*, or "good" + *-logy*), and *mineralogy* (the study of rocks).

When I Grow Up, I Want to Be an Ologyologist

Of course, there are the standard *-ology* words, such as *theology*, *psychology*, and *biology*, that end up in the names of university departments, but there are a host of others that are more obscure and, arguably, more interesting:

✳ *alethiology*—study of truth

✳ *angelology*—study of angels

✳ *balneology*—study of baths and bathing

✳ *codicology*—study of manuscripts for historical purposes

✳ *cosmology*—study of the universe

✳ *cryptozoology*—study of legendary animals, or animals not recognized by mainstream science

✳ *dittology*—a double meaning or interpretation, a double entendre

* *emetology*—study of the causes of vomiting

* *enology*—study of wine and winemaking (also *oenology*)

* *eschatology*—study of death, judgment, and the afterlife

* *ethology*—study of animal behavior

* *hierology*—sacred literature

* *iridology*—study of the eye to make diagnoses in various alternative medical disciplines

* *logology*—study of words

* *ludology*—study of videogames

* *oology*—study of bird eggs

* *parthenology*—study of virgins

* *philology*—study of a language and its literature

* *phrenology*—the derivation of a person's character traits by studying the shape of his or her skull

* *posmology*—study of fruit

* *psephology*—study of elections

* *scatology*—study of feces

* *selenology*—study of the moon

* *vexillology*—study of flags

* *xenobiology*—study of extraterrestrial life

This list is a sad one indeed without the addition of the most important of all the -*ology* words, *etymology*, which, as any word nerd knows, is the branch of linguistic science that is concerned with determining the origin of words.

One of These Things Is Just Like the Other

Human beings have an irrepressible tendency to compare things, to think in analogies. More than simply a figure of speech, an **analogy** *is a kind of logical argument created to demonstrate how two things are alike by pointing out shared characteristics.*

✳ ✳ ✳ ✳

ANALOGY EXISTS TO explain. The purpose is to make one unfamiliar thing understandable by showing how it is like something that is already familiar. For example: e-mail is to the twenty-first century what the telegraph was to the nineteenth. In other words, people today rely on e-mail as a means of cheap, instant communication as much as people depended on the telegraph for this in the later 1800s.

Analogy can explain a line of reasoning, which makes it useful in arguments of logic and law. In logic, analogy identifies a similarity between two things and then goes on to argue that they must be similar in other respects as well. The process moves from something familiar and agreed upon to aspects that are less familiar. The same process occurs in law, when the circumstances of one case or precedent are extended to cover new situations.

Chapter Is to *Book* as *Line* Is to *Poem*

Analogy can be used to demonstrate the relationships between the words of a language: *vixen* is to *fox* as *sow* is to *badger* (in both cases, the former is the female of the latter animal); *diurnal* is to *day* as *nocturnal* is to *night* (both are adjectives that relate to the noun); or *adjective* is to *noun* as *adverb* is to *verb* (in both cases, the former modifies the latter).

To conclude, here's an analogy from Irish poet, dramatist, and wit Oscar Wilde: "To recommend thrift to the poor is both grotesque and insulting. It is like advising a man who is starving to eat less." This is a good example of the use of an analogy to illustrate a point.

Get Outta Here

One humorous form of analogy relies on the use of the word *like* to link two things in an unexpected way. You've probably heard the phrases "Make like a tree and leave" and "Make like a banana and split." Here are a few more examples that may be new to you:

✳ Make like a bakery truck and move your buns.

✳ Make like a nut and bolt.

✳ Make like a dog and flea.

✳ Make like a hat and go on ahead.

✳ Make like a jacket and zip.

✳ Make like an atom and split.

✳ Make like a tire and hit the road.

✳ Make like rain and get the hail out of here.

✳ Make like a river and run.

✳ **In writing, certain figures of speech depend on analogy. A**
   simile ("as green as grass," "as snug as a bug in a rug") says
   that one thing is *like* another. *Metonymy* takes one part of a
   thing and uses it in place of the thing itself (e.g., using *the*
   ***stage* in place of *the theater*). *Metaphor* says that in some figu-**
   rative sense one thing *is* another: "It's raining cats and dogs."
   For more on simile, see page 94, metonymy page 652, and
   metaphor page 658.

Famous Last Words

✳   ✳   ✳   ✳

"Now comes the mystery."
> —HENRY WARD BEECHER, ABOLITIONIST (1813–1887)

"Why are you weeping? Did you imagine that I was immortal?"
> —KING LOUIS XIV OF FRANCE (1638–1715),
> SPOKEN TO HIS ATTENDANTS, WHO WERE CRYING AS HE LAY ON HIS DEATHBED

"Go on, get out. Last words are for fools who haven't said enough."
> —KARL MARX, REVOLUTIONARY (1818–1883),
> SPOKEN TO HIS HOUSEKEEPER WHEN SHE URGED HIM TO GIVE HER HIS LAST WORDS
> SO SHE COULD PRESERVE THEM FOR FUTURE GENERATIONS

"I am going in search of a great perhaps."
> —FRANÇOIS RABELAIS, PHILOSOPHER, SCHOLAR (C. 1483–1553)

"I'm bored with it all."
> —WINSTON CHURCHILL, STATESMAN (1874–1965),
> SPOKEN BEFORE SLIPPING INTO A COMA. HE DIED NINE DAYS LATER.

"I am not the least afraid to die."
> —CHARLES DARWIN, SCIENTIST, WRITER (1809–1882)

"All my possessions for a moment of time."
> —ELIZABETH I, QUEEN OF ENGLAND (1533–1603)

"Don't let it end like this. Tell them I said something."
> —PANCHO VILLA, MEXICAN REVOLUTIONARY (1878–1923)

"Turn up the lights, I don't want to go home in the dark."
> —O. HENRY, WRITER (1862–1910),
> QUOTING A POPULAR SONG

"How were the receipts today at Madison Square Garden?"
—P. T. BARNUM, ENTERTAINER/ENTREPRENEUR (1810–1891)

"Friends applaud, the comedy is finished."
—LUDWIG VAN BEETHOVEN, COMPOSER (1770–1827)

"I have offended God and mankind because my work did not reach the quality it should have."
—LEONARDO DA VINCI, ARTIST (1452–1519)

"Nothing but death."
—JANE AUSTEN, WRITER (1775–1817),
WHEN ASKED BY HER SISTER CASSANDRA IF SHE WANTED ANYTHING

"Beautiful."
—ELIZABETH BARRETT BROWNING, POET (1806–1861),
WHEN HER HUSBAND ASKED HER HOW SHE FELT

"Crito, I owe a cock to Asclepius; will you remember to pay the debt?"
—SOCRATES, PHILOSOPHER (469–333 B.C.)

"This is the last of earth! I am content."
—JOHN QUINCY ADAMS, POLITICIAN (1767–1848)

Index

✳   ✳   ✳   ✳

B

Double-crostic puzzles. *See* Acrostic puzzles.
Double-letter words, 623
Doublespeak, 65, 114–15, 506
Doublets, 270
Douglas, Norman, 76
Doyle, Sir Arthur Conan, 147, 490
Dreams, 472
Dr. Seuss. *See* Geisel, Theodor.
Dryden, John, 276, 459
Duh, 103
Dumas, Alexandre, 417
Dumb-denoting insults, 164, 556–57
Dunce cap, 557
Duns. *See* Scotus, Jon Duns.
Dysphemisms, 66–67, 425

E
Edison, Thomas A., 37, 113, 139, 413
Education, 226
Edwards, Jonathan, 218
Eggcorns, 17, 60–61, 255, 267, 482
Einstein, Albert, 47, 89, 293, 484
Eisenhower, Dwight D., 450
Eliot, George, 163, 215, 386, 390, 391, 514, 622, 655
Elizabeth I (queen of England), 686
Ellipsis, 298–99
Emerson, Ralph Waldo, 138, 226, 251, 275, 301, 398, 484, 606, 611, 627, 629
Endings, rare word, 308
Enthusiasm, 368
Epanalepsis, 677
Epictetus, 239, 408
Epiplexis, 83, 274
Epistrophe, 677
Epitasis, 641
Eponymous adjectives, 146–47
Eponyms, 16, 136–37, 146–47, 189, 198, 529, 633
Equivocation, 81
Ethelreda (Saint Audrey), 555

Euler's Day Off (word game), 47
Euphemisms, 59, 64–65, 66, 67, 114, 141, 202–03, 356–57, 368, 425, 506, 648
Euripides, 162, 342, 548
Eustress, 422
Exaggerations, 112–13. *See also* Hyperbole.
Excursus, 656–57

F
Fables, 642–43
Facebook, 515
Failure, 275
Faith, 536
False corrections. *See* Incorrections.
Family, 123
Famous last words, 42–43, 686–687
Fear of long words, 152, 181
Ferris Beuller's Day Off (1986), 633
Festivus, 478
Field, Eugene, 501
Fielding, Henry, 218, 584
Fillmore, Millard, 42
Flack, Gene, 373
Flaubert, Gustave, 267
Food, 118–119, 500–01
Football terms, 200–01, 204, 504
Ford, Gerald R., 190, 332
Ford, Ford Madox, 25
Ford, Henry, 275
Foreign words, borrowed, 168–69
Forgiveness, 644
Foss, Sam Walter, 472
France, Anatole, 472, 622
Franklin, Benjamin, 123, 184, 226, 246, 273, 398, 401, 523, 528, 561, 622
Freedom, 366
Free morph, 295
French words, borrowed, 588
Friendship, 138–39
Fuller, Margaret, 325, 522
Fuller, Thomas, 139, 522, 543

M

Macaulay, Thomas B., 76, 606
MacDonald, George, 536
Mac-Geoghegan, Abbe, 190
Mack, Connie, 490
Magic, 280
Mahaffey, John Pentland, 332
Mahler, Gustav, 33
Malapropisms, 16–17, 60, 90,
    482, 571
Malory, Sir Thomas, 528
Mandela, Nelson, 300, 484
Marlowe, Christopher, 517
Marriage, 184
Marx, Groucho, 80, 81
Marx, Karl, 686
Maxims, 78–79
McKinley, William, 42
Meh, 142–43, 585
Meiosis, 674, 678
Melville, Herman, 25, 275
Memory, 655
Menander, 408
Mencius, 484
Mencken, H. L., 41, 384
Merikare, the Teaching for, 391,
    606
Merismus (merism), 278–79
Metanalysis, 250–51
Metaphor, 112–13, 278, 302–
    03, 652, 658–59, 685
Metaplasm, 282, 290–91
Metonymy, 278, 652–53, 671,
    685
Milton, John, 163, 366, 374,
    390, 404, 484, 520, 594
Mind meld, 572
Miracles, 55
Mirror writing, 344–45
Misheard lyrics, 44–45
Misplaced apostrophes, 234–35
Mistakes, 62
Mixed metaphors, 90–91, 659
Mnemonics, 341, 669
    accept/except, 442–43
    affect/effect, 434
    allude/elude, 438–39
    alterior/ulterior, 465
    cite/sight/site, 224–25

complementary/complimentary,
    445
desert/dessert, 432–33
discreet/discrete, 270–71
eminent/immanent/imminent,
    456–57
eternal/internal, 468
foul/fowl, 440
imply/infer, 227
lay/lie, 228–29
manner/manor, 444
peace/piece, 253
peak/peek/pique, 248–49
pore/pour, 232
raise/raze, 460–61
stationary/stationery, 264
than/then, 240
threw/through, 259
Moby-Dick (Melville), 28
Modern period, 498–99
Molière, 258, 390, 501
Mondegreens, 44–45
Money, 562
Monroe, James, 366
Montaigne, Michel de, 55, 226,
    370, 472, 632
Montesquieu, Charles, 359
Montgomery, Lucy Maud, 62,
    309
Moodie, Susanna, 215
Moore, George, 325
Moore, Thomas, 59, 163, 655
More, Hannah, 271
Morris, William, 391
Mort words, 424
Murphy's Law, 559
    as adage, 78
    as eponym, 137
Music, 97
My Life (Chekhov), 131

N

Nabokov, Vladimir, 289
Names from occupations, 12–13
Napoleon Bonaparte, 188
Nature, 218
Navajo language, 608
Na'vi (language for *Avatar*), 129
Necro words, 425